A Festschrift for Jacob Ornstein

Studies in General Linguistics
and Sociolinguistics

S0-GQF-469

A Festschrift for Jacob Ornstein

Studies in General Linguistics and Sociolinguistics

Edward L. Blansitt, Jr.
Department of Linguistics

Richard V. Teschner
Department of Modern Languages

University of Texas, El Paso

6447147

P
26
O7
F4

Newbury House Publishers, Inc. / Rowley / Massachusetts / 01969

1 9 8 0

WITHDRAWN FROM
OHIO UNIVERSITY
LIBRARY

Library of Congress Cataloging in Publication Data
Main entry under title:

A Festschrift for Jacob Ornstein.

  Bibliography: p.
    1. Linguistics--Addresses, essays, lectures.
  2. Sociolinguistics--Addresses, essays, lectures.
  3. Ornstein, Jacob--Addresses, essays, lectures.
  I. Ornstein, Jacob.   II. Blansitt, Edward.
  III. Teschner, Richard V.
  P26.07F4   410   80-18025
  ISBN 0-88377-172-X

NEWBURY HOUSE PUBLISHERS, INC.

Language Science
Language Teaching
Language Learning

ROWLEY, MASSACHUSETTS 01969

Cover design by Jean Ploss.

Copyright © 1980 by Newbury House Publishers, Inc. All rights reserved. No part of this book may be reproduced or transmitted in any form or by any means, electronic or mechanical, including photocopying, recording, or by any information storage and retrieval system, without permission in writing from the Publisher.

First printing: November 1980
Printed in the U.S.A.   5   4   3   2   1

ACKNOWLEDGMENTS

For typing services so ably rendered, this volume owes a considerable debt of gratitude to Ms. Kathy Early, senior secretary, Department of Linguistics, the University of Texas at El Paso, and to the chairman of that department, Dr. Ray Past, for generously permitting Kathy to work on our project. Thanks also go to Servicios Misceláneos Arvití for pinch-hit typing on various occasions.

                                        E.L.B., Jr.
                                        R.V.T.

El Paso, October 1, 1979

TABLE OF CONTENTS

vii

PROFESSOR JACOB ORNSTEIN— BIOGRAPHY

RICHARD V. TESCHNER

University of Texas—El Paso

Jack Ornstein was born August 8, 1915 in Cleveland, Ohio, the son of Yiddish-speaking immigrants from Polish Galicia who had settled in the Mid-West. His early education took place in Cleveland and Painesville, Ohio, typically in immigrant-neighborhood schools where many of his classmates were mother-tongue speakers of Russian, Hungarian, Polish, Ukrainian, German and Italian-- languages which in addition to Spanish, French and Portuguese constituted the focal points of Jack's many scholarly activities throughout his long career as researcher, civil servant and teacher.

Following the receipt of two degrees from Ohio State University (a B.S. in Education in 1936 and an M.A. in Spanish the next year), he enrolled in the doctoral program of the Department of Spanish and Portuguese at the University of Wisconsin-Madison where in 1940 he earned his Ph.D. under the direction of the renowned medievalist Lloyd A. Kasten; there he was also awarded the prestigious "Antonio G. Solalinde Award for Excellence in Spanish Studies" in 1938. After a summer with the Universidad Nacional Autónoma de México (1940), Jack received the first of the many dual appointments that were to characterize the professional life of our unstoppable honorandum-- as an Intelligence Officer (linguistic specialist and interrogator) with the U.S. Army, and as an instructor in Spanish and Latin American Civilization with Washington University of St. Louis. In 1942 he made his first transfer to Washington D.C. to work directly for the Office of Strategic Services. The following year he was relocated to the Mediterranean Theater of Operations (chiefly in North Africa and Italy, with the 2677 HQ. Regiment), where he again

1

served as an interrogation officer.

It was in Italy in 1945 at the age of thirty when Jack came down with the severe case of polio that was to keep him confined to a wheelchair permanently, and to a hospital until 1947, when, with movement largely restored to head, neck, and arms, he accepted a full-time post as teacher of Spanish and other languages at Waldorf College (Forest City, Iowa). The first stage of his twice-born teaching career ended prophetically with two years (1949-51) at New Mexico State University (then College), located in Las Cruces, just 43 miles north of the city where in later years he was to make such a mark as the nation's foremost researcher into the sociolinguistics of Mexican-Americans.

The years 1951-1968 were again spent in Washington D.C. as Jack's second or "Slavic" career saw him at work as an Associate with the Russian Research Center at the Department of Defense, where he also served as Scientific Linguist and Department Head. It has always been typical of Jack that he was never content to let his higher education remain fixed at lower peaks; thus the summer of 1955 found him at work in Advanced Intensive Russian at Colby College, the academic year of 1957-58 at Harvard for post-doctoral studies in General and Slavic Linguistics, and the summer of 1965 at the University of Washington (Seattle) for the Linguistic Society of America's Summer Institute; in addition he took part in an instruc tional programmer course offered April-June 1966 at Lackland Air Forc Base Training Command in San Antonio, Texas. While working and study ing, Jack also taught courses in Portuguese and "Languages of the World" in the evening graduate division of the U.S. Department of Agriculture from 1951-1963, and courses in linguistics at Georgetown University's School of Languages and Linguistics from 1964-68.

It was the third or "El Paso" period (1968-), however, that served to establish Jack's international reputation as a student of the languages and language behavior of the Chicano or Mexican-American population of the United States Southwest. When Jack moved to El Paso in the summer of 1968 with his wife Janet and their daughter Denah, it was inevitable that someone of his wide-ranging intellectual curiosity and dauntless energy should be drawn to research on the speech and especially on the sociolinguistics of the millions and millions of varyingly-bilingual Hispanophones who up to that moment in history had indeed constituted an "invisible minority" but whose impact on the national consciousness was then increasing daily. Throughout the Southwest, issues of language planning and language loyalty, bilingualism and bilingual education, ethnic co-existence and ethnic conflict were front-page news, yet as of 1968, little if any scholarly response to this "news" had come forth from linguists or Hispanists. It was indeed the case (to quote from the title of one of Jack's many conference papers) that Mexican-American sociolinguistics could be called "a well-kept public and scholarly secret." Almost alone for a while, he labored long and laudably to declassify the secret, as his voluminous list of publications convincingly demonstrates (see the BIBLIOGRAPHY which follows).

By no means have Jack's labors ended with his many publications.

Dubbed on one memorable occasion "the Sol Hurok of Southwestern Sociolinguistics," he has effectively promoted a multitude of conferences, workshops, seminars, sessions, roundtable discussions and miscellaneous meetings in his seven years as Professor of Linguistics and Modern Languages at the University of Texas-El Paso and in the four years since being awarded emeritus status here (1975). Foremost among his many "promotional" activities has been the co-directorship (with Prof. Z. Anthony Kruszewski of UTEP's Department of Political Science) of the Cross-Cultural Southwest Ethnic Study Center, funded through a $63,000 grant from the Spencer Foundation of Chicago. (Funds from the Hogg Foundation for Mental Health awarded to Jack were also used to finance Center activities and other scholarly ventures.) Among the several conferences organized by Jack at UTEP alone, I can cite the June 1975 "Symposium on Bilingual/Bicultural Education: Effects on the Language, Individual and Society," which brought together (as his conferences always manage to do) 40 or 50 linguists, Hispanists, educationists, anthropologists, sociologists, librarians and literary scholars from three or four continents and scores of universities.

Jack has also planned, directed, and taken part in the 12th and 13th International Congresses of Linguistics, the 2nd and 3rd International Congresses of Applied Linguistics, the First International Symposium on Language Acquisition, the 9th International Congress of Anthropological and Etymological Sciences, the 12th International Congress of Americanists, various conferences of the Asociación de Lingüística y Filología de la América Latina, and many others. His generosity as a promoter and a catalyst is matched only by his willingness to serve as a consultant, as he has done on numerous occasions, for organizations such as the Southwest Cooperative Educational Laboratory, the Educational Testing Service, the Language and Linguistics Research Center, the National Science Foundation, and the National Endowment for the Humanities. He is a member of the editorial board of Language Problems and Language Planning, was assistant managing editor for the Modern Language Journal from 1961-64, and even served as a "stringer" to the New York Times education page from 1960-64. His active memberships in linguocentric associations require feet as well as hands to count, and include LSA, LASSO (Linguistic Association of the Southwest, of which he was a founding member; the same is true of SWALLOW--the Southwest Areal Language and Linguistics Circle, which first met in 1972 in El Paso under Jack's sponsorship), LACUS, the American Dialect Society, PILEI, TESOL, AATSP, ALFAL, MLA, and others. Nor has Jack failed to make his mark in service to the community, as can be seen from a long list of talks on language, bilingualism and ethnic problems at the El Paso Jewish Community Center, Kiwanis, Lion's, and various Protestant and Catholic church groups. He has also served as advisor to the UTEP Armadillo Club of disabled students.

It goes without saying that given the nature of his permanent handicap, Jack's professional life has been little short of remarkable, and is vivid and enduring testimony to the triumph of mind over matter, spirit over infirmity, will over adversity. It is

also hardly necessary to add that in Jack we have a scholar who is
truly concerned with the advancement of his discipline, and concomitantly, the careers of all who have had the good fortune to come
in contact with him over the decades. He is the soul of selfless-
ness, ever inventive, ever innovative. (In this latter context it
should be noted that in 1979 he legally changed his name to Jacob
Ornstein-Galicia to honor both the land of his parents' birth--
Polish-Ukranian Galicia, and the similarly-spelled region of NW
Spain from whence proceeded so many of the New World's colonial
Hispanic settlers.) Jack will long be remembered wherever linguists
gather. To Jacob Ornstein, then, on the occasion of his 65th birthday, this volume is respectfully, affectionately dedicated.

PROFESSOR JACOB ORNSTEIN— BIBLIOGRAPHY

CONTRIBUTIONS TO SCHOLARLY JOURNALS AND TO ANTHOLOGIES

1941. Brazilian or Lisbonese? Hispania 24.406-8.
1942. Castilho e as suas adaptações portuguesas de Molière. Hispania 25.416-8.
1942. An emergency language program. Curriculum Journal 13.221-2.
1942. Misogyny and pro-feminism in early Castilian literature.
Modern Language Quarterly 3.221-34.
1942. A pre-test on Latin America. Educational Method 11.344-5.
1942. Problems in the teaching of Portuguese. Modern Language
Journal 26.512-6.
1944. Notas preliminares para um estudo de Aluizio Azevedo. Revista
Iberoamericana 7.391-9.
1949. Foreign languages and the postwar era. Junior College Journal
19.250-2.
1949. A pre-test on things Slavic and East European. Bulletin of
the American Association of Teachers of Slavic and East European Languages 6.
1949. A Romance language instructor looks at the Slavic languages.
Modern Language Journal 33.185-92.
1949. (with Stanley Johnston.) The use of audio-visual materials
by foreign language classes in junior colleges of the north
central states. Modern Language Journal 33.36-41.
1950. Facts, figures and opinions on the present status of Portuguese. Hispania 33.251-5.
1950. Medieval Spanish studies at the University of Wisconsin.
Bulletin of Hispanic Studies 27.88-93.
1950. (with J.Y. Causey.) Novels and novelists in present-day
Spain. Books Abroad 24.245-7.
1951. The archaic and the modern in the Spanish of New Mexico.
Hispania 34.137-41. Reprinted in: El lenguaje de los chicanos:
Regional and social characteristics . . . , ed. by E. Hernández-
Chávez et al., Arlington VA: Center for Applied Linguistics,
1975, pp. 6-12.

1951. A decade of Russian teaching: Notes on methodology and text-
       books. Modern Language Journal 35.263-79.
1951. The literary evolution of Ramón Sender. Modern Language Forum
       36.33-40.
1951. (with J.Y. Causey.) Una década de la novela española contem-
       poránea. Revista Hispánica Moderna 17.128-35.
1952. Desiderata in eighteenth century Spanish scholarship. Hispania
       35.296-300.
1953. Breve panorama de la novela chilena reciente. Revista Ibero-
       americana 17:36.336-44.
1953. (with J.Y. Causey.) Camilo José Cela, Spain's new novelist.
       Books Abroad 27.136-7.
1953. Labor hispanista de la Biblioteca del Congreso Norteamericano.
       Clavileño 21.39-43.
1954. A birdseye view of Brazilian-Portuguese studies in the United
       States. The Americas 10.463-70.
1954. Facilities and activities of the Library of Congress in the
       Slavic and Eastern European field. American Slavic and Eastern
       European Review 12.549-54.
1954. Russian teaching materials: new texts and further pedagogical
       needs. Modern Language Journal 38.66-76.
1958. Foreign language teaching in the Soviet Union--A qualitative
       view. Modern Language Journal 42.382-92.
1959. Soviet language policy. South Atlantic Bulletin 24:4.12-4.
1959. Soviet language policy: theory and practice. Slavic and
       East European Journal 17.1-24.
1959. (with J.A. Van Campen.) Alternative analyses of the Bulgar-
       ian phoneme. Language 25.264-70.
1959-60. Crisis in language training. American Scholar 24.75-81.
       (Reprinted in Education Digest 25.25-7, May 1960.)
1960. Ferment in the Polish classroom. Journal of Central European
       Affairs 20.69-83.
1960. Passport from Babel. Texas Quarterly 3.150-5.
1960. Seven steps to a second language. English Digest 63.22-4.
1960. Structurally oriented texts and teaching methods since World
       War II: a survey and appraisal. Anthology for use with a
       guide for teachers in NDEA language institutes, ed. by Simon
       Belasco, Boston: D.C. Heath, pp. 29-38.
1962. English the global way. Modern Language Journal 46.9-13.
1962. New frontiers in language learning. Modern Language Journal
       46.110-5.
1963. Contemporary patterns of language planning. Proceedings of
       the Washington Linguistics Club 1:1.7-10.
1963. Foreign language teaching (in the Soviet Union). Current
       Trends in Linguistics, vol. 1: Soviet and East European ling-
       uistics, ed. by Thomas A. Sebeok, The Hague: Mouton, pp. 143-
       91.
1964. Africa seeks a common language. Review of Politics 26.205-14.
1964. Patterns of language planning in the new states. World Poli-
       tics 17.40-9.
1967. (with Robert Lado.) Research in foreign language teaching
       methodology. International Review of Applied Linguistics (IRAL)
       5.11-25.

1968. Soviet language policy: continuity and change. Ethnic minorities in the Soviet Union, ed. by E. Goldhagen, New York: Prae-
ger, pp. 21-46.
1969. (with E.L. Blansitt, Jr.) Tagmemics and string grammar. Anthropological Linguistics 11.167-76.
1970. Once more: programmed instruction in the language field:
the state of the art. Language Learning 20.213-22.
1970. Sociolinguistics and the study of Southwest Spanish. Studies
in Language and Linguistics 1969-70, ed. by R.W. Ewton, Jr. and
J. Ornstein, El Paso: Texas Western Press, pp. 127-84.
1971. Language varieties along the U.S.-Mexican border. Applications of linguistics: selected papers of the Second International Congress of Applied Linguistics, ed. by G.E. Perren
and J.L.M. Trim, Cambridge GB: Cambridge University Press,
pp. 349-62.
1971. Sociolinguistic investigation of language diversity in the
U.S. Southwest. Modern Language Journal 55.224-9.
1972. Toward a classification of Southwest Spanish nonstandard
variants. Linguistics 93.70-87.
1972. Toward an inventory of interdisciplinary tasks in research on
U.S. Southwest bilingualism/biculturalism. Bilingualism in the
Southwest, ed. by Paul R. Turner, Tucson: Univ. of Arizona
Press, pp. 321-39.
1974. Sociolinguistic changes viewed within a tagmemic framework.
Proceedings of the Eleventh International Congress of Linguists,
ed. by Luigi Heilmann, Bologna: Il Mulino, vol. 1, pp. 197-222.
1974. (with R.J. MacIntosh.) A brief sampling of west Texas teacher
attitudes toward Spanish and English language varieties. Hispania 57.920-6.
1974. (with R. Paul Murphy.) Models and approaches in sociolinguistic research on language diversity. Anthropological Linguistics
16.141-67.
1975. Sociolinguistics and the study of Spanish and English language
varieties and their use in the U.S. Southwest (with a proposed
plan of research). Three essays on linguistic diversity in the
Spanish-speaking world ... , ed. by J. Ornstein, The Hague:
Mouton, pp. 9-45.
1975-76. Notes on a diachronic view of the development of sociolinguistic practice and theory in the American Southwest.
Journal of the Linguistic Association of the Southwest (LAS-
SO) 1:1.5-21 (August).
1976. Constraints on lexical borrowing in Tarahumara: explorations
in langue and parole. Anthropological Linguistics 18.70-93.
1976. A cross-cultural sociolinguistic investigation of Mexican-
American bilinguals/biculturals at a U.S. border university.
La Linguistique 12.131-45.
1976. The need for a sociolinguistic marking system: and a proposal. The Second LACUS Forum, ed. by Peter A. Reich, Columbia
SC: Hornbeam Press, pp. 514-27.
1976. (with G. Valdés-Fallis and B. Dubois.) Bilingual child-
language acquisition along the United States-Mexico border:
the El Paso-Ciudad Juárez-Las Cruces triangle. Word 27:1-3.
386-404 (April-August-December 1971-1976) (Special Issue on
"Child Language--1975," ed. by W. von Raffler-Engel).

1976, (with G.D. Bills.) Linguistic diversity in Southwest Span-
     ish. Studies in Southwest Spanish, ed. by J.D. Bowen and
     J. Ornstein, Rowley MA: Newbury House, 1976, pp. 4-16.
1976. (with David Gold.) A note on the Slavic impact on Yiddish.
     Orbis 25.121-8.
1976. (with R. Paul Murphy.) A survey of research on language di-
     versity: a partial who's who in sociolinguistics. The Second
     LACUS Forum, ed. by Peter A. Reich, Columbia SC: Hornbeam
     Press, 1976, pp. 423-61.
1977. Reflections of a linguist on the unending quest for a world
     language: negatives, positives and prospects. ITL: Review
     of Applied Linguistics 38.1-30.
1977. Southwest Spanish. Readers' Encyclopedia of the American
     West, ed. by Howard R. Lamar, New York: Crowell, pp. 1134-5.
1977. The tagmemic model and language variation. Linguistics at
     the crossroads, ed. by Adam Makkai et al., Padova, Italy and
     Lake Bluff IL: Liviana Editrice and Jupiter Press, 1977, pp.
     167-93.
1977. (with W.F. Mackey.) Bilingual education as an ecology.
     Studies in Language and Linguistics 1977-78, ed. by John M.
     Sharp (The Bilingual Education Movement: Essays on Its
     Progress), El Paso: Texas Western Press, pp. 96-120.
1977. (with W.F. Mackey.) The bilingual education movement:
     patterns and prospects. Studies in Language and Linguistics
     1977-78, ed. by John M. Sharp . . . , pp. 1-35.
1977. (with W.F. Mackey.) Evaluating bilingual education pro-
     grams: critical variables. Studies in Language and Linguis-
     tics 1977-78, ed. by John M. Sharp . . . , pp. 48-83.
1977. (with W.F. Mackey.) The revolt of the ethnics. Studies in
     Language and Linguistics 1977-78, ed. by John M. Sharp . . . ,
     pp. 121-48.
1978. Relational bilingualism--a new approach to linguistic-cultural
     diversity and a Mexican-American case study. Ethnicity 5.148-66.

CONTRIBUTIONS TO POPULAR JOURNALS

1955. Mechanical translation: new challenge to communication. Science (Oct. 21).
1957. To win the 'language race' with Russia. New York Times Magazine (Sept. 15).
1958. Lame horse in the languages race. Kiwanis Magazine (May). (Reprinted in
         the Congressional Record, July 18, 1958.)
1958. The war of words. Ordnance (May-June).
1958. Start 'em young with a second tongue. Parents' Magazine (October).
1958. Language engineering. Popular Electronics (November).
1958. Why your child should learn a foreign language. Living (November).
1958. Breaking the language barrier. Think (December).
1959. Foreign language: chink in America's armor. Foreign Service Journal
         (February).
1959. Why can't your child speak a foreign language? Woman's Day (April).
1959. You ought to learn Russian. Popular Mechanics (May).
1959. America needs more technicians. Kiwanis Magazine (July).
1959. Foreign language is child's play. Rexall Reporter (September).

1959. Man against Babel. Western World (September).
1959-60. Crisis in language training. American Scholar (winter).
1960. Be your own interpreter. Think (February).
1960. Seven steps to a second language. English Digest (July).
1960. Overseasmanship--the urgent need for linguistic ability in international
       trade. Export Trade (Sept. 12).
1960. Half a million linguists in our grade schools. Today's Health (October).
1960. Our tongue-tied generation. Saturday Review (Nov. 26).
1961. (with A.E. Smith) Language escorts to the entire world. Foreign Service
       Journal (July).
1961. New recruits for science. Parents' Magazine (February).
1961. Russian fever. America (Sept. 15).
1962. Man against Babel. Kiwanis Magazine (June).
1963. Our linguistic buildup is slow. Washington Sunday Post (June 9).
1963. A frank appraisal of the foreign language program in our grade schools.
       Woman's Day (January). (Reprinted in Education Digest as "The FL
       program in grade schools," April.)
1964. The many-faceted approach to a world language. Washington Sunday Star
       (May 3).
1964. The tower of Babel compounded. Washington Sunday Post (July 12).
1964. Chinese, Urdu, Turkish... Washington Sunday Star ("Schools 1964" supple-
       ment, Aug. 23).
1964. How a lack of linguistic skills hurts the U.S. at home, abroad. National
       Observer (Sept. 28).
1973. New accents in foreign language teaching. Intellect Magazine (March).

REVIEWS

1949. von Gronicka-Bates. Essentials of Russian. Bulletin of the American
       Association of Teachers of Slavic and East European Languages 6.
1958. Pei. One language for the world. Saturday Review (July 19).
1959. Muller. Anglo Russkiy Slovar' (English-Russian Dictionary). Modern
       Language Journal 43.300-1.
1959. Lord. Beginning Serbocroatian. Modern Language Journal 43.360-1.
1959. Lunt. Fundamentals of Russian. Modern Language Journal 43.257-8.
1959. Magner. Manual of scientific Russian. Modern Language Journal 43.207-8.
1959. Zaimovsky and Litvinova. Russian-English, English-Russian pocket dic-
       tionary. Modern Language Journal 43.408.
1960. Borras and Christian. Russian syntax. Modern Language Journal 44.286.
1960. Byrnes. Bibliography of American publications on East Central Europe (1945-
       57). Modern Language Journal 44.375.
1960. Byrnes, ed. The non-western areas in undergraduate education in Indiana.
       American Slavic and East European Review 18.322-3.
1960. Hingley. Soviet prose. Modern Language Journal 44.369-70.
1960. Magner. The Russian alphabet. Modern Language Journal 44.242-3.
1960. Magner and Alexeev. The sounds of Russian. Modern Language Journal 44.371.
1960. Moore and Struve. Practical Russian, Book II. Modern Language Journal
       44.334.
1960. Morreale, ed. Enrique de Villena, 'Los doze trabajos de Hércules'. Sym-
       posium 14:2.143-5.
1960. Pei and Nikanov. Getting along in Russian. Modern Language Journal 44.52.

1960. Pressman. Conversational Russian. Modern Language Journal 44.193.
1960. Smirnitsky. Russko-Angliyskiy slovar' (Russian-English dictionary).
       Modern Language Journal 44.286.
1964. Kreusler. Teaching of modern foreign languages in the Soviet Union.
       Slavic and East European Journal 8.468-9.
1970. Rand. Constructing dialogs. General Linguistics 11.56-9.
1974. Steiner. Two centuries of Spanish and English bilingual lexicography
       (1590-1800). Linguistics 132.123-5.
1975. Makkai and Lockwood, eds. Readings in stratificational linguistics.
       Lingua 33.398-404.
1977. Currie and García. Sociolinguistics and the two American linguistic
       orthodoxies. Language in Society 6.75-8.
1977. Sánchez-Marco. Acercamiento histórico a la sociolingüística. Language
       53.949-52.

BOOKS AND MONOGRAPHS

1954. Luiz de Lucena, 'Repetición de amores.' Univ. of North Carolina Studies
       in Romance Languages and Literatures, No. 23 (Chapel Hill: Univ. of
       North Carolina Press).
1957. Slavic and East European studies: their development and status in the
       Western Hemisphere. Washington DC: U.S. Dept. of State (External
       Research Paper No. 129), March 29.
1960. Say it correctly in Serbo-Croatian. New York: Dover Publications.
1964. (with W.W. Gage.) The ABC's of language and linguistics. Philadelphia:
       Chilton Books. (2nd ed. with C.W. Hayes and W.W. Gage, Silver Spring
       MD: Institute of Modern Languages, 1977.)
1964. (with R.C. Howes.) Elements of Russian. Boston: Allyn and Bacon.
1970. (with Bonnie S. Brooks, Gary Brooks and Paul W. Goodman.) Sociolinguistic
       background questionnaire: instrument for measuring bilingualism. El
       Paso: Southwest Ethnic Study Center/Univ. of Texas-El Paso. (2nd ed.
       1972.)
1970. (ed., with R.W. Ewton, Jr.) Studies in language and linguistics 1969-70.
       El Paso: Texas Western Press.
1971. (with R.W. Ewton, Jr. and Theodore Mueller.) Programmed instruction and
       educational technology in the language teaching field. Philadelphia:
       Center for Curriculum Development.
1972. (ed., with R.W. Ewton, Jr.) Studies in language and linguistics 1971-72.
       El Paso TX: Texas Western Press.
1975. A sociolinguistic study of Mexican-American and Anglo students in a bor-
       der university. Border State Symposium Series, No. 3 (ed. by Will
       Kennedy) San Diego: Institute of Public and Urban Affairs Press/
       California State Univ.
1975. (ed.) Three essays on linguistic diversity in the Spanish-speaking world
       (the U.S. Southwest and the River Plate area). The Hague: Mouton.
1976. (ed., with J.D. Bowen.) Studies in Southwest Spanish. Rowley MA: Newbury
       House.
1978. (ed., with G.L. Gilbert.) Problems in applied educational sociolinguistics:
       readings on language and cultural problems of U.S. ethnic groups. The
       Hague: Mouton.

ON MARKEDNESS
AND SOCIOLINGUISTIC VARIATION[1]

JON AMASTAE

Pan American University

Bilingual communities are often of interest because they throw into sharper relief certain topics of linguistic interest. While language acquisition, sociolinguistic variation, and language change are present in every linguistic community, they assume a heightened focus in a bilingual community, and the ways in which they intersect become particularly interesting objects of study. Often the intersection of these three aspects of linguistics becomes like the psychologist's Necker cube or figure ground puzzle which is seen differently, e.g., as a chalice or as two faces in silhouette, depending where one focuses one's gaze, but which cannot be seen as both items at once. Thus a set of data may be interpreted, from the point of view of the individual speaker, as pertaining to language acquisition. Or, if the point of view is the community, it may be interpreted as pertaining to the analysis of synchronic variation. Or finally, to shift the gaze to the abstract system, that same data may be analyzed for what it shows about language change and the abstract linguistic system. In this brief paper I want to take data which, in its most narrow interpretation, pertains to synchronic variation, and show how such data may be of importance for what it reveals about both language acquisition and abstract structure.

Consider the variations in English consonants by a small sample of Mexican-American university students. These students

were all bilingual, and while English was perhaps the language
they had learned second and was not the language of their homes,
all were competent English speakers. The interview procedure
was designed to elicit variants of English sounds often noted to
cause difficulties for Spanish speakers and included various
types of elicitation procedures, including word list reading,
paragraph reading, and conversation (cf. Amastae 1978, 1979 ms. for
more complete description of the subjects and procedure).

After the interviews the data were tabulated to show whether
the speaker did or did not use, completely, the standard English
variant of each variable. The patterns of variance and invariance form a very interesting array, in which we can see a continuum from variance to invariance with respect to the use of
these variables. This method of treating data is the Guttman
scale, developed for use in linguistics by De Camp (1971),
Bickerton (1971, 1973), and Gatbonton-Segalowitz (1975). Though
none of the speakers interviewed conforms to a third possibility,
it exists nonetheless: an exclusive use of nonstandard variants.
These would appear to the left of an array such as Figure 1 (cf.
Amastae 1978, for a similar treatment of selected vowels, and
Amastae 1979 for a different perspective on the consonants).

		y	ð	ǰ	θ	š	C#	č	z
Speaker	7	2	2	1	1	1	1	②	1
	5	2	2	2	1	1	1	1	1
	1	2	2	2	1	1	1	1	1
	9	2	2	2	2	1	1	1	1
	6	2	2	2	2	2	1	1	1
	4	2	2	2	2	2	1	1	1
	8	2	2	2	2	①	2	1	1
	3	2	2	2	2	2	2	1	1
	2	2	2	2	2	2	2	2	1

Where 1 = incomplete use of standard variants
      2 = complete use of standard variant
coefficient of reproducibility = .97 all contexts

Figure 1

Remember that this is purely synchronic data, a frozen in-
stant so to speak, which simply places individuals in relationship to each other with respect to their use of certain linguistic forms. It is, however, susceptible to further linguistic
analysis.

Phonological theory since the Prague school has attempted to
incorporate a mechanism for analyzing the "intrinsic content"
(Chomsky and Halle 1968, ch. 9) of features. This is the theory
of markedness, which involves consideration of order in acquisition, perceptual salience, and frequency of occurrence in natural
languages. The theory of markedness, then, should be able to
provide us with explanatory descriptions of various factors in
natural language (cf. Chomsky and Halle 1968). In fact, however,
the theory of markedness has not been pursued much of late, and
has not fulfilled much of its early promise. We may ask, then,
how an array such as Figure 1 fits the concept of markedness,
and what it can tell us about possible revisions of the theory.
Consider the SPE marking conventions below in Figure 2. The
circled values are marked for each feature.

	y	ð	ǰ	θ	š	C#	č	z
low	-							
high	+							
back	-		(+)		(-)		(-)	-
anterior	-	+	(-)	+	(-)		(-)	+
coronal	-	+	+	+	+		+	+
continuant	(+)	-	(+)		(+)			+
delayed release		-	+	-	-		+	+
strident	(-)	+	(-)	+			+	+
voice	(+)	(+)	-	-			-	(+)

Figure 2

If the markedness is to explain acquisition, a simple approach here is clearly insufficient since it would predict that
segments with fewer marks would be learned before segments with
more marks, which is clearly not so, for ð and ǰ, each with 3
m's are "learned" by the speakers in Figure 1 before z, with only
one m.

Studies of English L₁ acquisition are interesting here.
Smith (1973) notes that at the age of 4 years 3 months the child
studied had acquired all the adult system except for /š ž θ ð/

(all replaced by /s/) and /z/, though [z] had been used as a
realization of various other phonemes.[2] Ferguson and Farwell
(1975) note for three children between 11 and 14 months that /z/
had not appeared. Burling (1959) notes that at 2 years 8 months
the child investigated had not acquired /z, ž, š/, all of which
were realized by /s/, nor had he acquired / ð θ /. Velten (1943)
notes that while [z] was used as the phonetic realization of various phonemes, it was not acquired as a full phoneme until late.
Dale (1976) also notes that it is extremely common for children
to devoice final voiced stops, e.g., bag > bak. That the affricates and interdental fricatives are acquired late is well known,
but it seems less widely acknowledged (though no less clear) that
/z/ is also acquired late by monolingual English speakers.

Though these acquisition data perhaps help explain why these
segments under consideration are troublesome, they do relatively
little to account for some of the orders among them, given the
SPE chart. Why the voiced ð is acquired before the voiceless θ,
for example, appears mysterious, given that voiceless obstruents
are generally less marked than voiced ones. Equally mysterious
is the position of final voiced stops in the learning continuum,
despite the tendency noted by Dale (1976). However, it is not
particularly surprising that ð θ are acquired before the disambi-
guation of š č since the dentoalveolars are less marked than the
alveolopalatals.

It might be proposed that function within the Spanish system
(e.g., functional load or another such concept) might be involved
here. At present I do not see how this could be so. For example,
ð occurs only allophonically, and θ does not occur at all in
American Spanish, while č certainly occurs phonemically (though
it is phonetically distinct from English č); š occurs allophonically in some dialects, including the one spoken by most of the
speakers considered here; [z] also occurs, though only as an allophone of [z] (e.g., desde [dɛzðe]). Why then are ð and θ acquired
before š, č and ž? Function in Spanish apparently provides no answer (cf. below, however).

Another possible factor is the frequency of occurrence in
English of these consonants. However, this seems not to be important. Wang and Crawford's (1960) collation of ten consonant
frequency studies (cf. fn. 2) shows that z occurs near the middle
in frequency, while ð occurs more frequently, and š and θ very
infrequently. (The affricates č ǰ are not included in the studies). Apparently, then, frequency of occurrence in the target
language explains no more than functional load in the first language.

In very interesting work, Williams, Cairns, et al. analyzed
the errors made on selected consonant phonemes by Standard
English-, Mexican-American English-, and Black English-speaking
school children in grades 1-12. In particular, the study was
focused toward using markedness theory to explain the errors
made, especially in the substitutions which occurred. The hypothesis that the substitution errors would be less marked than
the target sound was thought to be confirmed overwhelmingly for
the speakers of Standard English but less so for Mexican-American

or Black speakers of English, who were thought to have been influenced more by phonetic variation from a first language or
dialect.
  Nevertheless, several interesting things emerge from these
studies. Williams, Cairns, <u>et al</u>. were not concerned with de-
veloping continuums or with ranking troublesome phonemes, yet a
continuum of "errors" can be developed from their data, as they
give the total number of errors for each segment. The Williams/
Cairns continuum is (from fewest "errors" to most) for Mexican-

  n p r l b g ǰ d ð θ š č v z

Americans which, excluding sounds I have not investigated, is
exactly the continuum shown here, except for ǰ/ð. Thus the validity of the continuum is strongly confirmed.
  Moreover, there is a certain congruence between the rankings
for the three groups of speakers (that the segments for each
group differ slightly is due to the exclusion of those which had
"errors" below a certain threshold of occurrence):

  MAE: n p ð r l b g ǰ d ð θ š č v z

  SE: b m g t d n k p ǰ f č š s l ð v θ r z

  BE: m f t č s š n r z ǰ l g ð p b d v ð θ

These are very rough rankings, including "errors" of both substitution and omission, and thus are not totally comparable. The
MAE and SE rankings are generally congruent, but the position of
the voiced stops g b d seems to be a key difference. However, if
one realizes that these again are predominantly "substitution
errors" (k/g, p/b, t/d) in final position (again, devoicing of
final stops), then the orders begin to look much more similar.
  Williams, Cairns, <u>et al</u>. were led to their conclusion that
error sources for speakers of standard English are largely different from those for speakers of Mexican-American or Black
English by their examination of substitutions[3] and by their pre-
disposition to find feature unmarking, or a reduction in the number of marks, for the resulting segment. But although they do
not develop it, their own work contains the key to the essential
similarity of the three groups of speakers, and the key does have
to do with markedness.
  For all three groups of speakers, continuancy and stridency
are difficult features. Stops are the most natural obstruents,
and exclusive of final position, the earliest acquired. Con-
tinuants are in general acquired later, and the co-variation
among continuancy, stridency, and voicing is particularly problematic. Strident sounds are perceptually salient, and s, as
the unmarked strident continuant, is particularly salient. However, voicing appears to alter this salience considerably, making
z appear much less strident and, therefore, given the fact that
its stridency is keyed to its continuancy[4] (i.e., these features

are much less subject to alteration), perceptually indistinct.
Thus z is very likely to "become" s, or more accurately, voicing
will not be attached to continuancy and stridency until very
late.

Confirmation of this is found in work by Olmsted (1971)
which may be the most complete study of phonological development
of English speakers, in that it is based on extensive data from
100 children between 15 and 54 months. Olmsted performed extensive
calculations for various factors influencing the data collection
and analysis, such as ratios of successes/attempts, corpus size,
position in the utterance, etc. The consonants examined in the
present study were all shown by Olmsted to be acquired very late,
though direct comparisons are difficult because of the detail involved in Olmsted's work, particularly with respect to position
in the utterance. However as Olmsted notes (1971: 186), voicing
is advantageous in learning the first stops, but disadvantageous
in learning the later fricatives. Blache (1978) also notes in a
very elaborate statistical study that "stridency must be acquired
after continuancy," and that "features such as voicing and place
appeared to be working within major subclasses" (246).

The evidence from Black English speakers shows that the nature of a prior spoken language or dialect may alter the continuum
somewhat (ð θ rather than z are apparently the standard English
sounds adopted last by many Black speakers);[5] notice, however,
that the essential fact that continuancy, stridency, and voicing
are problematic is unchanged.

It seems, then, that markedness can explain all these continuums, though not if we look only for feature unmarking, and
not if we just count marks for each segment. We do see that an
approach based on features rather than on unit phonemes works
best in explaining second language acquisition as in phonology
generally.

We also see that, in effect, the SPE marking conventions
need revision, especially in that some way must be found to weight
features in their relationships with each other and to take account of position in the utterance, as for example with voiced
stops, which are in general acquired early, but not in word final
position. Lack of space prevents doing that here, and in any
event more evidence will be needed, but nonetheless the path
seems clear. It should be noted also that evidence from universal occurrence points in the same direction. A quick scan of
Ruhlen (1975) suggests that z is a relatively rare phoneme, as
are č, š, θ, ð.

Another need is for work on the mechanisms interrelating acquisitional and dialectal/sociolinguistic processes.[6] We infer
that Figure 2 replicates sequences of acquisition. But in a
given speech community some of these segments may become markers
of style or some other sociolinguistic trait, while others may
not. These may then show clear patterns of variation such as
those given by Labov (1972). With which segments will this occur,
and with which will it not occur? It makes intuitive sense to
think that similar constraints operate for the selection of fea-

tures to carry sociolinguistic meaning as for those to carry morphological meaning (unmarked, perceptually unambiguous), but this will need much more investigation. Just these several possibilities suggest interesting directions for future research into the connections between data provided by sociolinguistic variation and our understanding of language in general.

NOTES

[1]The research which is the subject of this report was supported in whole or in part by the U.S. Office of Education, Department of Health, Education and Welfare. However, the opinions expressed herein do not necessarily reflect the position of policy of the U.S. Office of Education, and no official endorsement should be inferred. The research reported here has been supported by an Advanced Institutional Development Grant OEG - 0 - 74 - 2511 to Pan American University, which support is gratefully acknowledged. I thank Nicholas Sobin for helpful comments.

[2]It is difficult in reading such studies to discern whether the author is discussing mastery of phonemic or phonetic segments, and, in discussing numbers of errors, whether a substitution of X for Y is one error (Y) or two (X and Y). This also makes comparability between studies difficult. Nevertheless, I proceed in spite of these problems, especially since the studies discussed below show remarkable consistency.

[3]Assuming of course that the Black and Mexican American speakers were actually attempting Standard English and that therefore the deviances were actually errors. Otherwise, Williams, et al. were simply seeing differences between Black English and Mexican American English and Standard English. See Amastae 1979 for much more detailed discussion of the relationship between social and acquisition factors.

[4]In Cairns' marking conventions, not SPE.

[5]The actual shape of 'substitution' (cf. fn.3) is what is covered by the concept of interference. We see here, however, that merely identifying substitutions is not terribly revealing in an overall linguistics sense.

[6]Bailey (1973) has done exactly this. Though he has a strong predilection to identify "natural" change with feature unmarking, he does note that other sorts of changes may leave segments more marked. Clearly what is necessary is research which will enable us to construct a model capable of unifying dialectal changes, language acquisition, and abstract linguistic structure, whether we are dealing with marking or unmarking. An example of variation "going the opposite direction" (again the focus of the view, individual or social--along with certain assumptions--determines the

"direction" of the choice: marked → unmarked or unmarked → marked) would be devoicing of final stops, common in many dialects and languages (e.g., German).

REFERENCES

Amastae, J. 1978. The acquisition of English vowels. To appear in Papers in Linguistics 11.
_____. 1979. Learner continuums and speech communities. (Manuscript.)
Bailey, C.-J.N. 1973. Variation and linguistic theory. Washington DC: Center for Applied Linguistics.
Blache, Stephen E. 1978. The acquisition of distinctive features. Baltimore MD: University Park Press.
Bickerton, D. 1971. Inherent variability and variable rules. Foundations of Language 72.457-92.
_____. 1973. On the nature of a creole continuum. Language 49.640-69.
Burling, R. 1959. Language development of a Garo and English speaking child. Word 15.45-68.
Chomsky, N. and M. Halle. 1968. The sound pattern of English. New York: Harper and Row.
Dale, P. 1976. Language development. New York: Holt, Rinehart and Winston.
Decamp, D. 1971. Toward a generative analysis of a post-creole continuum. Pidginization and creolization of languages, ed. by D. Hymes, pp. 349-70. Cambridge: Cambridge University Press.
Ferguson, C.A. and C.B. Farwell. 1975. Words and sounds in early language acquisition. Language 51.419-39.
Gatbonton-Segalowitz, E. 1975. Systematic variation in second language speech: a sociolinguistic study. PhD Diss., McGill Univ.
Labov, W. 1972. Sociolinguistic patterns. Philadelphia: Univ. of Pennsylvania Press.
Olmsted, D. 1971. Out of the mouths of babes. The Hague: Mouton.
Ruhlen, M. 1975. A guide to the languages of the world. Stanford CA: Stanford University.
Smith, N. 1973. The acquisition of phonology. Cambridge: Cambridge University Press.
Velten, H.V. 1943. The growth of phonemic and lexical patterns in infant language. Language 19.281-92.
Wang, W. and J. Crawford. 1960. Frequency studies of English consonants. Language and Speech 33.131-9.
Williams, F., H. Cairns and C. Cairns. 1971. An analysis of the variation from standard English pronunciations in the phonetic performance of two groups of non-standard English-speaking children. Austin TX: Center for Communication Research.
Williams, F., H. Cairns, C. Cairns, and D. Blosser. 1971. Analysis of production errors in the phonetic performance of school age standard English-speaking children. Austin: Center for Communication Research.

POSSESSIVE RELATIVE CLAUSES

EDWARD L. BLANSITT, JR.

The University of Texas at El Paso

1.   Characterization of possessive relative clauses

The basic subtype of relative clause (RC), including that
which is the topic of this paper, may be defined as a predicate-
headed structure (i.e., clause) which is a dependent of a nominal
or nominalized adjective which manifests, either totally or partially, one of the functions within the clause or within one of
the nominal groups within the clause. This definition is not
broad enough to include such clauses as which made her very happy
in John finally proposed to Alice, which made her very happy or
what you told Bill in I didn't like what you told Bill for lack,
in each case, of a governing nominal. It quite properly excludes that I might dance the tango in the idea that I might
dance the tango because, although there is a governing nominal,
it manifests no function within the dependent clause.
   A possessive relative clause (PRC) is a RC in which the function of the nominal governing the RC is that of a dependent of one
of the nominal elements in the RC to which it is semantically related as possessor to possessee. The RC whose sister Frank often
dates in that boy whose sister Frank often dates is a PRC.
   Possessive relative clauses, just as other RC's, may be
either restrictive or non-restrictive. The PRC whose latest

<u>novel is a best-seller</u> is restrictive in <u>John knows a writer</u>
<u>whose latest novel is a best-seller</u>, where the PRC completes the
identification of the writer, and non-restrictive in <u>John's wife</u>,
<u>whose latest novel is a best seller, is working on another one</u>.
Restrictive RC's are universal; non-restrictive RC's do not seem
to occur in some languages (Downing 1978:380).

In most cases, the referent of the governing nominal of a
RC is the sole participant corresponding to a particular gram-
matical function in the RC, but this does not hold in all cases.
I recently --at breakfast in a restaurant in Colorado City,
Texas-- overheard the following sentence:

1) She's marrying a boy that they went to high school
        together.

In this case, the governing noun <u>boy</u> only partially manifests the
function of subject in the RC; the total subject is <u>the boy and</u>
<u>she</u> = <u>they</u>. There is generally, as in this case, function revers-
ibility between intransitive subject and comitative and combin-
ability of intransitive subject and comitative as intransitive
subject with, in English, <u>together</u> manifesting comitative: he
<u>went to high school with her</u> ≡ <u>she went to high school with him</u>
≡ <u>they went to high school together</u>. I also find perfectly acceptable the sentences below which are introduced by the relative marker <u>that</u> and in which the governing noun is represented
anaphorically by the corresponding personal pronoun in a coordinated series.

2a) I have a friend that he and his brother married twins.

2b) *I have a friend who and his brother married twins.

2c) ?I have a friend whose brother and he married twins.

3a) I have a friend from Chicago that we're going to take
        him and his wife on a trip with us.

3b) *I have a friend from Chicago whom and his wife we're
        going to take on a trip with us.

3c) *I have a friend from Chicago whose wife and him we're
        going to take on a trip with us.

4a) I have a friend from Chicago that we're going to go
        with him and his wife on a trip.

4b) *I have a friend from Chicago with whom and his wife
        we're going to go on a trip.

4c) *I have a friend from Chicago with whose wife and him

we're going on a trip.

In all cases, I also find a coordination of relatives unacceptable.

4d) *I have a friend from Chicago with whom and whose wife
we're going to go on a trip.

4e) *I have a friend from Chicago with whose wife and whom
we're going to go on a trip.

Coordination structures link functionally equivalent elements or functionally equivalent sequences of elements. For this reason, it would not be expected that a relative pronoun, with two functions, might be linked in a coordination structure with another element which shares only one of those functions. This observation accounts for the unacceptability of who and his wife but not that of who and whose wife.

A relative clause may have no relative marker, although such cases are not very common, or it may have an overt relative marker which may be either pronominal or non-pronominal. In postnominal RC's the relative marker most frequently occurs initially in the RC; less commonly it occurs in the predicate or may even be discontinuous. In Somali, a SOV-postpositional language with postnominal RC's, a postposed nominal emphasis marker may be interpreted, when immediately following a verb, as a RC-final relative marker. A pronominal relative marker, i.e., relative pronoun, has double function. A relative pronoun may be overtly marked for function, with an adposition or case affix; a non-pronominal relative marker cannot be marked for function but is not necessarily invariant as it may show some kind of agreement with the governing nominal.

A tendency to avoid relative pronouns, and hence a preference for non-pronominal relative markers, seems to be universal. Unaccessibility for coordination is only one reason; less complexity in the always linear encoding process is the most powerful reason for the preference for single-function relative markers. In the case of a RC-initial relative pronoun, specification of the function of the governing nominal in the RC will also be required in the initial segment; in the case of a non-pronominal relative marker, function specification is delayed, generally until the position at which that particular function would be specified in a non-relative clause.

2. A common type of postnominal relative clause

2.1. Non-possessive relative clauses

Examples from Albanian, French, Irish, Moroccan Arabic, Scots Gaelic, Swahili, and Welsh show RC's introduced by non-pronominal relative markers and the governing noun represented pronominally as axis of a relator-axis structure. In formal Alba-

nian, formal French, and Moroccan Arabic, there are RC's in which
a preposition precedes a relative pronoun.

5a) ALBANIAN (colloquial)

    zotnija   qi   fjalosëm   dje   me'të

        man   rel. we-spoke   yesterday with-him

    'the man (that) we spoke to yesterday'

5b) ALBANIAN (formal)

    zotnija   me   të   cilin fjalosëm   dje

        man   with him   whom   we-spoke yesterday

    'the man with whom we spoke yesterday'   (Mann 1932: 69)

6a) FRENCH (colloquial)

    l'ami   que tu   vas   chez lui

    the friend rel. you   go   to-house-of him

    'the friend whose house you're going to'

6b) FRENCH (formal)

    l'ami   chez   qui tu   vas

    the friend to-house-of   whom   you   go

    'the friend to whose house you're going'

                    (Tesnière 1969: 570)

7) IRISH

    an   speal   go   mbaineann sé   an féar   léi

    the scythe rel. he-cuts   he the grass with-her

    'the scythe (that) he cuts the grass with'

               (Dillon and Croínín 1961: 147)

8) MOROCCAN ARABIC

    a) le-mkoḥla lli   qtelt   biha   s-sbeʕ

        the rifle rel. he-killed with-her the lion

        'the rifle (that) he killed the lion with'

    b) le-mkoḥla   b-aš   qtelt   s-sbeʕ

        the rifle with which he-killed the lion

                        (Harrell 1962: 164)

9) SCOTS GAELIC

    na   daoine   a dh'fhuirich   thu   aca

    the-pl. men   rel. you-stayed   you   with-them

    'the men (that) you stayed with' (MacLaren 1971: 110)

10) SWAHILI

    msichana ambaye nilikwenda sinema naye

     girl rel.3sg.an I-went   movies with-her

    'the girl (that) I went to the movies with'

11) WELSH

    y   wlad   y   daeth   ef ohoni

    the country rel. he-came he from-her

    'the country (that) he came from'   (Smith 1925: II,90)

The use of a personal pronoun in a RC as an anaphoric substitute
for the governing noun following, initially in the RC, a non-pronominal relative marker is probably the most common type of
structure when function must be overtly manifested by an adposition. In some languages, as optionally in English, no pronoun is
used and the adposition stands alone as an axisless relator; such
is the case in Acooli, Danish, Norwegian, Sonay, Swedish, and
Tarahumara. Just as in formal English and formal Albanian, an
imposed preposition + relative pronoun structure can be found in
literary usage in North Germanic languages; in Acooli, a SVO-post-
positional language, an alternative RC structure has the post-

position immediately following the initial relative marker, in which case the marker may reasonably be interpreted as a relative pronoun.

12) ACOOLI

òdeéro ma gĭyεέkó   kí bεεl

basket <u>rel</u>. they-sift with corn

'a basket (that) they sift corn with'

                     (Crazzolara 1938: 95)

13a) DANISH (normal)

en   ven   (som)   man kan stole på

a friend   (<u>rel</u>.)   one can count on

'a friend (that) one can count on'

13b) DANISH (literary)

en   ven,   på hvem man kan stole

a friend   on whom one can count

                (Koefoed 1958: 176)

14) NORWEGIAN

huset   som jeg bor i

the-house <u>rel</u>. I live in

'the house (that) I live in' (Berulfsen 1971: 49)

15) SONAY

  a) gobo   k'a   n'a   kar nda

     stick <u>rel</u>. he <u>perf</u>. he hit with

     'the stick that he has hit with'

  b) gobo   kaṅ   nda a n'a kar

     stick <u>rel</u>. with he <u>perf</u>. he hit

     'the stick with which he has hit'   (Prost 1956: 137)

16)   SWEDISH

       den person, (som) ni talar om

       the person (<u>rel</u>.) you talk about

       'the person (that) you're talking about

                        (Björkhagen 1962: 102)

17)   TARAHUMARA

       wià   ma ne gite cǎʔpimea

       rope <u>rel</u>. I with will-catch

       'the rope (that I will catch with)

                        (Brambila 1953: 57)

2.2. <u>Possessive relative clauses</u>

The double function of a possessive relative pronominal adjective makes a single-function relative marker desireable also
in PRC's. The problems are not so severe in a SVO language when
the possessee noun functions as subject in the relative clause.
In the cii) examples below, a single-function relative marker is
used.

18a)   ENGLISH: I know a man whose sister speaks French.

18b)   GERMAN: Ich kenne einen Mann dessen Schwester Franzö-
               sisch spricht.[1]

18ci) SPANISH (formal)

       Conozco a un hombre cuya hermana habla francés.

18cii) SPANISH (normal informal)

       Conozco a un hombre que su hermana habla francés.

The complications become much more severe, particularly in a NG
language, when the nominal group in which the governing noun as
possessee is rankshifted and functions as an element of structure
in another nominal group. German in this case is NG, but the relative pronoun itself remains in initial position of the RC preceded only by the preposition <u>von</u>; Spanish, which is always NG

except with a pronominal possessor, is forced to have the relative marker, in the structure used in the formal written language (ci)), far from RC-initial position.

19a) I know a man whose sister's mother-in-law speaks French.

19b) Ich kenne einen Mann von dem die Schwiegermutter von der Schwester Französisch spricht.[2]

19ci) Conozco a un hombre la suegra de cuya hermana habla francés.

19cii) Conozco a un hombre que la suegra de su hermana habla francés.

20a) I know a man whose sister's mother-in-law's best friend speaks French.

20b) Ich kenne einen Man von dem die beste Freundin von der Schwiegermutter von der Schwester Französisch spricht.

20ci) Conozco a un hombre la mejor amiga de la suegra de cuya hermana habla francés.

20cii) Conozco a un hombre que la mejor amiga de la suegra de su hermana habla francés.

Possessive relative clauses in Acooli, Irish, Maltese, Margi, Moroccan Arabic, Old English, Scots Gaelic, Swahili, Tswana, Welsh, and Yoruba are all introduced by a non-pronominal relative marker and the governing nominal appears pronominally as possessee in the RC.

21) ACOOLI

làcɔ̀ɔ̀ ma   gïwàŋò   ɔ̀dὲ

man <u>rel</u>.   they-burned   house-his

'the man whose house they burned'

(Crazzolara 1938: 95)

22) IRISH

an fear gur imigh a mhac go Sasana

the man <u>rel</u>. went his son to England

'the man whose son went to England'

(Dillon and Coínín 1961: 148)

23) MALTESE

il-kaptan   li   s-suldati   tiegħu telquh

the captain <u>rel</u>. the soldiers of-him deserted-him

'the captain whose soldiers deserted him'

(Aquilina 1965: 99)

24) MARGI

bzɛ́r kų́ dɛ́ hyájá aɓɛ́l

boy <u>rel</u>. leg-his broke

'the boy whose leg broke'   (Hoffmann 1963:   90)

25) MOROCCAN ARABIC

l-bent   lli   bbaha   mrid

the girl <u>rel</u>. father-her sick

'the girl whose father is sick'   (Harrell 1962: 164)

26) OLD ENGLISH

se wer, ðe his tohopa bið to Drihtne

the man <u>rel</u>. his trust will-be in Lord

'the man whose trust is in the Lord'

(Mitchell 1965: 74)

27) SCOTS GAELIC

am fear a thainig a mhac gu baile

the man <u>rel</u>. came his son to house

'the man whose son came to the house'

(MacLaren 1971: 110)

28) SWAHILI

mtu   ambaye mtoto wake anaongea lugha kumi

person <u>rel</u>. 3sg.an. child his speaks language ten

'the person whose child speaks ten languages'

29) TSWANA

monna yôdikgômo tsagagwê ditimêtseng

 man rel.-cattle his   have-strayed

'the man whose cattle have strayed' (Cole 1955: 181)

30) WELSH

y   weddw y lladdwyd ei gûr

the widow <u>rel</u>. they-killed her husband

'the widow whose husband they killed'

(Smith 1925: 91)

31) YORUBA

okùnrin tí mo wọ̀ sí ilé rẹ̀

 man   <u>rel</u>. I enter to house his

'the man whose house I entered'   (Rowlands 1969: 89)

In Sonay, the governing nominal is understood as possessor without a possessive pronoun.

32) SONAY

boro   kań fula go né

man rel. hat be here

'the man whose hat is here'   (Prost 1956: 73)

In the Tarahumara PRC, the possessive postposition níwara stands
as an axisless relator just as the instrumental postposition
gite does in 17), perhaps because Tarahumara has no special
third-person pronouns.

33) TARAHUMARA

(ŕejói) ma   čabé níwara wasi mu cigore

(man) rel. long-ago 's cow you stole

'(the man) whose cow you stole long ago'

(Brambila 1953: 58)

In Somali, there is no introductory relative marker; the nominal
emphatic particle, e.g. baa, which occurs at the end of a RC, actually has the effect when it immediately follows a verb of identifying the preceding predicate-headed structure as a RC.

34) SOMALI

ninkii geeliisii-ey   qabteen   baa (jooga)

man-the camels-his   they-seized ___ (is here)

'the man whose camels they seized (is here)'

(Bell 1953: 98)

In French, the non-pronominal relative marker possessive structure of colloquial French PRC's alternates with the possessive
relative pronoun of formal French.

35a) FRENCH (colloquial)

l'homme que j'ai vu son chapeau

the man rel. I've seen his hat

'the man whose hat I saw'

35b)   FRENCH (formal)

l'homme   dont j'ai vu   le chapeau

the man of-whom I've seen the   hat

'the man whose hat I saw'   (Tesnière 1969: 571)

The that...his type of PRC structure also occurs in English.

36)   The president is entitled to take up to Washington with
       him people that he has confidence in their loyalty.[3]

37)   There are people in this town that I would love to
       stand on their faces.[4]

In both 36) and 37), the relative pronoun their stands at some
distance from the relative marker that; the RC in 37) is "right-
extraposed." The that...his PRC type is probably uncommon in
English when the possessed nominal is the initial element of
structure in the RC.

3. Possessive relative clauses in Mexican Spanish

The approximately 33 hours of transcribed interviews with
educated native speakers of Mexico City Spanish found in El habla
de la Ciudad de Mexico   (henceforth HCM) offer a good opportunity
to discover the structural realities of cultured speech in this
very important Spanish dialect; the interviewees were unaware at
the time of the interviews that their speech was to be studied.

3.1. Nominal functions

3.1.1. Subject

A RC in Spanish in which the governing noun is subject could
hardly have a subject pronoun, just as it would not normally have
a subject pronoun if the same main clause and relative clause occurred as two separate but contiguous main clauses. There is one
example in HCM, however, in which the governing noun is actually
repeated in the subject slot of the RC, now with a definite article.

38)   un niño que, si no se le suministran todos los ele-
       mentos para vivir --calor, alimento...estímulos de
       toda naturaleza-- el niño podría morir (HCM: 344)

The verb in the RC in 39) is far removed from the relative marker
que, which probably accounts for the repetition of the governing
noun.

3.1.2. Direct object

In most cases, RC's in which the governing noun functions
as direct object do not have direct-object pronouns (lo, la, los,
las) agreeing with the governing noun; however, cases of such
direct-object pronouns are far from rare.

39) substancias, por ejemplo, que traen de la India, que las
        traen de la isla de Madagascar, de las islas de
        Borneo, Sumatra, de la China, de la India... (HCM: 40)

40) niños que los llevaban por rebeldes o por apáticos o
        por agresivos (HCM: 75)

41) esmeraldas que se las dio Joselito (HCM: 175)

42) la receta...que nos la dieron allá en...en Sevilla
        (HCM: 179)

43) una pirámide (allá arriba), que es muy interesante cono-
        cerla también (HCM: 195)

44) una fuenta (también), que de noche la iluminan
        (HCM: 199)

45) un hombre que nunca lo vi tirar palomas, no lo vi hacer
        causa común con el resto de...de salvajes que hay
        infestado dentro de la Universidad (HCM: 211)

46) las cosas que cuestan trabajo, que requieren una dis-
        ciplina, que esto...la gente las elimina fácilmente
        (HCM: 228)

47) un hilito que nada más lo metes a la tetera (HCM: 234)

48) una gente que quiero tanto, que la admiro tanto y me
        acuerdo tanto de ella (HCM: 253)

49) una mujer que la abandona el marido   (HCM: 273)

50) (non-restrictive) nuestra galaxia, que la...la dibujaré
        como una lenteja (HCM: 354)

51) una fuerte industria, que...que la has hecho por es-
        fuerzo propio (HCM: 399)

52) cosas que nos gustan, que las ponemos en un lugar y...
        allí viven eternidades (HCM: 416)

3.1.3. Indirect object

    The relative marker, when the governing noun functions as in-
direct object in the RC, is almost always the non-pronominal que,
especially in non-bitransitive RC's; preposition a + pronominal

relative marker (e.g., in masculine singular el que, quien or,
rarely, el cual), required in formal written Spanish, is occasionally found. In either case, the in-predicate indirect object
pronouns occur as they do in all types of clauses. In the following examples, only 60) and 61) have bitransitive RC's, with the
verb poner.

53)   aquellos otros que...que les gusta la cosa
          arqueológica   (HCM: 44)

54)   una persona que se interese o que sepa de todas esas
          cosas, que le guste la historia del arte, que le
          guste todo eso   (HCM: 50)

55)   un torero (--imagínate--) viejo, con reumas, y que nadie
          le haga caso   (HCM: 176)

56)   un hombre que le gustaba salir, que le gustaba que yo
          trabajara con él, que colabora y eso   (HCM: 220)

57)   gentes que les gusta, pero que a los dos, tres meses,
          les fastidia   (HCM: 228)

58)   (non-restrictive) la mujer mexicana, que le interesa muy
          poco cultivarse   (HCM: 229)

59)   una persona que le gustaba la lectura   (HCM: 230)

60)   (non-restrictive) la obra Landrú opereta, que Salvador
          Elisondo le puso la música que están oyendo en este
          momento   (HCM: 329)

61)   ampliaciones de fotografías que después se les puso un
          poco de color nada más   (HCM: 331)

62)   una muchacha que le encanta vestirse muy bien   (HCM: 404)

63)   muchos muchachos que no les gusta eso   (HCM: 443)

3.2. Adverbial functions

   When the function of the governing noun in the RC corresponds
to a prepositional phrase, indirect objects of non-bitransitive
clauses excepted, the RC is almost always introduced by the corresponding preposition + pronominal relative marker. Occasionally,
however, the preposition occurs non-initially followed by the
appropriate personal pronoun; an example has already been seen in
48), where una gente...(que) me acuerdo tanto de ella is used instead of una gente de quien me acuerdo tanto or una gente de la
que me acuerdo tanto. Such RC structures occur only occasionally
and may be considered slips or perhaps only marginally acceptable
structures by most speakers.

64)   (non-restrictive) un dicho (por ahí), que me acuerdo
        muy bien de él   (HCM: 284)

65)   maridos que se mueren de ganas de entrar, y que para
        ellos es su máxima ilusión, y que la esposa no
        quiere que entre   (HCM: 391)

3.3.   Possessor function

    In the 33 interviews of HCM, there are only two examples of
the use of the possessive relative pronominal adjective cuyo.
One is well-formed in a non-restrictive RC, 66); in the other example, 67), the speaker became confused and the possessive su
was inserted before he was able to stumble through his sentence.

66)   (non-restrictive) un hombre, cuyo nombre no vale la
        pena ni siquiera recordar   (HCM: 211)

67)   pueblos eminentemente no cristianos, cuya manera de
        pensar, cuya manera...su desenvolvimiento social y
        demás está tendiendo al amor libre   (HCM: 273)

The most common PRC structure in Spanish is introduced by the non-
pronominal que and has possession shown within the clause by the
possessive su.

68)   la parta griega, que se la robó el...un lord de esos
        que...ahorita no recuerdo su nombre   (HCM: 202)

69)   una gente que esta casada y sus ninos son chiquitos
                        (HCM: 223)

70)   un doctor que no recuerdo su nombre   (HCM: 381)

71)   cuántas gentes (conocemos) que su hijo va a la Prepara-
        toria   (HCM: 402)

In one example, 72), the PRC is introduced by a non-possessive
pronominal relative marker and possession is shown by su.

72)   una mujer a la cual le matan a su marido   (HCM: 394)

In another example above, 65), the definite article is used instead of the possessive pronoun (que la for que su).   Example 49)
above is subject to the same interpretation.

    In some cases, two relative clauses are used for a PRC, one
within another; in this case, the matrix RC contains in the predicate the unitransitive possessive verb tener.

73)   unos bloques de mármol que tienen unos reflejos color de
        rosa, que se ven preciosos en la tarde, al amanecer
                        (HCM: 202)

74)   una compañera enfermera que tiene un hijo -- que estuvo
        en los Amigos del Bosque   (HCM: 443)

4. Conclusions

The RC is most typically marked with a non-pronominal relative marker, and occasionally by no marker, zero. This is true,
and perhaps especially so, for PRC's.[5] One of the most important
reasons that pronominal, double-function relative markers are not
preferred is that they force specification of the function of the
governing noun in the RC in the initial segment. When a speaker
begins a sentence, except sometimes a very short one, he typically does not know how the sentence will end; the amount of
total linguistic anticipation will vary, although there has to be
a maximum possible amount which may vary from speaker to speaker.
A number of examples (false starts and other slips) in HCM
demonstrate that speakers frequently have not yet identified the
function of the governing noun when the RC is introduced; they
may use the wrong preposition, use a preposition where none is
indicated, or use no preposition where one is expected.

75)   (en la cual for que) una fábrica en la cual...este...
        Es un consorcio de fábricas   (HCM: 34)

76)   (que la for para la que) una tómbola que...que la vendemos el boleto en diez pesos   (HCM: 89)

77)   (que for en que) el hotel que estuvimos nosotros
        (HCM: 196)

78)   (que for con (el) que if antecedent is grupo; que for
        con las que or con quienes if antecedent is solteras)
        el grupo de solteras que alternaban antes   (HCM: 263)

79)   (que for con (las) que) las comedias sobre todo...
        este...bonitas, ligeras, que se divierte uno
        (HCM: 314)

80)   (sobre for en or entrar for hablar) una estructura sobre
        la cual...no se puede entrar con argumentos del tipo
        filosofico   (HCM: 354)

81)   (a for en) cosas a las cuales no debemos meternos
        (HCM: 400)

In some cases, speakers start anew and repair the slip.

82)   mucha gente que...de...de donde podría salir un buen
        deportista   (HCM: 226)

83)   una serie de hipóthesis, de elucubraciones, de análisis,
        de observaciones en las que...a las que me he dedicado durante los últimos veinte anos de mi vida

científica   (HCM: 352)

Slips such as the above would not occur if specification of the
function of the governing noun in the relative clause were delayed until the position corresponding to that function is
reached in the encoding process.[6]

I have stated (Blansitt 1979: 241), "Any theory which shows
complex semological sentences moving in single chunks into complex grammatical sentences is untenable." The term 'untenable'
is totally inadequate to describe a theory which fantasizes a
movement of complete semological sentences from an initial abstract form through a series of intermediate derivations. The
earlier evidence which I have given (Blansitt 1979) is based on
the frequent slips which are made in cataphoric agreement compared to the virtual absence of slips in anaphoric agreement; it
is not surprising to find that slips occur in the anticipatory
assignment of function as well as in the anticipatory assignment
of concord.

Evidence, not all of which is presented here, suggests the
following putative universals:
1) Possessive relative pronominal adjectives are not found
    in VSO languages.
2) If a language has a possessive relative adjective, then
    pronominal possessors precede possessees. In most
    cases, languages which have a possessive relative ad-
    jective are GN languages, so all possessors precede
    possessees; this may explain 1) above.
3) If a language uses a non-pronominal relative marker in
    non-possessive relative clauses, then it uses the same
    marker in possessive relative clauses, if any.
4) If a language uses a pronominal relative adjective in
    possessive relative clauses, then it uses a pronom-
    inal relative marker, i.e., relative pronoun, in
    non-possessive relative clauses.
5) If a possessive pronominal relative adjective is used in
    restrictive relative clauses, then it is also used
    in non-restrictive relative clauses, if any. The
    converse is probably not true.
6) In almost all cases, languages which always use a pronom-
    inal relative adjective, or for which no alternative
    is well-known, the possessive relative clauses
    have a morphological case system.

An additional universal may be derived from Downing's Universal P (1978: 396) and 4) above:
7) Possessive pronominal relative adjectives do not occur
    in pre-nominal relative clauses.

Although RC's are apparently universal, PRC's do not seem to
occur in Mandarin, a somewhat unusual language in its RC structure
as it is SVO and has pre-nominal RC's.[7] It would be premature to
speculate that the SVO--prenominal RC combination has anything to
do with the unexpected absence of PRC's. It is possible, in
fact, that PRC's may be far from universal, although few grammars

specifically observe their absence; that such RC's are not
attested in Mbum has been noted (Hagège 1970: 335). An utterance such as

84) mì màmá nzùk gûn à ké zí

I know man son of him come

'I know the man whose son came' (Hagège 1970: 335)

is two juxtaposed sentences: mì màmá nzùk and gûn à ké zí.
Mbum is SVO, prepositional, NA, NG, with postnominal RC's--
nothing unusual there; a statistically infrequent feature of
Mbum RC's, however, is the fact that the RC has both an initial
and a final relative marker, both demonstratives (ibid.: 334).

85) úì   àí mi zàŋzáŋ   nú   bèlbél

woman rel.$_1$ I run-into rel.$_2$ pleasant

'the woman (that) I ran into is pleasant' (Ibid.: 334)

In Spanish, it is necessary to recognize syntactic diglossia
in PRC's. The cuyo construction is maintained through the stub-
born persistence of normative grammar in formal usage, in spite
of the fact that its usage does not fit the typological characteristics of the language, but the que...su structure is normal
in informal conversation. Similar situations apparently exist
in several other caseless Indo-European SVO languages. The fact
that English pronominal relative adjective whose is more alive
than Spanish cuyo is probably due principally to the fact that
English is GN, plus the fact that interrogative whose has no
alternate form while interrogative cúyo disappeared long ago from
Spanish. English structures such as 36) and 37) above, however,
are predicted for English by Universal 3 above.
Many pronouncements of normative grammar are unquestionably
designed to promote structures which do not fit the typological
characteristics, i.e., the "genius," of the language, though it
would be a mistake to credit normative grammarians with knowledge
of this fact. In studying language typology and universals, a
distinction must be made between the real structure of the language, frequently scorned by normativists, and the artificial substitute proposed in normative grammars.

NOTES

[1]I am grateful to Ilse Irwin for the German (18b, 19b) examples.

[2]I am grateful to Helga Harries-Delisle for calling to my attention the dialect colloquial variants in which wo is used as an invariant non-pronominal relative marker: Ich kenne einen Mann wo die Schwiegermutter von seiner Schwester Französisch spricht (19b).

[3]I am grateful to Charles Elerick for calling this example to my attention. The speaker was presidential assistant Charles Kirbo in an interview seen on the CBS Evening News, January 22, 1978.

[4]This example appeared on the handout accompanying Michael B. Montgomery's paper at the 1978 Mid-America Linguistics Conference, from his corpus of Appalachian speech.

[5]Although English relative marker that may be omitted when the function of the governing noun is any clause-rank function other than subject, it seems to be obligatory when the function is possessor: He has an aunt in Fort Worth that he loves to eat her cooking; *?He has an aunt in Fort Worth he loves to eat her cooking. Relative marker that seems obligatory in any case in which the governing noun is antecedent of a personal pronoun in the RC: examples 1), 2), 3), and 4).

[6]An examination of false assignments of function in HCM reveals that the use of the wrong preposition seldom occurs before a noun phrase which appears in its most usual position in the clause. Often, after the correct function marker has been assigned, errors in cataphoric gender-number agreement are found; assignment of function must generally precede selection of the head noun.

[7]I am grateful to Ching-Ying Chen for information about the absence of PRC's in Mandarin.

REFERENCES

Aquilina, Joseph. 1965. Maltese. London: Teach Yourself Books, English Universities Press.
Bell, C. R. V. 1953. The Somali language. London: Longmans, Green and Co.
Berulfsen, Bjarne. 1971. Norwegian Grammar. Oslo: H. Aschehoug.
Blansitt, Edward L., Jr. 1979. The grammatically conditioned linearity of semantic processes. Forum Linguisticum 2:3. 231-245.
Brambila, David. 1953. Gramática rarámuri. Mexico: Editorial Buena Prensa.
Centro de Lingüística Hispánica (directed by Juan M. Lope Blanch). 1971. El habla de la Ciudad de México, materiales para su estudio. Mexico: UNAM.

Cole, Desmond T. 1955. An introduction to Tswana grammar. London: Longmans, Green and Co.

Crazzolara, J. P. 1938. A study of the Acooli language. Oxford: Oxford Univ. Press.

Dillon, Miles and Donncha Ó. Croínín. 1961. Irish. London: Teach Yourself Books, English Universities Press.

Downing, Bruce T. 1978. Some universals of relative clause structure. Universals of human language, ed. by Joseph H. Greenberg, volume 4, 375-418. Stanford CA: Stanford Univ. Press.

Hagège, Claude, 1970. La langue Mbum de Nganha. SELAF.

Harrell, Richard S. 1962. A short reference grammar of Morrocan Arabic. Washington, D.C.: Georgetown Univ. Press.

Hoffmann, Carl. 1963. A grammar of the Margi language. Oxford: Oxford Univ. Press.

Koefoed, H. A. 1958. Danish. London: Teach Yourself Books, English Universities Press.

MacLaren, James. 1971. MacLaren's Gaelic Self-Taught. Glasgow: Gairm.

Mann, S. E. 1932. A short Albanian grammar. London: David Nutt.

Mitchell, Bruce. 1965. A guide to Old English. London: Basil Blackwell.

Prost, A. 1956. La langue Soñay et ses dialectes. Dakar: IFAN.

Rowlands, E. C. 1969. Teach yourself Yoruba. London: English Universities Press.

Schwartz, Arthur. 1971. General aspects of relative clause formation. Working Papers on Language Universals 6.139-171.

Smith, A. S. D. 1925. Welsh made easy. Wrexham: Hughes and Son.

Tesnière, Lucien. 1951. Éléments de syntaxe structurale. Paris: Klinckseick.

NEOLOGISTIC PALATAL + AR VERBS IN MEXICAN-AMERICAN SPANISH

ELEANOR GREET COTTON AND JOHN M. SHARP

University of Texas at El Paso

It has long been noted that Mexican and Mexican-American Spanish differ in that the latter is characterized by a great many neologisms with both English and Spanish roots. The common explanation is that Mexicans emigrating to the United States have found themselves within a culture quite different from their own and for which, therefore, their original vocabulary was inadequate (Sharp, 1970). Faced with this problem, they solved it as speakers often do when suddenly immersed in a new environment: they either 1) accepted the new artifacts and other cultural innovations with their Anglo-American names or 2) adapted lexical items from Mexican Spanish, altering them in various ways.

These two processes of lexical expansion are, of course, historically commonplace in Spanish. When the Spaniards arrived in the New World, they at once began to absorb Indian words to designate neoteric New World flora, fauna, and cultural elements, adopting such terms as maguey, iguana, coyote, and cacique. There also occurred numerous adaptations of Peninsular Spanish words to New World conditions. The word álamo serves to illustrate. In Spain it means "poplar tree," but in Mexico "cottonwood." Apparently the Spaniards thought the two trees sufficiently similar for the name-transfer to occur. Another assumption gave rise to tabaco 'tobacco'. On his first voyage, Columbus observed an Indian on a Cuban beach smoking a cigar. Since Columbus was famil-

iar with the Arabic custom of inhaling smoke from the ignited leaves
of a plant called <u>tabbak</u> to cure a respiratory ailment, he misap-
plied the Arabic word to the American plant (Moliner, 1971).

The number of neologisms in Mexican-American Spanish precludes
the examination of all of them in a short paper, and an exhaustive
list would not be possible since the process is dynamic and continuous. Accordingly, the present authors narrowed their focus
to newly-coined verbs in which palatalization occurs before terminal -<u>ar</u> in the infinitive. Verbs of this phonological pattern
occur frequently in popular speech. Some neologistic verbs with
English bases include <u>monquear</u> (from <u>monkey</u>), <u>parquear</u> (from <u>park</u>),
and <u>tichar</u> (from <u>teach</u>); and with Spanish bases, <u>chistear</u> (from
<u>chiste</u>), <u>moquear</u> (from <u>moco</u>), <u>jacalear</u> (from <u>jacal</u>) and <u>sanchar</u>
(from <u>Sancho</u>). Verbs of this sort are created by the application
of several rules.

Rule (1): If the base ends in -<u>i</u> or -<u>e</u>, add -<u>ar</u>:

<u>monqui</u> › <u>monquiar</u>; <u>chiste</u> › <u>chistear</u>.

Rule (2): Where the final vowel of the stem of these verbs
is -<u>e</u> it becomes -<u>i</u> (/y/) when it is unstressed, and palatalization results: <u>chistear</u> › <u>chistiar</u>.

Rule (3): If the base ends in a vowel other than -<u>i</u> or -<u>e</u>,
delete this vowel and insert -<u>i</u> or -<u>e</u> and apply rules (1)
and/or (2): <u>jaina</u> › <u>jaine</u> + -<u>ar</u> › <u>jaini</u> + -<u>ar</u> › <u>jainiar</u>;
and <u>moco</u> › <u>moque</u> + -<u>ar</u> › <u>moqui</u> + -<u>ar</u> › <u>moquiar</u>.

Rule (4): Where the base ends in a non-palatal consonant,
add -<u>i</u> or -<u>e</u> and apply rules (1) and/or (2): <u>parqu</u> + -<u>e</u>
+ -<u>ar</u> › <u>parqu</u> + -<u>i</u> + -<u>ar</u> › <u>parquiar</u>; and <u>jacal</u> + -<u>e</u> + -<u>ar</u>
› <u>jacaliar</u>.

Rule (5): Where the base ends in a palatal consonant, <u>ch</u>
(/ĉ/), <u>ñ</u>, <u>y</u>, or <u>ll</u> (/y/), add -<u>ar</u>. Rules (1) and (2) do
not apply, and a final -i (/y/) is not inserted since
Spanish phonology constrains the use of a palatal immediately following another palatal. Applied to English bases,
rule (5) can be exemplified by: <u>tich</u> + -<u>ar</u> › <u>tichar</u>.[1] Applied to Spanish bases, rule (5) has a preliminary require-
ment: with a base containing a palatal followed by a vowel,
delete the vowel and then add -<u>ar</u>: <u>Sancho</u> › <u>sanch</u> + -<u>ar</u> ›
<u>sanchar</u>.[2]

These rules appear to be as old as the Spanish language itself, dating back as they do to Vulgar Latin (see Menéndez Pidal,
1941). While -<u>ear</u> and -<u>iar</u> verb classes were kept distinct in
<u>la lengua culta</u>, they tended in common speech to coalesce into a
single class or to vary freely. Menéndez Pidal cites words such
as <u>colorear</u> from <u>color</u> + -<u>i/e</u> + -<u>ar</u> and <u>camear</u> from <u>cambiar</u>.
The form <u>camear</u> is an early one, used consistently throughout <u>El</u>

Cantar de Mio Cid.   That the dynamic has continued is attested
to by modern Standard Spanish verbs such as zapatear (base:
zapato) and telefonear (base: teléfono). Santamaría (1978)
attributes many of these verbs to semantic or phonologic variation in popular Mexican Spanish, puristically labeling them as
corriente, vulgar, or lengua soez y baja.
     What of these verbs in Mexican-American Spanish? Do their
semantics cast any light on the Mexican-Americans' acculturation
to a society dominated by Anglo-Americans? Specifically, in what
area of social interaction has the Mexican-American felt a need
for new verbs of this type? Conversely, in what areas have Spanish-based verbs been preferred?
     In an attempt to answer these questions, data were gathered
from Galván and Teschner (1975), González (1967), Baker (1966),
and from Mexican-American informants in the El Paso area. The
resultant sample consists of 368 lexical items plus definitions.
Where one lexical item has two widely divergent meanings, it is
counted twice in view of the importance of semantic shift as a
basis for the creation of neologisms. For example, machetear
is counted twice because it means both "to eat voraciously" and
"to botch a job."
     Analysis not only confirmed previous assumptions but also
resulted in some surprising findings. For example, contrary to
our expectations, more of the verbs in this sample are derived
from Spanish than from English: 221 verbs or 60% of these entries are Spanish-based while only 147 or 40% contain English
roots. Among those with Spanish bases, 151 or 68.3% are based
on nouns, whereas those based on other verbs number only 46, or
20.8%, and, of the latter, 84.4% are semantic or phonological
variants of Standard Spanish forms. Adjective bases are found
in only six verbs(2.7%). Only one verb is either noun or verb-
based, and one is based on a verb phrase. Among those with English bases, however, 127 or 86.4% are verb-based while only 20
or 13.6% are based on nouns; 17.7% are ambiguous: two counted as
noun-based and 24 counted as verb-based might actually be considered either noun- or verb-based, i.e., verbs like comb, step,
and work. However, it seems more likely that they were borrowed
as originally labeled. Moreover, if the percentage of ambiguous
verbs is subtracted from the total that seem definitely to be
verb-based, the remaining percentage of verb-based verbs is still
quite large--68.7%.
     It is evident from these figures that the percentages of
noun-based verbs and verb-based verbs are almost exactly the
opposite in the case of Hispanic versus English coinages. How
does one explain this difference? One may surmise that Spanish-
dominant speakers are inclined to create new verbs based on nouns
they already know, while merely copying verbs to which they are
exposed in the Anglo culture. Surely it is easier to be creative
in one's own language, and, contradistinctively, a necessity to
limit oneself to imitating forms of a second language imperfectly controlled.
     Another difference among these verbs is that those with Span-

ish bases come from sources that are linguistically more varied
than those with English bases, which are largely Germanic. The
Spanish bases are derived from Medieval ("archaic") Spanish, e.g.,
camear; from Standard Spanish (modified semantically and/or phonologically), e.g., linear, brujear, lambuzquear; from Standard
Spanish slang, e.g., caldear; rogue slang, e.g., muraguear; Na-
huatl (apapachar); and Pachuco slang (entacucharse); some are
calques (e.g., lamparear).

Perhaps the most interesting difference between the Spanish-
based and the English-based verbs is the contrast between their
respective areas of semantic application, as shown in Table 1.
These figures show that of the verbs in category I ("Behavior"),
the number with Spanish bases is three times greater than that of
verbs with English bases. In categories II ("Sports and Play")
and III ("Work"), English-based verbs predominate by a ratio of
2 to 1. Terms in categories IV, "Weather," and V, "Medical," are
all Spanish-based, and category VI, "General and/or Unclassifiable," is split 50-50.

Table 1. Semantic categories according to language base

Semantic Category	Spanish Base	English Base
I Behavior	77.4%	22.6%
II Sports and Play	33.3	66.6
III Work	34.3	65.6
IV Weather	100.0	0
V Medical	100.0	0
VI General and/or Unclassifiable	50.0	50.0

Of the 221 Spanish-based verbs in the sample, how many fall
within each of these six semantic areas? How does their semantic
distribution compare with that of the 147 English-based verbs (see
Table 2)? The figures in Table 2 indicate that approximately
three-fourths of the verbs with Spanish bases concern behavior
while slightly less than one-third of the English-based verbs
have to do with this area. Terms for sports and play in the
Spanish sample account for only 7% but there are three times
that many among the English-based verbs in this category. In
the case of the third category, "Work," there is a large dis-
proportion between the Spanish-based verbs and the English-based
verbs in that only 15% of the Spanish total fall into this category while 44% of the English total refer to work. A very small
percentage of the Spanish total can be found in categories IV,
"Weather," and V, "Medical," and there are no English-based verbs
at all in these categories. Category VI, "General and/or Unclas-

sifiable,"is very small, representing less than 2% for bases from both languages.

General category I ("Behavior") is divided into the subcategories of (A) personal behavior, domestic setting; (B) personal behavior, general; (C) interpersonal behavior, general; (D) interpersonal behavior, social formulas; and (E) socially-disapproved behavior, ranging from idle gossip to crimes of violence. There are 161 verbs with Spanish bases in this category. In subcategory (A), personal behavior, domestic setting, there are 10 terms for (1) eating and drinking; three of these are synonyms of <u>comer</u> "to eat"; six more refer to manner or means of eating; the remaining one refers to drinking. In this same category there are 10 terms for (2) grooming and dressing, all or most of which refer to the activities of women. Half of them refer to grooming and half to dressing, among which four out of five mean "to dress up," demonstrating the traditional Spanish interest in dressing for festive occasions. The English-based terms in the category are fewer (only half as many) and less specific. Only two of the seven grooming and dressing terms apply to women. It would seem that behavior in this area is more tradition-oriented than adopted from Anglo-American culture except when it involves technological artifacts, such as <u>permanentear</u> and <u>tatu(y)ar</u> that would not have been common in rural Mexico.

Table 2. Language base according to semantic category

Semantic Category	Spanish Base: % of Total	English Base: % of Total
I Behavior	72.8%	31.9%
II Sports and Play	7.2	21.7
III Work	15.4	44.2
IV Weather	1.3	0
V Medical	1.8	0
VI General and/or Unclassifiable	1.3	2.0

In subcategory I.B, "personal behavior, general," there are 36 Spanish-based terms, for the most part dealing with physical activities. Many of these concern self-expression, such as <u>cara-quear</u>, "guffaw" and <u>jirimiquear</u>, "complain" or "whine"; four have to do with locomotion, three describe relaxation, two mean "excel,"

two mean "go crazy," and the others refer to a variety of activities. The English-based verbs in this category number only seven
but they refer to some of the same activities denoted by the
Spanish-based verbs here, such as manners of locomotion--stepear
("step"), shoflear ("shuffle")--and laziness, e.g., bonquear
"sleep". As is true of "personal behavior in a domestic setting," these more general terms are for the most part adapted
and not acquired.

As can be expected, there are many Spanish-based verbs (37)
in subcategory I.C, "interpersonal behavior, general." More than
one-fourth of them refer to amatory activities; two of these refer solely to courtship activities and seven to acts more carnal
in nature, ranging from cachumbear, "neck," to chopetear, "have
sexual intercourse." It is not surprising, then, that there are
also a number of terms concerning child-raising. Among the other
terms in this category, three refer to positive, 13 to
negative, and three to neutral interrelationships. A positive
interrelationship may be exemplified by ahuichotear, "encourage
or stimulate"; a negative one by azorrillar, "frighten"; and a
neutral one by cotorrear, "converse."

The English-based verbs of "interpersonal behavior, general,"
although fewer in number (12) than their Spanish-based counterparts (37), comprise almost the same percentage (25%) of the total
for this category. Moreover, these verbs have semantic referents
that are very similar to those of the Spanish-based verbs and also
occur in similar proportions: three refer to sex and three may
refer to children (although not to child-raising as is the case
with the Spanish-based verbs). Also like those with Spanish
bases, the greater number of remaining items with English bases
refer to negative interpersonal relationships(5), and, as with
the Spanish bases, there are the same number which refer to
positive and to neutral relationships (two and two). Still, it
is to be noted that the comparatively large proportion of English-
based verbs in this semantic area suggests that the Mexican-
American's interpersonal relationships have been modified by
life in a bicultural setting.

The largest category of verbs, both Spanish-based and English-
based, is that of "socially disapproved behavior." These lexical
items account for 40.9% of the Spanish-based total and include
items that are general (E.1) (46 verbs) and terms that refer
specifically to criminal activities (E.2) (23 verbs). Subcategories within the "general" contain derogatory verbs referring
to sex (13), betrayal (7), unacceptable types of conversation
(5), fighting (3), loafing (3), driving someone crazy (3), going
on a spree (2), flatulence (2), and miscellaneous types of anti-
social conduct (8).

Lexical items concerning socially-disapproved behavior (general and criminal) account for 29.7% of the English-based total.
Within the category "general" there are only eight terms; of
these, two refer to sexual activities, two to fighting and the
four remaining refer to various kinds of undesirable social behavior.

There are 23 verbs with Spanish bases that refer to criminal
behavior, and these can be divided on the basis of semantic reference into five subcategories: (a) general crime, (b) larceny, (c)
crimes involving narcotics, (d) crimes in which a knife is used,
and (e) crimes in which other weapons are used. In "general
crime," three of these terms involve interrelationships between
the criminal and the police, and three are miscellaneous. Referring to larceny, there are four terms, all of which mean "to steal."
In crime involving narcotics, there is only one term, pildorear,
"to ingest narcotics." In the category of crime in which a knife
is used, there are at least seven verbs with Spanish bases, and
possibly eight, if one includes pacotear ("to stab in the back").
Terms for crimes in which other weapons are used include two for
firearms and one for a blackjack or other heavy weapon; plomear
("to fill with lead") may be derived from cowboy language.
     Among the nine terms with English bases that refer to criminal
behavior, there are four in the "crime, general" subcategory, two
of which describe activities between the criminal and the police
and two describing activities of the criminal alone. Referring to
larcenous activities there are two items, both of which mean "to
steal." In crime involving narcotics there are two terms. There
are no English-based terms referring to cutting or stabbing and only
one referring to crime with a gun. This disparity between Spanish-
based and English-based verbs suggests that in traditional Hispanic
culture there has been more prestige attached to the use of a blade
to settle differences than there has in the English-speaking world.
Further, many of the English-based verbs in this subcategory refer
to types of illegal activity to which the Mexican-American might
have been exposed in a United States urban environment: terms
such as estulear ("to stool"), freimear ("to frame"), joslear
("to hustle"), requetear ("to steal," with a suggestion of gang
or "racket" activity), and rolear ("to roll someone").
     In the next large category, II, "Sports and Play," there are
twice as many verbs of English derivation (32) as there are with
Spanish roots (16). Considering that the English sample (147)
is only three-fourths the size of the Spanish sample (221), this
category would seem to be English-dominated. The largest subcategory among the English-based items in this semantic area contains verbs naming activities typical of team sports. Of these,
the greatest number, six, pertain to baseball, three to football-
soccer, three to basketball, one to any team sport, and one (gol-
fear) to an activity playable by groups or alone. The preponder-
ance of English bases here possibly reflects the fact that team
sports have only recently achieved popularity in Latin America
with the exception of soccer. These sports with their accompanying terminology have been acquired by Hispanic countries--not only
Mexico but Venezuela, the Dominican Republic, and others--from the
English-speaking world. Verbs with Spanish bases here are capotear
("to snatch the ball or leave a team scoreless") and garrotear ("to
defeat"), not only limited in number but less specific than their
English counterparts. Analogously, terms for boxing and wrestling
are more numerous (6 to 1) and more specific if they are based on

English words and less so if based on Spanish, as in the English-based fletear ("to flatten") contrasted with the Spanish-based tironear ("to pull at someone's limbs"). Again, these sports, probably introduced by Anglophones, are extremely popular and widespread in Hispanic countries these days, and the terminology which accompanies them is commonplace. For instance, one frequently sees naquear ("to knock out") on the sports pages of newspapers in Mexico City.

The next subcategory of "Sports and Play" contains terms for card-playing and gambling. Here, too, English-based verbs are in a majority (4 to 1); two English-based terms refer to poker, one to dealing, and one to betting. The sole Spanish-based verb, barajear ("to play cards" or "to shuffle"), is a phonological variant of the standard barajar.

Spanish-speaking people have been playing cards since the late Middle Ages, and the Spanish lexicon is replete with card-playing terms. Why, then, has the Mexican-American felt a need to borrow such terms from English? The answer may be that the rural Mexican did not play Anglo-American-style card games; thus the immigrants to the United States acquired new terms along with the new games learned here.

In the subcategory of lexical items concerning social amusements, II.D, English-based verbs again predominate (6 to 3). Here too, the English-based verbs tend to be specific, referring to types of amusements such as cabaretear, "to be nightclubbing," campear, "to go camping for pleasure," and swimear, "to go swimming" that would probably not have been indigenous to rural Mexican culture (or to dry-land culture in the case of the last item).

There remain two subcategories in "Sports and Play": general terms and terms for dancing. In the general subcategory we find Spanish-based fonchar, "to cheat at marbles" and the English-based (?) jonchar "to move a marble closer to its goal," i.e., to cheat.[3] Also of this type are trampear and trapear, both of which mean "to hunt and trap animals."

The subcategory of items referring to dancing, II.D, is especially interesting because it contains six Spanish-based verbs and no English-based verbs at all, probably because love of dancing is a long-standing Hispanic cultural trait which continues to be of major importance in the social life of Mexican-American teenagers. The Spanish-based terms here are both general (three verbs) and specific, as in polquear and valsear, both phonological variants of Standard Spanish referring to particular dances.

Highly revealing of both traditional cultural values and activities acquired from Anglo-American society are the new verbs in category III, "Work." There are only about half as many Spanish-based verbs as English-based verbs in this category (34 as opposed to 65). Furthermore, the sub-categories which contain the largest number of English-based verbs are often those which contain the smallest number of Spanish-based verbs. Subcategory III.A, with terms referring to technological work, is the largest in verbs with English bases and relatively small in the verbs with Spanish bases, in a ratio of 15:7. Among the Spanish-based verbs in the

"automotive" subcategory 1, three are adaptations of Standard Spanish terms for horsemanship. Arrear, which originally meant "to say
'giddap' to a horse," in Mexican-American Spanish means "to start
a car." Manear, originally "to hobble a horse," has the new meaning
of "to put on the brakes," and talonear, once "to spur a horse," has
the new meaning of "to step on the gas, to hurry." The terms pilo-
tear ("to drive a car") and orillar ("to park a car alongside a
curb") are of nautical origin. All the Spanish-based verbs concerning technological work refer to motor vehicles. This is not
true of the English-based verbs in this subcategory. Although the
English-based verbs which do concern automobiles are numerous (15)
there also exist six terms for secretarial work from the English
bases check, dial, sign, tape, type, and staple. There is one electrical term from English plug and one military term from English
machine gun. A contrast may also be noted between the Spanish-based
and English-based automotive terms. A majority of the former have
to do with driving a car in general, whereas most of the English-
based verbs refer to more specific automotive activities, such as
starting a car, choking it, braking it, and to various malfunctions
or activities designed to remedy them such as ponchar ("to puncture,
said of tires"), bompear ("to bump into"), requear ("to wreck"),
puchar ("to push"), yequear ("to jack up"), and güeldear ("to weld").
This is to say: the Spanish-based verbs are adapted from pre-
technological practices while those with English bases reflect the
rural Mexican-American's acculturation to the age of the machine in
the United States.

While terms involving automotive work suggest male agents, the
second subcategory, III.B, domestic work, suggests activities cus-
tomarily performed by women. The nine Spanish-based verbs in this
area refer primarily to the preparation of food whereas the 13
English-based verbs have to do primarily with cleaning chores. One
might assume that the Spanish-based verbs have been coined by bilingual speakers while English-based verbs originated from communication between Anglo-American housewives and their Spanish-speaking
maids.

A third subcategory of "Work," III.C, educational terms, appears
to be age-group oriented, not gender-oriented, since most of these
terms seem to have been created by youngsters. There is only one
Spanish-based verb in this subcategory as opposed to 15 with
English bases. These verbs reflect life in a typical Anglo-American
school, referring as they do to such activities as juquear ("to play
hooky"), espeletear ("to spell"), impruvear ("to improve"), testear
("to test"), and tichar ("to teach").

The fourth subcategory of terms dealing with work, III.D., "financial transactions," seems independent of gender-age notions although these terms concern actions most probably performed by adults.
Among the four Spanish-based verbs, two mean "to pay" and two "to
make change." Among the three English-based verbs, two concern
credit. The four Spanish-based verbs are non-institutional in reference, while those with English bases involve Mexican-American
dealings with institutions often dominated by Anglo-Americans.

Anglo-American economic dominance is again reflected in the

subcategories III.E and III.F. In III.E, terms concerning labor
relations, there are none with Spanish bases; of the four with
English bases, two, cuitear ("to quit") and discharchar ("to dis-
charge"), have to do with unemployment, either voluntary or involuntary; while the other two, estraiquear ("to strike") and pique-
tear ("to picket"), concern labor disputes. In III.F (terms referring to manual labor), four verbs have Spanish bases and only one an
English base; "to shine" appears with a Spanish base in bolear and
with an English base in shainear.

In subcategory III.G (general terms having to do with work)
there are only two English-based verbs but nine with Spanish bases.
Those with English bases are extremely general: pulear ("to pull")
and güerquear ("to work"). Those with Spanish bases are more interesting. Camear and chambear mean simply "to work," but three
refer to doing work incompetently: cachuquear, chambonear, and
machetear. One means "to contract for work," reganchar, and one
means "to complete a job," cabulear. Another contains, again, the
notion of economic subjugation: cascarear "to work for low pay."

There remain three major categories, all containing a small
number of verbs and two containing Spanish-based verbs alone. The
first of these, IV, "Weather," is comprised of three Spanish-based
terms that refer to precipitation; two concern sleet and one rain.
Since bad weather is a universal phenomenon, there would be no need
for the rural Mexican-American to coin verbs based on meteorological
terms in English. The second of these categories, V, "Medical,"
contains four Spanish-based verbs, three of which have to do with
injuries and one with heat stroke; all were surely experienced by
the rural Mexican-American before his introduction to urban Anglophone culture. In the final category, VI ("General and/or Unclassifiable"), there appear three verbs with Spanish bases (afra-
ñar, "to understand," cantear, "to incline," and costear, "to be
worthwhile") and three with English bases (capear, "catch or tattle,"
craquear, "crack," and cheiquear, "shake or agitate").

Altogether, our examination of neologistic verbs has confirmed
that base (+ palatal) + -ar is a highly productive pattern. Semantically it can be shown that when Mexican-American adaptation to
Anglo-American mores, economic structures or artifacts was desirable
or necessary, new words based on English were coined to the extent
that the rural Spanish lexicon did not provide the needed terms.
Conversely, where the Mexican-American was able to retain his culture of origin (as in the realms of dancing, dressing up, and other
personal/interpersonal relationships), he created neologisms from
the appropriate Hispanic bases.

NOTES

[1]The verb tichiar indeed exists, but here the i is not palatal
(/y/) but vowel (/ī/).

[2]It should be borne in mind that any -ar verb in Spanish may be made frequentative by the insertion of e between the stem and -ar, provided the meaning permits, for example trotar, "to trot," trotear, "to keep trotting." Some of the verbs in this sample probably result from this process. It would be extremely diffi-cult to identify most of these frequentatives, however; thus such an attempt has not been made.

[3]Fonchar and jonchar may be doublets since they are both synon-ymous and also phonetically similar; note the well-known tendency for Spanish /f/ to aspirate.

REFERENCES

Baker, Paulline. 1966. Español para los hispanos. Skokie IL: National Textbook Company.

Galván, Roberto A. and Richard V. Teschner. 1975. El diccionario del español de Tejas/The dictionary of Texas Spanish. Silver Spring MD: Institute of Modern Languages.

González, Rafael Jesús. 1967. Pachuco: the birth of a creole language. Arizona Quarterly winter 343-56.

Menéndez Pidal, Ramón. 1941. Manual de gramática histórica espa-ñola. 6th ed. Madrid: Espasa-Calpe.

Moliner, Marina. 1971. Diccionario de uso del español. Madrid: Gredos.

Santamaría, Francisco J. 1978. Diccionario de mejicanismos. 2nd ed. México D.F.: Porrúa.

Sharp, John M. 1970. The origin of some non-standard lexical items in the Spanish of El Paso. Studies in Language and Linguistics, 1969-1970, ed. by Ralph W. Ewton, Jr. and Jacob Ornstein. El Paso: Texas Western Press, pp. 207-32.

APPENDIX A

LEXICAL ITEMS WITH SPANISH BASES

I.   Behavior

   A.   Personal behavior, domestic setting

      1.   Eating and drinking

1)	*cusquear*	pick up with a utensil
2)	*gusjear*	eat
3)	*jaspear*	eat
4)	*lambuzquear/lambizquear*	eat between meals
5)	*machetear*	eat voraciously
6)	*martiar/martillar*	eat
7)	*mastiquear*	chew
8)	*pistear*	drink alcohol
9)	*sopear*	use tortillas or bread instead of spoon
10)	*tortillar*	eat tortillas

      2.   Grooming and dressing

1)	*alinear/linear*	get dressed
2)	*chapear*	put on rouge
3)	*chapetear*	put on rouge
4)	*entacucharse*	dress up
5)	*floriar*	dress up
6)	*laquear*	spray hair
7)	*pintorreguear*	use cosmetics to excess
8)	*pirfantear*	dress up
9)	*polvear*	powder self or nose
10)	*trajear*	dress up

   B.   Personal behavior, general

1)	*anclear*	settle down
2)	*bostecear*	yawn
3)	*brujear*	go without sleep
4)	*cacaraquear*	guffaw
5)	*cacarear*	cackle
6)	*calcear*	go barefoot
7)	*carajear*	laugh heartily
8)	*coyotear*	goof off
9)	*chanquilear*	walk
10)	*chapear*	blush
11)	*chicanear*	do one's thing/act like Chicano
12)	*chicotear*	excel
13)	*chisquear*	go crazy
14)	*chistear*	complain

15)	*chivear*	be bashful
16)	*chorrear*	soil
17)	*chotear*	use to excess
18)	*frajear*	smoke cigarette
19)	*jainear*	make love
20)	*jirimiquear*	complain
21)	*lamparear*	eye
22)	*moquear*	drip at the nose
23)	*moretear*	bruise self
24)	*nortear*	go crazy
25)	*papalotear*	excel
26)	*periquear*	talk incessantly
27)	*petatear*	die
28)	*planchar*	sleep
29)	*sofacear*	lie on sofa
30)	*sombrear*	move into/stay in shade
31)	*talonear*	hurry
32)	*temponear*	be used to
33)	*titiritear*	shiver
34)	*tomatear*	stare at
35)	*torear*	make an attempt
36)	*totachar*	speak in Chicano slang/talk in mixed English and Spanish
37)	*trafiquear*	walk/ride

C. Interpersonal behavior, general

1)	*ahuichotear*	encourage/stimulate
2)	*apapachar/papachar*	spoil a child
3)	*azorrillar*	frighten
4)	*babiarse (por)*	covet another's belonging
5)	*baratear*	mix with a crowd
6)	*barbear*	flatter
7)	*borruquear*	confuse
8)	*cachetear*	slap
9)	*cachumbear*	nick a dish/neck
10)	*caldear*	anger/make love
11)	*carrerear*	hurry someone
12)	*colear*	grab/borrow/color
13)	*corretear*	run someone ragged
14)	*cotorrear*	converse
15)	*changuear*	imitate
16)	*chiplear*	spoil a child
17)	*chiquear*	pamper a child or pet
18)	*chistear*	hush someone up
19)	*chivear*	back down
20)	*chopetear*	have intercourse
21)	*chotear*	pet heavily
22)	*chulear*	caress/speak sweetly
23)	*encantonear*	marry
24)	*enseñar*	show one's bad side
25)	*esquinear*	assent/agree
26)	*nalguear*	spank a child

27)	*ningunear*	debase/kill
28)	*pafuelear/pajuelear*	whip/excel
29)	*pajarear*	keep an eye on
30)	*pandear*	retract
31)	*pichonear*	engage in sexual foreplay
32)	*rayarse*	repeat/excel
33)	*sacatear/zacatear*	dodge
34)	*serenatear*	serenade
35)	*sonajear*	spank child
36)	*tironear*	pull at limbs of another in fun, fight, or love
37)	*tortillar*	slap

D. Interpersonal behavior, social formulas

| 1) | *matrimoniar* | marry |
| 2) | *sentenciar* | warn of revenge |

E. Socially disapproved behavior, general

1)	*abolillar*	act like gringo
2)	*acarrear*	gossip
3)	*cachuquear*	double cross
4)	*casquetear*	masturbate
5)	*corbear*	sponge/freeload
6)	*chacotear*	behave lewdly
7)	*chancear*	commit adultery
8)	*chapetear*	fornicate
9)	*chapucear*	cheat
10)	*chaquetear*	betray
11)	*chismolear/chismorrear*	gossip
12)	*chisquear*	drive someone crazy
13)	*chotear*	defame, make fool of someone
14)	*chulear*	pimp
15)	*disgracear*	impregnate/injure/ruin
16)	*enchinchar*	fill with bed bugs
17)	*engarruñar*	brawl/shrink in anger
18)	*garrotear*	beat up
19)	*huevonear*	be lazy
20)	*idear*	daydream
21)	*jacalear*	gossip
22)	*jetear*	pout
23)	*lambuzquear/lambizquear*	be hypocritically courteous
24)	*lamparear*	ogle
25)	*maderear*	flatter/brag
26)	*manosear*	paw
27)	*manzanear*	bribe
28)	*maromear*	betray
29)	*mirojear*	peek lustily
30)	*mitotear*	raise Hell
31)	*nortear*	drive someone crazy
32)	*pacotear*	betray

33)	*patalear*	kick someone in rear
34)	*pedrorrear*	warn/scold/fart consistently
35)	*pepeyendo*	farting (according to Galván and Teschner the gerund is the only form of the verb used)
36)	*politiquiar*	play politics
37)	*puñetear*	masturbate
38)	*putear*	act as if on the make
39)	*rajolear*	back down
40)	*retobear*	(child) sass an adult
41)	*sanchar*	commit adultery
42)	*tamboretear*	beat up
43)	*tontear*	be foolish
44)	*torear*	go on spree

2. Socially disapproved behavior, criminal

    a. Crime, general

1)	*alinear/linear*	go straight
2)	*colear*	tail somebody
3)	*maraguear*	murder
4)	*putear*	solicit, as prostitute
5)	*torear*	defy the law
6)	*trampear*	enter without paying

    b. Crime, stealing

1)	*babiarse (por)*	steal
2)	*coyotear*	steal
3)	*mañanear*	steal
4)	*talonear*	steal/hustle

    c. Crime, with dope

1)	*pildorear*	ingest narcotics

    d. Crime, with knife

1)	*alfilear*	cut someone with knife
2)	*canalear*	cut someone with knife
3)	*charrasquear*	cut someone with knife, leave scar
4)	*filerear*	cut someone with knife
5)	*filetear*	cut someone with knife
6)	*garranchar*	cut someone with knife
7)	*navajear*	cut someone with knife

    e. Crime, with weapon other than knife

1)	*cuetear/quetear*	shoot someone

2)	*macanear*	strike over head with heavy object
3)	*pacotear*	stab in back
4)	*plomear*	shoot someone

II. Sports and play

A. Team sports

1)	*capotear*	snatch ball/leave team scoreless
2)	*garrotear*	defeat

B. Boxing

1)	*tironear*	pull at limbs in wrestling

C. Card playing and gambling

1)	*barajear*	play cards

D. Social amusements

1)	*banquetear*	have good time
2)	*maromear*	somersault
3)	*tortear*	applaud

E. General

1)	*fonchar*	cheat at marbles
2)	*pichonear*	easily defeat a novice
3)	*trampear*	hunt animals

F. Dancing

1)	*bolevear*	dance
2)	*borlotear*	dance
3)	*chanclear*	dance wildly
4)	*polquear*	dance polka
5)	*taconear*	dance
6)	*valsear*	dance waltz

III. Work

A. Work, technological

1. Automotive

1)	*arrear*	start car
2)	*carruchar*	ride
3)	*manear*	brake
4)	*mecanear*	do mechanical work

5)	*orillar*	curb car
6)	*pilotear*	drive car
7)	*talonear*	step on the gas/hurry

2. Secretarial

3. Domestic (See IIIB: Work, domestic below.)

4. Electrical

5. Military

B. Work, domestic

1)	*asear*	clean up
2)	*cocinear*	cook
3)	*copetear*	fill glass
4)	*chicharronear*	burn to crisp
5)	*lamprear*	roast
6)	*tasajear*	slice
7)	*trapear*	dust
8)	*trastear*	wash dishes
9)	*tortear/tortiar*	make tortillas

C. Work, educational

1)	*colear*	color

D. Financial transactions

1)	*cambear*	make change
2)	*feriar*	make change/better
3)	*pagulear*	pay
4)	*rayar*	pay wages/write checks

E. Labor relations

F. Manual labor

1)	*azadonear*	hoe
2)	*bolear*	shine shoes
3)	*pegostear*	spread with sticky substance
4)	*sarruchar*	saw

G. Work, general

1)	*cabulear*	complete a chore
2)	*cachuquear*	blow a job
3)	*cambalachar*	hawk
4)	*camear/camillar*	work
5)	*cascarear*	work for low pay
6)	*chambear*	work

7)	*chambonear*	do job awkwardly
8)	*machetear*	do job clumsily
9)	*reganchar*	contract for work

IV. Weather

1)	*candelear*	sleet
2)	*chipear*	light rain
3)	*grajear*	sleet

V. Medical

1)	*asolear*	have heat stroke
2)	*falsear*	sprain knee
3)	*moretear*	bruise
4)	*sangrear*	bleed

IV. General and/or unclassifiable

1)	*afrañar*	understand
2)	*cantear*	incline
3)	*costear*	be worthwhile

APPENDIX B

LEXICAL ITEMS WITH ENGLISH BASES

I. Behavior

   A. Personal behavior, domestic setting

      1. Eating and drinking

1)	*bironguear*	drink beer or other alcohol
2)	*liquear*	lick
3)	*lonchar*	eat lunch

      2. Grooming and dressing

1)	*combiar*	comb
2)	*mechar*	match
3)	*permanentear*	give a permanent
4)	*setear*	set
5)	*shainear*	shine
6)	*tatu(y)ar*	tattoo
7)	*trimear*	trim

   B. Personal behavior, general

1)	*bloquear*	block
2)	*bonquear*	sleep
3)	*chusear*	choose
4)	*guachar*	watch
5)	*shoflear*	shuffle
6)	*stepear*	step
7)	*toriquear*	talk

   C. Interpersonal behavior, general

1)	*chatapear*	shut up
2)	*espatear*	spot/recognize
3)	*flipear*	flip/go crazy
4)	*flirtear*	flirt
5)	*fulear*	fool
6)	*pinchar*	pinch
7)	*tisear*	tease
8)	*tochar*	touch
9)	*tritear*	treat
10)	*trostear*	trust
11)	*yonkiar*	junk, throw away

   D. Interpersonal behavior, social formulas

1)	*pronuncear*	declare that something is so

E. Socially disapproved behavior

   1. Socially disapproved behavior, general

1)	*canquear*	beat someone up
2)	*mochar/muchar*	mooch
3)	*monquear*	monkey around
4)	*parquear*	overstay one's welcome
5)	*pinchar*	pinch
6)	*pompear*	fornicate
7)	*ponchar*	punch
8)	*swinguear*	swing

   2. Socially disapproved behavior, criminal

     a. Crime, general

1)	*estulear*	stool on someone
2)	*freimear*	frame
3)	*joslear*	hustle
4)	*licorear*	look over/case the joint

     b. Crime, stealing

1)	*requetear*	steal
2)	*rolear*	roll/steal

     c. Crime, with dope

1)	*capear*	put heroin in capsules
2)	*estufear*	sniff residue of narcotics

     d. Crime, with knife

     e. Crime, with weapon other than knife

1)	*chutear*	shoot

II. Sports and play

  A. Team sports

1)	*batear*	bat
2)	*cachar/quechar*	catch
3)	*cañonear*	throw a cannonball pass
4)	*chutear*	shoot
5)	*driblear*	dribble
6)	*estraiquear*	strike at and miss/strike someone out
7)	*fanear*	fan/strike out
8)	*fildear*	play position of fielder
9)	*golear*	make a goal
10)	*golfear*	play golf

11)	*pichar*	pitch
12)	*rachar*	rush
13)	*swinguear*	swing
14)	*quiquear*	kick

B.   Boxing and wrestling

1)	*catear*	give someone an uppercut
2)	*fletear*	flatten someone
3)	*naquear/noquear*	knock out
4)	*ponchar*	punch
5)	*ringuear*	ring a bell
6)	*soquear*	sock

C.   Card playing and gambling

1)	*betear*	bet
2)	*blofear*	bluff
3)	*dilear*	deal
4)	*poquear*	play poker

D.   Social amusements

1)	*cabaretear*	go night clubbing
2)	*campear*	go camping
3)	*clapear*	applaud/cut in, while dancing
4)	*plujear*	plunge
5)	*swimear*	swim
6)	*trapear*	go hunting

E.   General

1)	*escrachar*	scratch, eliminate
2)	*jonchar*	move marble shooter closer to target

F.   Dancing

III.   Work

A.   Work, technical

1.   Automotive

1)	*baquear*	back
2)	*bompear*	bump
3)	*brequear*	brake
4)	*choquear*	choke
5)	*crenquear*	crank
6)	*draivear*	drive
7)	*estarear*	start
8)	*fletear*	flatten a tire

9)	*güeldear*	weld
10)	*parquear*	park
11)	*ponchar*	puncture a tire
12)	*puchar/apuchar*	push
13)	*raitear*	give or get a ride
14)	*requear*	wreck
15)	*yequear*	jack up

2. Secretarial

1)	*chequear*	check
2)	*dailear*	dial
3)	*esteiplear*	staple
4)	*sainear*	sign
5)	*taipear*	type
6)	*teipear*	tape

3. Domestic (See III B: Work, domestic below.)

4. Electrical

1)	*ploguear*	plug in

5. Military

1)	*machinganear*	shoot, with machinegun

B. Work, domestic

1)	*clinear*	clean
2)	*cuquear*	cook
3)	*dompear*	dump
4)	*dostear*	dust
5)	*flochar*	flush
6)	*guarear/warear*	water (plants)
7)	*laquear*	lock
8)	*mopear*	mop
9)	*mixear*	mix
10)	*polichar*	polish
11)	*pompear*	pump
12)	*teipear*	tape
13)	*waxear*	wax

C. Work, educational

1)	*copear*	copy
2)	*cuitear/quitear*	quit
3)	*charpear*	sharpen (pencil)
4)	*chitear*	cheat
5)	*dropear*	drop (course)
6)	*espelear/espeletear*	spell
7)	*esquechar*	sketch
8)	*fielear*	skip

11)	*flonquear/flankiar*	flunk
12)	*impruvear*	improve
13)	*instructear*	instruct
14)	*juquear*	play hookey
15)	*mistear*	miss
16)	*practicear*	practice
17)	*ringuear*	ring (bell)
18)	*testear*	test
19)	*tichar*	teach

D. Financial transactions

1)	*buquear*	enter a purchase as debit against future wages
2)	*cleimear*	claim
3)	*charchear*	charge

E. Labor relations

1)	*cuitear/quitear*	quit
2)	*discharchar*	discharge
3)	*estraiquear/straiquear*	go on strike
4)	*piquetar*	picket

F. Manual labor

1)	*shainear*	shine

G. Work, general

1)	*güerquear*	work
2)	*pulear*	pull

IV. Weather

V. Medical

VI. General and/or unclassifiable

1)	*capear*	catch/tattle on someone
2)	*craquear*	crack
3)	*cheiquear*	shake

THE CONTEXTUAL VARIETIES OF *YOD*:
AN ATTEMPT AT SYSTEMATIZATION

JERRY R. CRADDOCK

University of California, Berkeley

It has been said that science advances not only when the
correct solutions are proposed, but also when the right questions
are asked. The development of Spanish vowels before palatal glides
and obstruents constitutes to the present day a very difficult and
even confused chapter in the historical grammar of Hispano-Romance.
In this essay I wish only to point out what I consider to be the
major anomalies present in this development, in other words, by
asking the pertinent questions, to demarcate as sharply as possible well established sound shifts from those that seem to depart
from a general pattern. The chief protagonist in the drama, the
glide traditionally labeled yod, can be described in phonetic terms
as vocalic, non-syllabic, palatal and close, a phone most commonly
symbolized as [j]. It is very like the close (high) palatal (front)
vowel [i], except that the latter is syllabic, and similar to the
voiced palatal fricative [y], which, however, is non-vocalic, i.e.,
consonantal. In what follows, I will draw a further distinction,
so as to separate the yods that occur in the syllabic onset from
those that appear in the syllabic coda; in traditional terminology,
the former [j] is a semiconsonant while the latter [i̯] is a semi-
vowel. Many Spanish consonants behave quite differently according
to whether they occur in the syllabic onset or coda, so I assume
that the distinction at issue would add no new baggage to the phonological grammar of Spanish. The four phones [i]/[i̯]/[j]/[y] all

have different syllabic distributions: [i] is exclusively nuclear, as in Sp. pino 'pinetree'; [i̯] is obligatorily the first, and most often only, member of the syllabic coda (Sp. peine 'comb' [péi̯ne]); [j] is the last, never the first, member of the syllabic onset (Sp. piedra 'stone' [pjéðra]); [y] occurs only as a syllabic onset (Sp. payo 'churl'). In structural terms, only one phoneme may be involved, though I have no desire to enter into that rather jejeune debate.

The broad pattern of historical development involves the phenomenon of assimilation, normally by way of anticipation: a vowel adopts, in the course of its development from Vulgar Latin to Old Spanish, one or more features of a following palatal glide or obstruent, specifically, closure and palatality, more often the former than the latter. This assimilatory adjustment occurs in three environments: (1) a glide [i̯] occurs immediately after the vowel as the initial part of the syllabic coda; (2) a glide [j] occurs in the onset of the following syllable; and (3) a palatal obstruent, e.g., [y], occurs as the onset of the following syllable. The effects of assimilation vary according to the nature of the vowel undergoing the influence of the palatal glide or obstruent. The open (low) vowel [a] experiences both palatalization and closing; the mid vowels are subject only to closing, the velar (back) mid vowels being more susceptible to extreme closure than the palatal (front) vowel in certain environments; finally, the close vowels lie beyond the range of any potential impact the palatal glides or obstruents might have had. Hispano-Romance shows little or no trace of the palatalization of back vowels of assimilation to a palatal glide, a phenomenon so characteristic of the Germanic family.

The foregoing should suffice as prolegomena; it is now my purpose to describe the assimilations that have occurred in Spanish, with the intention of emphasizing which cases constitute major anomalies. I consistently compare Spanish with Galician-Portuguese forms, since the latter are so often illustrative of archaic stages of evolution.[1]

The open vowel [a] reacts only to the first environment mentioned above, i.e., when it comes into contact with a following [i̯]; in the resulting diphthong [ai] the nuclear vowel is palatalized and partially closed, yielding [ei̯], a stage preserved in Galician-Portuguese and Western Asturian. In Spanish the off-glide [i̯] disappeared in preliterary times. The diphthong [ai̯] was not a regular part of the Latin vocalic apparatus after æ was monophthongized. It arose from a number of phonological processes, to wit: (1) the suppression of hiatus (Lat. laicus 'layman' > VLat. [lai̯ku] > Ptg. leigo [léi̯gu], Sp. lego); (2) from loss of a consonant (Lat. cantaui 'I sang' > VLat. [kantái] > Ptg. cantei, Sp. canté); (3) from metathesis of a glide [j] in the following syllable (Lat. ārea 'threshing floor' > VLat. [árja] > [áira] > Ptg. eira, Sp. era; (4) from the vocalization of a velar consonant in the syllabic coda (Lat. lac, lactic 'milk' > Vlat. [lákte] > [láite] > Ptg. leite, Sp. leche [léče]; Lat. mataxa 'raw silk' > VLat. [matáksa] > [madái̯sa] Ptg. madeixa 'hank, skein', OSp. madexa

[madéša]). Note that in Spanish, the glide [i̯] palatalized the
following consonants [t] and [s], while in Portuguese, it palatalized only the latter. The development just summarized is not
dependent on word stress--compare Lat. maxilla 'jaw' > VLat.
[maksɛlla] (with suffix change) > [maisɛ́lla] > OGal. meixela
'cheek', OSp. mexiella [mešjéλa], or, with [i] surfacing in the
wake of vocalic syncope, Lat. maiorĭnus 'of the larger sort' >
VLat. [mayorínu] > [mairíno] > Ptg. meirinho 'bailiff', Sp merino.
     The well-known transformation of [ai] > [ei] > [e] is paral-
lel in every respect to the developmental sequence [au̯] > [ou] >
[o] (Lat. paucus 'little' > VLat. [páu̯ku] > Ptg. pouco [póu̯ku],
Sp. poco), and is not, when viewed as an exclusively vocalic phenomenon, a controversial subject.
     The open vowel [a] resisted assimilatory pressure in the other
two environments mentioned above: (2 -- [j] in the following syllabic onset) Lat. *capreus, unattested derivative of capra 'goat'
with the presumed meaning 'goat-like', figuratively as a sustantive
'support, prop' > VLat. [káprju] > Sp. cabrio 'rafter, joist', Ptg.
caibro (with late metathesis); Lat. rabia 'rage' > VLat. [rábja] >
OSp. rauia [ráβja], Ptg. raiva (likewise with late metathesis);
Lat. flaccidus 'flabby' > VLat. [flákǩedu] > [flátsjo] > OSp. lla-
cio 'lank, limp' (> lacio; Portuguese cognate wanting); (3 -- [y]
as the following syllabic onset) Lat. mai-us, -ōris 'greater,
older' > VLat. [mayóre] > Sp. mayor (compare Sp. merino, above),
OPtg. maior (> maor > moor > mor). The palatal fricative [y] may
also arise through consonant loss: Lat. radius 'spoke, ray' >
VLat. [rádju] > [ráyu] > Sp. rayo, Ptg. raio; Lat. (māteria) fāgea
'beech (wood)' > VLat. [fágja] > [fáya] > OSp. faya, Ptg. faia.
     At this point I would like to admit into consideration two
more palatal obstruents, the lateral [λ] and nasal [ŋ], offspring
of their alveolar counterparts [l] and [n] in contact with yod.
Though initially the relevant environments resembled types (1) and
(2), the concrete effect in Hispano-Romance has, by and large,
been identical to that of environment (3). Observe the following
sets: Lat. palea 'chaff' > VLat. [pálja] > Ptg. palha [páλa], OSp.
paja [páža] (with the peculiarly Spanish shift [λ] > [ž]); Lat.
arānea 'spider' > VLat. [aránja] > Ptg. aranha, Sp. araña; Lat. tam
magnus 'so great' > VLat. [tammágnu] > Ptg. tamanho, Sp. tamaño;
Lat. coāgulum 'rennet' > VLat. [kwáglu] > Ptg. coahlo [kwáλu], OSp.
cuajo [kwážo]. The integrity of the open vowel [a] preceding [λ]
and [ŋ] in Hispano-Romance suggests that at no time could the diphthong [ai̯] have arisen as a significant factor in the pattern of
development, say in intermediate stages such as *[tramáinu] or
*[kwáilu]; or, if [i] did crop up in such situations, its existence
must have been so ephemeral as to leave the preceding vowel untouched. The reader will learn below, however, that the components
([y]/[λ]/[ŋ]) of the redefined environment (3) do influence the development of the mid vowels in important ways.[2]
     The non-low vowels that preliterary Spanish and Portuguese in-
herited from Vulgar Latin were mid-open [ɛ]/[ɔ], mid-close [e]/[o],
and close [i]/[u]. The first pair regularly diphthongized in
Spanish to [jé]/[wé] when stressed, while the other two pairs are
maintained. The operation of palatal glides and obstruents, viewed

abstractly, might have been either to produce a merger of all three
pairs into a single close set [i]/[u], or at least to have closed
each set by one step where possible, such that [ɛ]/[ɔ] and [e]/[o] >
[i]/[u]. In general, the second of the two alternatives seems to
have prevailed with important exceptions, not all of them satis-
factorily explained.

With regard to the palatal series of vowels, the evidence is ample that diphthongization fails to occur in environment (1), i.e.,
when [ɛ] is immediately followed by [i], of whatever provenience:
Lat. māteria 'wood' > Vlat. [matɛrja]^ > [madɛira] > Ptg. madeira,
Sp. madera; Lat. ceresia 'cherry' > VLat. [k̑erɛsja] > [tserɛiza] >
Ptg. cereja, OSp. ceresa [(t)seréza] (> cereça); Lat. lectus 'bed,
couch' > VLat. [lɛ́ktu] > [lɛ́ito] > Ptg. leito, Sp. lecho; Lat.
integ-er, -rum ' untouched' > VLat. [entɛ́gru] > [entɛ́iro] > OPtg.
enteiro, Sp. entero. In the diphthong [ɛi], the stressed vowel
is closed one step to [éi], becoming, in the process, indistinguish-
able from the products of [ai].

In environments (2) and (3), diphthongization likewise seems
blocked, though the evidence is scantier: Lat. superbia 'pride'
> VLat. [sopɛrbja] > OSp. soberuia, OPtg. sobêrv(i)a; Lat. neruium
'sinew' > VLat. [nɛ́rvju] > OSp. neruio, OPtg. nervho; Lat. grex,
gregis 'flock' > VLat. [grɛ́ge] > [grɛ́ye] > Sp. grey, Ptg. grei;
Lat. sedeat 'let him/her sit' > VLat. [sɛ́djat] > [sɛ́ya(t)] > Ptg.
seja [séža], OSp. sea (~seya); Lat. speculum 'mirror' > VLat.
[spɛ́klu] > Ptg. espelho, OSp. espejo [espéžo]. If Sp. viejo 'old'
< VLat. [vɛ́klu] < Lat. vetulus can be taken as analogical to OSp.
viedro 'old' < VLat. [vɛ́tru] < Lat. uet-us, -eris, then I know of
no really troublesome exceptions.

The palatal mid-close vowel [e], against the basic trend, maintains its quality in environment (1): Lat. ceru-isia, -esia 'beer'
> VLat. [k̑ervésja] > [tserveiza] > Ptg. cerveja, OSp. cervesa
[(t)servéza] (> cerveça); Lat. strictus 'close, tight' > VLat.
[(e)stréktu] > [estréito] > Ptg. estreito, Sp. estrecho; Lat.
dictatum 'dictation' > VLat. [dektátu] > [deitádo] > Sp. dechado
'model' (Ptg. ditado shows the influence of the p.-ptc. dito
'said'). One might be tempted to suspect a dissimilatory motive
for the failure of [ei] to become [ii] (which would have merged into
a simple vowel [i]). In any case, the relevant generalization is
that [i] produced closure only up to the point where merger would
have ensued. The merger just speculated on can be observed in
the following sets: Lat. frīctus 'fried' > VLat. [frík̑tu] > [friito]
> Ptg., Sp. frito; Lat. fīctus 'fixed, driven in' > VLat. [fík̑tu] >
[fiitu] > Ptg., OSp. fito. Note that the coalescence of [ii] into
[i] must have occurred with sufficient suddenness so as to preclude
in Spanish any palatalization of the following [t].

Environment (2), on the other hand, regularly produces a closing
effect: Lat. sepia 'cuttlefish' > VLat. [sépja] > OSp. xibia [šíbja],
Ptg. siba; Lat. uitreus 'glassy' > VLat. [vétrju] > Sp. vidrio 'glass'
Ptg. vidro; Lat. limpidus 'clear' > VLat. [lémpedu] > [lémpjo] >
Sp. limpio, Ptg. limpo.[3] In Spanish, this effect is frequently pro-
voked by the onset of the diphthong [jé] in the following syllable: [4]
Lat. pigmenta 'coloring' > VLat. [pegmɛ́nta] > Sp. pimienta 'pepper'.
With few exceptions, the mid-close vowel [e] appears proof against
closing influence of environment (3); Lat. uideat 'let him/her see'

> VLat. [védjat] > [véya(t)] > Sp. vea, Ptg. veja; Lat. corrigia
'shoe lace' > VLat. [korrégja] > [korréya] > Sp. correa; Lat.
cilia 'eyelids' > VLat. [ǩélja] > Sp. ceja 'eyebrow', Ptg. celha(s)
'eyelash(es)'; Lat. ligna 'firewood' > VLat. [légna] > Sp. leña,
Ptg. lenha. The two exceptions I have noted, Sp., Ptg. porfía
'stubborness' < VLat. [perfédja] < Lat. perfidia 'treachery' and
Sp., Ptg. navío 'ship' < VLat. [navégju] < Lat. nauigium, may have
been deflected from their normal development by approximation to
the common abstract suffixes -ía (Sp., Ptg. alegría 'happiness')
and -ío (Sp., Ptg. gentío 'mob, crowd').

To sum up the evidence presented so far: with the exception
of the potential shift [ei̯] > [ii̯], perhaps thwarted by a natural
resistance to producing a vocalic cluster of such phonetically similar elements, environment (1), involving [i̯], is the most powerful catalyst of the three, since it affects a vowel [a] otherwise
impervious to the influence of neighboring palatal articulations;
next in line comes environment (2), in which the glide [j] both
blocks diphthongization, and closes mid vowels; finally environment
(3) seems efficient only in impeding the diphthongization of the
original mid-open vowel [ɛ]. Now let us see to what extent the
back vowels conform to this pattern.

The mid-open velar vowel [ɔ], with some crucial exceptions,
behaves like its palatal counterpart in all three environments:
(1) Lat. octō '8' > VLat. [ɔ́kto] > [ɔ́i̯to] > Ptg. oito, Sp. ocho;
Lat. coxus 'lame' > VLat. [kɔ́ksu] > [kɔ́i̯so] > OPtg. co(i)xo, OSp.
coxo [kóšo]; (2) Lat. ostrea 'oyster' > VLat. [ɔ́strja] > OSp.
ostria (> ostra), Ptg. ostra; Lat nouius 'newish' > VLat. [nɔ́vju]
> Sp. novio, Ptg. noivo (with late metathesis); (3) Lat. podium
'balcony, terrace' > VLat. [pɔ́dju] > [pɔ́yo] > OSp. poyo 'stone
bench', Ptg. poi-al (with suffix); Lat. hodie 'today' > VLat.
[ɔ́dje] > [ɔ́ye] > Ptg. hoje, Sp. hoy (via [ɔ́e]); Lat. folia 'leaves'
> VLat. [fɔ́lja] > Ptg. folha 'leaf', OSp. foja [foža]; Lat. oculus
'eye' > VLat. [ɔ́klu] > Ptg. olho, Sp. ojo [óžo].

The most remarkable of the exceptions hinted at earlier pertains to environment (1): Lat. corium 'hide' > VLat. [kɔ́ruju] >
[kɔ́i̯ro] > Ptg. coiro, Sp. cuero. The Portuguese reflex is perfectly normal, but in the Spanish form, how is one to account for
the presence of the diphthong [wé], the regular outcome of [ɔ́] when
its diachronic trajectory is not perturbed by palatal attraction
(e.g., Sp. puerta 'door' < VLat. [pɔ́rta] < Lat. porta)? It will be
necessary to return to this set later, but before going on, I should
point out another possible exception with regard to environment (3):
Lat. somnium 'dream' > VLat. [sɔ́nnju] > Ptg. sonho, Sp. sueño. The
Spanish form is, of course, intimately related to a homonym containing a legitimate diphthong, i.e., Spanish. sueño 'sleep' < VLat.
[sɔ́nnu] < Lat. somnus (the Spanish palatalization of [nn] is
relatively late and has no effect on preceding vowels, cf. Ptg.
sono. However, it will become clear below that the palatal nasal
constitutes one of the environments in which aberrant developments
of velar vowels takes place.

The mid-close velar vowel [o], unlike its palatal counterpart
[e], readily succumbs to the closing effect of the glide [i̯] present in environment (1), there being no articulatory impediment

to a shift [oi̯] > [ui̯], since the two elements of the vocalic cluster remain sufficiently distinct through their opposing velar and
palatal features: Lat. luctat 'he/she struggles' > VLat. [lóktat]
> [lói̯ta(t)] > OGal. loita, OPtg. luita (> luta), Sp. lucha; Lat.
multum 'much' > VLat. [mṍltu] > [mṍuto] > [mṍi̯to] > OGal. moito,
Ptg. muito, Sp. mucho, muy 'very'; Lat. impulsat 'he/she pushes,
strikes' > VLat. [empólsat] > [empóu̯sa(t)] > [empoi̯sa(t)] > Ptg.,
OSp. empuxa [empúša]. In environment (2), closure is likewise consistent: Lat. rubeus 'reddish' > VLat. [róvju] > OSp. ruuio
'blond', Ptg. ruivo (with late metathesis); Lat. pluuia 'rain' >
VLat. [plóvja] > Sp. lluvia, Ptg. chu(i)va; Lat. turbidus 'muddy'
VLat. [tórvedu] > [tórvjo] > OSp. turuio, Ptg. turvo.
    Environment (3), whose lack of influence on the mid-close
palatal vowel has already been noted, yields a more complex pattern
with regard to the mid-close velar vowel: before [y] and [ŋ] clear
cases of closure are extant, but before [λ] the vowel maintains its
quality. Lat. fugiō 'I flee' > VLat. [fógjo] > [fóyo] > Ptg. fujo
OSp. fuyo; Lat. cuneus 'wedge' > VLat. [kónyu] > Sp. cuño 'die for
stamping coins', Ptg. cunho; Lat. pugnus 'fist' > VLat. [pógnu] >
Sp. puño, Ptg. punho; contrast Lat. genuculum dim. 'knee' > VLat.
[ɡɛnóklu] > OSp. e-, i-nojo (> finojo), OPtg. geolho (> joelho).
In pretonic position, both solutions can be documented: Lat.
mulie-r, -ris > VLat. [moljɛ́re] > OSp. mug(i)er, Ptg. mulher; Lat.
cōle-ō, -ōnis 'testicle' > VLat. [kolpóne] > OSp. cojón [kožón],
Ptg. colhão.
    In Spanish, the alternative to closure is not usually, as one
might expect in view of the Portuguese cognates, the mid-close
vowel [o], but rather the diphthong [wé], as in the case of Sp.
cuero mentioned above: Lat. augurium 'omen' > VLat. [agórju] >
[agói̯ro] > Ptg. agoiro, Sp. agüero; Lat. cicōnia 'stork' > VLat.
[k̆ekónja] > Ptg. cegonha, Sp. cigüeña. The diphthong in Sp. agüero
evolved out of a vocalic cluster [ói̯] whose stressed vowel was
never subject to diphthongization; hence it is reasonable to argue
that neither Sp. cuero nor agüero can have anything directly to do
with the regular diphthongization of [ɔ́] to [wé]. To allege that
cuero involves such diphthongization would be to claim that the
glide [i̯] at one and the same time both prevents diphthongization
(Sp. ocho < [ɔ́i̯to]) and causes it (Sp. cuero < [kwéi̯ro] < [kɔ́i̯ro]).
    The crucial difference between the development of Sp. ocho,
lucha, on the one hand, and Sp. cuero, agüero, on the other, lies
evidently in the fact that the glide [i̯] was absorbed by the following palatal obstruent [č] in the former two instances, but remained
for a time intact in the latter two, since the flap [r] was not
subject to palatalization. This relatively long-lived [ói̯], perhaps
also [úi̯], became [wé] without regard to the original quality [[ɔ́]
or [ó]) of the nuclear vowel.
    The most intractable enigma does not involve the cases just
mentioned, but rather those in which [wé] arose in contact with
the palatal nasal [ŋ], i.e., Sp. cigüeña. The violation of the
broad pattern is two-fold: the stressed vowel behaves as though
placed in environment (1), i.e., before [i̯] (like agüero <
[agói̯ro]) when in all other instances [ŋ] constitutes an environment of type (3), thus araña; but even granted that cigüeña must

go back to a form involving a type (1) environment ([(t)segóịŋa]),
in all other cases where the glide [ị] stands before a palatal
obstruent, it is speedily absorbed, as in lucha, empuxa, and, indeed, cuño. This last form, in fact, is based on a Vulgar Latin
prototype whose stressed vowel stands in an immediate environment
identical to that of the stressed vowel in the Vulgar Latin fore-
bear of cigüeña: [kónju]/[kekónja].

Without underestimating the importance of the aberrations
just mentioned, the velar vowels nevertheless show a high degree
of conformity to the pattern observed with respect to palatal vowels, especially if one is willing to allow for certain departures
attributable to their different basic features (palatal/velar);
for instance the shift [ei] ˃ [iị] is blocked, while [oị] ˃ [uị]
enjoys a relatively free course. Even the quite different developments of the diphthongs [eị] and [oị] when not immediately reduced
by absorption of the glide into a following palatal obstruent can
be regarded as sharing a certain basic parallelism in that off-
glide diphthongs are consistently eliminated ([eị] ˃ [e]: Sp. era
˂ [éịra], madera ˂ [madéira]; [oị] ˃ [wé]: Sp. cuero ˂ [kóịro]).
The latter change still lacks a definitive explanation though its
rigorous similarity to another diachronic sequence in Spanish has
been noted ([éụ] ˃ [jó], see Malkiel 1976); the former possesses
a well known pendant in [oụ] ˃ [o]. It is the origin and development of [oị] in the environment _____ [ŋ] that remains entirely exceptional when viewed in the perspective I have attempted to lay
out.

To conclude: by identifying the three characteristic environments involving the element traditionally called yod and by ob-
serving in turn the effects these environments have on open, mid-
open and mid-close vowels, one gains a more precise understanding
as to which developments appear to fit a broad pattern and which
must be considered aberrant. Once the broad pattern has been
securely established, the linguist can turn his full attention to
the exceptions.

NOTES

[1]For Spanish examples I have relied chiefly on Menéndez Pidal
1941 and Corominas 1954-57, and for Portuguese specimens, Williams
1962, Machado 1952-59, and Lorenzo 1968. The evidence presented
is highly selective, meant only to illustrate, rather then ex-
haustively document, the phenomena studied.

[2]In an effort to conform to the limitations of space suggested
by the editors, I have left out of consideration one other relevant
environment, consisting of a syllable-final nasal followed by a
palatal or palatalized obstruent: Lat. tangit 'he/she touches'
VLat. [tánget] ˃ OSp. tañe 'he/she plays (an instrument), Ptg.
tange.

[3]In Sp. tibio 'warm,' OPtg. tiv(i)o < [tɛ́pjo] < VLat. [tɛ́pedu]
< Lat. tepidus, an original mid-open [ɛ] has undergone complete
closure. The contrast with the Hispano-Romance descendants of Lat.
superbia and neruium may require the assumption that a two-stage
evolution occurred, first [tébjo] with blocked diphthongization,
then tibio at a later, though still preliterary, date, since the
glide [j] continued to exercise its influence, having been neither
absorbed into the preceding consonant, nor metathesized into the
preceding syllable. I further speculate that this later influence
could not operate when a consonantal coda existed in the stressed
syllable, as in Sp. soberbia and nervio.

[4]The labiovelar glide [w] had a like effect in Spanish: Lat.
aequālis 'equal' > VLat. > [ɛkwále] > OSp. egual [egwál] > igual.

REFERENCES

Corominas, Joan. 1954-57. Diccionario crítico etimológico de
    la lengua castellana. 4 vols. Bern: Francke/Madrid: Gredos.
Lorenzo, Ramón. 1968. Sobre cronologia do vocabulário galego-
    português. Vigo: Galaxia.
Machado, José Pedro. 1952-59. Dicionário etimológico da língua
    portuguesa. 2 vols. Lisbon: Confluência.
Malkiel, Yakov. 1976. From falling to rising diphthongs: the
    case of Old Spanish ió < éu. Romance Philology 29.435-500.
Menéndez Pidal, Ramón. 1941. Manual de gramática histórica
    española. 6th ed. Madrid: Espasa-Calpe.
Williams, Edwin B. 1962. From Latin to Portuguese. 2nd ed.
    Philadelphia: Univ. of Pennsylvania Press.

ROLE ENACTMENT
AND VERBAL STRATEGIES
IN THE U.S. VIRGIN ISLANDS

ROBERT J. DI PIETRO

University of Delaware

The usefulness of a speech continuum in describing polylectal
grammars has been recognized.[1]   However, we are now in need of an
equally detailed theoretical tool with which to approach the strategic use of language in creolized societies. Grammars are limited
in general to what they can cover. The ways in which humans manipulate language for personal ends are not easily incorporated into
grammatical description, no matter how socially sensitive the description might be. The use of verbal strategies is especially
evident in societies which have undergone extensive language contact. In such societies, people are usually conscious of the social
and cultural constraints uniquely placed on their interactions.
Frequent code-switching is one result of language confrontation.
    In order to initiate a fruitful approach to the strategic use
of language, it is proposed that linguistics be expanded to include
a dramaturgical point of view. Speakers become role-players and
speech events are redefined as "episodes" in on-going real-life
dramas. Three episodes involving the use of verbal strategies in
the U.S. Virgin Islands are recounted and analyzed. Several implications are drawn not only for linguistic theory and the future
directions of creole language studies, but also for second language
learning.

1. The speech continuum and verbal strategies

Thanks to the work of scholars such as Derek Bickerton and
David DeCamp, among others, we have found a clear way to explain
the polymorphous yet rule-governed organization of language in
creole societies. Although the idea of a speech continuum had been
known by creolists for some time, it was only at a meeting of the
Society for Caribbean Linguistics in 1971 that Bickerton provided
a detailed and formal exposition of how the varieties or 'lects'
of a speech community could be arranged across a single continuum
from basilect to acrolect (see Bickerton 1973 for a published version of his formulations). In addition to its obvious power of
description, the dynamic nature of the continuum yields many implications for the basic principles of language change. It can
be shown, for example, that the array of variations in form displayed synchronically in a given speech community also reflects
the history of linguistic change undergone by that community.

To be sure, a good deal of the future research of linguists
can be put to good purpose in uncovering the speech continua of
diverse communities. In the process, many elaborations will doubt-
lessly be forthcoming, with even newer insights into the nature of
language change. There is, however, an aspect of linguistic inquiry which is not being touched, even within the context of the
latest approaches to language theory. Many sociolinguists are
apparently content to take grammar statement as the one and only
goal of their work. The major difference between the "straight"
linguist and his hybridized colleagues in sociolinguistics and
creole studies has come to rest on where to look for the data and
how to collect and organize it. There is a larger principle which
we linguists, regardless of our specialization, never seem to question, namely that the grammar of a language is the theoretically
correct way to account for all the linguistic capacities of its
speakers. To put the issue in the form of a question: do speakers
have abilities with their language which cannot be somehow subsumed
in the rules of grammar? Obviously no one has succeeded in writing
a total grammar of a language and no individual speaker in a speech
continuum has all the competence of all the other speakers sharing
the continuum. These are not the matters which should concern us,
at any event. Powerful grammars generate a rich assortment of
well-formed utterances. By the same token, sociolinguistic grammars
produce utterances which are appropriate to the social status of
their speakers. This paper poses no argument with either of these
notions.

There is an aspect of linguistic competence which does not
respond to grammatical statement, regardless of how sophisticated
that statement might be. Grammar relates to form and not directly
to a use of language which can be termed "strategic." If we could
agree that people enter into verbal transactions with each other
simply because they have to exercise some innate drive to phonate
or to respond to a given social structure, grammars would be enough.
In fact, if language were only for the exchange of factual information, we would not even need the intricate grammars that we now have.

The decision to speak is also a commitment to participate with others in the socializing process. As a result, every speaker develops a competence of some sort in the use of utterances to gain desired ends. Speaking is a risky business. It entails potential harm to the psyche of those engaged in this particular expression of socialization. The ends desired by a speaker may be foiled by other speakers who are more skillful in their use of language.

Creole societies are especially appropriate places to study verbal strategies. Such societies are or recently have been the scene of intensive language contact. In the American Virgin Islands, for example, the need to interact with people of distinct linguistic and cultural groups is as pressing today as it has been throughout the known history of the islands. Only the groups themselves have changed. Under the Danish flag, a Dutch-based creole was spoken. Since the islands have passed to the possession of the United States the older creole has been replaced by an English-based one. In addition to waves of tourists from mainland U.S.A., the islands have witnessed the influx of Spanish-speaking immigrants from Puerto Rico.

Rather than enumerate the many other groups that have come and gone, it is sufficient to say that participation in Virgin Island society has always required a good number of distinct verbal strategies. In addition to the customary human needs for communication, individuals functioning in Virgin Island society are constantly reminded of who they are, who the persons being addressed are and what is the setting in which the interaction is taking place. For example, a participant in a seminar for librarians which the author conducted at the College of the Virgin Islands identified herself as a native of St. Thomas' Frenchtown. Upon hearing this, an effort was made to initiate an informal conversation with her in French, hoping to elicit responses which would reflect her local creole. Although it was of some difficulty to her, she insisted on speaking an acrolectal form of standard French and avoided all traces of the local variety. Of course, there are several possible interpretations for this "avoidance strategy" on her part. The one I favor is that she remained mindful of the fact that we were in a college setting. I was the teacher whom she, as a special student and a librarian by profession, would ultimately have to impress with her educational expertise. The purpose of my seminar was to present the rudiments of linguistics to librarians and she, along with the other participants, found themselves facing a potentially threatening array of new concepts about language. Under such circumstances, a volunteering of forms in a speech variety which is not acrolectal would be clearly counterproductive. (For an example of St. Thomas French dialect and its use, see Highfield 1976.)

The following is an illustration of a strategy which is apparently employed by many speakers throughout the English-speaking Caribbean. A native Thomian professionally employed as a teacher of English on the island confided that the inter-island differences in speech which were made so much of by local inhabitants are disregarded when Virgin Islanders travel on the North American mainland and encounter people from other Caribbean islands. Insular peculiarities which would quickly be noted at home lose their sig-

nificance as societal markers when the islanders find themselves con-
fronting a larger and potentially more alien mainland society.

Mainlanders who have become residents of the Virgin Islands
have provided various examples of the use of basilectal or mesolectal creole by natives for strategic purposes. Faced with a mainlander who has become established on the islands, natives will
often engage in a form of language testing to gauge how integrated
into island society the mainlander has become. Mesolectal forms
are purposefully used in conversation to appraise the mainlander's
comprehension of what is being said. Once the degree of comprehension has been determined, the natives know the extent to which
intimate topics can be discussed in the mainlander's presence.
With the mastery of lects located toward the basilectal pole of
the continuum comes the implication of sympathy with local social
and political issues.

People living in language contact situations become agile code-
switchers. The mainland wife of a teacher on St. Croix recounted
the instance of two natives walking towards her on the street, engaged in discussing some private affair. As they approached her,
they shifted from the near-standard acrolectal English they had
been using to a speech variety further down on the continuum toward
the basilect. On passing her and believing themselves to be once
more out of earshot, they moved back into the acrolect. This particular example illustrates quite neatly the distinction between
the realm of verbal strategies and that of grammatical statement.
This code-switch, with its purpose of assuring privacy in a public
place, exists as part of the repertoire of the speakers' verbal
strategies. Recognizing that fact is quite independent of determining how the speech forms used were generated by the social context and located at points along the continuum. Both should be
equally legitimate pursuits for the linguist. (See Di Pietro 1977
for a study of code switching as a strategy among bilinguals.)

2. Some necessary definitions

Before going any further into the matter of the strategic use
of language by Virgin Islanders, it is crucial that we understand
some basic concepts and the novel descriptive approach being undertaken here. The term 'verbal strategy' has already been introduced.
Summing up what we have said about it into a working definition, we
can call it 'that aspect of linguistic competence which comprises
speakers' ability to manoeuvre conversation to desired ends'. Verbal strategies are executed through manipulation of the mechanics
of grammar and also by prosodic elements and all the vocal quali-
fiers associated with speech performance. Di Pietro 1976 provides
a discussion of the strategies used by children to manipulate the
verbal behavior of adults. Verbal strategies apparently reflect
not only maturational differences but all the other variables,
psychological and social, which affect performance as well

When a strategy becomes ritualized in a society, it is rela-
beled a 'speech protocol.' The expression "excuse me" is a protocol
in use in standard English-speaking societies for both passing and

bumping into people. In Spanish, these two situations have led to
the development of distinct protocols. One who bumps into someone
in Mexico, for example, is expected to say "perdone." Passing by
someone entails the use of "con permiso." Speech protocols become
so ritualized in a society that failure to execute them attracts
more attention than their use. It may also be that most utterances
have more significance as strategies and/or protocols than they do
as conveyors of information. As Adrienne Lehrer (1975) has pointed
out, a man describing the qualities of a wine over a candlelit din-
ner may be more successful in impressing his female companion with
his savoir faire than in providing information of a substantive
nature about the liquid contained in their glasses.

   Some sociologists have recognized the strategic significance
of language use in society. Ernest Becker (1975), for example,
employs the term 'linguistic basis of power' in referring to the
social function of language. The individual who knows how to say
"I'm terribly sorry" or "Good show!" at the right times, with the
desired effects, has achieved a measure of control over his social
environment. The parent who reminds the child to say "thank you"
to an adult is introducing the child to one of the ways of gaining
control over others.

   The choice of 'role enactment' as the term to describe the
participation of individuals in speech events is an effort to shift
the focus of attention away from people seen as possessors of innate linguistic knowledge to a view of them as active shapers and
creators of meanings in the social context. The perception of what
roles are being played by the participants in a situation contributes essentially to the semantic interpretation of their utterances. The resolution of ambiguity which has figured so importantly
in the theoretical linguists' approach to sentences loses much of
its significance in real life. The 'role players' in real speech
events assign meanings to utterances in terms of how these utterances match the projected motives of the speakers. The librarian
on St. Thomas who was reluctant to volunteer specimens of her native
French creole was enacting the role of the professional in an educational setting. The author, as the other player in this episode,
was forced to abandon all intentions to play the role of linguistic
field worker and stay within the boundaries of his 'college professor' role. In retrospect one can wonder at how many persons throughout the world have been labeled as 'poor informants' by linguists
who have neglected to take into consideration the roles being played by them.

   In keeping with this admittedly dramaturgical approach to the
study of language use, the term 'episode' is preferred over the
more familiar one of 'speech act.' Human lives are not disjointed
social acts. The times when we find ourselves engaged in conversation with others do not have neat, clear-cut boundaries. Speech
acts are integral parts of the episodes which we link together to
form the extended allegory of our lives. Without this larger
meaning to our interactions, we risk losing the ability to make
anything we say functional. Following are several episodes which
will illustrate the dramatic nature of human acts, the strategic

value of the language used in those acts and the episodic nature
of speech events.

3. <u>Three episodes with accompanying analyses</u>

In each of these episodes the author was either an active participant or an observer. All three took place in St. Croix, U.S.
Virgin Islands.

<u>Episode no. 1</u>: The scene is the post office lobby. Several
customers, natives and non-natives alike, are queued up in front of
the stamp window. A mainlander enters the lobby and gets in line
behind a native policeman who also has a number of letters to mail.
Obviously impatient with the delay, the mainlander leans forward to
address the policeman. He asks if the stamp machine located in the
corner of the lobby is working. There is no answer from the policeman. A female tourist standing in front of the policeman overhears
and volunteers the information that the machine is not operational.
The mainlander eventually leaves the post office, expressing to his
friends the opinion that the policeman was rude to him.

<u>Analysis of Episode no. 1</u>: There is a protocol used by native
Virgin Islanders to open conversations with strangers. It takes the
verbal form of "Good morning," "Good day," or "Good night," depending on the time of day. If a native approaches a stranger without
prefacing his request for information by one of the above saluta-
tions, the stranger is under no social obligation to hear the request. If there is any rudeness it is on the part of the question-
er for failing to use the proper opening protocol and not on the
part of the addressee who does not answer. On the other hand, the
native policeman must interact with many aliens and tourists from
the mainland in his daily work. In very short order, he must realize that they are unfamiliar with the native protocol for opening
conversations. If he were to adhere to the expected protocol he
would be responding very rarely to questions asked of him. Not
responding to the improperly posed requests for information while
on duty would endanger his effectiveness as an officer of the law
in a locale annually inundated by tourists. In the post office,
however, he was "off duty." Although still in uniform, he was no
longer playing the role of official "information supplier." Therefore, he could ignore the enquiry on the grounds that the expected
politeness in talking to a stranger was not extended to him. In
this way, the native policeman has functioned strategically to his
own advantage. By enacting the role of a native private citizen,
he could invoke the native protocol to justify his choice of not
answering the outsider's question.

<u>Episode no. 2</u>: The scene is the Antilles Airline landing
station. The waiting area is jammed with people waiting for the
seaplane to take them to the other islands. Veteran travelers appear to be unusually excited because of the crash of a seaplane
with great losses just the week before. Delays between flights

seem longer than usual possibly because of the extra caution taken
by the personnel of the airlines. One man who has remained silent
for some time is slowly walking back and forth, staring at people.
Then he begins to speak in Spanish, at first in short, almost in-
audible bursts. Gradually his utterances become louder. Singling
out a mainlander dressed in jacket and tie, he shouts at him: ¿Qué
más quiere? ('What more do you want?'). He also begins to proclaim
evangelical slogans in Spanish, such as ¡Cristo no anduvo por el
mundo con una pistola! ('Christ didn't go through the world with
a pistol'). His belligerence appears to be increasing. He turns
to other people in the waiting area and asks them: ¿Qué quiere
que haga yo? ('What do you want me to do?'). Then he gets down
on his knees, stretches out his arms and shouts: ¡Mátenme si
quieren! ('Kill me if you wish!'). At this point, most conversation has ceased. People look at each other nervously and no one
attempts to talk to this 'crazy man'. However, someone does call
the clinic. Within a few minutes an ambulance arrives and a native
nurse approaches the man who, in the meantime, has loudly declared
that he is from Santo Domingo. The nurse speaks gently to him in
standard English. He appears to become docile. Taking him by the
arm, she leads him to the ambulance. As they go off, he remarks
to her: ¿Qué puedo hacer? Estoy loco. ('What can I do? I'm
crazy.'). After they leave, people in the waiting area begin to
comment on the episode. Eventually conversation returns to its
original level.

    Analysis of Episode no. 2: This episode could easily be en-
titled "A Caribbean Approach to Acting Crazy in a Public Place."
Erving Goffman (1971, footnote, p. 32) has described the ambulatory
schizophrenic who is sometimes found in public places in North American cities sitting in an open telephone booth facing the door
and speaking aloud to no one in particular. Goffman has also provided some analysis of how to display normalcy in public. The behavior of the 'crazy man' in St. Croix included several violations
of the same constraints discussed by Goffman, especially that of
staring. The added ingredient to enacting the 'crazy man' role in
the Virgin Islands was the choice of language. The main protagonist in this episode chose to use Spanish rather than a lect located
at some point along the English-based creole continuum. The native
nurse chose standard English in playing her part of caretaker. In
this way, she was successful in recasting the 'crazy man' in the
role of patient under medical care. His recognition of this recasting was evidenced by his final remark about his mental state. His
self-appraisal was more fitting to a therapeutic setting in a hospital than to a public place. If the 'crazy man' had originally
used some variety of the English-based creole, he might have been
approached by a native. The use of Spanish gave him center-stage
in this particular language-contact situation. While several persons had been using Spanish in their private conversations, none
of them attempted to approach the crazy man. Would one's use of
Spanish in talking to a crazy man who is also speaking Spanish have
given the impression to the English-speakers that the crazy man is

travelling in one's company? The use of the crazy man's own language might have entailed some unwanted responsibility in the event
that violence were to ensue. Our inability to go any deeper into
the strategic use of language in this episode reflects the need for
linguists in general to extend their considerations of language contact to include such public enactments.

    <u>Episode no. 3</u>: The scene is the library of a public school.
In an effort to give the author, as visiting professor, an idea of
how natives speak their creole in settings where outsiders are unlikely to be present, three teachers of English decide to enact the
script of a play written entirely in Crucian creole. The episode
chosen by the teacher-players takes place in the native market. The
conversation centers around the preparations for a forthcoming native
celebration. The taped dialogue yields the following exchanges
among the three (including stage commentary, which is marked 'S.C.'
in the transcription):

1.	<u>S.C.</u> A: ein yu spoz ta rîd?	Aren't you supposed to read?
	teik yo taim.	Take your time.
	(A laughs, B joins in.)	
2.	<u>S.C.</u> C: bigin agin.	Begin again.
	(more laughter)	
3.	A: wa yu no?	What do you know?
4.	B: Estella, wel yu ar? hau ting?	Estella, how are you? How're things?
5.	A: ting no gud, tšail. a bin hîr for a marnin and a no sel a ting.	Things are not good, child. I've been here all morning and I haven't sold a thing.
6.	C: tšail, yu lēt! yu ein no wa hapnin?	Child, you're late! Don't you know what's happening?
	(laughter)	
7.	Λ, B: wa?	What?
	(laughter)	
8.	C: al dī pîpl getn redi	Everybody is getting ready

for dī semi-sentainl. dē
ein spendin moni an fūd
dīz deiz. al goin en
klat.

for the semi-centennial.
They're not spending mon-
ey on food these days.
(It's) all going into that.

9. B: eh! daes tingin tong!
      let mi hīr abaut it,
      budi! . . .

Hey, that's news! Let me
hear about it, buddy!

(B breaks out into laughter)

10. C: wel, evribodi takin baut
       goin in a trump aen dei
       sei dat de goin, dat de
       goin be big pareid an
       ting.

Well, everybody's talking
about going in a "trump"
(tramp/troop) and that
there's going to be a big
parade and other things.

11. B: mi tšail ...

My child ...

12. C (cuts in): mi tš ...

My ch ...

13. S.C. B: daets mai part!

That's my part!

14. B: mi tšail, ay go si if ai go
       get in wan trup. ay go aks
       mi fren if ši gat trup.

My child, I'll go see if I
can get into a troop. I'll
ask my friend if she's got
a troop.

(at this point, B drops a line, in which she
is supposed to express the hope that A makes a
sale)

15. A: so long, Margaret. taenk
       yu!

So long, Margaret, thank
you!

16. S.C. C: natš yu yet!

Not (you) yet!

		hīr yu start.	You start here.
		(laughter)	
17.	C:	Kom an, Stella.	Come on, Stella.
18.	S.C. C:	but no, ai haef ta sei dat firs.	But no! I have to say that first.
19.	C:	so long, Stella, houp ya meik a seil!	So long, Stella, I hope you make a sale!
20.	S.C. A:	di end!	The end!
21.	S.C. C:	no, yu sei it nau: 'so long'.	No, you say 'so long' now.
22.	A:	so long, Margaret. taenk yu.	So long, Margaret, thank you.
23.	S.C. C:	no, yor pars [for] a litl wail der.	No, your part lasts a little while more.
24.	A:	wel, mi darlin, diz aur baed dei tadei. ai beta go hōm.	Well, my darling, this is our bad day, today. I'd better go home.
		(B, C laugh)	
25.	S.C. C:	ha, ha an daz di end. ha, ha.	Ha, ha, and that's the end. Ha, ha.

   Analysis of Episode no. 3: The most interesting linguistic aspects of this episode are not in the script itself but in the stage commentary. Although the play-acting was originally intended to serve as an illustration of the forms of the local creole, the actors have also provided--perhaps inadvertently--some striking examples of how native speakers can shift up and down the continuum for strategic reasons. For example, the opening line (ein yu spoz ta rīd? teik yo taim.) is delivered in a variety of the creole located somewhere below the acrolectal pole. Just prior to this utterance, A had been talking to me, the observer, in her acrolect. The suggestion to 'take your time' is apparently meant to relax all the players, in-

cluding A herself, and help them get into their stage roles. The
sharing of laughter plays the same strategic function.

As the scene develops, C will take charge of directing the other
players. With the second line (bigin agin) she has already begun to
exert herself. At line 12, C cuts in on B who reprimands her with
line 13 (daets mai part!). The scolding given to C by B is made more
effective by B's shift up the continuum toward the acrolect. This
shift is clearly indicated by her use of the copula and by the pronunciation of part with [r] rather than the long vowel. After the
reprimand, B gets back into the character she is playing. In re-
suming her play-acting, she also shifts back to the basilectal
language which goes with her part (see line 14). C's stage directing in line 16 (natš yu yet! hïr yu start.) does not entail a shift
so far up the continuum toward the acrolect as B's reprimand. By
remaining closer to the basilectal syntax, she can exert control
without sounding imperious. However, lines no. 21, 23 and 25 clearly show the extent to which she has taken command. All the players
use both the lects of their creole continuum and the various intonational elements at their disposal in order to enact their strategies. Thus, C uses a soft tone of voice in no. 21, so as to tone
down her style of directing.

4. Conclusions

The proposal of a continuum for creole speech communities has
not incorporated the possible effects of human interaction on polylectal grammar. While speakers may stand at various points along
the structural continuum, they are also susceptible to modifications
of their lects due to interaction with speakers at higher and lower
points, going both toward more basilectal and more acrolectal forms.
We must not forget that participants in creole society not only
speak to each other, but they also overhear others speaking. In
view of this state of affairs, it should come as no surprise that
many creole speakers are good code-switchers.

If we are to understand the dynamic forces affecting the shape
of polylectal grammars, we will have to delve into the ways in
which linguistic expression serves the demands of the speakers'
psyche. The off-duty policeman standing in the post office line
found a way to protect himself from the encroachment of tourists
into his private life. He simply applied the rules of discourse
which pertain to his intimate interactional style. The school
teachers in the last episode play the parts of native marketwomen
but remain nonetheless conscious that they are performing for an
audience with very specific interests. Their playful laughter
derives, at least in part, from having cast themselves in roles
which stereotype their own customs and speech styles. Their
interactions become mildly regressive as they employ language
which is reminiscent of the affect-laden aspects of their lives
(note, for example, C's closer in line 25). In going through the
educational process to become teachers, they have had to move up
through the continuum to professional 'acrolect' use. The play-
acting before the professor was like a divesting of professional

garb and a slipping into a more intimate native dress. This change
of social wardrobe in public was no doubt the motivation for the
embarassed laughter.

The dramaturgical approach to the language use of creolized
and multilingual societies carries several implications for linguistic theory beyond its potential for a fuller description of grammar.
In the quest for an understanding of all the factors contributing
to the birth of creole languages, we must look beyond the grammatical artifact itself. The theories of unmarking which have been
suggested to explain the origins of pidgins relate to form and not
to use. The conventionalization of linguistic forms is motivated
by the need to communicate and communication, itself, grows from
the enactment of social roles.

There are also implications for second language learning. Not
only do rules of form block the acquisition of new rules of form,
as Bickerton (1973) has pointed out, but also the need to invoke
strategies may lead to the formation of new verbal content for those
strategies. Let us all look forward to the day when we will develop
formal descriptive mechanisms for verbal strategies which are as
sophisticated as those we already have for grammar.

NOTES

[1]An earlier version of this paper was read at the Conference on
New Directions in Creole Studies of the Society for Caribbean Lin-
quistics, University of Guyana, August 11-14, 1976. The author
wishes to express his gratitude to Professor Shaligram Shukla of
Georgetown University and to Professor Arnold Highfield of the
College of the Virgin Islands for their critical and helpful
readings of drafts of this paper.

REFERENCES

Becker, Ernest. 1975. Socialization, command of performance, and
    mental illness. Life as Theater, ed. by D. Brisset and C. Edgley.
    Chicago: Aldine, pp. 292-301.
Bickerton, Derek. 1973. The nature of a creole continuum. Language
    49.640-69.
Di Pietro, Robert J. 1976. The strategies of language use. The
    Second LACUS Forum, ed. by P.A. Reich. Columbia SC: Hornbeam
    Press, pp. 462-67.

_____. 1977. Code switching as a verbal strategy among bilinguals. Current themes in linguistics: Bilingualism, experimental linguistics, and language typologies, ed. by F.R. Eckman. New York: John Wiley, pp. 3-13.

Goffman, Erving. 1971. Relations in public. New York: Harper & Row.

Highfield, Arnold. 1976. The French dialect of St. Thomas, U.S. Virgin Islands: A descriptive grammar with texts and glossary. PhD Diss., Ohio State Univ.

Lehrer, Adrienne. 1975. Talking about wine. Language 51.901-23.

PHONOLOGICAL VARIATION IN CHICANO ENGLISH: WORD-FINAL (Z)-DEVOICING

MARTIN J. DOVIAK AND ALLISON HUDSON-EDWARDS

University of New Mexico

Introduction[1]

A commonly observed characteristic of the English spoken by
Chicanos is the variable realization of either a voiced or voiceless segment at the ends of words in which careful standard
English has categorical or near categorical [z]. For example,
the word 'tigers' can variably be pronounced as [taygr̩z] or
[taygr̩s], and the word 'washes' may be pronounced either [wašəz]
or [wašəs].

A pilot study by Edwards (1975) found that word-final (z)-
devoicing by 10 fourth-graders in the Martineztown barrio of Albuquerque was influenced by several features of the linguistic environment though not by speech context. The purpose of the present study is to investigate for a larger sample the effects of
linguistic, stylistic, and social variables on (z)-devoicing among
Chicano children.

Methodology

The study resulted from the researchers' participation during
the spring of 1975 in a larger investigation of the language domi-

nance and language use patterns of children in a bilingual elementary school in the Martineztown barrio of Albuquerque. The findings of this latter investigation are reported in Teitelbaum (1976).

Subjects. Twenty-eight fourth-grade students from Longfellow Elementary School in Martineztown provided the speech samples for this analysis. Half of these students were boys and half were girls. All of the students were Spanish-surnamed, as is 95% of the school population. Most of the children come from bilingual homes in which Spanish is the most commonly used language. English use appears to predominate among friends in school and on the streets and playgrounds of the community (Teitelbaum 1976).[2]

Interview. After an initial period of casual observation and interaction with the children, a modified version of the Spolsky Language Dominance Test was administered to the children (Spolsky, Murphy, Holm, & Ferrell 1972, Teitelbaum 1976). In addition to its function as an assessment device, the interview was constructed in such a way as to elicit a corpus of speech in a variety of interview contexts in both Spanish and English. The tape-recorded interview consisted of (1) a sentence repetition task, (2) a word naming task, in which subjects were asked to name as many objects and activities associated with particular domains as they could, (3) a picture description task, and (4) a structured interview concerning the child's language use in various domains. All subjects were interviewed both in Spanish and in English. Only the English interviews were used in this analysis.

Coding procedure. Every occurrence of word-final (z) in the speech samples was transcribed and coded in terms of the following properties: (1) its realization as either a voiced or voiceless segment, (2) its morphological function, if any, (3) the nature of the surrounding phonological environment, (4) the interview context in which it occurred, (5) the formality of the utterance as signalled by various channel cues, (6) the identity of the individual speaker, (7) the speaker's sex, and (8) the speaker's language dominance score as determined from his/her performance on the word naming task.

The coded morphological functions of (z) were: (1) plural marker, (2) possessive marker, (3) third person singular present tense marker, (4) contracted copula or auxiliary, and (5) non-morphemic status. Both the preceding and the following phonological environments were coded for presence or absence of the following class of segments, as suggested by the pilot study: (1) voiced segments, (2) vowels, (3) consonants, (4) obstruents, (5) sonorants (vowels, liquids, and nasals), (6) glides, and (7) non-segments (phonetic pauses).

There were five interview contexts, consisting of the four components of the interview discussed earlier plus free speech, which was defined as recorded speech which occurred either before or after the formal interview or during an interruption of the interview. The picture description context was divided into four sub-contexts, with each of the three most commonly used pictures treated as distinct contexts and all other pictures coded as 'other.'

As a check on the possibility that stylistic conditioning of

(z)-devoicing might have been missed because the interview contexts may not have been sufficiently diverse to provide a wide
enough range of formality, a second measure of formality was used.
Utterances were marked for the presence or absence of eight contextual and channel cues (Labov 1972) which the researchers' own
experience in the interviews had indicated were associated with a
more casual style of speaking. These channel cues were: (1)
changes in rate of speech, (2) changes in loudness of speech, (3)
changes in pitch, (4) changes in breathing patterns, (5) laughter,
(6) audible gestures such as hand clapping, (7) volunteered speech
beyond that required to answer any question, and (8) topics involving particular emotional power or excitement for 10-year-old
children, such as death or games. Any occurrence of a variable
within an utterance which was both marked for the presence of at
least one channel cue and was also subjectively judged by the
transcriber to be casually delivered was coded as casual; all
other occurrences were coded as non-casual.

    Analysis. Variants of (z) were crosstabulated by all features
and combinations of features of the linguistic environment, by interview context, and by contextual style as indicated by the
channel cues. Pearson correlations were computed between the variable (z) and the sex and language dominance of the speakers.

Results

    The variability of (z)-devoicing. The crosstabulations show
that, except for a few environments in which a few individuals
have categorical non-application of the devoicing rule, (z)-de-
voicing is applied variably in all linguistic environments and in
all contexts and styles. Given the linguistic environments used
in this study, no way has been found to fit the data into a model
calling for individual speakers to categorically apply or not apply
the rule in highly specific linguistic environments (Bickerton
1971). It is possible, of course, that linguistic environments
were not discriminated finely enough and, consequently, that cate-
goriality could underlie the variability which was observed. This
seems extremely unlikely, however, due to the frequency with which
subjects would in the same breath repeat a word in identical linguistic environments, realizing the (z) variable as [s] in one instance and as [z] in the other.

    The variable rule. The data for the sample as a whole were
analyzed according to a variable rule model (Cedergren & Sankoff
1974, Labov 1969). This approach yielded a hierarchy of six phonological constraints whose predicted ranking of the frequency of
(z)-devoicing in each environment shows remarkably good fit with
the data. The morphological status of (z) was not found to have
any effect on devoicing.

    Of the total of 3086 instances of word-final (z) in the speech
sample, 31.3% were pronounced as voiceless [s]. The six phonological constraints and their effects on (z)-devoicing are shown in
Table 1. The considerable effect of a following voiceless segment
on (z)-devoicing can be seen from the data in column 1. Of the
1760 instances of word-final (z) in this environment, 46.6% were

Table 1. Percentages of word-final (z)'s devoiced in linguistic
          environments arranged in heirarchical constraining
          order. The symbol (+) before a number indicates that
          the percentage represents the rule output in the pre-
          sence of the feature named in a given column; the symbol
          (-) indicates that the percentage represents the output
          in the absence of that feature. An asterisk in a cell
          indicates a logically impossible combination of features.
          Numbers in parentheses represent the number of utterances
          on which each percentage is based.

1 __##[-vcd]	2 [+cns]__	3 __##[-seg]	4 __##[+cns]__	5 [-son]__	6 __##[+son]
+ 46.6 (1760)	+ 55.4 (965)	+ 57.1 (801)	+ *	+ *	+ *
					- *
				- *	+ *
					- *
			- 57.1 (801)	- 61.8 (152)	- *
					- 61.8 (152)
				- 55.9 (649)	+ *
					- 55.9 (649)
		- 47.6 (164)	+ 47.6 (164)	+ 50.0 (22)	+ *
					- 50.0 (22)
				- 47.2 (142)	+ *
					- 47.2 (142)
			- *	+ *	+ *
					- *
				- *	+ *
					- *
	- 36.0 (795)	+ 38.3 (454)	+ *	+ *	+ *
					- *
				- *	+ *
					- *
			- 38.3 (454)	+ *	+ *
					- *
				- 38.3 (454)	+ *
					- 38.3 (454)
		- 32.8 (341)	+ 32.8 (341)	+ *	+ *
					- *
				- 32.8 (341)	+ *
					- 32.8 (341)
			- *	+ *	+ *
					- *
				- *	+ *
					- *

1 __##[-vcd]	2 [+cns]__	3 __##[-seg]	4 __##[+cns]	5 [-son]__	6 __##[+son]
10.9 - (1326)	14.1 + (589)	+ *	+ *	+ *	+ *
					- *
				- *	+ *
					- *
			- *	+ *	+ *
					- *
				- *	+ *
					- *
		14.1 - (589)	14.6 + (226)	+20.5 (44)	+ 22.2 (27)
					- 17.6 (17)
				-13.2 (182)	+ 16.2 (74)
					- 9.0 (108)
			13.8 - (363)	+13.3 (60)	+ 13.3 (60)
					- *
				-13.9 (303)	+ 13.9 (303)
					- *
	8.3 - (737)	+ *	+ *	+ *	+ *
					- *
				- *	+ *
					- *
			- *	+ *	+ *
					- *
				- *	+ *
					- *
		8.3 - (737)	10.4 + (336)	+ *	+ *
					- *
				-10.4 (366)	+ 12.3 (146)
					- 9.1 (220)
			6.2 - (371)	+ *	+ *
					- *
				-6.2 (371)	+ 6.2 (371)
					- *

devoiced--substantially more than the over-all percentage of 31.3%.
In contrast, in the 1326 instances where the (z) variable was not
followed by a voiceless segment, it was devoiced only 10.9% of the
time. It is obvious, therefore, that the presence of a following
voiceless segment is an important constraint favoring application
of the (z)-devoicing rule.

The second most important constraint on (z)-devoicing is the
presence of a consonantal segment preceding (z), as shown in column
2. When the following segment is voiceless and when the preceding
segment is consonantal, that is, when the first and second constraints on the rule are both present, (z) is devoiced in 55.4% of
the 965 instances found in this environment. However, (z) is devoiced in only 36.0% of the instances where the following segment
is voiceless and the preceding segment is non-consonantal. The
consonantality of the preceding segment has a similar effect on
(z)-devoicing in the absence of the primary constraint. When the
following segment is not voiceless and the preceding segment is
consonantal, 14.1% of the 589 instances of (z) in this environment
are realized as [s]. However, when both the primary and secondary
constraints are absent, (z) is devoiced 8.3% of the time.

In a similar fashion, the third most important constraint
favoring the application of the (z)-devoicing rule was determined
to be the presence of a non-segment, or phonetic pause, following
(z). The effects of this constraint are shown in column 3. The
fourth-order constraint on (z)-devoicing is the presence of a
following consonantal segment, shown in column 4. The fifth- and
sixth-order constraints both refer to the sonorance of the surrounding segments: the fifth-order constraint specifies that non-sono-
rance in the preceding segment favors devoicing and the sixth-order
constraint specifies that sonorance in the following segment does
so as well.

It is clear that each of these six phonological constraints
affects the devoicing of word-final (z). It is not immediately
obvious, however, that these constraints must be ordered as they
are in Table 1, i.e., that the environment heading column 1
necessarily has the greatest effect, that the environment heading
column 2 has the next greatest effect, and so on. The justification for this ordering of constraints is to be found in the geometric ordering of the output frequencies in all combinations of
these environments (Labov 1969).

The claim of geometric ordering of the output of variable
rules specifies that, controlling for higher order constraints, if
any, a rule will always apply more often when a given constraint
is present than when it is absent. Thus, an examination of Table
1 reveals that the frequencies of (z)-devoicing in all environments
when the primary constraint is present are higher than the frequencies of (z)-devoicing in all environments when the primary constraints are absent. That is, all of the percentages in the top
half of Table 1 are higher than those in the bottom half. The
secondary constraint is defined as that constraint which, controlling for the presence or absence of the primary constraint, causes
the rule to apply more often when it is present than when it is
absent, whether lower order constraints are present or not. That

is, all the percentages in the top quarter of Table 1 are higher than those in the second quarter, and all the percentages in the third quarter are higher than those in the bottom quarter. Once the ordering of all the constraints of a variable rule is determined in this fashion, the ideal result is a perfectly decreasing order of percentages in each column of the table. Evaluated in this way, the pattern of percentages determined by the six constraints on the (z)-devoicing rule is extremely regular, although it contains a few minor reversals.

The only reversals in the pattern are found in the lower half of columns 5 and 6. Examined closely, column 5 is found to contain two ordering reversals, which are carried over into column 6. These reversals occur in the column 5 cells with the misordered percentages 13.2%, 13.3%, and 13.9% and in the column 6 cell with 9.0% devoicing. These are very slight reversals, easily attributable to chance, especially when one considers both the overwhelming regularity of the entire array and the fact that the reversals occur in constraints of a lower order than are normally even included in variable rule analyses. The additional order introduced into the array by the fifth- and sixth-order constraints clearly outweighs the disorder to be found in these few cells; these constraints both have a regular effect on the devoicing of word-final (z).

It is obvious, then, that in any formulation of a rule for word-final (z)-devoicing, the six phonological constraints given/ in Table 1 would somehow need to be included. The effects of these six constraints on (z)-devoicing can be summarized in a variable rule of the following form (Cedergen & Sankoff 1974, Wolfram & Fasold 1974):

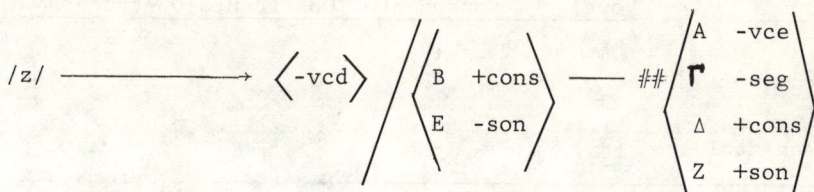

$$\text{/z/} \longrightarrow \left\langle \text{-vcd} \right\rangle \Bigg/ \Bigg\langle \begin{matrix} \text{B} & \text{+cons} \\ \text{E} & \text{-son} \end{matrix} \Bigg\rangle \text{---} \,\#\# \Bigg\langle \begin{matrix} \text{A} & \text{-vce} \\ \Gamma & \text{-seg} \\ \Delta & \text{+cons} \\ \text{Z} & \text{+son} \end{matrix} \Bigg\rangle$$

The angle brackets indicate variability in the rule output and in the constraining effect of environmental features; the upper-case Greek letters are used to indicate the hierarchical ordering of the constraining features. The rule can thus be read:

(z) is always devoiced more frequently when the A-constraint is present than when it is absent. Controlling for A, (z) will always be devoiced more frequently when the B-constraint is present than when it is absent. Controlling for A and B, (z) will be devoiced more frequently when the Γ-constraint is present, and so on; (z) will be devoiced least when none of the constraints is present.

Discussion

Principles explaining the constraints on (z)-devoicing. In
spite of the apparent heterogeneity of the sound classes specified
by the constraints on the (z)-devoicing rule, all the constraints
may be explained by appealing to two phonological processes: assimilation and resyllabication.
    The process of assimilation is most obviously at work in the
primary constraint: (z) devoices most often before a voiceless
segment. Essentially the same type of assimilation explains constraints two through five, although this relationship is obscured
by the traditional use of only binary distinctive features in discussing assimilation. The principle which unites the processes
acting in constraints one through five is that sound classes can be
ranked relative to one another along a dimension of 'sonority'
(Hankammer & Aissen 1974, Vennemann 1974). Each of the features
'voicing,' 'sonorance,' and 'non-consonantality' serves to locate
sound classes along this sonority continuum, as shown in Figure 1.

Figure 1.   Sound classes ranked according to sonority as defined
             by the features of voicing, sonorance, and non-
             consonantality.

Defining Features	Most Sonorous			Least Sonorous
	Vowels	Sonorant Consonants	Voiced Obstruents	Voiceless Obstruents
Voiced	+	+	+	-
Sonorant	+	+	-	-
Non-Consonantal	+	-	-	-

These features, although distinctive at the autonomous phonemic
level, seem to be related to each other at a more abstract level
via the concept of sonority. This is a plausible relationship,
given that the features of voicing and sonorance are intimately
related by definition and that the voicing of obstruents is different from the spontaneous voicing of vowels and other sonorants
(Chomsky & Halle 1968:300-302). Thus, vowels, which are voiced,
sonorant, and non-consonantal, are most 'sonorous' and voiceless
obstruents, which are voiceless, non-sonorant, and consonantal,
are least 'sonorous.' Sonorant consonants and voiced obstruents
are intermediate in terms of sonority. This more abstract concept of sonority allows (z) to devoice in order to assimilate not
just to a following voiceless segment, as specified in the primary constraint, but also to a preceding or following consonantal

segment, specified in the second- and fourth-order constraints, and to a preceding non-sonorant, specified by the fifth-order constraint.

The effect of the tertiary constraint can be interpreted in a similar way. A phonetic pause is certainly voiceless and also embodies extreme values of some of the same properties that distinguish consonants from vowels. It interrupts voicing at least as emphatically as any voiceless consonant, and it stops the flow of air more thoroughly than any stop. It is not surprising, therefore, that a rule which assimilates a sound to the voicelessness and consonantality of surrounding segments will also assimilate it to corresponding properties of a following non-segment. Therefore, these data suggest that voicing, along with non-consonantality and sonorance, is an important component of sonority, and that voicing assimilation may be more generally thought of as assimilation along a more abstract dimension of sonority.

The sixth-order constraint is the only constraint which does not act as part of this general sonority assimilation process. In this case, the presence of a following sonorant favors (z)-devoicing, unlike the presence of a preceding sonorant. This constraint seems to be best explained by a process of resyllabication which is facilitated by (z)-devoicing in certain environments.

Syllabication rules have been posited by a number of people in order to account for the phonetic grouping of segments in connected speech (Hooper 1972, Pulgram 1970, Vennemann 1972). In connected speech, word boundaries effectively disappear, and the two important phonetic units beyond the segment level are now syllables, often smaller than one word, and larger 'breath groups' or 'sections' (Pulgram 1970) which are usually composed of more than one word. Within these 'sections,' syllabication rules apply to regroup segments into syllables, often reassigning a segment from one word to an adjacent word. These syllabication rules obey language-specific constraints on permissible consonant clusters and syllable contours, but follow certain universal principles of syllabication. One such principle is that syllable onsets will consist of the maximal number of consonants permitted by the word-initial cluster constraints of a given language (Hoard 1971:137-138, Hooper 1972:535-536, Pulgram 1970:50). Another principle specifies that whenever it is impossible to avoid violations of either word-initial or word-final sequential constraints, the violation will occur in the coda preceding the syllable boundary rather than in the following onset (Hoard 1971:138, Pulgram 1970: 51). Both of these principles are concerned with achieving an ideal form of syllable onsets.

These principles of syllabication, along with the possibility of assigning segments to syllables without regard to word boundaries, are relevant to the process of (z)-devoicing. They introduce the possibility that resyllabication rules may assign word-final (z)'s to the initial syllable of the following word and that it is more likely for a devoiced (z) to be so reassigned than a voiced (z). Keeping in mind the necessity of maintaining permissible initial consonant clusters in syllable onsets, it is clear that [z] may be phonologically reassigned to the following word only if it begins with a vowel. [s], on the other hand, may be phonologically reassigned to the following word if it begins with a vowel, a nasal consonant, [l], or a voiceless stop. If one of the functions of resyllabication is to assign a maximal number of consonants to the syllable onset, (z)-devoicing will facilitate this process by providing a more usable segment--[s].

Certain constraints on the (z)-devoicing rule appear to favor devoicing in order to permit resyllabication. The sixth-order constraint, for example, specifies that (z)-devoicing is more likely to occur when the following word begins with a sonorant; as noted above, [s] may occur syllable-initially before any consonant except [r]. Since the presence of the sixth-order constraint automatically implies the presence of the fourth-order constaint, resyllabication is facilitated by the fourth-order constraint as well. The other sound class which may occur after syllable-initial [s] is that of voiceless stops. This class is partially specified by the presence of the first-order constraint, with the fourth-order constraint redundantly present. Clearly, then, the first-, fourth-, and sixth-order constraints operate to produce a situation in which resyllabication is more likely to be able to apply.[3] Since the environments favoring resyllabication are environments which also favor (z)-devoicing, it seems that information which is available as input to the (z)-devoicing rule must include the fact that resyllabication is likely to occur if (z) devoices. This suggests that global rules may be needed in phonology, as well as in syntax (Lakoff 1970). In other words, it appears that not all phonological rules apply blindly, without information regarding the application (or possibility of application) of other rules in a derivation. If this is true, current phonological theory needs to be revised to account for this situation.

Proposed models of linguistic variation. There have been two major paradigms advocated in the literature for the analysis of linguistic variation such as (z)-devoicing. The dynamic paradigm (Bickerton 1971, Bailey 1973) calls for categorical production by individual speakers in all environments except in one environment in which change may be in progress. The quantitative paradigm (Labov 1969), on the other hand, allows for ordered percentages of variability in all environments. The variability of (z)-devoicing in all environments even for individual speakers suggests that Bickerton's model is not appropriate for describing all types of linguistic variation. On the other hand, Labov's claim (1966, 1972) that greater regularity is to be found in communal grammars than in individual grammars is not borne out by the data either. An investigation of (z)-devoicing in the four environments defined by the first two constraints showed that the hierarchical ordering of the sample as a whole was replicated in 18 of the 28 speakers. Seven of the remaining 10 individual arrays have low enough occurrences of the variable in the deviant cells for the reversals to be due to chance. There is no immediate obvious explanation for the deviant arrays of the three remaining speakers, but the possibility should not be discounted that individual deviations from the group norm might be accounted for by more detailed sociological variables than were included in this study. Given an adequate speech sample and pertinent sociological information, and assuming the identification of the relevant linguistic features in the environment, the description of the speech of individuals should in fact prove to be even more regular than the description of the speech of the group as a whole.

The effects of speech context. The five interview contexts were established under the hypothesis that the sentence repetition task would elicit the most careful, standardized speech, followed by the word naming task, the language use interview, the picture description task, and free speech, in that order. It was further predicted that an emotionally-charged picture of a cat killing a bird would elicit more excited and, therefore, less formal or standardized speech than the other pictures. The actual data, which are shown in Table 2, confound these original expectations concerning stylistic stratification.

Table 2. Percentages of word-final (z)'s devoiced in different interview contexts.

Context	% Devoiced (z)	N
Sentence repetition	23.2	517
Word naming	37.2	950
Picture description	30.8	1066
Cat eating bird	23.3	365
Airplane	34.2	237
Zoo	35.2	403
All others	32.8	61
Language use interview	36.5	469
Free speech	23.5	149

The context expected to elicit the most formal speech, sentence repetition, has a percentage of devoicing slightly over 23%, which is almost identical to those in the two hypothetically most casual contexts--the description of the cat-and-bird picture and free speech. The other contexts are all grouped in the 32% - 37% range, in which even the maximal difference is not statistically significant (χ^2 = .47, p>.49). These results closely replicate the findings of the pilot study with respect to contextual variables (Edwards 1975).

There is no way to interpret these groupings of interview contexts in stylistic or situational terms. However, they can be explained in terms of the linguistic environment characteristic of each context. The contexts of sentence repetition, the cat-and-

bird picture, and free speech have in common the fact that whatever speech they elicit is connected speech, with few pauses after
words. The other contexts elicited predominantly one-word responses.
The difference between the percentages of (z)-devoicing in the
connected-speech contexts and in the one-word contexts is highly
significant (χ^2 = 53.10, p<.001). The most likely explanation for
the higher percentage of (z)-devoicing in these contexts is that
one-word responses are followed by pauses, which fit both the
first- and the third-order constraints on the devoicing rule, rather
than that the speakers are attending to any situational features of
formality or informality.

    Also contrary to original expectations, the percentage of (z)'s
devoiced in casual speech as determined by the channel cues (27.1%)
is slightly lower than that for non-casual speech (33.2%). While
the difference is not as great as that between the two linguistic
types of interview context discussed above (χ^2 = 8.60,p<.01), it is
best explained in the same way. Non-casual speech contains a relatively higher proportion of slow, halting, disconnected speech
with many pauses which favor (z)-devoicing. For these fourth-
graders, then, (z)-devoicing is phonetically conditioned and does
not appear to function as an indicator of style.

    The effects of the social variables. The percentage of (z)-
devoicing failed to correlate significantly with the speakers' sex
and language dominance as calculated on the word-naming section of
the interview. The lack of a correlation with a speakers' language
dominance is especially interesting, since it precludes the possibility that (z)-devoicing might be simply due to interference from
Spanish. Rather, it suggests that the English spoken by (some or
many) Chicanos is an internally consistent variety of English which
is learned by Chicano children whether or not they have any knowledge of Spanish.

Summary and Conclusions

    The investigation into the nature of word-final (z)-devoicing
in the English of Chicano children leads to the following conclusions:

    (1) Linguistic factors are of primary importance in condi-
tioning the realization of (z) in Chicano English. There is no
evidence that social or stylistic variables condition (z)-devoic-
ing.

    (2) Word-final (z)-devoicing in Chicano English can be de-
scribed by a complex variable rule involving at least six phonological constraints. This rule can be explained in terms of the
natural phonological processes of assimilation and resyllabication.

    (3) The assimilatory behavior of (z)-devoicing in terms of
an abstract sonority continuum suggests that the phonological component of a grammar must account for ways more abstract than traditional binary distinctive features of ranking sound classes relative to each other.

(4)   Phonological components must also account for the inter-dependencies among rules of resyllabication and other phonological rules.

(5)   A model involving categorical application or non-application of rules in finely restricted linguistic environments does not fit the (z)-devoicing data as well as one which involves probabilities of application in many environments.

(6)   Automatic appeals to psycholinguistic interference from Spanish in order to explain a speaker's Chicano accent are misguided; members of a Chicano speech community produce characteristics of Chicano English according to group norms regardless of their knowledge of or ability in Spanish.

NOTES

[1]A preliminary version of this paper was presented at the Session on Bilingualism at the LSA Annual Meeting in San Francisco, December, 1975. The authors are grateful to Dennis Muchisky and Daniel Doorn for their long hours of assistance in transcribing and coding the data and expecially to Alan Hudson-Edwards for his valuable comments and suggestions throughout the length of this study. His objective and critical ear was a great help during the final revision of this paper, and the time he spent in editing and typing the final draft is greatly appreciated.

[2]A more detailed discussion of language use in the Martinez-town community can be found in Hudson-Edwards and Bills (this volume).

[3]There are two variables which are relevant to the resyllabication process but which unfortunately were not coded in the present analysis. One of these is the stress of the following syllable. Hoard (1971:137) claims that only stressed syllables attract maximal permissible onset clusters. The second variable is the tenseness of the vowel, if any, preceding (z). Pulgram (1970) notes that a lax vowel may not be left in an open syllable, which would prevent the reassignment of (z) to the following syllable if it is preceded by a lax vowel.

REFERENCES

Bailey, Charles-James N. 1973. Variation and linguistic theory.
    Arlington VA: Center for Applied Linguistics.
Bickerton, Derek. 1971. Inherent variability and variable rules.
    Foundations of Language 7.457-92.
Cedergren, Henrietta J. and David Sankoff. 1974. Variable rules:
    performance as a statistical reflection of competence.
    Language 50.333-55.
Chomsky, Noam and Morris Halle. 1968. The sound pattern of English.
    New York: Harper and Row.
Edwards, Allison. 1975. A variable rule analysis of one aspect
    of Chicano English phonology. Paper read at the Symposium
    on Bilingual-Bicultural Education, University of Texas-El Paso.
Hankamer, Jorge and Judith Aissen. 1974. The sonority hierarchy.
    Papers from the parasession on natural phonology, ed. by
    Anthony Bruck, Robert A. Fox and Michael W. LaGaly. Chicago:
    Chicago Linguistic Society, pp. 131-45.
Hoard, James E. 1971. Aspiration, tenseness, and syllabication
    in English. Language 47.133-41.
Hooper, Joan B. 1972. The syllable in phonological theory. Lan-
    guage 48.525-40.
Hudson-Edwards, Alan and Garland D. Bills. Intergenerational
    language shift in an Albuquerque barrio. (This volume.)
Labov, William. 1966. The social stratification of English in
    New York City. Arlington VA: Center for Applied Linguistics.
_____. 1969. Contraction, deletion, and inherent varia-
    bility of the English copula. Language 45.715-62.   .
_____. 1972. Sociolinguistic patterns. Philadelphia:
    University of Pennsylvania Press.
Lakoff, George. 1970. Global rules. Language 46.627-39.
Pulgram, Ernst. 1970. Syllable, word, nexus, cursus. The Hague:
    Mouton.
Spolsky, Bernard, Penny Murphy, Wayne Holm and Allan Ferrel. 1972.
    Three functional tests of oral proficiency. TESOL Quarterly
    6.221-35.
Teitelbaum, Herta. 1976. Assessing bilingualism in elementary
    school children. PhD Diss., University of New Mexico.
Vennemann, Theo. 1972. On the theory of syllabic phonology.
    Linguistische Berichte 18.1-18.
_____. 1974. Words and syllables in natural generative
    grammar. Papers from the parasession on natural phonology, ed.
    by Anthony Bruck, Robert A. Fox and Michael W. LaGaly. Chicago:
    Chicago Linguistic Society, pp. 346-74.
Wolfram, Walt and Ralph W. Fasold. 1974. The study of social dia-
    lects in American English. Englewood Cliffs NJ: Prentice-
    Hall.

LITERATURE CITATION
IN BIOMEDICAL SCIENCES

BETTY LOU DUBOIS

New Mexico State University

Introduction

It is commonly acknowledged that in scientific prose, particularly as we approach the acrolect, i.e., the lect appropriate to journal articles, the focus is on fact rather than on discoverer.[1] The high incidence of the passive in academic writing (see Dubois 1972) confirms that intuition. More generally, we have only to read articles and style sheets to see that the belief is correct. Nowhere is the point more clearly made than in the literature citations of introductions to articles that report experiments, of which the following (from Bernstein 1976) might be termed a classic example of identifying source within parentheses:

It has now been shown by direct measurement that, in fish crows at rest, O_2 extraction exceeds by as much as two-fold the values for O_2 extraction calculated for mammals of the same mass (Bernstein and Schmidt-Nielsen, 1974).

Birds in steady-state flight consume O_2 at rates which may exceed by an order of magnitude or more the rates observed in birds under basal conditions (Lasiewski, 1963; Tucker, 1968, 1972; Berger and Hart [,] 1972; Bernstein et al., 1973).

Nevertheless, we do encounter instances of sentences in which investigators are brought into active-voice relationship to the information they are responsible for by using them as subjects of
sentences; thus Cascarano et al. 1976:

Hochachka et al. (1975) found that succinate accumulated tissues of diving vertebrates when oxygen
availability became limited. DeSilva and Cazorla
('73) found that the succinate level in heart,
liver and kidney of altitude acclimated guinea pigs
was higher than sea level controls when animals
were subjected to acute anoxia.

Moreover, although one paper may maintain a consistent citation
form throughout (see Magaria et al. 1976), another will vary
(Bernstein 1976).

It is possible, certainly, that shift in citation form is
nothing more than free variation: Sometimes we list the author
first, sometimes we list him last, within parentheses. However,
I claim that choice of citation form is functional, i.e., meaningful, as the subsequent demonstration of patterns will attempt to
show.

Materials

During the spring semester of 1978, in preparation for teaching a course in the development of spoken and written scientific
materials at professional level for the trainees of the Minority
Access to Research Careers Program at New Mexico State University,
I asked the other faculty participants, all biomedical scien-
tists, to send me copies of journal articles in the students'
areas of specialization. In response, I received five articles
from five journals in biochemistry and nine from five journals
in physiology, mainly avian respiratory physiology. It is the
literature citations from the introductions of the fourteen papers
which serve as the basis for the results which follow.

Results

Considering the above-labeled "classic" citation form (parenthetical source information) to be the unmarked (predictable)
form, we note that two (bibliography items 6 and 9) of the five
biochemical papers (40%) and three (7, 8, and 10) of the nine
physiological papers (33.33%) have literature citation exclusively in the unmarked form (in all, 35.61% of the total papers).
Within this group, the two biochemical and two (8 and 10) of the
remaining papers employ what might be termed the unmarked form:
a number, either as superscript or parenthesis, referring to a
numbered list of references. The final paper (7) in the group
consistently employing unmarked citation form uses name and date:
"The sperm whale can outdo the Waddell seal, while aquatic tur-
tles can dive routinely for many hours and possibly for over a
day (Jackson, 1978; Kooyman, 1972)."[2]

By contrast, the marked form of literature citation mentions

a researcher, most often by name: "Fillingame and Morris[12] used
low concentrations of MGBG to block the increase in spermidine
and spermine levels normally observed in bovine lymphocytes stimulated with concavalin A." (11) Sometimes, especially in topic
sentences, a group is mentioned: "Several investigators (20, 22,
36) have reported increases in DNA synthesis and the mitotic
rate in the host tissues of tumor-bearing animals." (12) The
most normal sentence position for the researcher(s) is subject;
in one instance, it occurs as object of preposition: "This results [sic] is in disagreement with the conclusions of Lutz et
al. (1973)." (13) One paper (14) is very nearly the mirror
image of the group described in the preceding paragraph, in that
nine references are cited in marked form in consecutive order,
from the beginning of the introduction. The tenth citation, to
a paper by two of the three authors, is made in a way which might
cause a careless or uninformed reader to attribute the results to
the scientist most recently named, one V.A. Tucker. The remainder of the articles, eight in all, contain both marked and unmarked forms of literature citation. Some instances of the marked
from occur relatively early in the introductions, other relatively late.

Discussion

It will be convenient to begin discussion with the instances
of marked citation form, divided into early and late occurrences.
The early marked citations are, with one exception, to works
which are not reports of laboratory experiments. The following
three types are found:
        (1) literature review: ". . . the literature
has recently been surveyed by Dawson and Hudson
(1970), Richards (1970) and Lassiewski (1972)." (2)[3]
        (2) popularized account of scientific expedi-
tion: "Hunt (1954), describing the 1953 British
expedition to Everest, mentions that birds were observed flying at altitudes above 7940 m. (26,000
feet)." (15)
        (3) development of laboratory test: "Gale (7)
measured CO_2 evolution manometrically, and Leclerc
(9) used a CO_2-phenolphthalein system in an auto-
mated procedure." (5)
The single exception (to the principle that early citation with
mention of person in text, where both marked and unmarked forms
co-occur, is not to the result of an experiment) embodies a deliberate attempt[4] to heal the breach between two camps by emphasizing their main area of agreement (1); it is all the more
striking because it is the opening sentence of the paper.
        Schmidt-Nielsen et al. (1969) and Scheid and
        Piiper (1970) have shown how patterns of air and
        blood flow in the avian lung could permit the
        fraction of available O_2 removed from respiratory
        air (O_2 extraction) to be considerably greater in

birds than in mammals.

Next, we consider late-occurring marked forms. The overwhelmingly common pattern of literature citation in the scientific articles studied begins with a more or less general survey
of the background information for the experiment to be reported,
with literature cited in unmarked form. As the section draws to
an end, citation may shift to the marked form, which denotes
studies directly related to the experiment at hand, forming a
continuous pathway leading from older to newer work. Perhaps
the most interesting and finely tuned example is one which, by
its use of marked and unmarked forms, establishes the two groups
of studies mentioned in its topic sentence, those of the marked
group leading directly to the authors' work (3):

The last important piece of supporting evidence
for these mitochondrial processes in mammalian cells
is that succinate accumulation occurs in a variety
of anoxic tissues, in addition to heart (Penney and
Cascarano, '70), in the presence or absence [the
groups to be distinguished] of exogenous precursors.
Anaerobic guinea pig brain slices incubated in
glucose plus pyruvate resulted in the accumulation
of succinate (Weil-Malberbe, '37). Goldberg et al.
('66) found that succinate accumulated in cerebral
tissue of mice during short periods of ischemia.
Anaerobic liver perfused with labeled fumarate
produced labeled succinate (Hoberman and Prosky, '67).
Succinate accumulated in muscle of rats during
intense exercise (Kondrashova and Chahovets, '71).
Hochachka et al. ('75) found that succinate accumulated in tissue of diving vertebrates when oxygen
availability became limited. DeSilva and Cazorla
('73) found that succinate level in heart, liver and
kidney of altitude acclimated guinea pigs was higher
than sea level controls when animals were subjected
to acute anoxia.

The grouping is summarized thus:

PRESENCE (unmarked)	ABSENCE (marked)
(Weil-Malherbe)	Goldberg et al.
(Hoberman and Prosky)	Hochachka et al.
(Kondrashova and Chahovets)	DeSilva and Cazorla

In the papers where citation of experimental results continues throughout in unmarked form, two tendencies are at work.
If, as we have seen, the shift to marked indicates immediate
close relevance to the matter being presented, it is no surprise
that continuation of unmarked indicates the opposite: that the
results being published represent, to a degree, a departure from
the works cited as below (2):

Concerning the consequences of the thermal tachypnea
on gas exchanges and the acid-base balance, several
experiments have shown that, during severe heat
stress, most avian species sustain a considerable
hypocapnia and alkalosis (Calder and Schmidt-Nielsen,
1966, 1968; Frankel and Frascella, 1968), although
the ostrich, a non-flying bird, does not develop
alkalosis after panting for up to 8 hr (Schmidt-
Neilsen et al., 1969). Whether panting causes
alkalosis during moderate heat loads [the research
question to be reported on] remains undocumented.
The departure has been foregrounded by the authors themselves
through the use of italics. A summary of this principle operat-
ing in three other papers follows:

TOPIC OF CITATION	TOPIC OF RESEARCH
prolonged diving	energy source for muscle activity (7)
body-brain temperature ratios of certain birds and mammals	ratios for other, more heat-tolerant species (8)
inhibition of putrescine in bacterial and mammalian cells	correlation of polyamines and proliferation of mammalian cells (9)

The break with previous research, or shift in direction, may be
underlined lexically (other [8]; however [6, 9]), although less
frequently than would be expected in other registers of exposi-
tory writing. The second tendency appears a desire to maintain
consistency, since a shift in relatedness is not indicated by
shift in form (2, 10).
    In summary: Leaving aside cases of what seem to be indivi-
dual preference (2, 10, 14), we find that the choice of citation
form is informative. Early use of the marked form most typically
indicates that the citation is to some work other than an experiment. Late use of marked form indicates works which are felt to
be particularly close to the work being reported. Where there is
a shift from unmarked to marked, information is given about the
relevance of the work cited. Failure to shift ordinarily indicates that no work mentioned is felt to be a direct fore-runner
of the results being reported. Literature citation can occur
throughout a scientific paper, notably in the final section,
which relates reported findings to other findings. It remains to
be shown whether the principles for introductory sections operate
elsewhere in scientific papers.

Applications

    As far as I can determine, specific courses to teach students
the principles of scientific writing at the most advanced, i.e.,

research, level are very nearly nonexistent, at best extremely
rare. Perhaps that is because they are unnecessary, for by the
time a student reaches the point at which he writes an article
for submission to a journal, he will have read enough similar
articles to acquire the lect in a natural way. On the other
hand, if the current lament over the inability of students to
write has a basis in fact, then there is a clear and present need
to teach advanced scientific writing, using information such as
that presented here. The need will grow as more and more under-
prepared students reach our universities and, in addition, as
English becomes the language of scientific discourse throughout
much of the world. Knowledge of the structure of scientific
English may find its greatest use at slightly lower levels, in
assisting upper-division undergraduates and lower-division graduate students to begin to read scientific articles--no easy task.

NOTES

[1] The study was partially funded by NIH Grant #5T32 #GMO
07667-02. My thanks go to Glenn Keuhn, biochemist, and Marvin
Bernstein, avian respiratory physiologist, who patiently explained enough of their specialties to enable me, however pain-
fully, to get through the papers they sent and who confirmed at
least some of my results.

[2] The use of unmarked or unmarked unmarked form is determined
by the journal itself.

[3] The nature of the articles cited forces the form here,
since it is not possible to summarize a literature review in one
sentence, as one can the findings of an experiment.

[4] Personal communication.

REFERENCES

Bernstein, Marvin H. 1976. Ventilation and respiratory evapora-
    tion in the flying crow, corvus ossifragus. Respiration
    Physiology 26.371-82.
Bouverot, P., G. Hildwein, and D. Le Goff. 1974. Evaporative
    water loss, respiratory pattern, gas exchange and acid-base
    balance during thermal panting in pekin ducks to moderate
    heat. Respiration Physiology 21.255-69.
Cascarano, Joseph, Ibrahim Z. Ades, and John D. O'Connor. 1976.
    Hypoxia: A succinate-fumarate electron shuttle between
    peripheral cells and lung. Journal of Experimental Zoology
    198.149-54.

Dubois, Betty Lou. 1972. The meaning and distribution of the per-
    fect in present-day American English prose. Ph.D. diss.,
    Univ. of New Mexico.
Goldschmidt, Millicent C., Betty M. Lockhart, and Katherine Perry.
    1971. Rapid methods for determining decarboxylase activity:
    Ornithine and lysine decarobxylases. Applied Microbiology
    22.344-49.
Harik, Sami I., Morley D. Hollenberg, and Solomon H. Snyder.
    1974. Ornithine decarboxylase turnover slowed by α-
    hydrazino-ornithine. Molecular Pharmacology 10.41-7.
Hochachka, P. W., T. G. Owen, J. F. Allen, and G. C. Wittow. 1975.
    Multiple end products of anaerobiosis in diving vertebrates.
    Comparative Biochemical Physiology 50B.17-22.
Kilgore, Delbert L., Jr., Marvin H. Bernstein, and Knut Schmidt-
    Neilsen. 1973. Brain temperature in a large bird, the rhea.
    American Journal of Physiology 225.739-42.
Mamont, Pierre S., Peter Böhlen, Peter P. McCann, Philippe Bey,
    Francis Schuber, and Chantal Tardif. 1976. α-methyl
    ornithine, a potent competitive inhibitor of ornithine de-
    carboxylase, blocks proliferation of rat hepatoma cells in
    culture. Proceedings of the National Academy of Science 73.
    1626-30.
Margaria, R., R. D. Olivia, P. E. Di Prampero, and P. Cerretelli.
    1969. Energy utilization in intermittent exercise of supra-
    maximal intensity. Journal of Applied Physiology 26.752-56.
Newton, Nancy E., and Mahmoud M. Abdel-Monem. 1977. Inhibitors
    of polyamine biosynthesis. 4. Effects of α-methyl-(±)-
    ornithine and methylgloyoxal bis(guanylhydrazone) on growth
    and polyamine content of Ll210 leukemic cells in mice.
    Journal of Medicinal Chemistry 20.249-53.
Noguchi, Tamio, Atsunori Kashiwagi, and Takehiko Tanaka. 1976.
    A factor responsible for increases in ornithine decarboxy-
    lase activity in the livers of tumor-bearing mice. Cancer
    Research 36.4015-22.
Scheid, Peter, and Takeo Kawashiro. 1975. Metabolic changes in
    avian blood, and their effects on determination of blood
    gases in pH. Respiration Physiology 23.291-300.
Taylor, C. Richard, Knut Schmidt-Nielsen, and Jacob L. Raab.
    1970. Scaling of energetic cost of running to body size
    in mammals. American Journal of Physiology 219.1104-07.

ON THE FORM
OF BILINGUAL GRAMMARS:
THE PHONOLOGICAL COMPONENT

CHARLES ELERICK

University of Texas at El Paso

During the past decade in the United States the level of interest in the phenomenon of bilingualism has reached previously unknown levels. This has come about mainly because of the attention that has been turned to the special educational needs of ethnic minorities and the implications of bilingualism for the educational process. Hundreds of scholarly papers dealing with various aspects of bilingualism have been presented at professional meetings or published in journals.

And for the past two decades the main concern of linguists has been to devise and verify, as abstractly accurate, formal representations of internalized monolingual competence. It has been a period in which fierce arguments have raged over the question of the relationship of these formal representations to psychological and neurological reality and, at the same time, a period in which more linguistic data has been critically scrutinized by trained linguists than in any other comparable period in history. The result has been a quantum leap in our understanding of human language and a door ajar on other exciting questions concerning the human mind.

During the second decade of the "great linguistic awakening," of data sifting and theory building, and new-found interest in bilingualism on the part of some, one development did not take place. No sustained effort seems to have been made to construct a model of bilingual competence which would serve as a formal point of departure for discussions of many issues central to the study of bilingualism, such as its role in promoting or directing linguistic change, though some roughly-conceptualized representations of language interaction in the mind of the bilingual (Swain, 1972) have been published. It is the purpose of this paper to present a restricted demonstration grammar that purports to represent certain aspects of the competence of a Spanish/English bilingual. As suggested by the title of the paper, this fragment will treat aspects of the phonology of such a grammar.

The premise underlying the work to be presented here is as follows. There are certain items in English and Spanish that are similar, semantically and phonologically, to the extent that they would have to be recognized by anyone who speaks both languages as the "same word." Such a pair is 'biology' and biología. This linguistic knowledge presumably takes the form of 1) a common interlingual lexical item which, phonologically, consists of a compromise representation composed of segmental material drawn from an inventory that is somewhat distinct from that which would be drawn on to represent underlying forms for items posited for a monolingual grammar of either language, and 2) some special phonological rules which reconcile these more than normally abstract lexical representations with their two manifestations, one Spanish and one English. For the Spanish/English bilingual I assume that these union lexical entries number in the many hundreds and perhaps more.

For purposes of this demonstration grammar I assume an ideal bilingual, one for whom neither the availability of Spanish or English data nor the matter of dominance is an issue. I consider the construction of such a heuristically motivated device a necessary baseline-establishing exercise. I have demonstrated elsewhere (Elerick, 1978) that the innovation of gasolín in the Spanish of Spanish/English bilinguals in the United States can be understood as having been the result of the replacement, in the grammar of the speaker who innovated this form, of a lexical representation underlying 'gasoline' and gasolina by one which underlies 'gasoline' and gasolín and that such replacement effects both lexical and derivational economies. It is especially for the purpose of comparing and better understanding innovative aspects of bilingual English and bilingual Spanish that I have constructed and am presenting here this fragment of an optimum bilingual grammar.

Displayed below are forty English/Spanish pairs, together with the putative underlying representation for each. Note that the representations are more fully specified than the lexical representations that derivationally precede them would be, since the operation of redundancy rules is assumed to have taken place.

The symbols used to represent the underlying segments reflect, for the most part, conventions that are widely used. The macron is used to indicate a tense vowel, except in 16) /teřitōryo/ and 26) /kařo/ where it is also used to indicate a trilled non-lateral resonant. The symbols /I E A O U/ represent a series of tense vowels which in English are manifested as [ay

īy ēy ūw aw] respectively. Most readers will recognize this phenomenon as essentially recapitulating the Great Vowel Shift. These
segments are always manifested in Spanish as [ī ē ā ō ū]. In the
Spanish derivations the underlying segments will be rewritten by
convention since in truth /I E A O U/ simply represent tense vowels
that happen to be marked as undergoing a phonological process in
English that does not occur in Spanish.

1)	soup	sopa	/sOpa/
2)	humor	humor	/hūmor/
3)	hymn	himno	/himno/
4)	east	este	/Este/
5)	fiber	fibra	/fIbra/
6)	theater	teatro	/θEatro/
7)	temple	templo	/templo/
8)	zone	zona	/zōna/
9)	fame	fama	/fAma/
10)	remedy	remedio	/remedyo/
11)	tank	tanque	/tanke/
12)	nation	nación	/nAsyon/
13)	hammock	hamaca	/hamaka/
14)	panther	pantera	/panθera/
15)	type	tipo	/tĪpo/
16)	territory	territorio	/teritōryo/
17)	style	estilo	/stIlo/
18)	throne	trono	/θrōno/
19)	rythm	ritmo	/riðmo/
20)	origin	origen	/ōriɣen/
21)	liter	litro	/litro/
22)	glory	gloria	/glōrya/
23)	gasoline	gasolina	/gasolīna/

24)	energy	energía	/eneɣia/
25)	portion	porción	/pōrsyon/
26)	car	carro	/kařo/
27)	blouse	blusa	/blUsa/
28)	station	estación	/stAsyon/
29)	spy	espía	/spIa/
30)	perfume	perfume	/perfūme/
31)	theme	tema	/θEma/
32)	total	total	/tōtal/
33)	use (n.)	uso	/ūso/
34)	impulse	impulso	/impulso/
35)	fruit	fruta	/frūta/
36)	ruin	ruina	/ruina/
37)	capital	capital	/kapital/
38)	mule	mula	/mūla/
39)	hero	heroe	/hEroe/
40)	debate	debate	/dEbAte/

The phonological rules--a set of English rules and a set of
Spanish rules--will be presented forthwith. These rules link each
underlying representation to its manifested forms, one English and
one Spanish. In the interest of ready intelligibility and for the
benefit of those readers whose training allows them to follow the
general outline of this argument but not formal generative phonological rules, these will be presented in less than rigorous form.
The reader is reminded that these rules apply in the following
manner. The first rule specifies a rewriting of the underlying
representation if the structure of this representation coincides
with that set forth in the rule. The resulting representation--
either the unchanged form if the rule does not apply, or the form
resulting from the application of the first rule if it does apply--
is then subject to modification according to the instructions com-
prising rule 2). Each rule is applied, in order, to the latest
representation, the last being the surface form. Some low-level
phonetic detail such as the aspiration of unvoiced stops in some
environments and the glides that occur with non-low tense vowels

in English and relative tenseness of vowels in Spanish is not specified. The mode of analysis and presentation of findings follows essentially that set forth in Chomsky and Halle (1968). The numbers following the rules refer to items affected by each.

English Phonological Rules

EPh.   1)   All final vowels are deleted.

(1, 3, 4, 5, 6, 7, 8, 9, 10, 11, 13, 14, 15, 16, 17, 18, 19, 21, 22, 23, 24, 26, 27, 29, 30, 31, 33, 34, 35, 36, 38, 39, 40)

EPh.   2)   The second of two successive nasal consonants in word final position is deleted.

(3)

EPh.   3)   r and r̄ become ɹ (retroflex 'r').

(2, 5, 10, 14, 16, 18, 19, 20, 21, 22, 24, 25, 26, 30, 35, 36, 39)

EPh.   4)   A word final sonorant (semi-vowel or resonant consonant) which follows a consonant becomes syllabic. I.e., y→i, n→n̩, etc.

(5, 6, 7, 10, 16, 19, 21, 22)

EPh.   5)   A high front oral glide (y) is inserted before a tense high back vowel (ū) when this vowel is word initial, follows h, or any labial or velar consonant.

(2, 33, 38)

EPh.   6)   A vowel that precedes another vowel is tensed.

(36)

EPh.   7)   All items are stressed by a complex of rules that will not be presented in this paper.

EPh.   8)   a becomes æ in syllables with primary stress.

(11, 14, 23, 37)

EPh.   9)   Word final non-low vowels are tensed.

(10, 16, 22, 24, 39)

EPh.   10)   Lax vowels in unstressed syllables become ə.

(2, 6, 10, 12, 13, 14, 16, 20, 23, 24, 28, 30, 32, 34, 36, 37)

EPh.   11)   A resonant consonant coalesces with a preceding ə to form a syllabic resonant of analogous articulation.

(2, 12, 14, 20, 24, 38, 30, 32, 34, 36, 37)

EPh.   12)   γ becomes ǰ.

(20, 24)

EPh.   13)   Vowel shift: I→ay, E→Ī, A→ē, O→ū, U→aw.

(1, 4, 5, 6, 9, 12, 15, 17, 27, 28, 29, 31, 39, 40)

EPh.   14)   e→i before a nasal consonant that is followed by a syllabic segment.

(10, 24)

EPh.   15)   sy→š

(25, 28)

EPh.   16)   n→ŋ before a velar.

(11)

EPh.   17)   t→d between two syllabic segments, the second of which does not carry primary stress.

(6, 21, 32, 37)

After presentation of the Spanish rules, exemplary side-by-side derivations which show the effects of the operation of both sets of rules will be offered. Some readers may wish to consult the English derivations at this point.

Spanish Phonological Rules

SPh.   1)   r becomes r̄ in word initial position.

(10, 19, 36)

SPh.   2)   All instances of h are deleted.

(2, 3, 13)

SPh.   3)   All items are stressed by a complex of rules that will not be presented in this paper.

SPh. 4) e is inserted before an initial s which is followed by
          a consonant.

SPh. 5) u→w before í.

      (36)

SPh. 6) All fricatives are devoiced.

      (8, 19, 20, 24)

SPh. 7) θ→t.

      (6, 14, 18, 19, 24)

SPh. 8) n→ŋ before a velar.

      (11)

SPh. 9) All vowels are tensed. I E A O U are rewritten ī, ē,
          ā, ō, ū, by convention.

   The exemplary derivations that follow trace the steps through
which the manifested forms proceed from the underlying representations. Each stage of the derivation is represented and the rule
that effects each successive form is indicated. The left hand
column traces the English derivation and the right hand the
Spanish.

	/hūmor/		
hūmoɹ	(EPh 3)	ūmor	(SPh 2)
hyūmoɹ	(EPh 5)	ūmór	(SPh 3)
hyū̃mòɹ	(EPh 7)	ūmō̃r	(SPh 9)
hyũ̄mə̀ɹ	(EPh 12)		
hyũ̄mị̀	(EPh 13)		
'humor'		humor	

	/θEatro/		
θEatr	(EPh 1)	θEatro	(SPh 3)
θEatɹ	(EPh 3)	tEatro	(SPh 7)
θEatɹ̣	(EPh 4)	teā̃trō	(SPh 9)
θÉatị̀	(EPh 7)		
θEətị̀	(EPh 12)		
θī̃ətị̀	(EPh 13)		
θī̃ədị̀	(EPh 17)		
'theater'		teatro	

/spIa/

spI	(EPh 1)	spIa	(SPh 3)
spÍ	(EPh 7)	espIa	(SPh 4)
spáy	(EPh 13)	ēspĪā	(SPh 9)
'spy'		espía	

/riðmo/

riðm	(EPh 1)	r̄iðmo	(SPh 1)
˻iðm	(EPh 3)	r̄íðmo	(SPh 3)
˻iðm̩	(EPh 4)	r̄íθmo	(SPh 6)
˻íðm̩	(EPh 7)	r̄ítmo	(SPh 7)
		r̄Ītmō	(SPh 9)
'rhythm'		ritmo	

/eneɣia/

eneɣi	(EPh 1)	eneɣía	(SPh 3)
ene˻ɣi	(EPh 3)	enerxía	(SPh 6)
éne˻ɣɪ̀	(EPh 7)	ēnērxĪā	(SPh 9)
éne˻ɣĪ̀	(EPh 9)		
éneə˻ɣĪ̀	(EPh 10)		
én̗ɣĪ̀	(EPh 11)		
én̗jᵛĪ̀	(EPh 12)		
ín̗jᵛĪ̀	(EPh 14)		
'energy'		energía	

/ruina/

ruin	(EPh 1)	ruina	(SPh 1)
˻uin	(EPh 3)	r̄uína	(SPh 3)
˻ūin	(EPh 6)	r̄wína	(SPh 5)
˻ū̃ìn	(EPh 7)	r̄wĪnā	(SPh 9)
˻uə̀n	(EPh 10)		
˻ū̃ǹ̩	(EPh 11)		
'ruin'		ruina	

Some questions regarding the adequacy of this grammar will certainly occur to some readers, aside from the obvious incompleteness of the treatment of the Spanish/English lexicon. One question

concerns the advisability of assuming recapitulatory Great Vowel
Shift. It should be noted that to posit underlying vowels that
have shifted manifestations for a Spanish/English union grammar
is a different matter from theorizing Vowel Shift for a monolingual grammar of English. Patent alternations abound in the
data on which the first type of grammar is based in contrast to
the second. Still, some investigations (Moskowitz, 1973) have
found operational evidence supporting synchronic Vowel Shift even
in a monolingual grammar of English, although not the SPE formulations (Chomsky and Halle, 1968). The use of the abstract systematic phoneme /ɣ/ may trouble some readers who suscribe to
theories of phonology that disallow such constructs. I assume
that such abstract segments are available to speakers when they
are composed of features that are distributively employed in the
specification of other well motivated systematic phonemes, which
condition is met for a Spanish/English intersection grammar.
Finally, many will notice that the underlying forms posited here
are consistently more Spanish-like than English-like and that
accordingly, the English derivations are more complex than the
Spanish. This fact does not, in itself, reflect on the validity
of the analysis. Spanish just happens to be more conservative,
phonologically, than English and to the extent that synchronic
rules recapitulate the history of the language, the derivations
of items in the former are simpler than those in the latter.
These questions of immediate adequacy aside, the grammar fragment
presented here is serviceable for a large segment of the Spanish/
English lexicon with little alteration. The bilingual reader will
have no difficulty finding many additional pairs which can be related by using these rules over appropriately-devised underlying
representations. However, a study of the lexicons of the two
languages will also turn up many other pairs which at first seem
amenable to this type of treatment but which involve problems
that have not been dealt with here. Below is a brief survey of
these problems.

Some word-final vowels must be treated as special. Most
pairs support English word-final vowel deletion ('tribe'/tribu;
'pole'/polo) but some English forms retain the vowel ('radio'/
radio; 'menu'/menú) while others delete both the final vowel and
the preceding semi-vowel ('abundance'/abundancia; 'bible'/
biblia). In order to handle such pairs the grammar will have to
be complicated to a not inconsequential extent.

Some pairs seem relatable but with ever increasing abstractness in the underlying representation. The constant question of
how much abstractness to allow is at issue in positing /botelya/
for 'bottle'/botella and /egzæmplo/ for 'example'/ejemplo.

Some pairs are phonologically relatable but are slightly
skewed, semantically. Such is the case for 'frontier'/frontera
('national boundary') which otherwise would be simply /frontEra/
and 'stranger'/estranjero ('foreigner') which would have the
underlying form /strAnɣero/, both leading to the appropriate surface forms via the rules supplied above. Should we assume that
intersection grammars include special semantic extension, adjust-

ment and limitation rules?

There are derivational complexes in the two languages that suggest complication of the union grammar. Such a case is 'electric'/'electricity'/ /eléctrico/electricidad. It is not at all clear how this phenomenon should be handled or what the implications for bilingual grammars are.

The ideas and analysis presented in this paper obviously reflect a line of investigation still in its infancy. In addition to the specific issues I have just skimmed over there remain broader questions which must be posed. Are there other situations in which bilingualism promotes the internalization of union grammars? This might well be the case wherever there are in contact two closely related languages or two languages, one of which has undergone extensive cognate relexification, the case of English vis-à-vis Spanish. How well, if at all, does a grammar of the sort presented here reflect neurological competence? Does such an abstract approach have applications to pedagogy?

Mindful of the pitfalls, or at least some of them, I have presented this material in the hope that others will be stimulated to examine and question the general concept and specific findings and begin to elaborate more ambitious and more finely tuned models of bilingual competence.

REFERENCES

Chomsky, N. and M. Halle. 1968. The sound pattern of English. New York: Harper and Row.

Elerick, Charles. 1978. The bilingual lexicon and linguistic innovation. Approaches to the Romance lexicon, ed. by Frank Nuessel, Jr. Washington DC: Georgetown Univ. Press.

Moskowitz, B. A. On the status of vowel shift in English. Cognitive development and the acquisition of language, ed. by Timothy E. Moore. New York: Academic Press.

Swain, Merrill. Bilingualism as a first language. 1972. Ph.D. Diss., Univ. of California, Irvine.

LANGUAGE SPREAD: IMPLICATIONS
OF AN INTERNATIONAL CONFERENCE
FOR THE SOUTHWEST

JOSHUA A. FISHMAN

Yeshiva University

The recently concluded "Conference of Language Spread"[1] is
of relevance to the American Southwest and to Jack Ornstein's
work there. It began with Robert Cooper's keynote: a distinguished attempt both to learn from diffusion theory and the
study of the spread of innovations, and to modify that theory to
accomodate language spread through the introduction of such considerations as language characteristics and functions. The concepts presented by Cooper may, indeed, be too new, too involved,
too far from other perspectives to be soon or easily digested.
As a result, the conference did not succeed in addressing his
proposed framework in the other papers or discussions that
followed the keynote. Nevertheless, Cooper's is a paper that
will often be turned to, both to be admired and to be attacked,
if only because it reveals that much more sociolinguistic sophis-
tication concerning general theories of social history and social
change are necessary in order to advance the topic 'language
spread'.
   The very first set of papers to follow Cooper's keynote immediately sharpened the question of whether we were to arrive at
a general theory, especially by comparing case studies, or to re-
fine or apply and test an already available theory. We did both--

114

though some participants favored one approach over the other--
but did neither to any great extent: those seeking to build a
theory were unable (and appropriately so) to arrive at a general
framework during the period of the conference; those attempting
to use existing theories (particularly, conflict theories, economic determination theories) were perhaps not given enough en-
couragement and were inundated with data or interpretations which
their chosen theory could not handle.

The conference generally reflected the adage that in a new
field "variety is the spice of life." For example, the methodological approaches and sources of data noted in papers and discussion included: census data, sociolinguistic survey data, library and archival records, some from thousands of years ago,
and data from informants and observation. Substantially, data
ranged from school performance, to attitudinal, to usage (reported and actual), to knowledge (awareness and factual), to demographic, to social class data. Little mention was made of experimental data pertaining to language spread--but it too is
available (see, e.g., Cooper, Fishman, Lown, Schaier and Seckbach).[2] The array, which was presented to illustrate language
spread, included languages numerically large and small, ancient
and modern, fully and partially recognized, languages growing
and languages approaching extinction, written and spoken forms of
languages, mother tongues and second languages. A few specific
omissions should be noted however, in view of this general interest: Arabic (other than Juda), Hebrew, and Cornish.

It was clear from each of the papers and discussion (and no
matter what the topic, methodological approach or exemplifying
language) that language spread is related to, and "interpene-
trated with," concomitant social change beyond itself. Languages
spread as peoples experience change--real or anticipated changes
in their roles, interactions and opportunity or rewards. Change
is due to many factors--economic, commercial, political, socio-
cultural, religious, demographic--and each change provides a new
context for other factors. What we lack is understanding about
combining all of these factors, particularly as the factors coincide, intersect, co-occur, and provide new contexts for each
other.

Language spread, however, does not always lag behind, responding to changes in other contexts and factors. It can facilitate, foster and anticipate these other changes. We might have
done well in our discussion to have distinguished or considered
separately when and how language spread responds to or antici-
pates changes, when it follows such changes. Conscious, sponsored, planned and organized language spread is characterized by
"language as precursor;" both status and corpus planning are undertaken in order to initiate, advance or consolidate language
spread, as well as and because other things are expected to
follow from language spread. In considering all of the factors
involved, we must be aware, though, that what (context or factor)
helps foster one language may not foster others, and that language spread may foster some things and not others.

The (unexpected) concern for history evident in many of the

papers deserves to be applauded. Participants recognized that history cannot provide a full explanation of the present, but that it continues to be an influence. We talked, too, of the different types of data that might be provided by history and sociology and of the difficulty in bridging the gap between the two. We need to recall that even social history is restricted to the types of data which contemporaries chose to collect and preserve.

We addressed, too, the notions of non-spread, recession and even death as aspects of the general topic 'language spread.' These may all be realizations along a continuum of language change; they may all be going on simultaneously--in different functions, in the same or different networks of the same communities, or in competing communities. All--spread, recession, and death--are metaphors that need to be operationalized.

What, as a conference, did we accomplish? We rejected and saw the limits of simple solutions and concurred that a series of simple solutions would not add up to a complex, comprehensive one. We rejected the positive and negative domino theories: the language that is ahead stays ahead; the group that is powerless stays powerless. We agreed that the "power language" does not always triumph over "non-power languages," and that language spread is not always conflicted. Nationalism does not always foster language spread; religion does not always reinforce language maintenance and spread; urbanization and modernization do not always benefit or harm. We acknowledged that all of the factors are not always involved.

Yet, while we were able to recognize the limits in the validity of these solutions, we did not quite know what to construct in their stead. We are at an early stage, because of the limitations of our own fields and of the theory of diffusion. Social change theory, too, is limited and might not yet be able to help us.

However, at this first general conference on the topic of language spread, we were not entering into totally unknown territory. We know, singly and together, many of the partial concepts, and have travelled part of the way to the solution. We know particular instances of language spread; we have examined the role of a particular factor in a particular case; we know areas where we lack competence.

Our new task is to generalize what we know (and don't know) across cases, topics, and periods, and to integrate and interrelate more factors in order to build a more general, more powerful theory than the one we have now. We should persist, as the study of language spread is not only interesting but useful as well, in order to be able to predict and guide future language spread. Certainly for Wales-- where we met--the study of language spread is a highly important topic. Our conference profited from the contributions of its Welsh setting.

A conference on language spread in the United States might not only be a fitting follow-up to the one held in Wales but yet another admirable way of recognizing Jack Ornstein's contributions to this entire field of inquiry.

CONFERENCE ON LANGUAGE SPREAD
September 12 - 14, 1978
Hosted by The University College of Wales -- Aberystwyth
Organized by The Center for Applied Linguistics
with Support from the Ford Foundation and the
International Development Research Centre

<u>Program</u> (addresses/papers only)

September 12

8:45   COFFEE

9:00   OPENING REMARKS
            Carl Dodson, The University College of Wales -
                Aberystwyth
            G. Richard Tucker, Center for Applied Linguistics
            Charles A. Ferguson, Stanford University

9:30   KEYNOTE ADDRESS
            "A Framework for the Study of Language Spread"
            Robert L. Cooper, The Hebrew University of
                Jerusalem

10:45   SESSION I - PERSPECTIVES ON LANGUAGE SPREAD
            Chair: G. Richard Tucker
            "Language Spread as a Wave-like Diffusion Process:
                Arabic in Southern Sudan," Ushari Mahmud,
                Georgetown University
            "Language Spread: The Ancient Near Eastern World,"
                Herbert Paper, Hebrew Union College

1:30   SESSION I continued
            "Microsociolinguistics of Hungarian-Serbocroatian
                Bilingualism," Melanie Mikes, Novi Sad,
                Yugoslavia
            Discussion

4:30   SESSION II - FACTORS IN LANGUAGE SPREAD
            Chair: Braj Kachru, University of Illinois-Urbana
                and Elinor Barber, The Ford Foundation
            "The Spread of Manding," Louis-Jean Calvet,
                Université René Descartes, Paris
            "Forces Affecting Language Spread: Some Basic
                Propositions," Stanley Lieberson,
                University of Arizona

September 13

9:00   SESSION II continues
              "Language Spread in China: The Contribution of
                  Nationalism to the Mandarin Movement, 1900-
                  1949," Dayle Barnes, University of Pittsburgh
              "Acceleration, Retardation and Reversal in Language
                  Decay?", Wolfgang Dressler, Universität Wien

10:45   SESSION II continues
              "Lingua Francas as White Elephants: Political
                  and Socioeconomic Integration in Africa,"
                  Carol Scotton, Michigan State University
              "Castilianization and the Spread of Indigenous
                  Languages: The Case of Aymará," Shirley
                  Brice Heath, University of Pennsylvania
              Discussion

7:00   SESSION II continues
              "Attracting a Following to the 'H' Function for a
                  Diglossic 'L': The Role of the Tshernovits
                  Language Conference in the Rise of Yiddish
                  Prior to World War II," Joshua A. Fishman,
                  Yeshiva University
              "Religious Factors in the Spread of Arabic,"
                  Charles A. Ferguson, Stanford University

September 14

9:00   SESSION III - MOVEMENTS AND AGENCIES IN LANGUAGE
                  SPREAD
              Chair: Carl Dodson, University College of Wales
              "Language Spread and Recession in Malaysia and
                  the Malay Archipelago," Ashma H. Omar,
                  University of Malaya[3]
              "The Spread of Hindi," B.G. Misra, Central
                  Institute of Hindi
              "The Role of The Ford Foundation in Language
                  Spread," Elinor Barber, The Ford Foundation

NOTES

[1]Conference on Language Spread, sponsored by the Ford Foundation and the Center for Applied Linguistics, University of
Aberystwyth, Wales, September 12-14, 1978. The full program of
the conference is appended to this summary.

[2]Cooper, R.L., J.A. Fishman, L. Lown, B. Schaier, and F.

Seckbach. Language, technology and persuasion in the Middle
East: Three experimental studies, in H. Giles, ed., <u>Language,
Ethnicity and Intergroup Relations</u>. New York, Academic Press,
1977, 83-98.

[3]Not presented in Aberystwyth due to author's absence.

ON NEGATION
IN COMPARATIVE CONSTRUCTIONS

PETER H. FRIES

Central Michigan University

Jacob Ornstein has been interested for many years in the associations people have with the language used to express ideas. In this way he has been exploring the connotations associated with the use of particular languages, such as English and Spanish. In this paper I would like to discuss associations of a different nature, the connotations associated with a particular grammatical construction: the comparative of inequality. A long tradition of grammatical description connects comparisons of inequality (e.g., John is taller than Bill) with negation. Jespersen (1917:80), for example, says that 'every comparison with than really implies a negation idea (he has more than necessary implies "it is not necessary to have more," etc.)...' More recently, in an attempt to derive the comparative from more primitive concepts, linguists such as Bazell (1967), Ross (1969), Seuren (1969 and 1973) and Mittwoch (1974) have formalized Jespersen's analysis and placed a negation element within the deep structure of comparisons of inequality.[1] The arguments advanced to support this analysis include the impressionistic semantic argument mentioned in the Jespersen quotation above. They include the etymological facts advanced by Joly (1967) that than derives from OE **þon** + ne (where ne is a negative particle). Further, Jespersen and Joly both point out that certain dialects of English use nor instead of than in the expression of comparatives (e.g. John is bigger nor I) while other languages such as French and Italian often use explicit negatives in the expression of comparisons of inequality (Jespersen 1917:80 cites plus qu'il ne faut.).   While talking about languages other than English we might add that Longacre (1976:110) describes a language (Wojokeso) which has no structure that encodes comparison directly, but instead uses two sentences which encode contrast.   Thus, a meaning such as 'the sun is better than the rain' would be expressed in Wojokeso as That sun is good.   The rain is bad.   Sentences in contrast can be interpreted as implying, if not encoding, a negative.   Thus the sentence pair given above can be paraphrased as

     (I)   (a)   That sun is good.

           (b)   The rain is not good.

           (c)   It is bad.

in which what is explicitly said about the sun is first denied as true about rain, and then a characteristic which contrasts with good is supplied for rain.   In his studies of clause relations in English, Winter (1977 a and b) calls the relation which holds between such sets of clauses 'comparative denial.'   He believes that all instances of comparitive denial may be paraphrased as either II a or II b.

     (II)   (a)   What is true of X is not true of Y.

           (b)   What is true of X in respect A is not true

               of X in respect B.

Further, he says most instances of comparative denial contain a correction of the wrong information.   Thus the sentence pair translated from Wojokeso fits his typical pattern of comparative denial. The first sentence states what is true about the sun, and the second sentence denies that the same thing is true about the rain by supplying a contrasting true statement about the rain.

     Not only is the English comparison of inequality paraphrased in other languages by sentence groups which express comparative denial, it itself functions in English as an expression of comparative denial.   Comparisons of inequality may take part in the expression of comparative denial in two ways.   First, it may be used to anticipate a comparative denial.

     (III)   (a)   A false-hearted lover is worse than a thief.

            (b)   For a thief he will rob you and take what you

               have,

            (c)   but a false-hearted lover will lead you to the

               grave.

In IV the contrast is again anticipated by (a), but then the particulars of the contrast are given in (b), a single sentence which contains a comparison in inequality. Sentence (b) functions in this environment much as it would if it were a group of sentences which expressed comparative denial. (Compare IV b'.)[2]

(iv) (b') (i) The Seaspray has a length and width.

(ii) The Windjammer does not have the same length and width.

(iii) It has greater length and less width.

Such arguments as have been mentioned so far, suggestive though they may be, are not adequate motivation for syntactic analysis. What happens in other languages or in earlier forms of the same language may be a useful source of ideas for analysis, but cannot constitute an argument for or against a particular analysis. Similarly, impressionistic judgments and even textual distributions must be regarded with care. In the case discussed here, however, other more syntactic arguments have been offered to support the claim that comparatives contain a negative. Ross (1969:294) notes:

first ... words like any and ever may occur in than-clauses:

(21) He solves problems faster than any of my friends ever could.

But these words occur characteristically in negative sentences (and in questions and if-clauses), and are excluded in affirmative sentences:

(22) (a) *Any of my friends could ever solve those problems.

(b) Could any of my friends ever solve those problems?

(c) At no time could any of my friends ever solve those problems.

(d) If any of my friends ever solve those problems I'll buy you a drink.

Notice furthermore that negative elements cannot occur in than-clauses:[3]

(23) (a) *He is taller than nobody here.

      (b) *Bill ran faster than I couldn't.

These two factors strongly suggest that a negative element is present in the structure which underlies the than-clause.

Seuren (1973) adds several more examples of words and phrases which may or may not occur within than-clauses. He takes the list of positive polarity items and negative polarity items given in Baker (1970) and finds that the positive polarity items (e.g., already, still, would rather, just as well, pretty much, etc.) may not occur within than-clauses while the negative polarity items (e.g. much, bother, care to, need, could help, at all, etc.) may occur within than-clauses. He cites examples like those in V:

(V) (A) POSITIVE POLARITY ITEMS

     (1) (a) You have already got less support than he

               has.

          (b) *He has got more support than you already

               have.

     (2) (a) John still wants to buy more books than he

               can afford.

          (b) *John can afford fewer books than he still

               wants to buy.

     (3) (a) I would rather carry less than he does.

          (b) *He carries more than I would rather do.

     (B) NEGATIVE POLARITY ITEMS

     (4) (a) *The emperor was more inclined to do much

               for his country than to amuse himself.

          (b) The emperor was more inclined to amuse him-

               self than to do much for his country.

     (5) (a) *He will bother thinking about it.

          (b) That's more than he will bother thinking

about.

(6) (a) *I cared to drink that glass.

     (b) That glass holds more than I care to drink.

(7) (a) *John need run fast.

     (b) John runs faster than he need run.

I have arranged the examples in V in such a way that the (a) member of each pair gives an example of a positive or negative polarity item in a positive statement, while the (b) member of each pair places the same item within a than-clause. Seuren's point, of course, is that the positive polarity items are grammatical in the (a) examples but they are not grammatical in the (b) examples, while the reverse holds true for the negative polarity items.

Evidence such as that cited by Ross and Seuren is indeed good syntactic evidence and, should it stand close examination, constitutes a good argument for the analysis proposed. I believe, however, that the evidence does not stand up to close examination; in particular, the evidence of negative polarity items must be reinterpreted. The first indication that something is wrong comes from the fact that the argument applied very well to a construction for which no intuitive reason for positing a negative has been advanced. I am thinking here of the comparison of equality (comparisons with as -- as). The examples in VI[4] show exactly the same patterns of grammaticality and ungrammaticality as the patterns shown by comparisons of inequality.[5]

(VI) Comparisons of Equality

(1) *He has got as much support as you already

     have.

(2) *John can afford as many books as he still

     wants to buy.

(3) *He carries as much as I would rather do.

(4) The emperor was as inclined to amuse himself

     as he was to do much for his country.

(5) That is as much as I'm going to bother think-

     ing about right now.

(6) That glass holds as much as I care to drink.

(7) We travel as much as we need.

(8)   He solves those problems as fast as any of

      my friends ever could.

(9)   (i)   *He is as tall as nobody here.

      (ii) *Bill ran as fast as I couldn't.

Like comparisons of inequality, comparisons of equality do not
allow overt negation within the expression of the standard, nor do
they allow positive polarity items. Similarly, both constructions
allow negative polarity items within the expression of the standard without the presence of overt negation. The presence or absence of negative polarity items in the expression of the standard
of comparison does not change the presuppositions as to the fac-
tuality of the process described by that standard. Thus, the process expressed in the than-clause in VII 1 a is as likely (or unlikely) to have occurred as that expressed in the than-clause of
VII 1 b. Similarly, the presupposition for VII 2 a matches that
for VII 2 b.

(VII)

(1)   (a)   The emperor was more inclined to amuse himself

            than he was to do much for his country.

      (b)   The emperor was more inclined to amuse himself

            than he was to do something for his country.

(2)   (a)   The emperor was as inclined to amuse himself as

            he was to do much for his country.

      (b)   The emperor was as inclined to amuse himself as

            he was to do something for his country.

Though there does exist a similarity of pattern of what is or
is not grammatical and there does exist a similarity in interpretations of the negative polarity elements within the expressions
of the standard, the two comparative constructions behave quite
differently in connected text. We have seen that comparisons of
inequality may anticipate or express a relation Winter calls comparative denial and that the relation of comparative denial implies negation. Comparisons of equality, however, do not express
comparative denial. Thus, if we insert a comparison of equality
in example IV b the unacceptable sequence IV " results.

(IV ")   (a)   The two boats are quite different shapes.

          (b)   The Windjammer is as long and as wide as

<u>the Seaspray</u>.

Comparisons of equality express a relation which Winter (1977 a: 30) calls comparative affirmation. Winter suggests that comparative affirmation may be paraphrased with either VIII a or b.

(VIII)   (a) 'What is true of X is (also) true of Y.'

          (b) 'What is true of X in respect of A is also

               true of Y in respect of B.'

In contrast to the paraphrases of comparative denial neither paraphrase contains a negative.

IX A and B illustrate that comparisons of equality may anticipate (A) or express (B) comparative affirmations.

(IX) (A) (1) <u>Guydon is just as good as Bracy</u>.

          (2) (a) <u>Bracy shoots well from the outside</u>.

               (b) <u>Guydon does too</u>.

          (3) (a) <u>Bracy handles the ball well</u>.

               (b) <u>So does Guydon</u>.

     (B) (1) <u>The two boats are quite similar</u>.

          (2) <u>The Windjammer is just as long and as</u>

               <u>wide as the Seaspray</u>.

B 2 can be paraphrased roughly as IX B ' 2.

(IX) (B') (2) (a) <u>The Seaspray has a length and a width</u>.

                (b) <u>The Windjammer has the same length</u>

                     <u>and width</u>.

That is to say, 'What is true of the Seaspray is also true of the Windjammer'.

A second construction which casts some doubt on the Ross-Seuren analysis is a construction which has been called the amount relative clause. Carlson (1977) isolates a group of relative clauses which he distinguishes from restrictive relative clauses in part on the following grounds:

1) Amount relatives allow <u>there</u> insertion in the relative

    clause, restrictive relatives do not.

a) *Some man there was —— on the life raft died.

b) Everyman there was   on the life raft died.

2) Amount relatives may be introduced only by that.

Every man that there is in the room disagrees.

*who

3) Amount relatives may modify nouns that cannot be modified by restrictive relative clauses.

a) This weighs every pound that they said it would weigh.

b) The soldiers will exhibit all the courage that will be needed to conquer the palace.

c) Mary will do what traveling she wants to do tomorrow.

While amount relative clauses differ from the comparative constructions in that the amount relatives allow certain positive polarity items such as already and still, amount relatives resemble the two comparative constructions in that they do not allow the other positive polarity items nor do they allow overt negation, while they do allow negative polarity items.

(X) Amount Relatives

(1) What money there already is in the drawer should be taken to the bank.

(2) What money there still is in the house should be taken to the bank.

(3) *What money Max would rather spend is quite little.

(4) We never appreciate the people there are who do much for our country.

(5) What food we had bothered to bring was gone before we knew it.

(6) What food we cared to eat was always provided.

(7)   What books we need bring we can carry in

our hand luggage.

(8)   What errors there ever were were discovered by

this fabulous machine.

(9)   (i)   *What errors there never were were dis-

covered by machine.

(ii)   *What errors no one made were discovered

by machine.

(iii)   *What errors he didn't make were discovered

by machine.

While patterns of judgments of grammaticality in X do not totally parallel those for the two comparative constructions discussed so far, the judgments involving negations and the negative polarity elements are parallel in the three constructions. Again, however, I find no supporting semantic evidence to indicate that amount relative clauses contain a negative element within their structure.

Let us now consider a structure which involves a kind of comparison with respect to time: clauses introduced by before. The examples given in XI illustrate exactly the same patterns of judgments of grammaticality as were illustrated for comparisons of inequality and equality. As with the other two constructions, before-clauses do not allow overt negatives or positive polarity items, but they do allow negative polarity items.

(XI)   before-clauses

(1)   *He arrived before you already did.

(2)   *We should go there before he still works there.

(3)   *They serve supper before I would rather eat.

(4)   He died before he did much for the country.

(5)   The crisis came before we bothered to prepare

for it.

(6)   They served supper before I cared to eat.

(7)   He will leave before we need.

(8) <u>He left before anyone else ever got there</u>.

(9) (i) <u>*He left before nobody arrived</u>.

   (ii) <u>*He left before I couldn't</u>.

The similarity in judgments of grammaticality for the three constructions conceals a significant difference, however. When negative polarity items are included within the comparative constructions, the presuppositions involving the process described in the comparisons do not change. When negative polarity items are included within <u>before</u>-clauses, on the other hand, the presuppositions involving the <u>before</u>-clause do change. Examples like XII presuppose that both the process expressed in the <u>before</u>-clause and that in the main clause actually occurred.

(XII) (1) <u>John arrived before Mary did</u>.

   (2) <u>John arrived before Mary left</u>.

Because both processes are presupposed to have occurred, it is possible to measure the amount of time intervening between the two events as in XIII.

(XIII) (1) <u>John arrived two hours before Mary did</u>.

   (2) <u>John came three years before Mary left</u>.

   (3) <u>John arrived just before Mary left</u>.

When a <u>before</u>-clause contains certain negative polarity elements (e.g. <u>much</u>, <u>bother to</u>) on the other hand, it is presupposed that the process described in the <u>before</u>-clause did not take place.[6] Since in this case the <u>before</u>-clause does not describe an event, it is not possible to measure the amount of time intervening between the process described by the whole sentence. As a result, though the (a) sentences of XIV are grammatical, the (b) sentences are not.

(XIV) (1) (a) <u>He died before he did much for his country</u>.

      (b) <u>*He died two years before he did much for</u>

         <u>his country</u>.

   (2) (a) <u>The crisis came before we bothered to prepare for it</u>.

      (b) <u>*The crisis came just before we bothered to</u>

         <u>prepare for it</u>.

(3)   (a)   <u>They thought up the idea before I ever did</u>.

    (b)   *<u>They thought up the idea two years before</u>

       <u>I ever did</u>.

Given the evidence above, one can only conclude that <u>before</u>-clauses do not commit the speaker to the actual occurrence or non-occurrence of a process. The structure of <u>before</u>-clauses does not itself commit us to negation even though we cannot overtly negate <u>before</u>-clauses, and negative polarity items may occur within <u>before</u>-clauses with no overt negative element present. We cannot then use the mere occurrence or non-occurrence of these items in a structure as proof that the structure must contain a negative element.

In each case in which we compare the results of the syntactic arguments with our intuitive reactions as to what these structures really mean we find that if we blindly follow the syntactic argumentation followed by Ross and Seuren we arrive at counter-intuitive results. The only means to resolve the issue is to reinterpret the evidence. I believe the solution to the problem is suggested in Quirk and Greenbaum (1973:184 ff.). They note that items such as <u>yet</u>, <u>much</u>, <u>any</u>, etc., do not occur freely in positive assertions, but that they do occur in questions, conditionals and negatives. Rather than highlight merely one aspect of the distribution of these forms by calling them 'negative polarity' items they attempt to choose a term which describes the entire range of their distribution. Since none of the three structures cited above assert, they use the term 'non-assertive'.[7] This choice of terms is extremely interesting, for there is good reason to believe that expressions of the standard of comparison in comparisons of equality and inequality do not assert, but rather name a particular value.[8]

If that is true, then the non-occurrence of negatives and assertive forms (the positive polarity items) may be explained by the fact that none of these constructions are assertions, while the possible occurrence of the non-assertive forms (negative polarity items) may be explained by the same fact. There is, therefore, no syntactic evidence to support the claim that comparisons of inequality contain a negative element while comparisons of equality do not.

We are now left, however, with the problem of accounting for all the intuitive reactions to the effect that comparisons of inequality do involve negation while comparisons of equality do not. I believe we can achieve this by examining the semantics involved. Comparisons of equality focus on similarity while comparisons of inequality focus on difference. When we say that two items are similar we are saying that what is true about one is also (roughly) true about the other. When we focus on the difference between two items we are saying that what is true about one is not true about the other. The semantic interpretation of 'difference' or inequality implies some sort of negation. In other words, though the syntactic evidence for the existence of a negative element in comparison of inequality is not sufficient, there are strong reasons for saying that this structure qua grammatical structure is

associated with negation. I believe we have a good case here for
talking of a grammatical analog to connotative association on the
meaning of words. Just as words have meaning over and above their
defining properties, depending on who uses them and in what contexts they are used, so this construction gains an association
with negation derivable from its primary meaning 'difference' and
the use of this meaning in connected text.

NOTES

[1]While Ross and Seuren do not explicitly state they are only
treating comparatives of inequality, it is quite obvious from
their discussions that this was their intent.

[2]A further association of comparisons of inequality with comparative denial lies in the fact that a number of the conjunctions
which express comparative denial derive historically from comparatives. Jespersen (1918:347-8) points out that 'the Latin sed is
replaced by magis, Ital. ma, Sp. más, Fr. mais. The change in
meaning causes no difficulty; from "more" it is not great distance
to "sooner" which, like Germ. vielmehr and Eng. rather, is well
adapted for use in statements implying correction of contrast.'

[3]Actually Ross has made his statement too strong here. Negative elements can occur in than-clauses when they form part of
statements which make positive assertions. The examples he gives
are ungrammatical because they refer to a lack of people and an
inability to run at a given speed. Since one cannot normally
count the absence of something, neither of these is measurable,
and therefore these attributes cannot be used as a standard of
comparison. If, however, we use a negative to describe a measurable situation, then that negative may occur within a than-clause.
Thus, in shooting arrows at a target, I can count the number of
times that I didn't hit the target; the times that I didn't hit
that I didn't shoot don't count. So I can say 'I didn't even hit
the target ten times' and 'I didn't hit the target even more often
than Bill didn't hit it' and 'I hit the target about as often as
Bill didn't hit his.' Examples such as these lead to the conclusion that this restriction is semantic rather than grammatical.

[4]Examples 1-7 are adaptations of Seuren's examples, while
examples 8 and 9 are adaptations of Ross's.

[5]Mittwoch (1974) discusses comparisons of equality in some
detail, but since my judgments of grammaticality and interpretation differ substantially from hers I will discuss this construction again. I am in sympathy with her basic point that the two
comparative constructions differ. I believe, however, that the
analysis she proposes does not describe both the similarities
between the two constructions and their differences.

[6]Although <u>any</u> is often taken as the paradigmatic example of
a negative polarity item, in this construction it does not seem
to signal a negative presupposition in the same way that <u>much</u> and
other negative polarity items do. Thus <u>John arrived before anyone
left</u>, does not presuppose that no one left. As a result one also
may find <u>John arrived two hours before anyone left</u>, also <u>John arrived three years before anyone left</u>.

[7]A different approach to reinterpretation of negative polarity
items is suggested in Anthony (1977) in which he attacks the distinction between the suppletive alternate <u>any</u> which is said to replace <u>some</u> in negative sentences (as in (1)) and the distributive
<u>any</u> which may occur in positive sentences (as in (2)):

> (1) (Neg) <u>I bought some books today</u> > <u>I didn't buy any
>   books today</u>.
> (2) <u>Now any man can shave in the shower</u>.

If those two uses of <u>any</u> are found to be the same, clearly the status of <u>any</u> as a 'negative polarity' item is destroyed. While the
position taken in this paper is compatible with Anthony's, the two
positions are independent and cannot be used to support one another.

[8]Note, for example, the fact that the value named in the expression of the standard can be multiplied, as in
> <u>John is twice as strong as Bill is</u>.
or used as a point of reference for a measurement--
> <u>John is six inches taller than Bill is</u>.
See Fries (1977) for further arguments.

REFERENCES

Anthony, Michael. 1977. Some remarks on 'any'. Forum Linguisticum
     2.15-32.
Baker, C.L. 1970. Double negatives. Linguistic Inquiry 1.169-86.
Bazell, C.E. 1967. Notes on natural interpretation. Word 23.17-
     24.
Carlson, Greg. 1977. Amount relatives. Language 53.520-42.
Fries, Peter. 1977. English predications of comparison. Studia
     Anglica Posnaniensia 9.95-103.
Jespersen, Otto. 1917. Negation in English and other languages.
     (Reprinted in) Selected writings of Otto Jespersen, pp. 3-151.
     _____. 1918. Adversative conjunctions. (Reprinted in)
     Selected writings of Otto Jespersen, pp. 347-54.
     _____. 1962. Selected writings of Otto Jespersen.
     London: George Allen and Unwin, Ltd.
Joly, André. 1967. Negation and the comparative particle in English.
     Québec: Les Presses de l'Université Laval.

Longacre, Robert. 1976. An anatomy of speech notions. Lisse:
    Peter de Ridder Press.
Mittwoch, Anita. 1974. Is there an underlying negative element
    in comparative clauses? Linguistics 122.39-46.
Quirk, Randolph and Sidney Greenbaum. 1973. A concise grammar of
    contemporary English. New York: Harcourt, Brace, Jovanovich.
Ross, John. 1969. A proposed rule of tree pruning. Modern studies
    in English, ed. by Reibel and S. Schane. Englewood Cliffs NJ:
    Prentice Hall, pp. 288-99.
Seuren, P.A.M. 1969. Operators and nucleus: A contribution to
    the theory of grammar. Cambridge: Cambridge University Press.
_____. 1973. The comparative. Generative grammar in
    Europe, ed. by Kiefer and Ruwet. D. Reidel, pp. 528-564.
Winter, Eugene. 1977a. A clause-relational approach to English
    texts: A study of some predictive lexical items in written
    discourse. Instructional Science 6.1-92 (special issue).
_____. 1977b. Replacement as a function of repetition:
    A study of some of its principal features in the clause rela-
    tions of English. PhD Diss., Univ. of London, 1974. (Now avail-
    able through University Microfilms International, #77-70,036.)

CLASS BY VALUE SYSTEM: IMPLICATIONS FOR BILINGUAL EDUCATION

BATES HOFFER

Trinity University (San Antonio)

One of the most interesting developments in sociolinguistics follows from the definition of sociological class in terms of value systems. It is much easier to try to describe class membership by income, education level and so on, because these factors are quantifiable. But these quantifications cannot explain why contradictory attitudes, motivations and aspirations are held by two people sharing identical descriptors, or by two close siblings. The trend in sociology over the past few decades has been toward the use of intangibles to define the more important aspects of culture and class.[1] Attitudes toward family, work, religion, the future, self-satisfaction and other variables cluster in sets which can be used as working definitions. The clash of values across class lines is predictable from the diametric opposition of some variables. After a brief overview of some clash definitions, the clash of values will be exemplified in attitudes toward bilingual education.[2] Most of the furor--at least in San Antonio--can be attributed to class values, although the press persists in labeling the values clash an ethnic problem.

This article uses class names which differ from the traditional terms; thus the reader cannot automatically employ quantifiable features usually associated with 'low,' 'working,' 'middle,' and 'professional upper-middle.' The four classes to be treated here are the ACTION, the FAMILY, the UNIT and the SELF classes.

I should note that the following discussion of class is a theoretical one and that the classification scheme itself is broad-gauged; thus no one will find himself totally "fitting" one particular slot. My definition of class is not based directly on economic or social status factors (though they are ultimately part of the final picture) but on value systems. Certainly there are cultural factors, social "class" factors, ethnic factors and so on which must be studied and taken into consideration. Yet it is also true that some attitudes and behavior patterns are not predictable from those factors and can only be predicted in terms of value-system.

The ACTION class is characterized by a female-based family unit and a marginal male. The stable part of the family includes the females and the children. The action-seeking male may provide economic support but provides little or no affection or emotional support. He does not help in rearing children and provides only a negative model for the male offspring. The mother attempts to provide family stability; the father seeks gratification. For the purposes of subsequent discussion, the major factors of the ACTION class are mother dominance, the view of work solely as a means (for the male) of obtaining money for action or gratification, the negative view of education (since it is either too expensive or too time-consuming or both), and a generally fatalistic view of life in the sense that people (especially ACTION people) have no long term control over any aspect of their lives. In this class, however, the mother's values of stability and support are rather close to the value matrix of the class described immediately below.

The FAMILY class is characterized by values based on the extended family. Decisions about school, work and so on are based primarily on family solidarity and stability. The FAMILY class sees all outside forces as either supportive or destructive of the family system. It seeks itself as a unit apart from "society" and usually views outside structures with hostility. In loose terms, paranoia[3] can be said to characterize the FAMILY class during some periods of crisis; however, this does not mean the class is unbalanced, but that its values have been under constant attack for decades. Employment is usually viewed as the factor which allows full participation in family life. Those who become professionals or are successful in other fields but who stay within FAMILY behavioral patterns are still FAMILY regardless of income or social standing. Job success or economic mobility are accepted if not in conflict with the family. Rejection of a promotion which would mean relocation would not be uncommon. Education for the FAMILY class--and this point is crucial below--is seen as a means to maximize family satisfaction through the subsequently higher income or the benefits of the subsequent employment. Members of this class completely reject what has become the central idea of our educational philosophy, namely, that

> the student is an individual who should use his
> schooling to detach himself from ascribed relation-
> ships like the family circle in order to maximize his
> personal development and achievement in work, play,
> and other spheres of life.[4]

It is not too strong to state that such an educational goal is considered immoral by the FAMILY class. Educational programs which consciously or unconsciously are based on such a philosophy attempt by definition to destroy family bonds. In FAMILY values, the entire extended family or larger group with which it is identified must rise together or not at all. It is usually the case that the FAMILY class has the strongest religious values, the least amount of tension-related illness, and the highest job satisfaction level. For the discussion below, the important points are that the extended family is the dominant factor, that work is seen as that which facilitates family participation, that education is seen as that which can help family income and maintenance (but which constantly seeks to infect the young with selfish, egotistical ideas), and the outlook on society is that of detachment from a larger society.

The UNIT class is also family-based, but based on the nuclear family. When children marry or reach a certain age, they are expected and encouraged to become a separate nuclear unit. The UNIT sees itself as a part of the fabric of society and, to use a different metaphor, as a unit which should rise to its highest level in that society. This class actually holds two views of the family unit: in one sense the nuclear unit rises or falls together, but in another sense, children are seen as a sub-unit which is entitled to special treatment so that each child may later have a maximum social and economic mobility. Consequently the UNIT class is seen as the most child-ridden. The employment pattern of the UNIT class is not seen as a means to stabilize but as a series of positions moving ever higher on the social and economic ladder. As a corollary, education is viewed as a means to maximize opportunities for upward mobility. It is just this emphasis on "upward, ever upward" which suggests a loosely-defined term for the class, and that is the "neurotic class." Since the goal is upward mobility and there is no definition of a status or goal at the "top" of the mobility, the UNIT class never reaches a point which gives complete job or social satisfaction. In many ways it is the least satisfied class. One factor which is a major difference from FAMILY to UNIT is that the former is people/person-oriented and the latter is object/possessions-oriented. Instead of family/peer group goals, the UNIT class stresses object orientation, such as prestige, career, money and so on. The important factors for the purposes of the discussion which follows are that the nuclear family unit is the dominant force, that work is seen as a series of positions of ever-upward mobility, that education is primarily a means of upward mobility, and that the societal outlook is that the UNIT is part of the larger society and has some control over the future of the UNIT and society as a whole.

The SELF class sees society as a set of individuals who seek (or should seek) to maximize each other's status, prestige, income, life satisfaction, or any combination thereof. The philosophy of education given earlier fits here quite well. The SELF sees himself as only a temporary participant in a family structure. The school, the job and the social group are all means to individual development. In this class, as in related ones not treated here,

serial monogamy is one expression of "upward" mobility. Church affiliation often changes for personal advantage. The SELF strives
for more complete control of his future and spends more time in
schooling and training to achieve that success and control. For
the discussion below, the important factors are that the individual
is the dominant force, that work is seen as a means to individual
achievement, and that the view of society is that of controlling
one's high place and future in the societal fabric.

Let us now make use of the foregoing analysis for some comments on bilingual education and the way people view it. The most
obvious incompatibility in class value systems is between the FAMILY
and the UNIT/SELF. On one side, education is seen as a means for
children to maximize their eventual social distance from their
origins. This gulf is seen in moral terms. To the FAMILY the
attempts by a school to encourage a child to leave the community
later to "better" himself is seen as an immoral interference with
family rights and responsibilities. On the other side, the UNIT/
SELF see the FAMILY attempt to keep the child "down" by denying
him upward mobility as an immoral infringement on the child's
rights. Much of the controversy over bilingual education in the
Texas area, as over other educational engineering programs, is
based firmly on class grounds. Where maintenance of Spanish is
seen as supportive of the extended family and its peers, bilingual
education is held to be a moral right. Where English is seen as
the primary means of mobility, bilingual education is viewed as a
morally wrong means of preventing Spanish speakers from attaining
the necessary high proficiency in English requisite for maximum
mobility. Each group sees morality on its side. No platitudes
from the educational planners will solve the deep controversy
involved. One problem that arises in school district after school
district is that the justification for the bilingual program is
often in terms of the children's future mobility, an argument
which insures maximum opposition. The interesting fact is that
by law the parents through their elected school board have in one
sense control over the curriculum, but over and over again, programs are installed without sufficient information or support and
then defended against the very parents who are legally in charge.
The problem goes back to the goal of education quoted earlier.
Most educators, especially administrators, seem to be UNIT or
SELF and therefore view the parents as opponents whose children
need to be "properly" educated so that they break the bonds to
family and locality. The problem of bilingual education, then,
strikes to the core of the moral gulf between value systems.

One point that is so hard for many to accept is that you cannot predict class by income or occupation or other "outside" factors. Class as defined here is an internal value system, often
not consciously held and at different times overlapping with other
values. The key point is that a so-called working-class family
defined in occupational terms may contain individuals from two,
three, or all four of the above classes defined by value system.
It is commonly observed, for example, that the oldest child in a
large family tends to retain the value system of the parents while

the youngest children are less predictable. Brothers only a year
apart can have different class membership. The conclusion for bilingual curriculum planning is quite clear. You cannot use Spanish
surname, average income, neighborhood, etc., to predict values and
decide on programs. The parents should have a choice of programs
for their children, a choice guided by results of various proficiency tests and so on. Certainly we have passed the time when all
Spanish-surnamed children of a certain age should be thrown into
the same bilingual program.

There are many other implications possible in the treatment of
class by value system and they can be explored elsewhere. The
final part of this paper sets the exploration in context. It will
sound like a history of Jack Ornstein's work because in a way it is.
The research needed to optimize education (including bilingual education) should start with the linguistic "state" of the students.
Ornstein has dealt with the Spanish research[5] in various publications over the decades and has pushed for research on the English
of the Southwest. The next step is research into language as used
in various settings. Not only Jack's research into social setting
and factors of language use but also his ability to get others to
do research have contributed needed basic information. For example, his sociolinguistics background questionnaire has been used
in several forms as a basis for multiple research projects and educational programs. He has done and has called for more scholarly work,
but in addition he has reminded us that we deal with real people and
not merely "complex sociological groups." As we view programs such
as bilingual education, we should keep in mind his model. We need
to do much more with the linguistic descriptions and with the specification of language in actual situations, but in the last analysis we need to make sure that we work with students and colleagues
individually and with compassion for their values.

NOTES

[1] One source of easy access to this definition is H. Gans, The
working class, lower class, and middle class, Language and cultural
diversity in American education, ed. by R. Abrahams and R. Troike,
Englewood Cliffs NJ: Prentice-Hall, 1972, pp. 47-55.

[2] Much of the material is from my article, Mexican-American acquisition of English syntax: Ethnicity or class?, Bilingualism and
bilingual education: New readings and insights, ed. by J. Ornstein
and R. St. Clair, San Antonio TX: Trinity Univ., 1979.

[3] The term paranoia has been used in a suggestive sense and should
not be taken literally.

[4] Gans, op. cit., p. 48

[5] See e.g. his The archaic and the modern in the Spanish of New
Mexico, (reprinted in) El lenguaje de los chicanos, ed. by E. Her-
nández-Ch. et al., Arlington VA: Center for Applied Linguistics,
1975, pp. 6-11.

INTERGENERATIONAL LANGUAGE SHIFT IN AN ALBUQUERQUE BARRIO

ALAN HUDSON-EDWARDS AND GARLAND D. BILLS

University of New Mexico

Spanish is clearly the most prominent ethnic language spoken in the United States today. Waggoner (1976:5) reports that in July, 1975, 13% of the U.S. population age four and over lived in households in which languages other than English were spoken, and Spanish heads the list of languages spoken in those homes. Indeed, the 8.2 million Spanish speakers represent four and a half times the number of speakers of the next most widely claimed ethnic language, Italian. Furthermore, Spanish appears to be one of the most actively maintained ethnic languages. Among the national Spanish heritage population, 81% claim Spanish as their mother tongue, almost half live in households where Spanish is the usual language, and only a slightly smaller percentage, 44%, claim to speak Spanish as their usual language. Only Chinese and Korean equal or surpass Spanish in these figures (Waggoner 1976:9). The evidence of numerical strength and retention rates demonstrates that Spanish is among the healthiest of the nation's ethnic languages.

For the Spanish heritage population of the Southwest, the diagnosis based on the same kind of evidence is just as positive. In the five states of Arizona, California, Colorado, New Mexico and Texas, 17% of the total population are of Spanish heritage, and of these, 76% are of Spanish mother tongue (Bills & Ornstein 1976:5). Within the Southwest, the healthiest place for retention is clearly

New Mexico. In this state, 40% of the people are of Spanish heritage, with 81% of these claiming Spanish as their mother tongue (U.S. Bureau of the Census 1971:105).

However, the robustness of Spanish in comparison with other ethnic languages does not necessarily mean that Spanish will survive for ever among its present speakers. On the contrary, it is widely believed that the Spanish-heritage population throughout the Southwest presents yet another classic example of language shift in progress. Most observers readily perceive the societal shift from dominance in Spanish to Spanish-English bilingualism and, with diminished maintenance of Spanish, to English dominance and eventual English monolingualism. Typically, this perception is documented by demonstrating for successive generations significant changes in the proportions of ethnic mother tongue claiming, proficiency, or use. However, the process of language shift is considerably more complex than these statistical analyses alone suggest. The purpose of this study, then, is to probe a complex of data from a barrio of Albuquerque, New Mexico, in an effort to characterize in finer detail the mechanism of language shift.

The community examined here is generally labeled 'Martineztown' or sometimes 'Martineztown-Santa Barbara' in government reports. The more acculturated tend to call it simply 'Martínez.' It is one of the oldest areas of Albuquerque, located near the center of town, but somewhat isolated by major boundaries on all sides: interstate highways I-25 and I-40 to the east and north, Central Avenue to the south, and railroad tracks flanked by industrial-commercial areas to the west. Martineztown covers some 190 square blocks housing industrial sites, commercial establishments, schools, municipal buildings, churches, a hospital, a large cemetery, residential areas, and considerable vacant land. The residential area is about twenty blocks in length and ranges from two to five blocks in width. Although the city of Albuquerque is almost identical to the state in its proportions of Spanish heritage population and Spanish mother-tongue retention, this little barrio of approximately 605 households is estimated to be 96% Spanish surnamed by Johnson and Yates (1969:32). The total population of somewhat over 2,000 is reported to be 97% 'persons of Spanish language or surname' with an equally high percentage of Spanish mother-tongue retention (U.S. Bureau of the Census 1972:P-11).

A pilot survey was carried out in 1975 to explore the language situation in this ethnic community. This consisted of interviews in the homes of 61 families, a ten percent sampling. Although the target households were randomly selected in advance, absolute randomness was lost in a few situations for refusals and no responses; the close correlation of our results with comparable data in the 1970 census, however, indicates that this slight deviation from randomness had no significant effect on validity. Because of the high Spanish-surnamed population of the barrio, only local Chicanos were used as interviewers.[1] Two persons, usually a male and a female, conducted each interview, one actually interviewing and the other taking notes on responses. The average

interview lasted approximately thirty minutes and, except for two
instances of mechanical failure, all interviews were tape recorded.
    The survey was intended to gather a broad range of basic in-
formation, including the spoken language sample in the tape recordings. The survey questionnaire elicited information of three kinds:
demographic data, Spanish and English proficiency and use for all
household members, and the respondent's attitudes towards the two
languages.[2] A brief overview of the demographic data will give a
clearer picture of the community and set the stage for the examination of data relevant to language maintenance and shift.
    The overwhelmingly Chicano composition of the community re-
ported by Johnson and Yates (1969) and the U.S. Bureau of the Census (1972) is confirmed in our survey. Of the 61 households, 56
or 92% were of Spanish heritage. The other five households, all
Anglo, were clearly transient elements of the barrio. Since for
present purposes the inclusion of these Anglo households could only
have a distorting effect, the analysis which follows is limited to
the Chicano majority--specifically the 191 individuals in the 55
Chicano households for which we have complete tape-recorded interviews.
    In her anthropological study of Martineztown 10 years earlier,
Vincent (1966) emphasized the highly stable nature of the barrio.
This impression of stability is precisely one of the most striking
aspects revealed by the demographic information collected in the
present survey. Almost half of the 191 individuals were actually
born into the community and 92% were born in New Mexico; fewer
than four percent were born in Mexico, a sharp contrast with other
urban Chicano communities in the Southwest. Of the 55 respondents,
72% claimed ownership of their homes and only nine percent reported
plans to move from Martineztown. The average age for all individuals is 33 years, with one-fourth being over 50 years of age.
With regard to education, over one-third of the adults failed to
advance beyond the sixth grade, while only one in four completed
high school and fewer than one in 10 had any exposure to college.
Relatedly, half of the heads of households have no gainful employment, and the employed adults are largely at the low end of the
occupational scale. Demographically, then, this Chicano community
is poorly educated, lower blue-collar or welfare, and 94% Catholic.
Minimal in-migration and considerable out-migration of young
adults gives it the cast of an elderly community with rather small
households. In spite of its location in the center of New Mexico's
largest urban area, Martineztown--demographically and in many
other ways--has the character of an isolated rural village.
    This impression is further enhanced by the strong pressure of
the Spanish language. The use of language during the interview,
determined primarily by the respondents, sheds some light on the
roles of Spanish and English in this community. Fully 58% of the
interviews were conducted mostly or entirely in Spanish, almost
one-fourth in English, and 18% with roughly equal measures of the
two languages. Though the respondents are not representative of
the community, a point to be treated further below, this initial
piece of objective evidence clearly demonstrates both the prominent

role of Spanish and the highly bilingual character of Martineztown.
     In the following pages we explore a more comprehensive array
of evidence, specifically focusing on Spanish-English proficiency
and use and their relationships to generational data. We consider
three kinds of variables that blend into the notion of generation:
(a) age, somewhat arbitrarily divided into two groups at the 25
year point; (b) composition of household in terms of both number
of generations and presence of minor children, yielding a three
point variable to be explained below; and (c) individual generational relationship to the head of household, providing four groups
in this community: a 'parent' generation composed of parents of
household heads, a 'senior' generation that includes the heads and
their spouses and siblings, a 'junior' generation containing the
children of heads, and a 'grandchild' generation. On the language
side, we utilize just four variables from our data: (a) mother-
tongue, (b) speaking ability in Spánish, (c) speaking ability in
English, and (d) language use in the home. The following sections
explore intergenerational variation for each of these language
variables.

Mother Tongue

     The data presented in Table 1 show that Martineztown is a pri-
marily Spanish mother-tongue community. Fully two-thirds of the
individuals for whom information was available either claimed or
were reported to have acquired Spanish as their mother tongue. One
person in six acquired Spanish and English simultaneously while a
nearly identical number acquired English only. A distinction between those persons providing first-hand information on their own
language background and those for whom this information was reporte
by others shows that 84% of the former and only 59% of the latter
claim Spanish as their single mother tongue. This discrepancy is
to be attributed largely to the fact that the average age of the
respondents was 46 while the average age of the other persons reported upon was 27.
     A very clear negative correlation between age and Spanish
mother-tongue reporting is readily apparent in the data in Table
1. Virtually all individuals over 25 years of age claim
Spanish alone as their mother tongue. Of the 81 persons in the
younger age group, only 38% report their first language to be only
Spanish. When age is considered as a continuous variable and
mother tongue as a trichotomous one, the correlation between the
two is -.48. This negative relationship is not, of course, unexpected. López (1978) reports a smaller but nonetheless negative
correlation between age and Spanish as 'language of upbringing'
for second generation Chicanos in the Los Angeles area. The Martineztown data include seven persons born in Mexico; if they are
removed from the calculation, the correlation between age and
Spanish mother-tongue claiming rises slightly to -.50.
     The relationship of mother-tongue claiming to the composition
of the household is also clear from Table 1. Twenty-four persons
in the study sample were reported living in one-generational
families. The fact that none of these claimed English only as a

Table 1

Mother Tongues by Age, Composition of Household, and

Generational Relationship to Head, in Percentages

| | Mother Tongue | | | |
	Spanish	Both	English	n
Total Sample	67	18	16	177
Respondent	84	9	7	55
Non-respondent	59	21	20	122
Age				
1-25 Years	38	31	31	81
26+ years	90	7	3	92
Composition of Household				
1 Generation	92	8	0	24
2-3 Generations, Adults	78	11	11	37
2-3 Generations, with Minors	58	22	21	116
Generational Relationship to Head				
Parent	100	0	0	3
Senior	87	7	6	87
Junior	44	29	28	80
Adult Child	58	27	15	26
Minor Child	37	30	33	54
Grandchild	50	25	25	4

mother tongue and that only 8% claimed English and Spanish both is
no doubt due to the fact that all of these individuals were over
45 years of age. Members of one-generation households claim only
Spanish as the mother tongue with considerably greater frequency
than do members of multiple-generation households: 92% for the
former versus 62% for the latter. However, the difference between
the two- and three-generation household is negligible. For them,
a more important consideration by far is whether or not there are
children under the age of 18 present in the family. The data in
Table 1 indicate that 78% of the persons residing in either two-
or three-generational households having no minor children are reported to have Spanish as a mother tongue whereas the corresponding figure for persons in families with young children is only 58%.

Generational status within one's family can also be seen to
be a factor affecting the likelihood of claiming Spanish as a
mother tongue. Although the present study obtained information
on only three parents of heads of households, all three claimed
Spanish alone as their mother tongue. Among the next generation,
consisting of heads of households, their spouses, and siblings
living with them, the overwhelming majority, 87%, claimed Spanish
also. By the third generation, however, the proportion of persons claiming Spanish only as a mother tongue is virtually halved.
It is understandable in the light of the previous discussion of
composition of households that grown children in this junior generation were more likely to claim Spanish than were minor children.

Spanish mother-tongue claiming in Martineztown does not appear
to be radically different from that reported for the northern rural
village of Arroyo Seco, near Taos, New Mexico (Ortiz 1975). Among
178 persons for whom data were obtained in the latter community,
some 77%, a mere 10 percent more than in Martineztown, were reported to have acquired Spanish alone as their first language.
Among those over 20 years of age in Arroyo Seco, virtually all,
93%, claimed Spanish as their only mother tongue; the corresponding
figure for those over 25 years of age in Martineztown is 90%. In
Los Angeles, California, on the other hand, Spanish is claimed as
the 'language of upbringing' by only 42% of the subjects in a sample
of 397 second and third generation married Chicano women (López
1978:270). With respect to mother-tongue claiming, Martineztown
resembles the rural village far more than it does the large metropolitan area.

Language Proficiency

This section examines the data on proficiency ratings for both
English and Spanish in Martineztown. As is to be expected, current
English ability and current Spanish ability are inversely related,
though only partially so, the Kendall's tau correlation coefficient
for the two variables being just -.33. The reason for the relatively low correlation becomes apparent from an examination of the
data presented in Table 2. Of the 24 persons whose English ability
was reported to be 'weak' (a rating of 'none' or 'poor'), 21, or 88%
claimed to have a 'fluent' (a rating of 'good' or 'very good')
command of Spanish. Likewise, of the 28 persons with weak Spanish

Table 2

Relationship Between Spanish Ability

and English Ability

| | Spanish Ability | | | |
English Ability	None/Poor	Fair	Good/Very Good	Total
None/Poor	0	3	21	24
Fair	4	3	30	37
Good/Very Good	24	35	53	112
Total	28	41	104	173

ability, 24, or 86%, apparently spoke fluent English. However, a fluent command of both languages was reported for 53 individuals, more than twice the number reported to be weak in one or the other language. Thus, while it is clearly the case that a poor knowledge of one language implies fluency in the other, the reverse does not hold true, for Martineztown is populated by a substantial number of effective bilinguals.

Comparable data on language proficiency in other Spanish-speaking communities of the Southwest are not available. However, Skrabanek (1970:275) reports that in the 544 Mexican American families studied in the Texas counties of Atascosa and Bexar, 'not one person ... old enough to talk was found who did not speak Spanish fluently, and an overwhelming majority speak Spanish more fluently than English.' Also, in Arroyo Seco, New Mexico, Ortiz (1975:154) found that 53% of the individuals in his study reportedly feel more comfortable speaking Spanish than English, 41% are equally at ease in both languages, and only six percent are more comfortable speaking English. Insofar as these data may be interpreted as a reflection of relative langauge proficiency, they may be compared with the data in Table 2, which show that 54 persons, or 31% of the Martineztown subjects for whom information was available, rate their Spanish ability superior to their English ability, while 56 persons, or 32%, rate their English on a par with their Spanish, and 63 persons, or 36%, rate their English better than their Spanish. Though predominantly of Spanish mother tongue, the people of Martineztown show a marginal tendency toward English dominance.

Not surprisingly, the mother tongue data correlate more strongly with Spanish ability than with English ability. These relationships are clearly displayed in the crosstabulations presented in Table 3. With regard to speaking ability in Spanish, almost 80% of the 114 Spanish mother tongue claimants are reported to be fluent in Spanish. Among these claiming both English and

Table 3

Relationship Between Mother Tongue and Spanish and

English Ability, Reported in Percentages

	Mother Tongue		
Spanish Ability	Spanish	Both	English
None/Poor	5	16	59
Fair	16	65	22
Good/Very Good	79	19	18
n	114	31	27
English Ability			
None/Poor	20	3	0
Fair	30	10	0
Good/Very Good	50	87	100
n	113	31	26

Spanish, the modal response is 'fair.' Finally, the majority of
the English mother-tongue claimants are reported to be weak in
Spanish, though it must be added that only 15% reported no ability
in Spanish at all. On the other hand, English ability correlates
less well with mother tongue, for fluent English was reported for
the majority in each mother-tongue category, ranging from 50% of
the Spanish mother-tongue claimants to 100% of the English mother-
tongue claimants. It is revealing to note that among the bilingual
mother-tongue claimants, only one in five acquired fluency in
Spanish while almost nine out of ten achieved English fluency. In
all, the Kendall's tau correlation for mother tongue and English
ability is a modest .38, but for mother tongue and Spanish ability
it is a substantial and highly significant .55.

This strong relationship is also readily apparent when the
Spanish ability ratings provided in Table 4 are compared with the
mother-tongue reports in Table 1. Thus, for instance, just as 16%
of the total sample claimed only English as their mother tongue,
16% also claim little or no knowledge of Spanish. Similarly, just
as 67% reported only Spanish as their first language, 60% report
a fluent command of that language now.

Age is as highly correlated with Spanish ability as it was
with mother tongue. The great majority of those over 25 years of
age claim at least a good knowledge of Spanish. Those 25 and under

Table 4

Spanish Ability by Age, Composition of Household, and
Generational Relationship to Head, in Percentages

| | Spanish Ability | | | |
	None/Poor	Fair	Good/Very Good	n
Total Sample	16	25	60	177
Respondent	4	17	80	54
Non-respondent	21	29	51	123
Age				
1-25 Years	33	36	31	83
26+ Years	1	12	87	89
Composition of Household				
1 Generation	0	8	92	24
2-3 Generations, Adults	5	24	70	37
2-3 Generations, with Minors	22	28	49	116
Generational Relationship to Head				
Parent	0	0	100	4
Senior *	5	10	85	87
Junior	29	39	33	80
Adult Child	12	50	38	26
Minor Child	37	33	30	54
Grandchild	25	75	0	4

are fairly evenly distributed on this three point ability scale,
but it must be noted that only five percent of this younger group
were reported to have no knowledge of Spanish at all. Overall,
when Spanish proficiency is treated as a five point variable and
age as a continuous one, the correlation between the two is a very
high .63.

Household composition and individual generational status show
the same kinds of relationship with Spanish ability as might be
predicted from the mother-tongue data. Members of two- and three-
generation homes with minor children less frequently claim Spanish
fluency than do members of comparable households without minor
children. The latter, in turn, report less proficiency in Spanish
than members of single generation homes, almost all of whom maintain fluency in the language. Similarly, while all four of the
parents of heads of households report fluent Spanish ability, only
85% of the latter and their generational peers do so. Finally,
among the junior generation, only 33% maintain a fluent command of
Spanish. Recall, however, that 44% of this junior generation reportedly first learned to speak in Spanish. There is a strong
suggestion here that as many as one-fourth of these Spanish mother-
tongue claimants in the junior generation either did not continue
to acquire Spanish to the level of mature native speakers or else,
having done so, subsequently shifted to English at some cost to
their Spanish ability.

The high rate of English fluency in Martineztown is shown in
Table 5. Almost two-thirds of the sample as a whole is reported
to have at least a good command of English. For reasons discussed
earlier, persons reporting on their own behavior typically claim
lower proficiency in English for themselves than for other members
of their household. As is to be anticipated, a fluent knowledge
of English is claimed almost twice as frequently for younger members of the community as it is for persons over 25 years of age.
Once again, the expected relationship with household composition
is apparent. Of those persons living in families with minor
children, 77% are reported to be fluent in English whereas only
56% of those living in multiple-generation households without young
children are reported to be as fluent. Lastly, crosstabulation of
English ability with generational relationship to the head of household shows that members of the parent generation are less fluent in
English than members of the senior generation while the latter, predictably, are less fluent than their own children.

There is, however, one minor reversal in Table 5 that sheds
some light on the processes involved in language shift in a bilingual community. That is, the adult members of the junior generation are reported to have greater English fluency than the younger
members. Given the negative relationship between age and English
ability mentioned just above, it might reasonably have been predicted that grown children would have poorer English than minors.
Indeed, the contrary prediction for Spanish ability is borne out
in the data of Table 4, namely, that the older children report
better Spanish than the younger children. The data on English
ability claiming within the junior generation suggest that the
pattern of age grading is reversed due to the more extensive con-

Table 5

English Ability by Age, Composition of Household, and
Generational Relationship to Head, in Percentages

| | English Ability | | | |
	None/Poor	Fair	Good/Very Good	n
Total Sample	15	21	64	177
Respondent	17	34	49	53
Non-respondent	14	15	71	124
Age				
1-25 Years	5	10	86	84
26+ Years	24	32	44	88
Composition of Household				
1 Generation	42	42	17	24
2-3 Generations, Adults	19	25	56	36
2-3 Generations, with Minors	8	15	77	117
Generational Relationship to Head				
Parent	75	0	25	4
Senior	22	32	47	88
Junior	4	11	85	81
Adult Child	0	8	92	25
Minor Child	5	13	82	56
Grandchild	0	0	100	3

tacts of the grown members of this generation with the larger
English-speaking community. A similar explanation could, of course,
be advanced for the differential between group and minor children
in Spanish ability, but a more plausible interpretation is that
the pattern of age grading in Spanish ability in fact reflects
genuine language shift across time. In other words, while age
stratification in the case of English ability may be said to represent a developmental acquisition process, in the case of Spanish
ability it seems to represent diachronic shift.

Home Language Use

     Additional insight into the process of language shift as well
as maintenance is provided by the data on language use in the home
presented in Table 6. Despite the relatively high rate of Spanish
first language and Spanish ability claiming, fewer than half of
the individuals in the sample were reported to use Spanish as the
primary home language. A further 19% use English and Spanish
equally, and over one-third use English more than Spanish.
     The relationship between age and English use in the home is
rather more dramatic than might have been expected. Although more
than two-thirds of those 25 years of age or younger claim to use
English mostly or exclusively in the home, only five percent of
those over 25 do so. In fact, three-fourths of those over 25 years
of age reportedly use Spanish as the principal home language and
fully one-third of this age group use Spanish to the total exclusion of English in the home.
     Generational range in the household and the presence or ab-
sence of young children are also factors related to the maintenance
of Spanish as a language of the home. Both factors contribute in-
dependently, and in the predicted directions, to the home use of
Spanish, though once again the presence or absence of minor children
is the more critical variable. Combining the data for single generation and multiple generation adult households, three out of four
of the individuals living in homes without minor children reportedly
use mostly or only Spanish at home. Among those living in either
two or three generational households with young children present,
only 29% use Spanish more than English.
     Analysis of home language use by generational relationship to
head of household reveals the same asymmetrical distribution of
languages that has come to be expected of families caught up in
the process of language shift. Of the three parents of heads of
households in this sample, one uses Spanish and English equally,
one uses Spanish mostly, and the third uses Spanish exclusively.
The generation of the head of household differs from the earlier
one in that it is the first to have any members at all claiming
predominant use of English. The majority of the generation of
children, however, claim to use English as the primary home language.
     A force counteracting the process of language shift may be
signaled by the fact that the adults in the junior generation approximate their parents' language use much more closely than do the
minor children. Even though 92% of the grown children claimed

Table 6

Home Language Use by Age, Composition of Household, and

Generational Relationship to Head, in Percentages

	Home Language			
	Spanish	Both	English	n
Total Sample	46	19	35	178
Respondent	64	24	13	55
Non-respondent	37	17	46	123
Age				
1-25 Years	12	18	70	83
26+ Years	74	21	5	91
Composition of Household				
1 Generation	88	13	0	24
2-3 Generations, Adults	68	24	8	38
2-3 Generations, with Minors	29	19	52	116
Generational Relationship to Head				
Parent	67	33	0	3
Senior	66	23	11	88
Junior	23	16	60	81
Adult Child	48	22	30	27
Minor Child	11	13	76	54
Grandchild	0	0	100	4

fluent English, almost half of them use Spanish as the major home
language. This apparent manifestation of ethnic language loyalty
is not perceivable in the behavior of the minor children, fully
76% of whom show predominantly English use in the home. Of the
four language variables treated here, it is in home language use
that the adults and minors of this generation differ most strongly.
One possible explanation for this discrepancy may be attitudinal
factors of the sort that Labov (1963) noted on the island of
Martha's Vineyard. That is, the older members of this junior generation who made a point of remaining in the community into adult-
hood are likely to have been those who identified most strongly
with the community's values and orientation and, therefore, to have
made more of a commitment to the maintenance of Spanish in the
home.

Comparative statistics on language use in Albuquerque, or indeed anywhere in New Mexico, are difficult to come by. However,
an earlier socioeconomic survey of the model neighborhood area of
Albuquerque, which includes Martineztown, found that 70% of the
318 Spanish surnamed families for whom data were available used
Spanish mostly or exclusively in the home (Johnson & Yates 1969:
34). This figure approximates quite closely the findings of the
present study in regard to heads of households and their parents,
though it is substantially in excess of the percentage reported
here for the study population as a whole. Elsewhere in New Mexico,
Ortiz (1975) notes that in Arroyo Seco parents over the age of 40
typically report using Spanish most if not all of the time in domestic situations. Younger parents, however, typically report language use in the home to be more or less equally divided between
Spanish and English.

Somewhat comparable statistics are available for several Chicano communities outside of New Mexico. Thompson (1971) reports
on Spanish language use in the home among some 176 informants
living in a Mexican-American neighborhood in Austin, Texas.
Skrabanek (1970) reports similar data for 268 Mexican American
households in rural Atascosa County, Texas, and for a further 276
households in San Antonio, in adjacent Bexar County. Finally,
López (1978) provides detailed information on 890 Chicano women in
Los Angeles, California. The statistics provided by these researchers have been retabulated by the present authors and collated
for convenience in Table 7.

The reader is advised that the data from the various studies
represented in Table 7 are not strictly comparable in all respects,
but are presented there for the purposes of impressionistic comparison. The data for Los Angeles (López 1978) are based on married
Chicano women, not on heads of households. In Atascosa County and
San Antonio (Skrabanek 1970) and in Austin (Thompson 1971), separate
data for language use with parents and with children were averaged
together to obtain an approximate overall measure of language use
in the home comparable to that used in the present study. Also,
both in López (1978) and in Thompson (1971), 'generation' is defined as the generational distance from immigration to the United
States; in the present study it refers to generational relationship
to the head of the household. Finally, the age breakdown is dif-

Table 7

Percentage Distributions of Persons Reporting Predominant

Use of Spanish in the Home, by Location of Study

	Location				
	Martineztown	Los Angeles	Austin	San Antonio	Atascosa County
Heads of Households	66	50	59	61	73
Age					
Older	74	--	66	--	--
Younger	12	--	36	24-28	40-48
Generation					
First	67	84	96	--	--
Second	66	15	67	--	--
Third	23	4	49	--	--

ferent in all three studies for which data are available: younger people in the present study are 25 years of age and younger, in Skrabanek (1970) they are between 10 and 24 years of age, and in Thompson (1971) they are between the ages of 18 and 29.

In general, it can be seen in Table 7 that the degree of Spanish maintenance in the home on the part of heads of households in Martineztown is highly comparable to that in other locations in the Southwest. Maintenance appears to be lowest in Los Angeles, the most urban of the five locations, and highest in rural Atascosa County. Albuquerque, Austin, and San Antonio, being cities of intermediate size, also show intermediate levels of Spanish use in the home, though Martineztown most closely approximates the rural pattern.

Martineztown seems to be more urban, however, when the comparative data for age are considered. Of the four locations for which useable data are available, the younger people of Martineztown are most similar in home language use to the largest urban area, San Antonio, and least similar to the most rural area, Atascosa County. Furthermore, a comparison with the age group data for Austin, a city comparable in size to Albuquerque, suggests an exceptional lack of Spanish maintenance in the home by Martineztown youth.

The percentages of Spanish use reported for each of the generations in the various studies are not strictly comparable because of the different definitions of generational status. However, all three studies for which data are available agree that later generations employ noticeably less Spanish in the home than do earlier ones. In the case of Los Angeles, the drop between the first and second generations is quite dramatic, supporting López' claim that 'the pivotal shift [from Spanish to English] occurs during the second generation' (1978:271). By the third generation, Spanish is hardly used at all in the home. In contrast, the data for Austin show a more gradual decline in Spanish use from 96% of the first generation who claim to use Spanish most of the time to virtually one-half of the third generation who do so. In the Martineztown context there appears to be no difference in Spanish language use in the home between the oldest generation and the second oldest, though this is very probably due to the fact that only three persons were identified in the former category. The difference between the second and third generations is more reliable in view of the numbers involved and shows a precipitous decline in Spanish use in the home. In this respect, Albuquerque appears to be more akin to the situation in Los Angeles than to that in Austin.

The Mechanism of Language Shift

Comparison between numbers of ethnic mother-tongue claimants in successive generations, as typified for instance in Fishman and Hofman (1966), necessarily does not reveal the full, variegated process that is language shift. More precisely, language shift must be seen as a series of concurrent shifts in the rates of ethnic mother tongue transmission, individual maintenance of proficiency, and actual use. This process can be viewed in some detail in Mar-

tineztown with regard to those two generations for which the
greatest amount of data is available, namely, the generation of
the heads of households and that of the children of heads of
households.

The interrelationships between Spanish mother-tongue claiming,
Spanish proficiency, and Spanish home use are displayed for each
of these generations in Table 8. Spanish was reported as the
first language of 87% of the individuals in the senior generation
and, of these, fully 95% still maintain a fluent knowledge of the

Table 8

Interrelationships Between Types of Spanish Claiming,

by Generation

	Generation	
	Senior	Junior
Total percent Spanish mother tongue	87	44
Percent of Spanish mother tongue		
claiming fluent Spanish	95	50
Total percent fluent Spanish speakers	85	33
Percent of fluent Spanish speakers		
claiming Spanish home language use	75	31
Percent of Spanish mother tongue		
claiming Spanish home language use	76	43
Total percent Spanish home language use	66	23

language. However, of those members of the senior generation who
speak Spanish fluently, only three-quarters actually use it more
than they do English in the home. The cumulative effect of this
erosion of Spanish vitality is that only 66% of the senior generation continue to use it in the home with greater frequency than
they do English, thus limiting the opportunity for the immediately
succeeding generation to acquire Spanish as a first language.

In fact, only 44% of the junior generation are reported to
have acquired Spanish as their first language and, of these, only
one-half are professed to currently have a fluent command of the
language. Once more, it is obvious that there are some in this
generation for whom Spanish was claimed as a mother tongue but for

whom the environment did not support continued use of it. Many of
these speakers, as a result, may never have developed a real facility in Spanish and may, in fact, have witnessed a deterioration
of their proficiency with the passage of time. Moreover, of those
in the junior generation who <u>did</u> achieve or maintain fluency of
Spanish, a mere 31% continue to use it as their primary language
in the home. In sum, the junior generation is much more prone than
the senior one not to develop mature native-speaker competence in
Spanish despite having acquired it as a first language, and secondly,
to resort to the use of English as a primary language of the home
even in those instances where a fluent command of Spanish was maintained.

The encroachment of English upon the scene may also be viewed
in terms similar to those used to describe the decline of Spanish.
Fluency in English in the senior generation is not, of course,
limited only to those who acquired it as their first language. Although only six percent learned English as their first language,
47% attain fluency in it; however, only 24% of these fluent speakers
actually use English as their predominant home language. Among
the junior generation, all of those who acquired English before or
simultaneously with Spanish now speak it fluently while 64% of those
who acquired Spanish first also do so. Moreover, two-thirds of
those classified as fluent English speakers currently use it as
their main home language.

The inexorable advance of English becomes clearer still when
the process of language shift is viewed across linked generations,
that is to say, across successive generations within the same
family. The hypothesis that later generations would show more
Anglophone characteristics than earlier ones was therefore tested
individually for 38 multiple-generation families on the items relating to first language, Spanish ability, English ability, and
home language use. Out of 141 useable observations, 78 were found
to confirm the hypothesis in its most stringent form, namely, that
each successive generation within each family observed showed increasingly Anglophone traits. In an additional 10 cases, stability
was observed between two generations while a shift in the predicted
direction was found in the third. Stability across all generations
in the household was observed in 44 instances. Finally, in only
nine cases did a later generation show fewer Anglophone characteristics than the preceding one, and five of these were instances
where the adults in the family understandably claimed greater
English proficiency than their children. Predictably, overall
intergenerational stability was most in evidence in the case of
mother-tongue and English-proficiency claiming, less so in the
case of Spanish proficiency claiming, and least of all in the case
of home language use.

Conclusions

The picture drawn in the preceding pages of this report offers
scant consolation to those concerned about the maintenance of
Spanish among the urban Chicano populations of the Southwest. True,

the language is still very much alive in Martineztown, whether
judged in terms of mother-tongue acquisition, current ability, or
use in the home. Yet the signs of large-scale shift are every-
where in evidence. The children of heads of households claim
Spanish alone as a mother tongue with only half the frequency of
their parents' generation. They much less frequently claim a
fluent knowledge of Spanish and at the same time much more frequently claim a fluent knowledge of English. They claim to use
Spanish as their primary home language with scarcely more than a
third the frequency their parents do. While intergenerational
loss of Spanish in Martineztown may not be quite as precipitous
as in other, larger, urban centers such as Los Angeles, the sustaining effect of a continuous influx of Spanish-speaking immigrants is not felt in Martineztown to nearly the same degree as
in these other areas. Thus, although out-migration of nontradi-
tional youth may help somewhat to preserve the Spanish character
of Martineztown in the short run, the longer term prognosis for
the survival of the language appears dubious indeed.

Finally, in a more theoretical vein, the results of this
study strongly suggest that the process of langauge shift can be
detected in its early stages within a single generation when the
proportion of ethnic mother tongue claimants exceeds the proportion of fluent speakers of the language and when the latter, in
turn, exceeds the proportion of those using the ethnic tongue as
their primary home language. As López (1978) noted, this process,
once begun, accelerates in succeeding generations. Not only are
there fewer ethnic mother tongue claimants to begin with, but a
smaller portion of them advance to the point of mature native
speaker proficiency, and of those who do, a smaller proportion
than in the senior generation actually maintain the ethnic language as the primary language of the home.

NOTES

[1]The data collection for the community survey was carried out
by 11 University of New Mexico student volunteers: Lori Baca,
Tim Baca, Esmeralda Fraga, Josephine Hernández, Gaylord López,
Arturo Maes, Cecilia Montoya, Proceso Montoya, Elena Pizarro, Al-
fredo Vigil, and Charlotte Vigil. We gratefully applaud their
contributions and wish to give special thanks to Fred and Lori.
We also acknowledge with gratitude the funds for essential supplies
and equipment provided by the Faculty Research Allocations Commit-
tee at the University of New Mexico.

[2]Kravitz (1978) briefly reports on some aspects of the attitudinal data. This pilot project also included a survey of the
145 children in the local elementary school's bilingual education
program; a variety of results of this part of the project is reported by Teitelbaum (1976), and Doviak/Hudson-Edwards (this volume)

provide a thorough examination of the phonology of these children's English.

REFERENCES

Bills, Garland D. and Jacob Ornstein. 1976. Linguistic diversity in Southwest Spanish. Studies in Southwest Spanish, ed. by J. Donald Bowen and Jacob Ornstein. Rowley MA: Newbury House, pp. 4-16.

Doviak, Martin J. and Allison Hudson-Edwards. Phonological variation in Chicano English: word-final (z)-devoicing. (This volume.)

Fishman, Joshua A. and John E. Hofman. 1966. Mother tongue and nativity in the American population. Language loyalty in the United States, ed. by Joshua A. Fishman et al. The Hague: Mouton, pp. 34-50.

Johnson, Susan S. and Ann S. Yates. 1969. A joint report on a socio-economic and attitude survey: residents of the model neighborhood and the rest of Albuquerque. Albuquerque: City of Albuquerque and the Univ. of New Mexico.

Kravitz, Merryl. 1978. Grammatical judgments and standard Spanish in a Southwest community. The bilingual in a pluralistic society, ed. by Harold H. Key et al. Long Beach CA: California State Univ., pp. 76-87.

Labov, William. 1963. The social motivation of a sound change. Word 19.273-309.

López, David E. 1978. Chicano language loyalty in an urban setting. Sociology and Social Research 62.267-78.

Ortiz, Leroy I. 1975. A sociolinguistic study of language maintenance in the northern New Mexico community of Arroyo Seco. PhD Diss., Univ. of New Mexico.

Skrabanek, R.L. 1970. Language maintenance among Mexican-Americans. International Journal of Comparative Sociology 11.272-82.

Teitelbaum, Herta. 1976. Assessing bilingualism in elementary school children. PhD Diss., Univ. of New Mexico.

Thompson, Roger M. 1971. Language loyalty in Austin, Texas: a study of a bilingual neighborhood. PhD Diss., Univ. of Texas, Austin.

U.S. Bureau of the Census. 1971. Census of population: 1970. General social and economic characteristics. Final report, PC(1)-C33, New Mexico. Washington DC: U.S. Government Printing Office.

_____. 1972. Census of population and housing: 1970. Census tracts. Final report PHC(1)-5, Albuquerque, New Mexico, SMSA. Washington DC: U.S. Government Printing Office.

Vincent, María Girard. 1966. Ritual kinship in an urban setting: Martineztown, New Mexico. MA Thesis, Univ. of New Mexico.

Waggoner, Dorothy. 1976. Results of the survey of languages (supplement to the July 1975 current population survey). Unpublished paper read at the 5th International Bilingual Bicultural Education Conference, San Antonio TX.

CONTINUITY IN THE STUDY
OF SOCIOLOGICAL VARIETIES
OF LANGUAGE

WINFRED P. LEHMANN

The University of Texas at Austin

Among Jacob Ornstein's major contributions is his work on
the sociolinguistic situation in the Southwest, and his encour-
agement of others to participate in such work. In seeking "a
more exact description of the multilingualism of the area" he has
also hoped to avoid "becoming inextricably mired in theoretical
disputes raging in our field" (Ornstein 1969: 350). This hope
reflects some of the ambivalence that sociolinguistics had manifested in the field of linguistics. For example, Bloomfield's
Language, the theoretical work dominant at the time of Ornstein's
student days, placed sociolinguistics within historical linguistic
study. Bloomfield devotes several chapters to the topic, all in
the section on historical linguistics. Dialect geography, "the
study of local differentiation in a speech area...supplements the
use of the comparative method" (1933: 321). And the "various
features in the language of any one speaker" (1933: 444) are
treated in three chapters on borrowing which conclude the section
of Language devoted to historical linguistics. Sociolinguistics
then was a kind of supplement to one of the central sub-disci-
plines of linguistic study, through which one might gather data
without theoretical "disputes."
   Other linguists at the time located the field of linguistics
within sociolinguistic study, making it the larger field. Thus
Sommerfelt, trained in the school of Antoine Meillet, proposed in

his inaugural address on assuming his professorship that linguistics is a science sociologique (1932). Moreover, Sommerfelt's
major essay on the topic, "Language, society and culture" (1953),
assumes "there is today general agreement about the social nature
of language"; but like Ornstein he views the "more precise relations that exist between language, society and culture [as] controversial" (1962: 87). His essay proposes to clarify these relations. But such investigations regarding language and society
were soon eclipsed by the attention to generative transformational grammar.

In generative transformational grammar sociolinguistics was
virtually excluded from linguistic theory, inasmuch as this was
held to deal with the language of an ideal speaker, etc., according to the position so firmly propounded by Chomsky. Some
theoretical discussions continued, however, outside the transformational movement, which are not my primary concern here.
Rather, as Ornstein's contribution is reviewed, I reexamine the
position of earlier theoreticians with regard to the study of
language and its role in society.

The theoretician most explicit about language variation and
its effect on language is Hermann Paul, whose "Principles" have
unfortunately been neglected, in large part through overhasty reaction to Paul's treatment of the humanistic sciences as historical. A part of the neglect may be due to the shift of the center
of linguistic concern from Germany to France, shortly after the
time of Paul's 5th edition. The reaction against Paul is clear
in many publications, including Sommerfelt's (1962: 87-88). The
reasons for Paul's treatment will not be pursued here, apart from
the observation that all humanistic activities at the time were
treated historically rather than in abstraction from reality as
in generative transformational grammar, based in part on
Saussure's Cours. Much more pertinent insights into Paul's position may be gained from the concluding chapters in his Principles
on "mixture of languages" and a "common language." This conclusion of the major theoretical work through 40 and more years
of linguistic study demonstrates where Paul held one might "grasp
the actual processes of the life of language" (1891: 475). This
is not in history, in the sense of understanding language through
predecessors several millennia ago, but rather in its actual use,
where "as soon as any two individuals converse, a mixture of language is the result" (1891: 456). To understand language then,
a linguist must study the multiple forms of language used by
speakers, not simply the common language, let alone an ideal language, but language with interacting dialects as Ornstein proposes.

If this is indeed an accurate reading of Paul's Principles,
Paul by no means neglected the study of language in its social
setting. It is noteworthy too that Osthoff and Brugmann in their
neogrammarian manifesto recommend "a method of research" based
on a "clear idea of how human speech really lives, and develops"
(1976: 198). The conclusion of Paul's Principles indicates in
some detail what such a "clear idea" entails. It is remarkable

how closely this corresponds with the activities encouraged by
Ornstein.

In establishing goals for linguistic study at the end of
the 19th century, Paul found there was no phenomenon "of greater
importance than mixture of language" (1891: 456).   The first
avenue to its understanding is study of bilingualism, as in the
"situation of a community upon the confines of two linguistic
areas" (1891: 457).   One could scarcely find a more promising
community than that identified by Ornstein as the American Southwest (1971).   Yet clearly the position pursued by Paul was not
continued by linguists, at any rate until recently when it was
at least in part resumed.   In an effort to account for this lack
of continuity in theoretical linguistics, we may examine more
closely Paul's views and his aims, in contrast with those of his
successors.

Paul's discussion of the results of bilingualism can
scarcely be improved on.   A "person who speaks two languages
will...be liable to have each of these influenced by the other...
The influence of the [mother-tongue] will, as a rule, be stronger
than that of the [foreign language]" (1891: 459).   But if the
"foreign language and foreign culture is more highly prized than
the native language of the speaker," they may have a very strong
influence even on the native language.   The effects are spread
through a linguistic community, even to those who have no "direct contact with the foreign idiom" (1891: 459).   These effects
may be external, as in the adoption of words, or they may extend
to the "inner language form."   All these effects, phonological
as well as syntactic and semantic, are treated and exemplified.
Throughout the discussion in his second-last chapter, Paul develops the view that a mixture of language results as soon as
any two individuals converse.   Accordingly mixed languages are
the norm, whether in a bilingual or a monolingual community.   Inasmuch as "individual languages are the only ones which have any
real existence" (1891: 456), the study of language as used in
social groups is fundamental to an understanding of language.

While such importance is ascribed to "individual languages,"
Paul also recognizes "common languages," to which he devotes the
last chapter of his book on principles.   Such a common language
found "in all modern civilized countries" is however an "abstraction...merely an ideal norm prescribing rules for speech.   It has
the same kind of relationship to actual linguistic activity as
that of a particular code of laws to the entire legal activity in
the district to which the laws apply, or of a confession of faith,
or a dogmatic text-book, to the entirety of religious views and
feelings.   Regarded as such a norm, the common language, like a
code or dogma, is in itself unchangeable" (1901: 475).   In the
remainder of his last, relatively long chapter, Paul discusses
the sources of such a norm, in Germany the stage-language,
oftener the language of a particular area, as was Latin or the
Greek koine, and its use, both as a spoken and a written language, again in a completely unobjectionable manner.   He also admits change for the common language, as for legal codes and re-

ligious dogma; for in accordance with the last sentence of his
book, "development is inseparable from all linguistic activity"
(501). Nonetheless, even in change, the common language is not
the "natural language." Through education in modern societies,
individuals learn an "artificial" language nearer to the norm.
The "artificial" and the "common" languages are not to be ig-
nored, but linguistics is primarily concerned with the natural
language of the actual speaker-listener as it is used in society.

This position is no longer represented in a theoretical work
published four years before the final edition of Paul's Principles, Saussure's Cours de linguistique générale (1916). Like
generative transformational grammar, Saussure directed the primary attention of linguistics to langue rather than the natural
language of the individual. While "the subject matter of linguistics comprises all manifestations of human speech," the focus is clearly on langue, "the conventions that have been adopted
by a social body" (1919: 6, 10). Saussure's statement is not as
absolute as Chomsky's (1965: 5). Yet linguists are directed
away from the "natural language." The great influence of
Saussure was to have a significant impact on sociolinguistics.

The topics which we associate with sociolinguistic study
are one by one dismissed, when Saussure distinguishes between
internal and external elements of language, and excluded everything known as "external linguistics." Such matters as "the relations between language and political history" are admitted to
be important, as well as "the coexistence of several idioms."
To external linguistics he assigns also "conflicts" between the
literary language and local dialects, "geographical spreading of
languages and dialectal splitting." Though he admits that "the
study of external linguistic phenomena is most fruitful...to say
that we cannot understand the internal linguistic organism without studying external phenomena is wrong." (1959: 20-22)
Saussure concludes his insistence on "mandatory...separation of
the two viewpoints" with one of his well-known references to
chess. Only the system matters. Linguistics was set on its de-
dication to "what is internal."

As is widely known, Saussure's Cours had a delayed impact.
The effective expulsion of sociolinguistics was also gradual. We
have already noted Sommerfelt's maintenance of the views propounded by Meillet. A similar position is advanced by Jespersen,
especially in his genial little book Mankind, Nation and the Individual (1946). Jespersen had however read Saussure, and accordingly his position is diluted. Yet he goes to great pains
to point to the social side of language. By speech "the one person comes in contact with the other. All human beings are im-
pelled to seek the society of others...and that is where language helps" (1946: 9).

While he refers to Saussure's distinction between speech and
language and approves of it, his interpretation of Saussure puts
his own views into Saussure's mouth. Langue he sees as "the social side of the matter, something which the individual must take
as he finds it" (1946: 12). But as to the "distinction between

Speech and Language...[he feels] that they have got hold of a
truth but have unmistakably run it to extremes, and that it will
be well for us to bring things into their right relation."
(1946: 15) These, as Jespersen sees them, lie "in Saussure's remark that Language is the sum of the word-pictures that are stored
in the soul of all the individuals...But then...we have not established a gulf between 'language' and 'speech'" (17). Moreover, "speech is socially conditioned: an individual is never
completely isolated from his surroundings, and in every utterance of 'la parole' there is a social element" (19). Paul's
"common language," which Jespersen refers to as "national language" is "a sort of average of individual-tongues" (20). Where-
ever the linguist deals with language he finds "common to all...
the mutual play of individual and community" (1946: 220). In
short, Saussure's distinction between speech and language has
been sharply reduced. The linguist does not confine himself to
"what is internal" but must deal with language in society.

In this regard Jespersen was influenced by the anthropolo-
gist, Malinowski, who also had a strong influence on Firth. In
his little book, The Tongues of Men, Firth expresses views similar to those of Jespersen. "The study of meaning brings in
overwhelming masses of 'non-lingustic facts', such as the
people, things, and events in the context of situation...Seman-
tics requires a new sociological technique unobscured by categories serving any other purpose" (87-88). And he concludes his
book with general statements, such as the following: "The approach to speech must consequently be chiefly sociological"
(1964: 135). Yet in spite of the positions of Jespersen and
Firth, the viewpoint of Saussure prevailed. Linguistics concentrated on langue. This concentration obviates a sociological
approach. Subsequently linguistics and what was to become known
as sociolinguistics went their separate ways.

The gulf is now being reduced, but on different grounds from
those found in Paul, and subsequently in Jespersen and Firth.
Today sociolinguists are proposing that langue, or competence,
includes variable rules. Further, that speakers do not master
simply an "ideal language" but one which involves variation which
they interpret in accordance with statistical procedures. This
view has been most forcefully stated by Labov, according to whom
"human linguistic competence includes quantitative contrasts as
well as discrete ones" (1978: 13). If this view prevails, sociological varieties of language will once again be a concern of
linguistic theory. The problems treated by Paul, and by Ornstein, will be central to linguistic research. Saussure's theoretical position will be seen as an interruption in the study
of sociological varieties of language; this in turn will fill a
large role in the effort to understand the phenomenon of language.

REFERENCES

Bloomfield, Leonard. 1933. Language. New York: Holt.
Currie, Haver C. 1952. A projection of sociolinguistics: The
   relationship of speech to social status. Southern Speech
   Journal 18:28-37. [This is the first proposal of socio-
   linguistics.]
Firth, J. R. 1964. The tongues of men and speech. London: Ox-
   ford Univ. Press. [First published in 1937]
Jespersen, Otto. 1946. Mankind, nation and individual. London:
   Allen and Unwin. [The first printing in England of lectures
   given two decades earlier.]
Labov, William. 1978. Where does the linguistic variable stop?
   Sociolinguistic Working Paper 44. Austin: Southwest Educa-
   tional Development Laboratory.
Ornstein, Jacob. 1969. Language varieties along the U.S.-Mexican
   border. Applications of Linguistics: Selected papers of the
   Second International Congress of Applied Linguistics, ed.
   G.E. Perren and L.J.M. Trim, pp. 349-62. 1971. Cambridge:
   Cambridge Univ. Press.
_____. 1971. Sociolinguistic research on language di-
   versity in the American Southwest and its educational implications. Modern Language Journal 60.223-229.
_____. 1977. (With William F. Mackey and others.) The
   bilingual education movement: Essays on its progress. El
   Paso: Texas Western Press.
Osthoff, Hermann and Otto Brugmann. Preface to morphological investigation in the sphere of the Indo-European languages.
   (Trans. by Judith Haddon Bills.) A reader in nineteenth
   century historical Indo-European linguistics, ed. W. P.
   Lehmann, pp. 197-209. Bloomington: Indiana Univ. Press,
   1967.
Paul, Hermann. 1920. 5th ed. Prinzipien der sprachgeschichte.
   Halle: Neimeyer. (English translation: Principles of the
   history of language, trans. by H. A. Strong. London: Longmans, Green, 1891.)
Saussure, Ferdinand de. 1916. Cours de linguistique générale.
   Paris: Payot (1949). (English translation: Course in
   general linguistics, trans. by Wade Baskin. New York: Philosophical Library, 1959.)
Sommerfelt, Alf. 1962. Diachronic and synchronic aspects of language. The Hague: Mouton.

LA ESTRUCTURA DEL DISCURSO
EN CINCO ESCRITORES MEXICANOS

JUAN M. LOPE BLANCH

Universidad Nacional Autónoma de México / El Colegio de México

En otra ocasión he analizado rápidamente la estructura de la
lengua hablada, tanto en su manifestación popular cuanto en su
modalidad culta, y he constatado las diferencias más notables que
se advierten entre las cláusulas típicas de la expresión popular
y las del habla culta.[1] Quisiera presentar aquí, también muy
sucintamente, los resultados obtenidos a través de una confrontación de textos breves escritos por autores mexicanos de nuestro
tiempo. Ante todo, debo advertir que los resultados estadísticos
a que he llegado son de validez muy provisional, dado que, siendo
mi propósito fundamental ensayar un método de trabajo, más que
analizar pormenorizadamente los diversos estilos, el corpus de que
me he servido es de extensión muy reducida y no permitiría llegar
a conclusiones firmes ni definitivas.
He hecho el análisis sintáctico de dos fragmentos de novelas
o ensayos escritos por Alfonso Reyes, Martín Luis Guzmán, Agustín
Yáñez, Octavio Paz y Juan Rulfo. Como es natural, y dados los pro-
pósitos comparativos del trabajo, los textos estudiados tienen
todos la misma extensión.[2] La cual, a su vez, es equiparable a la
de los pasajes de la lengua hablada analizados en el artículo citado en la nota 1.
Las unidades lingüísticas de que me he servido para hacer el
análisis de esos textos han sido las siguientes:
  I. UNIDADES FORMALES
      A. Estructuras oracionales
          1. Oración: Unidad gramatical básica. Estructura

bimembre de carácter predicativo (del tipo que
Karl Bühler simbolizó mediante el esquema
[S → P]. Ejemplos: "Los hombres hablan";
"F. estaba agotado"; "Las cuentas, claras";
"Año de nieves, año de bienes"; "Los niños,
delante".

   2. Período: Sintagma bioracional o, a veces,
plurioracional en que se establece una relación sintáctica inmediata entre sus dos--o más--
miembros. Los períodos pueden formarse por
coordinación o por subordinación. Normalmente
son bimembres: período adversativo ("Se lo
dije, pero no me creyó"); período objetivo
("Te ruego que vengas"); período adjetivo
("Compré el libro que me recomendaste"); período condicional ("Si vienes, te lo daré"), etc.
A veces, pueden ser plurimembres: período copulativo ("Volvió a su casa, cenó frugalmente,
se dio un baño y se acostó en seguida"); período disyuntivo ("O me lo devuelves, o me lo
pagas o no te vuelvo a prestar nada").[3]

B. Estructuras no oracionales
   1. Frases: Expresión autosemántica no articulada
en [S] y [P], del tipo "Una limosna, por cari-
dad"; "¡La emoción de un viaje en barco!";
"Tanto trabajo para nada".
   2. Pro-oración: Lexema o sintagma que implica (reproduce mentalmente) la estructura oracional
expresada anteriormente. Ejemplos: "¿Quieres
café o té? -- Café."; "¿Dónde nos reuniremos?
-- En mi casa"; "Creo que lo hiciste tú. --
Sí."

II. UNIDAD DE MANIFESTACIÓN
   Cláusula: Expresión de sentido completo; esto es, elocu-
ción que "manifiesta cumplidamente el concibimiento
del hombre en el propósito que tiene tomado para
hablar".[4] Puede estar integrada por una sola oración, por uno o varios períodos, por una o varias
frases o pro-oraciones, o por alguna combinación
de estas diferentes estructuras expresivas. Ejemplos de esto último: "Tanto trabajo para nada,
pero no me desanimo, porque tengo fe en el porvenir"
o bien "Al llegar al atrio, nos asaltó una multitud
de mendigos que gritaban: '¡Una limosna, por cari-
dad!'"

La clasificación de los períodos utilizada en el análisis
de los textos es la siguiente:
A. Períodos paratácticos:
   1. Copulativo: "Estudia y trabaja".
   2. Ilativo y declarativo: "No lo creo, así que
puedes callarte".
   3. Distributivo: "Unos cantaban, otros bailaban,

otros dormían".
4. Adversativo: "Fui a su casa, pero no estaba".
5. Disyuntivo: "Me lo das o te pego".
B. Períodos hipotácticos:
    1. Sustantivo
       a. Sujetivo: "Quien calla, otorga".
       b. Predicativo: "Él fue quien lo dijo".
       c. Objetivo: "No creo que venga".
       d. Indirecto: "Se lo daré a quien termine antes".
       e. Prepositivo: "Me convenció de que lo hiciera".
       f. Adnominal: "Tengo miedo de que venga".
    2. Adjetivo
       a. Explicativo: "Se lo di a tu hermano, que tenía frío".
       b. Especificativo: "Aquí está el libro que me prestaste".
    3. Adverbial
       a. Circunstancial
          i. Temporal: "Lo haré cuando pueda".
          ii. Modal: "Lo haré como me enseñaron".
          iii. Locativo: "Lo haré donde sea más seguro".
       b. Cuantitativo
          i. Comparativo: "Trabajo más que tú".
          ii. Consecutivo: "Llovió tanto que todo se inundó".
       c. Causativo
          i. Causal: "Llora porque tiene hambre".
          ii. Final: "Llora para que le den su comida".
          iii: Condicional: "Si vienes, te lo enseñaré".
          iv. Concesivo: "Aunque lo jures, no te creerán".

Siguiendo estos principios de análisis, los resultados obtenidos--bastante sintomáticos, en mi opinión--han sido los siguientes:[5]

	A. Reyes		M.L. Guzmán		A. Yáñez		O. Paz		J. Rulfo		Lengua literaria	
Cláusulas	9		15		15		15		28		78	
Oraciones	39		52		51		43		63		248	
Promedio	4.3		3.5		3.4		3.9		2.2		3.2	
Relación entre cláusulas (Total)[6]	Nº	%	Nº	%	Nº	%	Nº	%	Nº	%	Nº	%
	7		13		13		9		26		68	
Yuxtaposición	6	85.7	10	76.9	12	92.3	6	66.7	21	80.8	55	80.9
Coordinación copulativa	-	-	-	-			1	11.1	3	11.5	4	5.9
" ilativa	-	-	-	-	-	-	1	11.1	-	-	1	1.5
" distributiva	.	-	1	7.7	-	-					1	1.5
" adversativa	1	14.3	1	7.7	1	7.7	1	11.2	2	7.7	6	8.8
Relación causativa	-	-	1	7.7	-	-	-	-	-	-	1	1.5
Total rel. nexual	1	14.3	3	23.1	1	7.7	3	33.3	5	19.2	13	19.1
Relación entre oraciones (Total)[6]	37		50		49		41		61		238	
Yuxtaposición	6	16.2	13	26	14	28.6	9	21.9	24	39.3	66	27.7
Períodos copulativos	4	10.8	10	20	9	18.4	6	14.6	8	13.1	37	15.5
" ilativos	-	-	-	-	-	-	1	2.4	1	1.6	2	0.8
" distributivos	-	-	1	2	-	-					1	0.4
" adversativos	1	2.7	1	2	3	6.1	3	7.3	5	8.2	13	5.5
" disyuntivos	-	-	-	-	1	2.0	-	-	-	-	1	0.4
Total yuxt. y coord.	11	29.7	25	50	27	55.1	19	46.3	38	62.3	120	50.4

	A. Reyes		M.L. Guzmán		A. Yáñez		O. Paz		J. Rulfo		Lengua literaria	
Períodos sujetivos	4	10.8	1	2	-		2	4.9	2	3.3	9	3.8
" objetivos	4	10.8	4	8	3	6.1	5	12.2	3	8.2	21	8.8
" indirectos	-		1	2	-		-		-		1	0.4
" adnominales	1	2.7	3	6	-		2	4.9	2	3.3	8	3.4
Total sustant.	9	24.3	9	18	3	6.1	9	21.9	9	14.8	39	16.4
Períodos adjet. explicativos	8	21.6	2	4	8	16.3	2	4.9	1	1.6	21	8.8
" " especificativos	5	13.5	6	12	3	6.1	6	14.6	3	4.9	23	9.7
Total adjet.	13	35.1	8	16	11	22.4	8	19.5	4	6.6	44	18.5
Períodos temporales	3	8.1	1	2	4	8.2	1	2.4	1	1.6	10	4.2
" modales	-		3	6	3	6.1	-		6	9.8	12	5.0
" consecutivos	-		1	2	-		-		-		1	0.4
" causales	1	2.7	1	2	-		-		1	1.6	2	0.8
" finales	-		2	4	1	2.0	2	4.9	2	3.3	8	3.4
" condicionales	-		-		-		1	2.4	-		1	0.4
" concesivos	-		-		-		1	2.4	-		1	0.4
Total adverb.	4	10.8	8	16	8	16.3	5	12.2	10	16.4	35	14.7
Total subordinación	26	70.3	25	50	22	44.9	22	53.7	23	37.7	118	49.6
Índice S^7	73%		54%		53.1%		61%		45.9%		55.9%	

Observaciones.

Una rápida confrontación de los datos reunidos en este cuadro estadístico permite hacer algunas consideraciones interesantes.

I) La estructura del discurso varía notablemente según que pertenezca a textos novelísticos o a ensayos.

1) En promedio, el número de cláusulas que integran los textos novelísticos (19)[8] es muy superior al de los ensayos (10),[9] lo cual significa que la cláusula de este último género literario es mucho más amplia que la de la novela, como hubiera cabido imaginar.

2) Ello depende de la mayor complejidad sintáctica de la cláusula usual en el ensayo. En efecto, la cláusula de Alfonso Reyes está integrada por un promedio de 4.3 oraciones gramaticales, y la de Octavio Paz, por 3.9 oraciones (promedio 4.1), en tanto que la de Yáñez abarca sólo 3.4 oraciones, la de Guzmán 3.5 y la de Rulfo 2.2 (promedio de 3 oraciones por cláusula). Todo ello implica, obviamente, que la oración usada por los ensayistas es más amplia--presenta más sintagmas complementarios--que la de los novelistas, la cual es más escueta, más descarnada.[10]

3) Los períodos hipotácticos son más frecuentes en el ensayo (70.3% en Reyes y 53.7% en Paz; promedio: 62%) que en la novela (44.9% en Yáñez, 50% en Guzmán y sólo 37.7% en Rulfo; promedio: 44.2%). En cambio, la yuxtaposición de oraciones es mucho más común en el estilo de los novelistas (promedio de 31.3%) que en el de los ensayistas (promedio de 19%).[11]

II) Las diferencias de estructura sintáctica entre unos autores y otros es, a veces, considerable:

1) Los estilos de Alfonso Reyes y de Juan Rulfo--en lo que a la estructura de la expresión se refiere--son casi antitéticos. En los textos de uno y otro considerados--de idéntica extensión, por supuesto--, Reyes organiza sólo 9 cláusulas, y Rulfo 29, o sea, más del triple. La precisión pormenorizada del ensayista (a través de cláusulas y oraciones amplias, complejas) frente a la pincelada sintética, impresionista, del narrador.

2) La naturaleza misma de la cláusula difiere notablemente en Rulfo y Reyes. Se sirve el primero de la yuxtaposición en un 39.3% de los casos, en tanto que Reyes sólo la utiliza en un 16.2% de las ocasiones. En contrapartida, la subordinación oracional duplica en la prosa de Reyes (70.3%) a la usual en Rulfo (37.7%).

3) También se observan acusadas discrepancias entre los tipos de subordinación preferidos por uno y otro escritor. Los períodos modales, que en Rulfo representan un 9.8% de las relaciones oracionales en total, no aparecen en los textos de Reyes ni una sola vez. En cambio, la subordinación adjetiva, que en la prosa de Reyes alcanza un pasmoso 35.1%, en la de Rulfo apenas llega a un modesto 6.6%.

4) Octavio Paz es, de los cinco escritores aquí considerados, el que mayor número de relaciones nexuales establece entre unas cláusulas y otras (33.3%), en tanto que Agustín Yáñez apenas recurre a esa forma de expresión (7.7%).

5) Juan Rulfo es, sin duda, el autor de estilo más di-
ferenciado. En un buen número de ocasiones, su sintaxis se aparta
de la de los demás escritores, para aproximarse nítidamente a las
estructuras propias de la expresión popular, de la lengua hablada
por el pueblo: cláusulas muy breves (constituidas en promedio por
sólo dos oraciones gramaticales) y frases u oraciones escuetas, in-
tensas, esenciales. Yuxtaposiciones frecuentes (39.3%), como en
el habla popular (41.6%); subordinaciones oracionales escasas
(37.7%), a la manera de los hablantes populares (30.#%); y, dentro
de ellas, subordinación adjetiva muy esporádica (6.6%), aún más
ocasional que en la sintaxis del pueblo (8.5%). Sin embargo, esta
aparente sencillez de la prosa de Rulfo no impide que en su construc-
ción sintáctica se produzca una elevada variedad de relaciones. De
los cinco escritores estudiados, sólo Martín Luis Guzmán le supera
en cuanto a la diversidad de los períodos incluidos en sus respec-
tivos textos: 15 clases de relación oracional en este último, y
13 en Rulfo, mientras que tanto en Agustín Yáñez como en Alfonso
Reyes sólo encuentro 10 tipos de relación.

6) El análisis sintáctico del texto literario permite
también apreciar la variedad interna del estilo individual. No
obstante la brevedad de las muestras aquí estudiadas, hallamos
claros testimonios de ello. Martín Luis Guzmán, por ejemplo, se
sirve en un momento dado (Muestra A) de 4 cláusulas consecutivas
formada cada una de ellas por una sola oración, para desbocarse in-
mediatamente después en una gigantesca cláusula constituida por 13
oraciones gramaticales. Y Agustín Yáñez, por su parte, organiza
la primera de las muestras consideradas con sólo 19 oraciones, dis-
tribuidas en 6 cláusulas, en tanto que en el otro pasaje--de igual
extensión que el primero--se sirve de un total de 32 oraciones gramaticales, correspondientes a 9 cláusulas. Sería necesario analizar con detenimiento la relación que puede existir entre estructura
sintáctica y situación argumental.

III) Desde un punto de vista exclusivamente gramatical, los
textos analizados también parecen proporcionar informaciones interesantes:

1) Aparte de la simple coordinación copulativa, los tipos
de relación oracional más comunes y frecuentes en nuestra lengua
parecen ser la adversación, la adjetivación y las subordinaciones
temporal y final. Períodos de esta naturaleza han aparecido en
todas las muestras analizadas, y en proporción nada desdeñable.

2) La relación adversativa, que entre oraciones alcanza
un 5.5% de promedio, es--además--la única que todos nuestros escritores establecen entre cláusulas contiguas.

3) Proporcionalmente, la subordinación adjetiva es la
más empleada en español literario (18.5%), tanto con función ex-
plicativa (8.8%), como especificativa (9.7%).

4) También los períodos temporales aparecen en todos los
textos estudiados, si bien permiten apreciar considerables diferencias entre la inclinación de unos u otros escritores hacia su
empleo: en tanto que Agustín Yáñez los utiliza con alta frecuencia
(8.2%), Octavio Paz restringe su uso (2.4%), y Juan Rulfo parece
evitarlos (1.6%).

5) La finalidad es, asimismo, consideración presente en el pensamiento de todos los escritores, aunque con frecuencia más baja (3.4%), pero en cambio la causalidad--que parece ser factor primordial en la lengua hablada[12]--apenas alcanza un índice de frecuencia del 0.8%, y no halla acogida en los textos de tres de los autores analizados: Reyes, Paz y Yáñez.

Al terminar estas breves y rápidas consideraciones--presionado por los límites impuestos a esta contribución--, no quiero dejar de insistir en el carácter enteramente provisional y sólo sintomático de los resultados obtenidos. Véase en estas páginas--repito--un simple ensayo exploratorio de un método de trabajo que podría ser provechoso en el análisis de ciertos aspectos del estilo literario. Pero de ninguna manera, un repertorio de conclusiones definidas y seguras.

NOTAS

[1]Véase Gramática y aprendizaje de la lengua materna, que se publicará en el Boletín de la Academia Puertorriqueña de la Lengua.

[2]Los fragmentos analizados pertenecen a las obras siguientes: A. Reyes, Cuestiones gongorinas, en la edición de Obras completas VII, México: Fondo de Cultura Económica, 1958, p. 156 (Muestra A), y Entre libros, en la misma edición y volumen, p. 259 (Muestra B); M.L. Guzmán, La sombra del caudillo, 5ª ed., México, Compañía General de Ediciones, 1957, pp. 44-45 (Muestra A) y pp. 232-233 (Muestra B); A. Yáñez, Al filo del agua, México, Editorial Porrúa, 1955, p. 22 (Muestra A) y p. 177 (Muestra B); O. Paz, El laberinto de la soledad, México, Cuadernos Americanos, 1950, p. 20 (Muestra A) y p. 108 (Muestra B); J. Rulfo, Pedro Páramo, México: Fondo de Cultura Económica, 1955, pp. 23-24 (Muestra A), y p. 146 (Muestra B).

[3]Está por demás decir que corresponde a lo que se suele llamar "oración compuesta", nombre este último un tanto equívoco y que creo que podría reservarse para dos tipos especiales de períodos: el sujetivo y el predicativo solamente. Tal vez pudiera añadirse un tercer tipo: el objetivo.

[4]Esta definición--difícilmente superable en su esencia--es la que proporcionó, ya en 1558, el Licenciado Villalón en su excelente Gramática castellana, publicada en Amberes. Cito por la reimpresión facsimilar de Constantino García, Madrid, 1971; ver p. 85.

[5]En la presentación de los datos estadísticos sigo una disposición similar a la que utilicé en el artículo citado en la nota #1. Así resultará fácil hacer la comparación entre las estructuras propias de la lengua hablada y de la escrita.

[6]La oración regente de cada cláusula (situada por lo general al comienzo de ella) no establece normalmente, como es lógico, re-

lación sintáctica alguna, pues no se vincula sintácticamente con ninguna otra oración a que pudiera determinar.

[7]Dentro de este índice S incluyo todas las combinaciones sintácticas que implican una relación significativa, que va más allá de la simple adición por yuxtaposición o por coordinación copulativa o ilativa. Una relación adversativa, por ejemplo, es tan pertinente, desde el punto de vista semántico, como puede serlo una causal o una comparativa.

[8]Esto es: 15 cláusulas en Agustín Yáñez, también 15 en Martín Luis Guzmán y 28 en Juan Rulfo.

[9]Sólo 9 cláusulas en Alfonso Reyes y 11 en Octavio Paz.

[10]En los textos de Reyes figuran sólo 39 oraciones gramaticales, y 43 en los de Paz (promedio: 41 oraciones), en tanto que Guzmán organiza 52 oraciones, Yáñez 51 y Rulfo 63 (promedio: 55).

[11]En Guzmán, 26%; en Yáñez, 28.6% y en Rulfo 39.3%, mientras que en Reyes es sólo de un 16.2%, y en Paz, de un 21.9%.

[12]Cf. los resultados obtenidos en el artículo citado en la nota 1: subordinación causal = 6.4%.

ENGLISH TENSE DEVELOPMENT
IN A SPANISH-DOMINANT CHILD

ANTHONY GERARD LOZANO

University of Colorado

Professor Jacob Ornstein has been one of the pioneers in the
study of bilingual phenomena and languages in contact in the American Southwest. We are pleased to follow in this tradition and
hope to show the viability and importance of such studies not
only to bilingual and sociolinguistic studies but also as theore-
ical contributions to linguistics. The following paper presents
observations on the acquisition of English by a Spanish-dominant
child. It pertains specifically to the acquisition of English ·
past and future tense and the processes which are involved. The
bilingual English/Spanish child is a product of the American
Southwest. By understanding the characteristics of the bilingual
child, we gain a deeper understanding of bilingual phenomena and
languages in contact since the child is not only the object of
study but the agent of future change.

Although this study is limited to two tenses and to 14
months, it involves a number of variables which complicate the
study. It is complex since it involves, in addition to others,
two variables: (1) time and (2) grammatical structures as they
appear at a given point. Let us take, for example, the past
tense in English including the auxiliary for negation as in the
past tense, e.g., "He didn't do it." Also involved are the auxiliaries for questions: "Could he do it?" We must also include

perfective terms, such as, "Has he done it?" A number of grammatical features are involved if the investigator considers just one of the tenses. Our topic involves a small child, who in November 1978 was five years, four months old, and four years, one month old when the study began in September 1977. We are dealing with the English speech of a child, and in a situation where English is the second language for the child. In itself the bilinguality of the child involves complex questions.

Three semantic categories were selected at the outset: past, present, and future. The categorization of specific examples is not easy, particularly when the child goes through processes of pidginization at the beginning, where there is interference from the other language, and where inter-language phenomena are concerned. A bilingual child who is learning the second language goes through a number of processes which are normal in the acquisition of a second langauge by anyone, but which are clearly seen displayed in this particular time span which covers approximately 14 months.

In a paper to appear in the Bilingual Review ("English-learning Strategies of the Spanish Dominant Child"), several such strategies are mentioned--pidginization, interference, inter-language, near-standard usages, and standard usages. These occur within the context of three language codes: English, Spanish and inter-language. These five processes do form a kind of sequence. However, it is not possible on an analysis of the data so far to be able to make statements as firm as those made by Dulay and Burt (1972, 1974) about invariant sequentiality in acquisition of grammatical patterns. It is not easy to say, definitively, that one given language structure (i.e., a given pattern) is learned before the next. There are general patternings that seem to occur. These processes I mentioned do seem to fall into a sequence, but obviously are very general patterns--pidginization, interference, inter-language, near-standard usages, and finally, standard usages. It is difficult to establish precisely the stages in the development.

The study is of Angélica, our own daughter. She started learning English at the age of four years, one month. That was in September 1977. In November 1978, she was still in the process of acquiring English. An overview is provided by examining the two appendices which present excerpts from her English development. Included are examples of future tense and substitutions for the future tense, use of past tense and substitutes for past tense. A tentative inclusion was made of substitutes for the future since it was hypothesized that an examination of the child's use of the concept of 'future' would explain constructions such as "I want you make her, my dolly". This is an example of a future concept which is not normally included in the study of 'future tense.' From a semantic viewpoint, we are probably dealing with elements of future tense. One should recall that there is a Spanish subjunctive which can be considered an unaccomplished subjunctive, an action that has not yet been realized. For example, Lo haré cuando llegue. The verb, llegue,

is explained as an action that has not yet been realized. Other
examples of construction with elements of futurity could also be
given. Another example with future meaning is "gonna" as in
"I'm gonna pick him up" (April 20, 1978).

As concerns the pidginization process, it occurred very
early, and ceased to be used in the sixth month. Other processes
have replaced it as of this writing. In the early recordings
(October 19, 23, 25, 1977) there appeared phrases such as "I'm
the water". Her intent was to say, "I'm going to the pool." At
that stage it was clearly pidginization. There is no way one
could interpret the latter unless the listener knew what the context was. Similar examples are "I want outside" (= I want to go
outside). From a study on negation (Alonso de Lozano, ms.) we
extract examples not pertaining to verbal tense but nonetheless
germane to the question of pidginization such as "Dana, no book,"
meaning "Dana, don't open the book." Pidginization, then, was
clearly an early phenomenon. Dulay and Burt would like to de-
emphasize the notion of interference as being the most important
facet in second language acquisition by a small child. However,
our data suggest that a stage occurred where one could identify
a process of interference. In other words, once pidginization
was out of the way, the next step was to use a grammatical structure taken directly from Spanish where the negation was simply
with a preverbal 'no' plus verb: "No do it," meaning "Don't do
it." A construction such as this was patently based on Spanish
syntax. Once pidginization ceased to be operant, the child went
on to what is generally known as the 'inter-language' stage in
which elements of both languages are perhaps involved but which
cannot be clearly established as either pidginization or interference. This is the stage that Burt and Dulay emphasize, a
stage of examples they term "unique features."

Let us turn now to the past tense which illustrates more
clearly some of the processes that occur since they are more
clearly identifiable. One of the problems involved in analyzing
future tense is that the overlap between future and present tense
in English is substantial. In fact there are many studies of
English based on the division of 'past/non-past.' Then non-past
is further divided up into present/non-present or present/future.
English, of course, does not have a clearly marked future tense
as does Spanish. Of course English has "I will do it," and furthermore possesses all semantic possibilities for the expression
of futurity; yet futurity is not as clearly marked as in Spanish
(e.g., Lo haré, Lo harás, Lo hará, etc.). In Spanish the para-
phrastic future ('voy a hacerlo') is probably used more frequently
than 'lo haré.' Child language probably demonstrates the para-
phrastic future for Spanish and the translation into English:
"I'm going to (= gonna) do it," "He's going to (= gonna) do it,"
etc.

In the data, past tense is not clearly established in the
early months--"One day this school snow" (October 11, 1977),
glossed as "One day it snowed at this school." Note also: "I
look in this book"--'I looked in this book.' A likely source of

present tense forms with past tense glosses is of course the
phonological grammar of Spanish, the child's dominant language,
since few consonants occur in Spanish in word-final position,
whereas many do in English. Obviously the semantic weight of
the consonant in word-final position is quite important for regular English past tense, e.g. "He walked, He talked." Thus we
realize that the phonological interference from Spanish is crucial. In other words, the Spanish-dominant child cannot produce
phonologically the word-final consonants in English at the outset of his learning. That may be one of the reasons why past
tense forms do not occur very frequently in the early months.
    There were two forms which would be identified after num-
erous examinations of the data. She said either, "I finish" or
"I finished [my picture]." It is impossible to say whether it
was present or past. Similarly the context was not clear for
"I put it right here." Does she mean past by put? It is not
possible to say definitely since put is glossable as either
'past' or 'present.' These forms, recorded on the 30th of November, 1977, were the only ones found in those first few months
that could be said to even remotely resemble the past tense.
    We begin to see a clearer appearance of the past tense six
months later. At that time a number of things took place. Here
are data from March and April, 1978: it was, we're [= we were]
making, opened, didn't want, didn't say, didn't have, did he
has, has seen, he was died. As to closed, a question mark in
the notes indicates a lack of clarity as to close or closed.
    The following forms appeared in a later stage with a past
tense meaning: run, eated, fall, wake, make, went, have, buy,
and took. In other words, the subject produced a number of irregular pasts. However, she has not rendered them phonologically
in the standard way. She has used the present instead of the irregular past forms of English.
    Approximately two months later, in late June and early July,
we begin to see a shift where she starts using the standard irregular past tenses. She says took, went, came, said, have, had,
didn't like, didn't do, didn't get, was, was going, we weren't,
was getting, was snowing.
    A later stage was observed on November 4, 1978: we have,
we scared, was, wanted, worked, forgot, did, went, found, said,
gave. But she has not quite mastered all of them; note the
following: He falled yesterday, He come yesterday. However, she
also produced: got, came out, brought, woke. In this stage she
is shifting into more standard usages of the language.
    A hypothesis that has been suggested is called the "inter-
ference hypothesis." This is the one that Burt and Dulay dis-
credited to some extent because they claim it is not that important, and there is another one called the "creative-construc-
tion hypothesis" where the individual creates new forms which
are based on both his languages. In fact both processess are involved, and each must be considered in any study of child language. Burt and Dulay also claim the existence of what they term
"invariant ordering," by means of which one particular grammar

feature occurs chronologically before another one, regardless of the language spoken. Even in the case of English and Spanish, which are both Indo-European languages, the details surrounding just one set of features such as regular and irregular forms, phonological interference and overlapping stages suggest that a claim in support of invariant ordering is questionable. An invariant ordering can readily be sidetracked by irregular forms, interference and semantic overlapping. When one considers the differences in syntax and semantics between two generally unrelated languages, invariant ordering becomes even more tenuous. The data show that general processing of development occur, but not in a lock-step method.

REFERENCES

Alonso de Lozano, Leticia. 1979. Strategies of a four year old girl learning English. (Manuscript.)

Dulay, H. C., and M. K. Burt. 1972. Goofing: An indicator of children's second language learning strategies. Language Learning 22.235-252.

Dulay, H. D., and M. K. Burt. 1974. You can't learn without goofing: An analysis of children's second language errors. Error analysis: Perspectives on second language learning, ed. by J. Richards. London: Longman.

Lozano, Anthony G. English learning strategies of a Spanish-dominant child. To appear in The Bilingual Review (circa 1980.)

Papers in second language acquisition: Proceedings of the Sixth Annual Conference on Applied Linguistics. 1976. Language Learning 26:4.

APPENDIX I

Use of Future Tense and Substitutes for the Future

Oct. 19, 1977   1. I'm the water. (I'm going to go to the pool.)
Oct. 23, 1977   1. I want outside.
Oct. 25, 1977   1. I'm going close the door.

Nov. 4, 1977   1. Amy, let's go like that. (Kneading sand like
                     bread.)
                 2. Daddy, I want you come now.
                 3. Can I have it?
                 4. I don't know want more.
Nov. 8, 1977   1. I going happy birthday. (I'm going to a birth-
                     day party.)
Nov. 24, 1977   1. You want doing for me cookies.(?)
Nov. 27, 1977   1. I go to sleep.(?)
                 2. I want go to sleep.
                 3. Please don't put your mask, it's scary.
Nov. 29, 1977   1. One day my birthday.
                 2. Is going the school one day.
Dec. 8, 1977   1. Are you please the table for me? (Will you
                     please set the table for me?)
                 2. I want you do it right here.
Apr. 6, 1978   1. Maybe he can turn in a butterfly.
                 2. I'm going to see the Man About the Mancha. (She
                     went that night.)
Apr. 23, 1978   1. You go hide there.
Apr. 30, 1978   1. I want you make (draw) her, my dolly.
                 2. I'll put her right here.
                 3. I'm gonna go pick him up. (Her pretend little
                     boy.)
                 4. I'm going to take the children to a party.
                 5. That's why he (Papa) not going.
June 1, 1978   1. Me and Jennika are going to go to Mexico.
                 2. I'm gonna try to make a new butterfly.
                 3. Sometimes you Daddy stay.(?)
                 4. I going swimming too.
                 5. Can I play with you?

June 27, 1978   1. I(ng) go get some more.
                 2. If you put more, it gets up to here.
                 3. Let's pretend we're going to make Cool-Aid.

July 8, 1978   1. I'm gonna eat you up.
                 2. I'm gonna read it myself.
                 3. Give me your hand and we'll get married.
                     (Repeated after her Dad.)

Uses of the Future Tense and Substitutes of the Future (cont.)

Nov. 4, 1978   1. I want you to help me find this stuff. (Bottle
                     caps)

2. I do want to go with my aunt Lisa.
3. Will you help me look for pennies under here?
4. I put mine in here. (Will put)
5. Make it go round this way.
6. I know what we could pick up.
7. I hope it feels good.
8. Can we invite Jennika to my house today?
9. Would you put on her pants?

Use of Past Tense and Substitutes for Past Tense

Oct. 11, 1977	1.	One day this school snow.
Nov. 8, 1977	1.	You put that.
Nov. 23, 1977	1.	I look in this book.(?)
Nov. 29, 1977	1.	Papa: Did Marina go to Mexico?
		Angelica: No, is going to school.
March 3, 1978	1.	She hurt his finger.
	2.	It was not very good.
	3.	He (Snow White) opened the door.
	4.	He eated it.
	5.	He was die.
	6.	He close his eyes.
March 12, 1978	1.	They were making his house. (The Three Little Pigs)
	2.	He went to the next one piggy house.
	3.	He fall down in the water hot.
April 6, 1978	1.	Has someone seen one thing like a turtle?
	2.	I went by myself.
	3.	He run away from you.
April 23, 1978	1.	Because I didn't have any lunch.
April 30, 1978	1.	Did he has classes?
	2.	Daddy, I have a nice day.
	3.	Look what else I buy. (She had already gone through the motions of buying a few minutes before.)
	4.	And I took this picture of you.
June 1, 1978	1.	I hear. (Heard)
	2.	That's what you said.
	3.	I wasn't going to do that.
	4.	You were my way.
	5.	Hey! I did it.
	6.	And I didn't either.
	7.	We were all sisters.
	8.	He used to be a little kid, but now he's not.
	9.	All the kids came to over here.
	10.	Pretend we were doctors.
	11.	He said I could play.
June 27, 1978	1.	I bring a lot of water. (Brought)
	2.	My mommy took it home.
	3.	I went to clean me and then I came back.
	4.	How come when I came back you said you were not my friend?

5. I had to make some ice cream for me.
6. Then I was going to be five, then two, then three.

July 8, 1978

1. She was sewing.
2. Then he cut his finger. (About Snow White's mother)
3. And the baby didn't get no mother.
4. He had a fairy godmother.

Nov. 4, 1978

1. I forgot. I forgot what I did yesterday.
2. I said, "You have to find your own."
3. Rudy gave me this one. (A quarter)
4. I wanted them to find their own.
5. It was showing day.
6. I fall like this. (Fell)
7. It was already teared. (So it's O.K. if I tear it again)
8. All her stuff came out.
9. When I was really little and I was in the hospital. (Picture of herself as a newborn)
10. He (Barbie) worked so hard in the morning.
11. Barbie woke up from her nap.

THE CREOLE DILEMMA

WILLIAM FRANCIS MACKEY

International Center for Research on Bilingualism

    Some of the most lasting legacies of colonialism have been
the languages the empire builders left behind. French, English,
and Spanish are still official languages in most of the former
colonies. (The present study is based on observations on the
Creole/French islands in the Indian Ocean and in the Caribbean
during my sabbatical of 1979.) These European languages are now
spoken in all quarters of the globe in varieties and accents
ranging from European metropolitan standard to local vernaculars
admixed with regional tongues.
    At this latter end of the scale are the local creoles--ap-
proximations to the master language resulting from sociolinguistic
conditions whereby the speech of a remote minority serves as the
only model for the language of an illiterate and subservient
majority. In many cases, this imperfectly perceived model became
the only means of intercommunication between individuals speaking
mutually incomprehensible tribal tongues in conditions of servi-
tude which obliged them to live and work together.
    In conditions such as these, it was inevitable that the mo-
del, which itself was often the regional dialect of semi-literate
European overseers, should be transformed into something far removed from the literary languages of France, England and Spain.
This was especially evident in cases where the language became

the oral and highly unstable vernacular of people who had evolved
under such conditions after the third and fourth generation for
which these admixtures became the one and only mother tongue.

To label such vernaculars, the term creole was appropriated
from the French word for certain Europeans born in the colonies.
If this term can be traced back to the word for create (Lat.
creare), the line of descent is as mixed as the people it has come
to designate. For it passes through the Spanish derivative criar
(to breed), to criado (bred), to its diminutive criadillo, indicating an offspring born and bred in the West Indies of Spanish
parents only, as distinguished from one of aboriginal, mulatto or
negro origin. The local variant criollo, from which the French
borrowed the term, was first used therefore to designate the local
thoroughbred colonists, those of "pure" blood. Today it means the
opposite. The word creole is invariably associated with some sort
of mixture--racial, cultural or linguistic.

A creole language is typically a mixed or composite dialect,
generally with a European base of English (Melanesian Pidgin),
French (Haitian), or Spanish (Papiamento). The mixture and dis-
tortion varies from one part of the globe to the next. The French-
based creoles of Haiti, Mauritius, Réunion, Louisiana, Rodrigues,
Trinité, Guyana, Dominica, Gaudaloupe, St. Lucia, Martinique, and
the Seychelles are all different one from the other. Their degree
of intercomprehensibility or interintelligibility and distance
from French has yet to be determined.[1]

Aside from geographical isolation and differences in the conditions of creolization, what adds to the distinction between
creoles with the same base are the widely dissimilar conditions
of literacy. In some cases much of the population has become literate through schooling in an unrelated tongue--English for example, in the case of St. Lucia, the Seychelles, and Louisiana.
In other cases, it has been the related colonial language but seldom to the same extent. In the Doms (départements d'outre-mer),
for example, where compulsory primary education exclusively in
French has resulted in the decreolization of the vernacular of the
younger generation, the creole is different from that of long-
independent French-speaking republics like Haiti where the level
of literacy, according to government estimates in 1978, has been
under 20 percent. In areas where a colonial language like
French has been used as the exclusive medium of instruction the
local creole is not a speech-variety representing a norm shared
by all members of the community, but rather a continuum of
mutually modifying practices ranging from very creole to very French.

In areas of subsequent mass settlement from Europe and general
education, first in missionary and later in government schools,
some of the creole-speakers were able to abandon creole in favor
of the European standard and to maintain that standard through contact with a large population for whom it was the only mother tongue.
In areas where no such massive contact was possible, the local
creole developed into a home language further and further removed
from the source. Not surprisingly, such was the case in many of
the ocean islands of the Pacific, the Atlantic and the Indian

oceans and in many parts of the East and the West Indies. As long
as such islands were parts of an empire, any education that did
exist was dispensed in the imperial tongue--English, French,
Spanish, Portuguese, Dutch, and even German.

When some of these islands became sovereign states, however,
they were faced with the question of what to do about their local
creole vernacular. Should they still consider it as a local
patois, to be irradicated through schooling in the imperial language? Or should they replace it by some form of the local creole,
standardized for purposes of education and mass media usage? If
so, to what extent and at what rate? While some of these new
states, with the world's lowest standard of living, have been concerned with the downgrading of the language of their colonial heritage, some of the old nation-states with the world's highest
living standards are upgrading the use of the same languages in
order to give their people a better and better mastery of the
means of international communication. Some European states like
Sweden, for example, have been putting more and more emphasis on
the use of English.

To policy makers in the freshly-liberated island republics,
it may not have occurred that their local creole--or patois, as
they call it--could conceivably play the role occupied up to then
by languages like English and French, had not some professional
linguists gotten into the act. In the science of linguistics, it
was explained to the locals, all languages are equal. The language of the community is its everyday speech and no matter how
it is spoken or used, it is as worthy of consideration as is anyone's everyday speech. It is that language which should be reduced
to writing and taught in the schools.

As long as the population was mostly illiterate and that all
schooling was in a standardized European language, there was no
problem of choice. The dilemma occurs when enough people achieve
literacy in the European language to study their past and to become concerned with such things as cultural identity. If people
reject a cultural identity with the colonial past, all that is
left is the creole reality. And this implied that the national
identity with creole be reflected in the language of schooling.[2]
But the only people capable of making a choice are those who
already enjoy the socio-economic and cultural advantages of literacy in the colonial language. It is the acculturated who campaign to make creole the national language. In the former French
colonies, for example, those who know no French consider their
local creole simply as a patois. French, on the other hand, is a
language, since it is the only vehicle of literacy and education.
Those who know some French often attempt to speak it to those of
their children who have reached school age.

In such cases, creole is considered as a bridge language.
The child must learn creole "in order to understand" French.
Like the purely oral regional dialects of France, the local
creole is referred to as the "patois" by those who speak it. The
term "petit-nègre" formerly used by Europeans who do not use
creole, is now seldom heard on the islands. Yet the fact remains

Jerry R. Craddock, "The Contextual Varieties of YOD: An Attempt at Systematization," in *A Festschrift for Jacob Ornstein: Studies in General Linguistics and Sociolinguistics*. Rowley, Mass.: Newbury House, 1980. Pp. 61-68.

ERRATA

Page 62, line 7:	jejune	
24:	vowels	
28:	vowels by means of	
8up:	[léigu]	
7up:	cantauī...	[kántai]
5up:	[áira]	
3up:	lactis	
1up:	> Ptg.	
63, 5:	[maisélla]	
8:	[mairⁿno]	
10:	[ou]	
30:	[n]	
15up:	coalho	

Page 67, line 1:	[tsegóina]
19:	[madéira]...
24:	[kóiro]
	[n]
8up:	than
3up:	touches' > VLat.

that the concept of a home-language (patois) unfit for use in school was imported from France and constitutes an element in the acculturation of the people. As in France, it has been a punishable offense to use the patois in school, and this has in itself contributed to the status of creole as a pre-school home language. French is the language used with superiors (except in anger) and with strangers. Strong emotions like anger and joy are seldom expressed in French-- except when courting when the more distinguished or polite language is called for. In tri-lingual Seychelles, however, this is not French, but English.

In Haiti, creole is dominant in the rural areas. Here the distinction between town and country is more marked than elsewhere. To become urbanized means to pass from the extended to the nuclear family, from illiteracy to literacy, from voodoo to christianity, from plaçage (a sort of polygamy) to mariage (monogamy), and from creole to French dominance. Upward mobility through urbanization is achieved in stages: from unilingual creole to creole speech plus French comprehension, from there to the use of creolized French until Standard French becomes most dominant and creole recessive. In reality these stages represent a continuum of bilinguality which generally, but not always, corresponds to racial, ethnic, social and economic continua. It would seem that the lighter the skin, the less the creole is used; also, the richer the family, the less the use of creole. This is because most creole islands have elites which are the descendants of the original European colonists. These families in some islands are called the Békés, speak French at home but learn creole in childhood from their colored nanny (called a da). Since the institution of the da is now dying out, the children in these local families learn creole later and later by association outside the home. Because of this, the children and adults in the richer families no longer have the option of being able to increase or decrease the social distance between themselves and those they address by the use of more or less creole. This option is now the prerogative of the newly urbanized who, in addition to being bilingual, are largely bicultural as well, tolerating such practices as religious synchretism (christianity combined with voodoo, for example).

The children of these families will move up the ladder and join the French-speaking elite, thus further isolating the speech-community of the creolophones. Those who are fluent in French and understand creole are continually reminded of the fact that the overwhelming majority of creole words are derived from French and cannot help considering the local patois as a by-product and therefore inferior form of speech. Having become literate and having learned the history of their people, they begin to associate creole with slavery and with past injustice.

They now know that the injustice was most often perpetrated by the subalterns or overseers hired by the planters--many of them outlaws, adventurers or former buccaneers--who had acted no better at home. Many were simply bent on making a quick fortune and going back to Europe. Yet it was this very class of subalterns with their disregard for the law and for the status quo of their superiors that led the Haitian war of liberation, one of the bloodiest on record.

Unlike the former African colonies, these fabulously successful colonial enterprises, meriting the name of la perle des Antilles, as Saint-Domingue (now Haiti) was called, did not experience the indulgence and aid of their former masters. In the Europe of 1804, no country dared to condone the defeat of Napoleon's soldiers by an uprising of colonials. Instead, some 20 years later France was encouraged to exact war reparations so punitive that they were to impoverish the young nation for many generations to come.

The present poverty of many creole-speaking nations has itself become a deterrent to their creolization and national language development. Preparing and printing materials in creole can be expensive and often difficult undertakings. In some cases they can even become counter-productive. In practice, even though it were possible and feasible in some cases to spend the entire national income on the production of reading materials in creole, it would be several generations before these could lead the population beyond the elementary school. If anything beyond primary education is considered, it must necessarily be (for the foreseeable future) in one of the languages of wider communication.

The educators in some creole countries have become somewhat more pragmatic in their outlook. They are questioning the wisdom of spending time in the schools learning to read and write a language in which only primary materials exist. The more time spent in primary school on creole, the less time there would be left for learning the standard European language. Since creole is only a form of this standard tongue (the thinking goes), why not spend school time in speeding up the transition to the written standard, as had indeed been done with the patois and dialects in France and England, ever since the advent of formal schooling.

Not all, however, share this attitude toward creole. In the French Antilles, for example, the attitude is simply a component of an over-all political doctrine. The integrationists favor diglossia, the Communists push bilingualism, and the separatists want creole as the national language. The latter do not, however, claim that creole can replace French nor that it would be possible to raise creole to the level of that superlanguage. They would be satisfied with a status similar to that of Danish in Denmark and Finnish in Finland.

Whatever language policy is eventually adopted, it is bound to have a profound effect on the education of the masses. Until recent times most formal education was the work of missionaries who taught in the language of their homeland--English, French, Spanish or Dutch as the case may be. Such education was accessible to a small percentage of the population. In Haiti, for example, it prepared the elite to further education in France. On the Seychelles, it was carried out, if at all, in French, and continued in that language within private institutions operated by Canadian missionaries, long after the island had fallen under British rule.

In the late 1930s, however, the Colonial Office in London had decided to institute modern public education, and a commission of investigation for the Seychelles recommended in 1938 (the Smith Report) that the schooling be done in English.   It was not until 1944, however, that the recommendations were implemented (the Giles Report).   From that time until 1970, English became the main, if not the only, language of instruction.   The argument for its use was that the creole home language of the pupils was a source of constant interference with French, the only other possible language, since the use of creole was at that time completely out of the question.

In this context both English and French became the prestige languages.   English was reserved for administrative use, schooling, mass media, communication with native speakers of English, and, strangely enough, for courting among the middle-classes.   In the upper classes, however, French remained entirely dominant.   In the late seventies, when the islands constituted themselves into an independent republic, French was gradually reinstated, first as a subject in primary school, then for oral use only, and later as a medium.   In 1979, the new republic elaborated a policy of tri-lingual education in creole, French, and English by introducing the use of creole in primary school, greatly upgrading the role of French, and downgrading the use of English.   The same year the Ministry of Education in Haiti announced that it was introducing the use of creole as a medium in the first two years of primary school, but only in a few schools and that on an experimental basis.   Since creole in Haiti had long been developed for adult literacy (ever since the UNESCO fundamental education pilot project of the forties and the well-publicized Laubach-McConnell literacy campaign), the caution on the part of the authorities is an indication of the nature and extent of the dilemma facing educators in creole countries.

Before creole can become a language of general education and function as such, many technical problems remain to be solved, among them the standardization of the written language, whether it be the creole of Haiti or that of the Seychelles.

Even decisions concerning orthography are bound to have non-linguistic overtones and some political repercussions.   If creole is to be elevated to the status of a national language, the newspapers, official documents and texts will all have to be printed in that language in such a way that the population at large and especially the people who count most can understand.   Since most of the people prone to read papers and documents of any sort have been taught to read only in the former colonial language, in this case French or English, the orthography of creole will be comprehensible only in so far as it approximates that language.   This supposes the use of an etymological orthography as the most easily understood by the adult population.   But what makes it easier for French readers to read makes it difficult for illiterate learners to learn. The latter would be better off with a phonological orthography based on a one letter/one phoneme principle.   Yet the application of such a principle masks the familiarity of everyday words which the people have come to recognize in the conventional French orthography.   Attempts at the use of mixed orthographies have been entirely satisfactory to no one.

Even after an orthography has been standardized in dictionaries and grammars, the production of materials remains a formidable task. Most of the literature produced in the French Antilles has been in French, the use of creole being reserved for certain types of dialogue, especially in situation comedies or for local color, with the two languages co-existing in a relationship of literary diglossia.[3] Should creole become a literary and national language, the diglossic roles of the two languages would be changed and the potential audience of the creole writer vastly reduced.

These are some of the dilemmas facing about ten million people scattered throughout the globe in young, emerging island nations, where the home language is a creole at the stage where French, Spanish and other languages had been during the early Middle Ages, when Latin was the dominant tongue throughout Europe. Are these new Romance languages (the rising creoles) destined to play a role similar to that of the language from which they were derived? Events quite outside the realms of linguistics and language planning will probably decide the future of these creole languages. Meanwhile, the wisest policy is likely to be one of tolerance and prudence in recommending solutions to the difficult dilemma facing the creole languages of the world.

NOTES

[1]Mackey, W. F. Distance interlinguistique et interintelligibilité des langues. Proceedings of the XIIth International Congress of Linguists. Innsbruck: University Press. (Forthcoming.)

[2]Mackey, W. F. Identité culturelle, francophonie, et enseignement du français en milieu plurilingue. Identité culturelle et francophonie en Amérique II, ed. by Hans Runte and Albert Valdman. Bloomington: Indiana University Research Center for Language and Semiotic Studies, 1976, 81-102.

[3]Mackey, W. F., Langue, dialect et diglossie littéraire. Québec: International Center for Research on Bilingualism, 1975. (=CIRB Publication B-54.)

"LEXICAL INSERTION" AS A SOCIO-PSYCHOLOGICAL EVENT: EVIDENCE FROM POETIC BEHAVIOR

ADAM MAKKAI

University of Illinois at Chicago Circle

The thesis of this paper is that we human beings are all poets, no matter if we actually practice poetry in a professional sense or not.[1] Whether one is engaged in a matter-of-fact prosaic transaction with a sales clerk, a waiter, or during a university lecture on linguistics, one is constantly confronted with the necessity of CHOOSING THE RIGHT WORD for what one has to say.

The choosing of the right word, however, is a mysterious process shrouded in theoretical obfuscation and controversy. I have no intention to arbitrate in this paper on whether the transformational-generativists are right or wrong in their various notions of 'lexical insertion,' and I will not take sides in the glamorous debate between the Chomsky-Katz type 'lexicalist-interpretivists' and the McCawley-Lakoff-type 'generative semanticists.' (If I had to choose between those two versions of TG, I would probably choose generative semantics, because even though its practitioners disavow such intentions, it seems to imply a greater likelihood for psychological realism by 'starting' the sentence generating process in the semantics and not in the deep structure. If 'creativity' and generation start in the deep structure, lexical insertion becomes, I think, an appendage of the syntactic string whereby the sentence structure chosen would seem to dictate the choice of words to be used, a possible consequence of TG which seems to me to be entirely

counter-intuitive.) Nor will this paper make any attempt to re-
deeming stratificationalism, a movement with which I have been
associated in a major way for some time (Makkai 1972, 1972).
Stratificationalism, I believe, suffers from the same deficiency
as the various versions of TG do: there is no believable model
offered regarding the mysterious relationship between SENTENCE
STRUCTURE and VOCABULARY.

Thus, when a generative grammarian comes up with a pre-lexi-
cal terminal string of the type

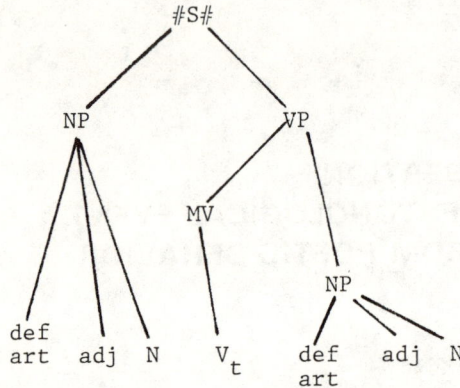

FIGURE 1

(this being a rough oversimplication for the sole purpose of illustration), there is never any convincing reason offered in the
literature to indicate whether this derivation is there because
one of the possible sentences it describes was virtually present
in the consciousness of the person (i.e., the linguist) who constructed it (e.g., *The naughty boy swallowed the ecstatic gold-
fish*) or whether it is this kind of structure which somehow elicits
vocabulary from the conscious and the subconscious mind of the
speaker. I am reasonably sure, of course, that the 'man-in-the-
street' would never find himself in the situation of having to find
suitable words for skeletal sentence structures, unless hired for
the explicit purpose by an experimenter. From an intuitive psychological point of view, it seems to me that sentence structures materialize quasi-automatically, in part after and in part simultaneously with our having selected the wording of what we are about
to say.

Similarly, stratificationalism gives us no indication regarding the precise nature, the timing, or the choices to be made
when a SEMEMIC RETICULUM is about to be realized as a lexemic network. (It doesn't matter, for the purposes of this discussion,
whether we draw relational networks or directed graphs. For simplicity's sake I will adopt here the latter.) Any sememic reticu-

lum that does not somehow exhibit actual WORDS in it remains unde-
codable, or multiguous.   Consider the following example:

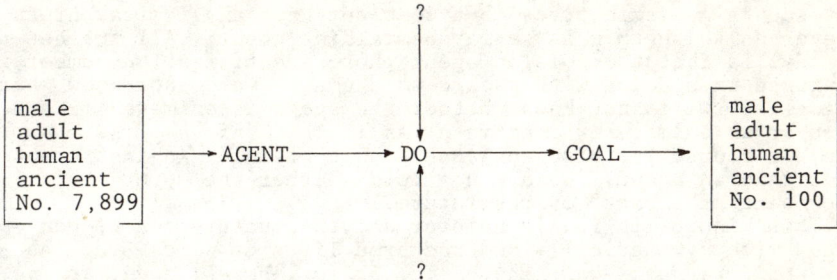

FIGURE 2

The only thing this network will tell the decoder is that the
agent is an ancient male human being (who can be further identified
if you look up his identification number) engaged in some doing,
the goal of which is another ancient male human being. We have no
idea what the doing entails; we do not know whether the doing takes
place in the past, the present, or the future (unless the word
'ancient' suggests the past, but we could deal with a contemporary
play which has not yet been performed); furthermore, not even this
much would be known, if we hadn't used the 'words' male, adult,
human, and ancient. One possible realization of this sentence is
Brutus killed Caesar, or, without any passive transformation,
Caesar was killed by Brutus, if we adjust the sememic focus (cf.
Lockwood 1972).

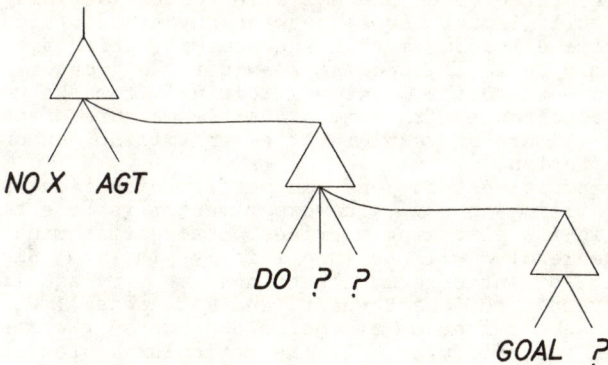

FIGURE 3

In another mode of stratificational representation, one does
not draw 'directed graphs' but 'relational networks' for 'sememic
traces.' Such traces, in simple cases, may consist of 'unordered
AND' nodes (also known as coincidence concatenations). Figure 3
shows such a 'sememic trace' but does not give any lexical hints
whatever as to what it is we may be talking about. All the network says is that there is an agent whose identification number is
X, engaged in a doing with regard to a goal. We do not know what
the goal is, we do not know whether the agent is animate, like a
person or an animal, or inanimate (as in *the wind shut the door*
which, of course, is also analyzable as containing an instrument
rather than an agent); we are not told whether the doing is in
the present, the past, or the future.

This kind of lexically uninformative structure can be contrasted with syntactically unstructured lists of words, such as
quick--police--dead--man; *man, dead, police, quick*; *dead, police,
man, quick*; *man, quick, dead, police*, or any combination of these
four words. Whereas, clearly, some ordering of these words will
sound more like what we expect for *quick, the police! The man's
dead!*, it is disproportionately easier to make sense of the four
words than it is to find out what the network of Figure 3 is
trying to tell us. Single words, without any syntax whatever,
may carry much richer communicative function than pages worth of
syntactically well-formed sentences. Compare the one word items
go!, *Fire!*, *Now!*, *Stop!* with some such elegant but semantically
empty sentence as "Previous information to the contrary notwith-
standing, the statements made in the case at hand will remain mere
allegations unless additional evidence can be adduced to support
dissident views on the matter."

The trouble is that, exactly as in the case of TG, the network makes sense after we know the sentence in question, but the
sentence, as given, is only one possible outcome of the network.
I am forced to conclude that all theoreticians have been either
deliberately joking or that they simply have not faced the fact,
which is that the communicative intent of normal people rests
with loosely structured words and not with lexical strings or sememic reticula. (If I must choose between any brand of lexical
string as a lexeme eliciting matrix and sememic reticula, I will
choose the sememic reticula, because they offer a greater freedom
of choice and seem to do the 'lexeme eliciting' from the unconscious more in accordance with some plausible measure of psychological realism.) I must now explain a few unfamiliar notions, such
as 'lexeme elicitation.'

This is an experiment any one can perform either on oneself
or on subjects willing to try. The experimenter is free to
choose between TG-ish eliciting matrices or stratificationally
styled ones; the results will be surprisingly similar. Since
surface structure-oriented terminal strings are very specific,
there is less freedom to insert words (and make sense); with the
sememic reticula one's freedom of choice depends on the specifications given in the reticulum. If the reticulum is reasonably
vague, the inserter's freedom remains proportionately larger; the
more specifications appear in the reticulum, the more compliance

in choice will be required on the part of the inserter. Both the
elicitor and the inserter have to be willing to play this game,
of course, but the benefits are considerable and the game is entirely harmless.

Let us try two different eliciting matrices, one in the
transformationalist style, and one in the stratificationalist mode.
An eliciting matrix is a set of instructions given by the analyst
(the elicitor) to his patient, the inserter, somewhat as if the
former were a psychiatrist, and the latter his patient, lying on
the office couch. I am reasonably certain that the eventual use of
such techniques by real psychiatrists on real patients would yield
valuable insight into personality structures, types of mental disorder, etc.

FIRST GAME, TRANSFORMATIONAL STYLE

Analyst: How many sentences can you make out of the simple the N
v-ed the N pattern?

Patient: Oh, that's easy! Here we go: *the boy threw the ball,
the man saw the girl, the girl saw the man, the elephant
trampled the grass, the tiger chased the tourist*.....

Analyst: You're slowing down...Anything the matter?...What were
you going to say?

Patient: (blushing): I was going to say *the boy hates the father*.

Analyst: That's all right. You can say anything you want.

SECOND GAME, TRANSFORMATIONAL STYLE

Analyst: How many sentences can you make out of the simple passive
pattern the N was v-ed by the N?

Patient: Oh, that's easy, too! Ok: *the boy was whipped by the
father, the rock was thrown by the boy, the dirt was
smeared by the boy, the tire was punctured by the boy,
the father was feared by the boy*....Why do I keep coming
back to that boy?

Analyst: That's what we're trying to find out. How many sentences
can you make of the somewhat more complicated pattern,
without thinking, the adj N which v-ed the adj N v-ed the
Ns.

Patient: Can you give me an example?

Analyst: Sure, take for instance: *the shaggy dog that stole the
old bone frightened the chickens*.

Patient: Ah, I get it... Let's see... *the angry father who whipped*

> *the boy shut the windows..... the crying mother who*
> *washed the dishes broke the jar.....the tired father who*
> *fixed the garage door moved the benches....the angry*
> *teacher who....*

Analyst: You're omitting the adjectives before your second noun.
Try again.

Patient: OK, let's see: *the angry father who whipped the crying*
boy shut the windows.....the crying mother who washed
the dirty dishes moved the benches..

     This can go on for an hour twice or three times a week, and
by the end of a month or two, the analyst would have a fairly good
insight into a variety of traumas the patient is carrying around
in his unconscious. The skeletal sentence structures, dubbed
'transformational style' here (although there is nothing truly
transformational about them, as they also seem perfectly straight-
forward as traditional grammatical categories) can start out as
very simple and gradually become more and more complex. Just how
many instructions an actual patient on an actual couch can absorb
will, of course, differ from person to person, but for the purposes
of our experiment(s) these can be two linguists who are not in an
analyst-patient relationship in real life, but colleagues on the
same campus. The faster the 'patient' has to reply, the better the
chances that some real, hard 'sense' will emerge from the eliciting
matrix and not some fanciful contrivance such as *the superannuated*
aardvark which denigrated the Chairman, circumambulated the edifice.
Note that this highly unlikely sentence is just as grammatical as
is the much simpler *the crying mother who washed the dirty dishes*
broke the jar; furthermore, they are exactly structurally identical,
or to use Gleason's term ENATE. The difference between the aardvark-
sentence and the mother-sentence is that the former lacks any real
socio-psychological reality and is a mere mental exercise; the
latter can be a real sentence reporting a real event from one's
suppressed or forgotten past, despite the present tense, as if view-
ing one's ·life on a movie screen, here and now.
     I will now try to show similar games in the 'stratificational'
style.

THIRD GAME, STRATIFICATIONAL STYLE

Analyst: Close your eyes. There is a doer, and a done to; technically an <u>agent</u> and a <u>patient</u>, and the doer does something to the done-to. What do you see?

Patient: *A boy throws a rock, the father spanks the boy, the*
mother is breaking the jar...

Analyst: Excellent, you've got it. Now try this: There is a
doer, an agent, who has certain qualities, technically
known as attributes. The done-to also has some qualities

or attributes. Bear in mind, though, that these qualities
or attributes can be a single item like <u>kind</u>, <u>noisy</u>,
<u>honest</u>, or <u>naughty</u>, or longer statements about something
they did in the past, for instance, <u>who loves gingerale</u>
or <u>who can't stand Coca Cola</u>, because both the short
items and these longer statements describe, and characterize that person. Got it?

<u>Patient</u>:   How about: *the angry father spanked the frightened boy,*
the father who drank too much spanked the boy who was
screaming for help, the mother who broke the jars scolded
the boy who was crying?

<u>Analyst</u>:   You've got it. Now let's try this: There is a doer, you
know, the agent, and the done-to, or the patient, but we
are more interested in the done-to than in the doer, so
we want to give him the courtesy, so to speak, to appear
first on the stage; think of the father spanking the boy,
but favor the boy in your statement. Can you do that?

<u>Patient</u>:   Let's see...*the boy.... the boy....* we want him first,
don't we?

<u>Analyst</u>:   That's right.

<u>Patient</u>:   *The boy was spanked by the father, the rock got thrown*
by the boy, the jars were broken by the mother...

<u>Analyst</u>:   You've got it.

FOURTH GAME, STRATIFICATIONAL STYLE

<u>Analyst</u>:   Imagine the following situation. There is a doer and a
done to, as before, and a doing which affects the done to.
They both have qualities, as before, and they can be short
item qualities or longer statement qualities. The difference is this: You don't want to tell me what happens,
but you're asking questions about it, trying to find out
if it really happened, then next you're denying that it
happened, and lastly you're trying to ask questions about
denying that it happened. Can you do this?

<u>Patient</u>:   (After several trials) *Did the father spank the boy?*
Did the father who drank too much spank the screaming
boy? Didn't the screaming father who drank too much
spank the miserable boy who ran away? Did the sad mother
break the jars? Didn't that sad, crying mother, who
broke the jars, scold the miserable boy who ran away?
The father didn't spank the boy...The sad mother didn't
break the jars...The sad boy, who was spanked by his
father who drank too much, didn't run away...

<u>Analyst</u>:   You mixed up the order a bit there--notice, that all your

denials were clustered at the end.   Does that mean something?

Patient: Maybe.   I made it, didn't I?   I didn't run away, in the long run, if you know what I mean...

And this is probably how it would go between our imaginary 'analyst' and 'patient.'   Notice that the 'analyst' here always provides the 'primary input'; once the 'transformationalist' or rather 'syntacticist' style, and once in the 'stratificationalist', or more accurately 'semanticist' style.   The 'patient', by verbalizing about his experiences takes the individual words, as they come to his mind, and 'inserts' them into the eliciting framework provided by the analyst.

But this is an artificial situation, one might object; a situation which is restricted to the practice (or a semblance thereof) of psychotherapy.   My reply to such an objection would be that the situation is only apparently artificial insofar as we actually put two people on the stage, dubbed here the 'analyst' and the 'patient.'   I would contend that ordinary people engaging in dialog, or in monolog, are in fact each other's (linguistic) 'analysts' and 'patients' when they converse with one another, and the analysts and patients of themselves, when they soliloquize.   The basic difference between our imaginary conversations above and what happens in real life is that people do not give each other grammatical hints when they talk and a person thinking out loud or writing is essentially unaware of grammatical constructions.   The analogy of the conversations between the 'analyst' and the 'patient' will become useful later: we shall see that in the process of encoding (verbalization) people unwittingly force themselves into grammatical structures which, then, exert a fair amount of tyranny on what is, or what CAN be said later.   The best known kind of association game is the single word elicitation method where grammatical structures and sentences are quite irrevelant.   An example follows below:

Analyst: Tell me what you think of when I give you the words I will pronounce, one by one.   Don't speculate.   Just try to see and feel what wants to come out and just enumerate these things.   I give you an example: I say lemon, and you say sour and yellow, get it?

Patient: Let's try it.

Analyst: Father.

Patient: *Angry, screams, booze, ...scared....bangs....money.... money....money....screams....not enough....*   Is that what you want?

Analyst: You're doing OK.   Just see, and enumerate, all right?

Patient: All right.

Analyst: School.

Patient: *Kids....boys.....snow-balls...chalk...math...scared....*
            hungry....lunchbag...empty....hungry....teasing....kids...
            teasing....hungry....math....scared...pushing....teasing...
            mud....snow....falling....hurts...bell...ringing...
            hungry...

Analyst: That was during the War in Europe, wasn't it?

Patient: You know it.

    (cf. Eric Berne, 1969)

It is becoming more and more widely known and generally appreciated that hemispheric lateralization may have a great deal to
do with the consious and the unconscious.[2] During sleep, when we
dream, associations flow freely and without logical control. We
can be in more than one place simultaneously, step out the window
and not fall down, but just float away, etc. These are generally
believed to be 'right hemispheric functions' (with the right hemisphere dominating the left hand and left eye, and being, generally,
the 'weaker,' or 'sinister,' artistic-feminine part of the person's
mind).[3] Passing a course in computer programming, driving a car
and stopping at the red light, ordering supplies over the telephone,
etc., are said to be 'left hemispheric functions' (Bolinger 1975,
Jaynes 1976). It makes sense to compare, by analogy, grammatically
correct sentence constructing and poetic free-association of single words to left (strong) and right (weak) hemispheres, respectively, and further to imagine that, somewhat as Julian Jaynes
suggests, a modern poet, when he turns his imagination loose and
writes a poem in the modern mode of stream-of-consciousness, is
relying more on right-hemispheric functions than on left hemispheric ones and that, conversely, when next day he rewrites his poem
'with a cold head,' he is more under the influence of the left
(sober, quasi-mathematical) hemisphere. But it doesn't really
matter if it doesn't quite work this way technically as far as the
biology of the brain is concerned; what matters from our point of
view here is that people do exhibit poetic behavior, something
which is, strictly speaking, 'superfluous,' or which seems to be
superfluous from the point of view of material survival. (I
firmly believe that we would actually die if we were always and
only logical and never allowed our brains to 'rest', by wandering
off in the direction of 'sleep', even when we are technically
awake.)
Thus we find ourselves giving each other and ourselves eliciting matrices which we then proceed to fill with words (=lexemes)
which are arranged in certain traditional ways. These eliciting
matrices range from the very exactly prosaic (*How much for that
pair of shoes? - Thirty nine dollars, Sir*) to the surrealistic and
the esoteric (*Who can see love in a rancid prune in February? -
Any one who has a wrinkled face.*) Abstract structures, such as

The <u>Adj. Ns. that/who V-ed the Adj. Ns.</u> 'elicit' variously eligible lexemes, while concrete lexemes, such as <u>lemon</u>, <u>father</u>, <u>school</u>, <u>war</u>, <u>love</u>, and <u>jail</u>, tend to 'elicit' word association sets and/or grammatical structures insofar as they materialize wearing these grammatical structures. It is as if grammar and lexis co-selected one another both consciously and unconsciously at a very rapid rate.

In the opening sentence of this paper I stated that we humans are all poets, whether we professionally engage in poetry or not. I hope that this statement is a little more meaningful now after what has been said, but I know that further elucidation is in order. I don't know of any better way to show what I mean than by retracing my own steps in what I did when I wrote what eventually turned out to be a sonnet. It appears in toto toward the end of the paper written out in the traditional fourteen lines, three quatrains and a couplet with an ABBA, BAAB, CCDD, AA rhyme pattern consisting of iambic pentameters (A=10 syllables, B+11 syllables; C=11 syllables; D=10 syllables).

The various 'matrices' that 'elicited' these 114 words (a word is defined as one graphic unit between spaces, i.e., <u>eight-foot</u>, <u>ain't</u>, and <u>I'd</u> are single words) involved physical events that took place, things I saw, certain tasks I had to perform, and certain monologs that started here and there during the performance of those tasks. I had absolutely no idea that I was about to write a sonnet, and once I got into it, I had no idea how it would start and how it would end, or how the lines and rhymes would exactly be organized. Nor was I conscious of writing well-formed clauses and sentences in the declarative, the negative, or the conditional--I actually became aware of these structures as the sonnet unfolded itself first in my head and later on paper. Here is what happened: I had to shovel an enormous amount of snow on my drive-way in order to be able to open the garage door and get the car out. I have a dog who has been cooped up inside the house for a long time; it's impossible to walk him over the 4-5 foot drifts. We take him out for a few minutes, put him in a hole in the snow, and then put him back in. The poor animal relieves himself where and how he can; the visible traces are greenish-yellow discolorations in the snow. I was thinking of Professor Ornstein's beautiful house in El Paso, Texas, where I spent an active and happy week in August of 1976 during the Third LACUS Forum (see Di Pietro and Blansitt 1976) and remembered what a precious commodity water was in the arid Southwestern desert climate and how beautifully green the vegetation was around the Ornstein home. The only green I could see now was the yellowish discoloration left by my miserable dog. The temperature was -20 F and I was in considerable physical discomfort. The two words, devoid of any syntactic role that kept coming back to me, were *snow*, and *green*, *green* and *snow; green*, *green*, *snow*, *snow*, *snow*, in a variety of orders and without any apparent logic. During a moment's pause my logical self rebelled against this colonization of my attention and I actually loudly spoke out the words *there is no such thing as green snow*. Then I shoveled some more and the words *green* and *snow* kept coming back. Then I asked myself the question: *Could there be such a thing as green snow?* The answer, after three shovels full of the white stuff, was *If snow were green it wouldn't be snow*. But then what would it be? *This is nonsense, let's get back to work*. I'll fix a cup of constant comment tea when I get inside. *If snow were green....! Wait! That's iambic! if SNOW were GREEN...if SNOW were GREEN....*I stopped and bent over the shovel. I felt hot. What else could snow be that it isn't? Why, hot, of course. It's terribly cold, yet I am hot, because I have to bend over shoveling the stuff. *If Snow were GREEN and HOT....that's iambic, too! Three feet, in fact.* But snow is neither, it isn't, it isn't. *It ain't.* That's inelegant; I teach how to avoid <u>ain't</u> to my foreign students. Of course the dean said it in a meeting a couple of weeks back, signalling, in a way, that he can afford to say <u>ain't</u> and that he was "cool" by using this form. *If SNOW were GREEN and HOT which it SURE AIN'T....not perfectly iambic, you can't say Which IT sure AIn'T, the natural way to say it is which it SURE AIN'T....How about which sure it ain't?* (That sounds better, now I have a good iambic line.) I felt a bit dizzy, and my pulse was racing. I am not going to pass out, not out here. *Faint, faint, faint!* somebody shouted inside my head, and I heard a full line answered by a ghost-line that ended in <u>faint</u>:

> *If snow were green and hot which sure it ain't,*
> *ta TUM ta TUM ta TUM ta TUM ta faint.*

I did not know what this was shaping up to be. I was glad that <u>ain't</u> and <u>faint</u> had announced their desire to be united as a rhyming couple but, not being at all sure what form this whole message was going to take, I felt resentment against the words. They're not going to tell me what to do![4]

As it happens, I watch a fair amount of television, especially on Thursday nights, when Hawaii Five-O and Barnaby Jones are aired. This was Friday, and the night before during the breaks a vegetable company ran their Jolly Green Giant ad, *à propos* of some green peas. So I suppose the JGG must have been on my mind subliminally, because without further ado I momentarily imagined that I became the JGG who blew all the snow away in one fell swoop. I suppose this further increased my resentment at the inexorable reality of the nearly eight-foot drift at the end of the driveway, as I overheard myself saying to the snow drift: *I feel mad and defiant, because I am not a giant.* It was time to go in. I took a piece of paper and jotted down in pencil:

> *If snow were green and hot (which sure it ain't)*
> *ta TUM ta TUM ta TUM ta TUM ta TUM defiant*
> *ta TUM ta TUM ta TUM ta TUM ta TUM ta giant*
> *ta TUM ta TUM ta TUM ta I will faint.*

But this is like the first quatrain of a sonnet, I realized; all right then, I might as well accept that challenge and actually make this into one. But sonnets have a structure, and therefore a will, of their own; any one wishing to write one must obey the dictates of the iambic pentameter, the rhyming scheme, etc.

At this point I made a deliberate decision: the second quatrain will use the same rhymes, except in the reverse order; instead of ABBA, I would use BAAB. While I was out in the snow, I
almost swore out loud a couple of times, but decided not to when
I saw one of my neighbors go by. This reminded me of the word
silent which, I found, would do for one of the rhymes with giant
and defiant, but I needed one more to fill the pattern. Why is
it, I wondered, that native speakers get away with using four-
letter words in mixed company, even evoking laughter, and immigrants usually don't? Is it the accent? Or could it be that it
is just not expected of a 'foreigner' to indulge himself in some
of the luxuries of the native? I know that when I hear a non-
native speaker of Hungarian proudly perform one of our obscenities
for my benefit, I feel embarrassed. It strikes me the wrong way;
it sounds too 'loud,' somehow, no matter how 'softly' spoken
otherwise....I've got it! My next word will be strident. A
colleague once observed that part of my foreign accent is that my
rate of speech is considerably faster than that of native Americans. (This would seem more natural if I were French or Italian;
not all Hungarians speak as fast as I do.) I now had silent and
strident as two elicitors placed in line-final strategic positions;
and they were conveniently polarized in meaning, somewhat like
soft is to hard or harsh. The A-rhymes quaint and restraint almost leapt out of the unconscious automatically and simultaneously;
I actually have no recollection of which came first. All I knew
was that I had moved out of the snow and into the area of language;
I was no longer concerned with snow at all, but rather with my
possible verbalizations on the subject of snow and how they might
affect my English-speaking listeners. I put down the rhymes in
the format:

$$I \begin{cases} \text{ain't} \\ \text{defiant} \\ \text{giant} \\ \text{faint} \end{cases} \quad II \begin{cases} \text{silent} \\ \text{restraint} \\ \text{quaint} \\ \text{strident} \end{cases}$$

I had, at this point, probably made two subconscious decisions
regarding syntax: the words faint and strident should be spoken
on a falling (period) intonation, indicating the end of a sentence each. I wasn't sure at all, though, whether there might be
just two full sentences in the first two quatrains, or more than
two. At this point I went back to the beginning, and for the
first time consciously realized that I had worked myself into an
if-clause in the present tense, contrary to fact. What, really,
would I do, if snow were green, which it sure ain't? I'd be glad,
I guess. That's all right, but I must end the line with defiant
which is an adjective. Maybe be defiant? Act defiant? No, be
less defiant, or act less defiant. But I needed a conditional
to answer to present condition contrary to fact and it must all
be in good iambic scansion. The words I'd leap for joy and would
be/feel less defiant seemed to fill the bill so I wrote down the
first two lines:

If snow were green and hot (which sure it ain't)
I'd leap for joy, and would feel less defiant....

But less defiant about what? Well, the snow, obviously; but I had
used the word snow already and repeating it is dull; there must be
other words to refer to it. What did I do out there? I attacked
snow mountains. One of them was well over my head, at least eight
feet. I wrote: when tackling eight-foot drifts. This made sense
with the would be less defiant of the previous line, but made me
make a period, and I was not having a full line ending in the
target word, giant. So I had to start a new sentence in mid-line.
Some sonnet writers regard this as bad form, while some actually
praise the practice and call the device enjambment, the art of the
grammatically run-on line whose syntactic boundary does not coincide with the metric line. So be it; I've worked myself into an
enjambment; let's see, how do I get out of it? Giant must be the
subject of the new sentence, but it must be introduced by three
syllables, otherwise I am falling out of the iambic pentameter,
one of whose tolerated poetic licenses is that choriambic, ana-
paestic, dactylic, and trochiac feet may occasionally be inter-
spersed with pure iambs. One doesn't do iambic scansion saying
onLY a GIant, the natural rhythm is ONly a GIant. What about
Only a giant grammatically, as a subject? Well, that's what I
wanted to be, to move the snow. The giant can move it. Only he
can move it. I had it: Only a giant-----can move this. Not me.
Faint. That's it; I will faint. *Only a giant can move it, I will*
faint. The words can move this, I will faint seemed to fill in
the last portion of the fourth line, but I needed four syllables
at the beginning of the fourth line. Maybe describe the giant,
I thought, and the words jolly and green went down on the paper
almost automatically. They are actually 'wrong', they should go
in scansion as joLLY and GREEN, while in fact they go JOlly and
GREEN ' . . '; a dactyl and a half spondee. With can move this:
I will faint, however, the iambs are restored, and sometimes un-
interrupted, pure iambs get to be monotonous. I felt thrilled,
for I now had a full quatrain:

If snow were green and hot (which sure it ain't)
I'd leap for joy, and would feel less defiant
when tackling eight-foot drifts. Only a giant
jolly, and green, can move this: I will faint.

I now had the four-word rhyming outline (silent-restraint-
quaint-strident) of the second quatrain. Have I said enough about
what I might do if snow were green and hot? What other magic
might one use to make the snow go away? When I was a nine-year
old boy, I was stricken by polio. It was the summer of 1945, and
we were in a village in the county of Somogy near Lake Balaton,
where my mother had a modest summer house that survived the end
of the war. All the local boys were climbing trees, swimming, or
playing soccer, the Hungarian national sport; I was sitting in a
wheel-chair and was reading books, whatever I could get my hands
on. My mother gave me the Kalevala in Hungarian translation. Its

principal hero, Vejnemöjnen, is a magician who makes things happen
by verbal incantations. When faced by people physically much
stronger then he, he sings an incantation at them, and they are
drilled into the ground up to their necks and cannot get out for
several days. 'What a neat trick', I used to think; what he cannot do with his body, he does through the power of words. I became a precocious, somewhat smartallecky and overly verbal young-
ster who would flail his tongue at older men, stronger boys, any-
body who was foolish enough to listen, and when they wanted to
slap me for my arrogance, I accused them of cruelty and base igno-
bility for maligning a poor polio victim. In short I was black-
mailing and punishing the world for the great wrong that had be-
fallen me, and I considered verbal prowess to be the best means
to get even. Going into linguistics instead of comparative literature after graduation from Harvard (where I first met Dr. Ornstein, who was the first American to speak to me in fluent Hungarian, out of his wheel chair, he being a less fortunate victim of
polio than I was) may have had to do with an unconscious desire
to master the language better before I tried my hand at writing
literary prose or poetry in it; I don't know for sure. But this
was all subliminally in the background for the next line, *If singing melted snow, I'd sing*. I am not a good singer; I have a
hoarse tenor voice mixed with infelicitous falsettos. Aha! I
had just worked myself into yet another enjambment. Not too bad;
this gives me a chance to start a new sentence with silent; all I
need is a syllable. OK, it's *a*, the indefinite article. I now
had *If singing melted snow, I'd sing*. *A silent* - a silent what?
Whatever it will be, it must lead to restraint, because I put that
word down there as a milestone which I must reach. What should
restraint be? The end of a sentence? The direct object of a sentence? Maybe a new subject? I had no idea. 'A silent what?', I
continued. I thought of various delectable expletives including
'hell' and other, less printable ones; I visualized these as ap-
pearing between quotes in order to indicate that these are the
silent exclamations I am making inwardly so that only I can hear
them. Then it occurred to me that perhaps I don't have to cite
an exclamation: unspoken swear-word materialized rather soon and
without much conscious speculation. I now had a sentence start
which read a silent, unspoken swear word. What am I to do with
this so that I can let the line end in restraint? Predicate them
to one another? As I said the word restraint out loud a few times,
I realized that it sounded best when I imagined that it was an
order, sort of an exhortation, said to me encouragingly and warning-
ly, by some one else. I wrote: -------"Restraint / my boy!" I
now saw that restraint was both the beginning of a new sentence
and quoted rather than direct speech; this must be my social super-
ego talking to me through another person. That's fine; but I still
haven't finished the sentence with a silent, unspoken swear-word.
What can a silent, unspoken swear-word do or be? What should it
do or be? Must it do or be anything? I am trying to disallow myself to shout out loud, therefore the silent swear word must be
enough; it must do. I tried: a silent swear-word must be enough.
I didn't like the sequence must be enough; it was too choppy and

dactylic. What other way is there to say 'be enough' in English?
The adjective <u>sufficient</u> came to mind; a moment later the verb
<u>suffice</u>. I now wrote:

> *If singing melted snow, I'd sing. A silent*
> *unspoken swear-word must suffice: "Restraint*
> *my boy!"*

and looked at what I had so far. I was now into the third line of
the second quatrain, and my goal was to reach the word <u>quaint</u> to
close the second stanza. Someone here, perhaps my super-ego, my
parental ego-state, is warning me not to swear out loud, but to
swallow my anger. It's a privilege of native speakers to use
four-letter words; I have to be on my best behavior. What is
going to be quaint? The foreigner's use of 'hell' or some of its
fellow four-letter words? A fellow graduate student once, back
in 1962, after a two-hour car ride from Boston to New Haven, told
Professor Isidore Dyen, who sat in the back seat: 'Adam speaks
a quaint brand of English.' Mr. Dyen was laughing. The student,
Al Stevens, explained: 'He compared the Indonesian lady, Mrs.
Dardjowidjodjo, to an "apparition"... He meant that she was very
pretty.' I was laughing, too, and asked my riders: 'Would you
please tell me what <u>quaint</u> means? I never heard the word.' This
was true. 'Does it mean funny?' More laughter. 'Keep guessing,'
they said. 'Awkward' - I volunteered. 'No, not really.' 'Anti-
quated?' - more laughter. 'Well,' I asked, 'tell me, Mr. Dyen,
is Al praising me, or is he criticizing me?' They were roaring
with laughter. Mr. Dyen said: 'It is mildly offensive, Adam.
Look it up in a good dictionary when you get home.' We were driving back to Yale from the Ninth International Congress of Linguists which was held at M.I.T., and people generally didn't make
allowances for me in their speech. 'I take you as a straight American, Adam', Mr. Dyen said, 'that's why it jars us when you
don't know a common word.' I doubt that I was consciously aware
of all of this, but I caught myself writing: *Your friends may
find your English quaint - your accent jars, your speech is fast
and strident."* But this is two full quatrains already! Let's
see what I've got here:

> *If snow were green and hot (which it sure ain't)*
> *I'd leap for joy and would feel less defiant*
> *when tackling eight-foot drifts. Only a giant*
> *jolly and green, can move this: I may faint.*

> *If singing melted snow, I'd sing. A silent*
> *unspoken swear-word must suffice: "Restraint,*
> *my boy! Your friends may find your English quaint - - -*
> *your accent jars, your speech is fast and strident."*

I was getting quite annoyed at myself. What is this poem
about, anyway? Who am I kidding? I start out with snow, my desire to get rid of it; I think of the Jolly Green Giant, and then,
suddenly, find myself feeling sorry for myself because I cannot

swear gracefully in English? I had no intention of talking about
my accent and what it means to me; I was going to talk about snow
and how I hate it. I've got to get back to that snow somehow.
This is imperative if there is to be any cohesion to this inane
text.   Snow, snow, snow --- but I am talking about language, aren't
I? My own language, my accent, and my feelings about it.
      'What's wrong with this term paper, Mr. Dyen?,' I once asked
my respected teacher, and he answered: 'It's a snow job.' 'I am
sorry,' I said, 'I don't understand.' He explained. I acquired
the expressions to snow someone under, to do a snow job; later I
also learned that snow can refer to cocaine.
      I suddenly saw the light. It is no accident that I have
drifted into a discussion of language from the snow shovelling;
it had to happen that way. Talking about actual snow was a 'snow-
job'; I was just warming up to the occasion to express my feeling
of estrangement in Midwestern suburbia where I live. I belong,
and I don't. I get invited to my neighbors' cocktail parties, and
I manage to entertain them; but I never really feel truly relaxed
with them; I don't know what they think of me. One of the most
difficult things here in Lake Bluff is to explain to the ortho-
dontist, the real estate broker, the lawyer, the physical thera-
pist, the medical supplies wholesale dealer and importer, the
commodities trader, and the retired Navy Captain what my wife and
I do for a living: we are linguists. 'What is that?' they invariably ask us, and since theory would instantly put them to
sleep and a flat assertion such as 'we teach English to foreigners'
would really be underselling ourselves, we sometimes indulge in
stories about the Summer Institute of Linguistics and how the
missionary tagmemecists create alphabets for unwritten languages,
translate the Bible, and bring penicillin to preliterate peoples
in strange corners of the world. This gets some attention and
exclamations of the sort 'Oh, how interesting! You must like to
travel a lot? Have you been to Africa? My husband and I went
to Kenya's Serengeti for a safari last year...'
      I was penning out the four corner-stones of the third quatrain,
reasonably sure that my neighbors must be mentioned. I wrote:
neighbors - arbitrators - hot, and Hottentot. But how shall I
start the third quatrain? This is an important point in the unfolding of a sonnet's internal plot; something new must come in.
But the something 'new' cannot be disconnected from what I started
with; I must get back to that snow out there. No. Not out there.
The line jumped at me like a tiger from behind a bush: The snow's
inside. Maybe I AM a snow-artist, as Mr. Dyen suggested in one
of his intimidating moods. If I was, I probably wouldn't be able
to admit it. If I admit that I must act that way sometimes, maybe
I'll get free of it eventually. At any rate, I must change the
focus of the scenery. I'll make this the semantic axis of my
story; here is where I'll really shift pace. All right then. What.
do I do with the 'snow' (my loose talk about my profession) that
affects my neighbors? I throw it at them, not with a shovel, of
course, but at 4th of July parties with a drink in my hand. I
wrote:

The snow's inside. I throw it at my neighbors,
these gentle and bewildered arbitrators - - - - -

arbitrators of what? I looked at the line-final call-word, and
saw that it was hot. This reminded me that I had used hot
earlier, in line I, in its primary sense 'high in temperature.'
Next to it, in line 1, is the word green also in its primary
physical color sense. Can it mean anything else? I thought of
Chomsky's colorless green ideas sleep furiously and all the fun
we have had with it during these past 20 years. Dell Hymes
had rhymed it forwards and backwards in a variety of sonnets;
John Oller interpreted it psychiatrically as meaning 'bleak,
immature ideas lurk in the unconscious ready to break out and
attack;' and I interpreted it once similarly for a Hungarian
audience in Szeged in 1972. 'Immature', 'juvenile' (as in green-
horn) is a good sense of green, and so is boasting of foreign
travel and the excessive seeking of adventures abroad. Cool in
its socio-psychological sense of 'detached, elegant, unhurried,
relaxed, clever,' etc., announced its availability by juxtaposi-
tion to hot, and so before I knew it I wrote:

of why it's "cool" and yet so "green" and "hot"
selling linguistics to the Hottentot - -

except I didn't know whether to make a period or to go on. What
makes people decide to make a period or to go on? Does any one
know? Does Chomsky know? My dilemma was solved by my great
desire to bring the sonnet to a close with a couplet. I am a
frustrated musician; I play rather mediocre piano, and when no
one is around, I indulge in composing songs. I like recapitula-
tions. So I wrote down faint and ain't, which made me ask the
question, who is fainting? I already said that I would; maybe
the Hottentot should faint. But if he faints, Hottentot can't end
the sentence and I am going to be stuck with a who- clause. So
be it: selling linguistics to the Hottentot / who ta TUM ta TUM
ta TUM ta TUM would faint. All right, let's see what this adds
up to: who TUM ta TUM ta TUM would surely faint. What would
make a Hottentot faint that is connected to snow (or "snow", as
the case may be) and that is somehow connected to linguistics?
Chances are that Hottentots never see real snow; if they saw it,
without previous explanation, they wouldn't know what it was. It
would literally (as well as figuratively) snow them under. Then
I looked at the words in the first line and saw snow, green, and
hot, in that order. 'Maybe I could just reverse them and see what
I get,' I thought, and wrote:

who, - - - - - - - - - - - - would surely faint,
hot words are snow that's green (which it sure ain't).

This, however, didn't make sense. The trouble was that it was
unclear who thinks or says the last line. If I say it, it doesn't
make any sense at all; but the Hottentot can't say it either. So

maybe a third person must enter and talk to the Hottentot, whereby the last line can become quoted speech. I put quotation marks
around the last line, changing <u>it</u> to <u>they</u>, and now had:

> who - - - - - - *would surely faint:*
> *"hot words are snow that's green" (which sure they ain't).*

But what am I to do with - - - - -? Everything depends on it. I
tried various things, such as <u>if some one told him</u>, <u>if he found
out</u>, and many more. What I need is five syllables that introduce
what I've got between quotation marks as quoted speech: what
about <u>if he heard the truth</u>? I penned out the whole sentence
from <u>I throw it at my neighbors</u>, reinserting <u>it</u> again for <u>they</u>:

> *I throw it at my neighbors,*
> *these gentle and bewildered arbitrators*
> *of why it's "cool" and yet so·"green" and "hot"*
> *selling linguistics to the Hottentot*
> *who, if he heard the truth, would surely faint:*
> *"hot words are snow that's green" (which sure it ain't).*

I had to see it in a variety of formats, which appear above in
scattered parts. Later I changed the format to a solid, indented
block of 14 lines and altered details here and there. I also
added a title and a subtitle:

> The Mad Foreign Linguist Speaks to His
> <u>Straight American Neighbors During Chicago's</u>
> <u>Great Blizzard of '79 in Commemoration of</u>
> <u>Jack Ornstein's 65th Birthday.</u>

> If snow were green and hot (which sure it ain't)
> I'd leap for joy, and would feel less defiant
> when tackling eight-foot drifts. Only a giant
> jolly, and green, can move this: I will faint.
>   If swearing melted snow, I'd swear. A silent
>   regurgitation must suffice: "Restraint,
>   my boy! Your friends may find your English quaint - -
>   your accent jars, your speech is fast and strident."
> The snow's inside. I throw it at my neighbors,
> these gentle and bewildered arbitrators
> of why it's "cool" and yet so "green" and "hot"
> selling The Grammar to the Hottentot
>   who, if he heard the Truth, would surely faint:
>   <u>"hot words are snow that's green"</u> (which sure they ain't).

    I have no illusions about the intrinsic literary merit of this
text and I certainly don't expect a great emotional reaction from
the reader as one might in the case of less structured heart-poetry.
I have edited out the line <u>if singing melted snow, I'd sing.</u> A

silent / unspoken swear word and substituted if swearing melted
snow, I'd swear. A Silent / regurgitation must suffice. Trans-
incantation (not to be found in any dictionary) for regurgitation may say more for 'verbal magic'; regurgitation, however,
better explains what immigrants do to vocabulary primarily used
by natives. It is like forced feeding that has difficulty set-
tling to the stomach. My goal was to illustrate, by writing, explaining and editing this sonnet, what the phenomenon of 'lexical
insertion' might look like in a performance model that seeks to
attain maximum psychological realism. None of the attendant
circumstances were invented; "ALL IS TRUE," as they used to say
on the front page of certain historical novels.

    Situations correlate with certain institutionalized bundles
of meaning (sememes). One, two, or more lexemes, idiosyncrati-
cally or logically relevant to a given situation tend to line up
in the conscious and the unconscious, thereby forming two kinds
of 'elicitors' at once: a word-association elicitor (unconscious), and a more deliberate phrase, clause, and eventually
sentence elicitor (see the various possible games described
earlier in this paper). A person indulging in poetic behavior
is simultaneously his own analyst and his own patient and the game
is played in terms of soliloquy or internal monolog eventually reinforced by paper and pencil or typewriter. Once a combination of
words is put down on paper, they assume a force of their own bring-
ing to mind suggestions and possibilities of which the 'poet' was
not at all, or only most vaguely, conscious at the beginning.
Most poetry is like finding a shiny button on the street, falling
in love with it, and then having a coat tailored to suit the
button. This being the case, the notion of 'lexical insertion'
evaporates in thin air, if viewed as a part of poetic behavior,
if by lexical insertion we mean a reasonable specific deep structure and/or surface structure derivation replete with categorical
markers which then somehow conjure up real lexemes in order to become real sentences. Note that there is something of this sort
going on, insofar as the text, as it evolves, creates certain
patterns which then need to be filled. The search for the right
word becomes quite deliberate in these cases as I have tried to
show above, but this is actually incidental to the poetic process. Lexical insertion, however, can be interpreted entirely
differently. Let us imagine a high school chemistry laboratory:
there is a thin, tall jar, filled with water that has a high concentration of salt in it. The teacher INSERTS A THREAD from the
top and tells the students that a few days later, when they re-
move the string, small salt crystals will be visible along the
string. The string is usually called a catalyst during such
simple demonstrations. The body of lexical knowledge a fluent
speaker has of his/her language may be compared to the solution
containing the high concentration of NACL (kitchen salt), and
the inserted string to a number of actual situations; conversely,
the physical chemistry of the kind of salt in use may be compared
to the speaker's unconscious knowledge of his grammar, and the
inserted string may be compared to association-set call-words.
Both analogies leak, and both contain a fair amount of truth.

Looked at with tolerance and dialectical stereo-vision, they reveal something about language that we, as speakers, all know intuitively, but as linguists have a hard time facing and explaining. The truth is that a single word can be a syntactic event, and the entire grammar can be viewed as a collection of words. At the same time, of course, a single word can, and frequently must, be seen as an isolated item in an inventory, and the grammar can be seen as a highly complex network of relations (if one is stratificationally oriented) or as a large body of rewrite rules (if one is transformationally oriented). Words tend to create their own syntax, and syntactic patterns cause words to crystallize in the right places. Words secrete tactic patterns and tactic patterns cause words to crystallize at crucial junctures. Lexical insertion, I suggest, ought to be renamed LEXEMIC CRYSTALLIZATION and syntax ought to be renamed LEXEMIC SECRETION.

The 'chemistry' of it all is enormously complex. Involved in it are the speaker's self-image as a member of society; his self-image as a complex bundle of emotions; his ability or inability to avail himself of certain lexemes, all of which are social products and bear distinguishing marks of prestigious stigmatized, colloquial, technical, common, or rare status (Ornstein 1975). The grammar, of course, has its own tremendous complexities, but it must be seen as strictly secondary in importance during the communication process. This is not to downgrade grammar. Without it, lexis can only limp along, as if on crutches. Frequently, of course, two steps will do the job--would you drive a Cadillac to your neighbor's house 20 yards away to borrow two eggs? The single utterance /mmmmmmmmmm!/ as produced by my ten-month old daughter achieves most things she cares to achieve; by pointing at the milk bottle and the bread, she orders us to give them to her; it can also mean 'get me out of the high chair,' 'change me,' 'I am sleepy,' and a variety of other manipulatory functions (see Halliday 1975). To call /mmmmmmmmmm!/ a lexeme, a morpheme, a word, a sentence, or a proposition would be just as absurd as denying that it contains germinally all of these and, given her social situation in the family, it delivers her all the goods and services she wants.

But ARE we all poets, in fact, as I suggested? I think we are. Certainly my ten-month old is. Beside her command word /mmmmmmmmmm!/ and a more recent /dæ - dæ - dæ/ (on a rising intonation) meaning something like 'what is the name of that?,' she plays a number of vocal games with us at the breakfast table. She looks at me and says /ghaaaaaa/. I look back at her and /ghaaaaaa/. She smiles, happily, and now says /ghaaaaaa/, /ghaaaaaa/. I repeat after her /ghaaaaaa/, /ghaaaaaa/. We go up to three or four /ghaaaaaa/s, make them at lower and higher pitches, of shorter or longer duration. It is an intense and lively exchange, everyone gets involved, and it makes us feel good. Sometimes we call it the 'Let's be Lions' game, or just /ghaaaaaa/. There are no words, no lexemes, and no grammatical patterns to act as 'elicitors' or as 'insertions'; /ghaaaaaa/ just HAPPENS, it just

IS. She can get carried away with /ghaaaaaa/; when I am receiving
a long distance phone call and she won't stop, it is downright
irritating: /ghaaaaaa/ can be felicitous, and it can be mal à
propos.
    Maybe it is a poem.

NOTES

[1]This paper owes a good deal to Charles F. Hockett, William
M. Christie, Jr., and Michael Eric Bennett who have given me
valuable suggestions on how to improve the original version. They
are not to be blamed for any errors, over-simplifications, and the
like, which remain in here solely as my own fault; nor do they
necessarily agree with my presentation and my conclusions.

[2]I may be technically wrong about this, though it is one logical inference to be drawn from Jaynes 1976. Insofar as dreams
are 'unconscious' rather than 'conscious' (which sounds intuitively sensible to me) and insofar as dreams are typical 'right hemisphere activity,' the correlation seems to exist. This is not to
deny that certain 'right hemisphere activities' such as car driving
or typing cannot become 'unconscious' due to routine activities,
overrepetition, and the like. I have come across people who add
up long columns of numbers while talking on the phone quasi-uncon-
sciously. Future research not available to me at the present will
have to settle the physiological loci of conscious and unconscious
and the above statement should be taken metaphorically.

[3]'Mind' is used here in its general or sloppy sense since I
cannot use 'brain'; mentality, outlook, personality and consciousness all say too much and too little; thus the sloppy sense of
'mind' offers the least offensive intersection of the senses I
need.

[4]Professor Hockett points out (personal communication) that
in the literature of aesthetics there are several important statements regarding how poets feel about the interaction between the
piece they write and their own intentions. To Robert Frost, for
instance, the making of a genuine poem was that it had to be a
discovery in the poet's experience with the language, as surprising to the poet as to his audience. It is rather rare in world
literature to find a major master who actually also wrote a doctoral dissertation on how he composes, but this is the case with
Hungary's undisputed leading poet laureate, Sándor Weöres (1913-   ),
who translated most of Western lyrics into Hungarian. In his
doctoral dissertation The Birth of the Poem (A vers születése,
Pécs 1933, published as Weöres 1970) under the chapter 'The Development' W. contrasts Coleridge's Kubla Khan and Poe's The Raven as
two types of poems that had attendant circumstances well documented
in the literature. Coleridge wrote in a trance, almost unconscious-

ly, while Poe himself describes The Raven as a precalculated and almost mathematical progression. Weöres points these out as two extremes and suggests that most poets use both intuition and premeditation. An English translation of W's dissertation is in progress and will reach print within a year. The phenomenon also exists in musical composition and the visual arts; both compositions and paintings as well as sculptures have a way of unfolding themselves to the utter surprise of the artist at work.

REFERENCES

Berne, Eric. 1969. What do you say after you say hello? New York: Grove Press.

Bolinger, Dwight L. 1975. Aspects of Language. 2nd ed. New York: Harcourt, Brace, Jovanovich.

Christie, William M., Jr. 1977. A stratificational view of linguistic change. Edward Sapir monograph no. 4. Lake Bluff IL: Jupiter Press.

Dell, Gary S. and Peter A. Reich. 1976. A model of slips of the tongue. The third LACUS forum, ed. by R. Di Pietro and E. Blansitt. Columbia SC: Hornbeam Press, pp. 448-55.

Di Pietro, Robert J. and Edward L. Blansitt, Jr., eds. 1976. The third LACUS forum. Columbia SC: Hornbeam Press.

Halliday, M.A.K. 1975. Learning how to mean. London: Edward Arnold.

Jaynes, Julian. 1976. The origin of consciousness in the breakdown of the bicameral mind. Boston: Houghton Mifflin Co.

Lamb, Sydney M. 1966. Outline of stratificational grammar. Washington DC: Georgetown University Press.

Lockwood, David G. 1972. Introduction to stratificational linguistics. New York: Harcourt, Brace, Jovanovich.

Makkai, Adam. 1971. Degrees of nonsense, or transformation, stratification, and the contextual adjustability principle. Comparative Literature Studies 7.479-92.

——————. 1972. Idiom structure in English. The Hague: Mouton.

——————. 1973. A pragmo-ecological view of linguistic structure and language universals. Language Sciences 27.9-23.

Ornstein, Jacob. 1975. The need for a sociolinguistic marking system and a proposal. In Di Pietro and Blansitt 1976, pp. 514-28.

Sándor Weöres. 1970. A vers születése ("The birth of a poem"). Összegyüjtött írások ("Collected writings"). Budapest: Magvető könyvkiadó.

BILINGUALISM
OF MEXICAN-AMERICAN CHILDREN:
LANGUAGE CHARACTERISTICS

JOSEPH H. MATLUCK

University of Texas—Austin

In 1973 Betty Mace and the present author reported an extensive
description of the language characteristics of Mexican-American
children (Matluck and Mace 1973). Since that time we have greatly
extended our research on Mexican-American bilingualism. So much
has been published in this area in recent years that we would now
like to summarize our previous description, to report on the results of our own research since that time, and also present an up-
dated assessment of some of the more recent work that is now available both in and out of print in this very timely, interesting,
and complex field of research.

We had pointed out that the Spanish which bilingual Mexican-
American children are exposed to is a legitimate dialect of Spanish,
as attested to previously by a host of investigators (Espinosa 1917a,
1917b; Cárdenas 1970; Clegg 1969; Lance 1969; González 1968, 1970;
and many others) and that, as suggested by Cárdenas (1970:20) in
dividing the U.S. Southwest into four dialect zones, we believe that
"it is safe to suggest that the greatest majority [of the original
migration patterns from Mexico to the U.S.] came from the North
[of Mexico] and the Central High Plains," and that the daily in-
fusion of influence from the former zone has, over the years, resulted in an educated standard of the Spanish Southwest resembling that
of the Northern Zone of Mexico. Our mentions of 'standard' will
therefore use that zone as point of reference. We maintained, further, that this dialect, like many others, is a regional variety of
Spanish which has all the basic structures of that language, but
because of particular geographical, sociological, and linguistic
circumstances, has a most powerful overlay of English which sets

211

it apart from all other Hispanic dialects except, perhaps, the Puerto Rican.

That it is recognized as such a dialect is obvious in the recent writings of many investigators such as Bills and Ornstein (1976), Lozano (1974), Keller (1976), Troike (1968), González (1973), Ornstein (1972), Bowen (1974), and a host of others. Rosaura Sánchez (1972:47) classifies it as the Mexican-American Spanish dialect group of the U.S. since it is a subgroup of a language used within certain geographical limits, and she agrees with this author that it shares various characteristics with other Hispano-American dialects, with its distinctive features coming from the contact with English. She refers to this English influence as interference, a concept which many linguists refuse to consider appropriate with respect to this dialect. There is, of course, much controversy over whether certain features of Mexican-American English or Spanish are a result of "interference" from the other language. That polemic is beyond the scope of this presentation. We shall classify certain features of Mexican-American Spanish and Mexican-American English as being purportedly or apparently developmental or acquisitional in nature, others as purportedly or apparently deriving some influence from the other language. It appears clearer and more logical to discuss them in this way, but here we are interested only in whether the influence from the other language is present rather than how or why it "got there."

Over the past five years we have been collecting data on the language of bilingual children and now have a large archive of taped material that was collected during the field-testing of an oral language assessment instrument. In 1973-74 we developed the MAT-SEA-CAL Oral Proficiency Tests (Matluck and Mace-Matluck 1974), a series of comparable tests (designed for use in grades K-4) in English and five other languages, one of which, of course, was Spanish. These tests were extensively field-tested in western Washington and Idaho, in California, and in Texas, with over 6,000 tests administered over a three-year period. About 2,000 bilingual children were tested with the instrument in English and Spanish in the above-mentioned areas. The various validation studies conducted during this field-test stage (Talbott 1976; Doyle 1976a, 1976b, 1976c; Matluck and Mace-Matluck 1975, 1976, 1977; Matluck 1976, 1978) have indicated high reliability and strong indications of validity, so that numerous research projects have been undertaken using the test results and the in-process analysis as a data base.

The tests were designed as a diagnostic instrument and the significant grammatical structures of each language were placed, for scoring and analysis, into eight semantic categories which we considered to be the basic communication concepts that a child must handle (in any language) in order to perform in a school setting, i.e., the skills of identifying, classifying, quantifying, interrogating, and negating, and of showing important relationships such as spatial, case, and temporal.

We then determined which grammatical manifestations of the language--English, for example--the child must handle in order to comprehend or communicate these concepts. The other languages express the same concepts as does English, but each one almost always

does so in different ways (i.e., with different grammatical structures).

We have prepared, for several school districts which uséd the
tests in Texas and Idaho, an analysis of the errors of their bilingual children on the Spanish and English tests. These errors
were categorized in terms of the eight semantic categories, and
an inventory of the language manifestations of each of the grammatical structures causing difficulty was prepared for each child,
each classroom, and each school district. We have analyzed these
errors in terms of descending order of difficulty, not only by
grade level, but by proficiency level within each age-grade group.
Proficiency levels were determined on the basis of total test score
as follows: Level I, 30%-50%; Level II, 51%-70%; Level III, 71%-
93%; Level IV, 94%-100%. Thus far, in this pilot-study stage we
have been able to analyze the errors of 59 children in grades K-2
on the Spanish test and 119 children in grades K-1 on the English
test for three school districts in Texas and Idaho. In a very
short time, our data reduction system should provide us with this
kind of data for 2,000 bilingual Spanish-speaking children across
grades K-4.

Our analysis of these errors across two-to-three grade levels
leads us to believe that we have data which provide a very promising
view of both developmental and acquisitional trends in the language
patterns of Mexican-American children.

Characteristics of Spanish spoken

In the article previously referred to (Matluck and Mace 1973)
we discussed various aspects of the languages of five-to-six year
old Mexican-American children. Among those cited with respect to
Spanish were: 1) developmental, 2) influences of a second language
(English) at all structural levels--lexical, morphological, phonological, and syntactical, but with special emphasis on the latter,
3) internalization of ruralisms and popularisms used by adults in
the region, 4) the language of peers, 5) trends in linguistic
change, and 6) code-switching.

Developmental

We would now like to focus our attention primarily on a discussion of the developmental aspect, concentrating on the evidence
we have gathered from our own firsthand research, with supporting
evidence from other recent studies. In our research we analyzed
the pattern of errors in the spoken Spanish of the 59 K-2 bilingual
children from two points of view: 1) by semantic category, and
2) within each of the semantic categories.

A. Errors by semantic categories

1. In kindergarten the categories that produced the greatest
number of grammatical errors were Temporality (above all), Classification, Number, and Interrogation. Negation, Case Relationship,
and Spatial Relationship were next in the order of difficulty. Al-

ready diminishing as a problem area was the category of Identification (see Appendix for our definition of these semantic categories).

2. By first grade, the only notable change was a substantial decrease in the percentage of errors in the category of Number.

3. By second grade, the Temporality and Classification categories were still causing great difficulty, while problems in Negation, Spatial Relationship, and Interrogation were greatly diminished in either extension or frequency of occurrence, and the errors in Identification, Case Relationship, and Number were fast disappearing.

B. <u>Errors within semantic categories</u>

1. <u>Temporality</u>. Structures within this category which persisted in difficulty throughout all three grades, as manifested by frequency of occurrence, were the regular preterites (saltó, regalaron, vio) and the present perfect (ha estado enfermo). Troubles with irregular preterites (such as fue) were also still present throughout, but at grade two show definite signs of diminishing in difficulty.

Many errors of very high frequency at kindergarten virtually disappear as a source of difficulty at subsequent grade levels. Some of these are the periphrastic future (va a comer), the imperfect (jugaba, vendía), the future of conjecture (la llevará) and the subjunctive in adverbial clauses (después de que lave).

2. <u>Classification</u>. Among persistent difficulties in this category were structures involving gender, noun-adjective agreement (esa cuerda), object pronouns (la veo--referring to inanimate objects, in this case casa), and the word order of postposed descriptive adjectives (la oreja izquierda).

Errors diminishing to a very low incidence after kindergarten were omission vs. inclusion of definite and indefinite articles (¿Es médico el señor alto?), diminutive infixes (perrito), comparative constructions (más bonito que), possessive adjectives vs. pronouns (su/suyo), word order of adverbial and adjective modifiers (una flor muy bonita), prepositional phrases indicating mode of conveyance (en bicicleta), and the subjunctive in adjective clauses (No veo ninguno que sea rojo).

3. <u>Interrogation</u>. Errors in this category were among the most persistent in K-1, but most of them cease to be troublesome at subsequent grades, except for two structures: problems with the intonation marker in yes-no questions drop off markedly at grade two, at which grade level the contrast between question words such as ¿Adónde?/¿Cuándo?/¿En qué? still cause great difficulty. Errors in tag questions (Es amigo suyo el bajito, ¿no?; No dice "miau," ¿verdad?) and the ¿Qué?/¿Quién? contrast (¿Quién es?) were quite noticeable in kindergarten, but diminished in frequency at other grade levels.

4. <u>Negation</u>. Only the sino/pero contrast remained high in difficulty throughout. Other structures such as the double negative (no veo ninguno) and the negative particle followed by the verb negator (No, no fue eso) were major problems only in kindergarten.

5. <u>Spatial Relationship</u>. Difficulties which were particularly presistent throughout all three grades were the éste/ése demonstra-

tive pronoun contrast and adverbial phrases such as <u>por debajo de</u>, <u>encima de</u>, although divergence from the standard in the latter structures may not be developmental in nature, since <u>abajo de</u>, <u>adentro de</u>, <u>arriba de</u>, etc., are very frequent in the speech of adults. Directional pronouns such <u>a</u>, <u>de</u> were troublesome only for kindergarten children.

     6. <u>Number</u>. This category contains structures presenting considerable difficulty at the kindergarten level; they begin to taper off at the upper proficiency levels of kindergarten, but do not really diminish until Grade Two. Troubles with syllabic noun plurals (<u>pinceles</u>) hang on the longest, but by Grade Two are almost under control. Some of the difficult structures for kindergarten children but which no longer seem to bother children in Grades One and Two are the following: mixed plurals (<u>hijos</u>), object pronoun number (<u>la/las</u>), demonstrative pronouns (<u>ésta/éstas</u>), noun-adjective agreement (<u>sus perritos</u>), and pronoun-adjective agreement (<u>yo - grande</u>; <u>ellos - pequeños</u>).

     7. <u>Case Relationship</u>. Of moderate difficulty at kindergarten, most of the structures in this category present minimal problems in subsequent years, to wit: the pronoun subject/object contrast (<u>la</u>, <u>las</u> / <u>ella</u>, <u>ellas</u>), the syntactic pattern for unplanned occurrences, ethical dative, etc. (e.g., <u>se le cayó</u>), and the dative/accusative contrast among object pronouns (<u>le/lo</u>, <u>la</u>). The only exception was the postposed possessive adjective (<u>amigo suyo</u>) which persisted as a source of error even at Grade Two.

     8. <u>Identification</u>. Problems in this category occurred with appreciable frequency only at the kindergarten level. Some of these were: action verbs such as <u>comprar</u>, <u>ponerse</u>; count nouns (<u>un escritorio</u>); agreement of subject pronoun and verb (<u>soy - yo</u>; <u>son - ellos</u>); the neuter demonstrative pronoun <u>eso</u>; and the prepositional phrase indicating destination (<u>para su cumpleaños</u>).

C. <u>Summary</u>.

     A good many of the errors in structures not controlled by kindergarten children but which seem to cause relatively few problems for children at subsequent grade levels may well be related to maturation and concept development as well as to language growth. The structures which continue to cause difficulty for many children beyond the kindergarten level may well be indicative of those which develop late in the acquisition process of Spanish. This would certainly seem to be the case with the perfect tenses, noun and pronoun gender, and to some extent, number marking and/or agreement.

     Consistent with our findings are those reported by various investigators. With respect to the perfect tenses, González (1970) shows that these tenses were the last to appear in the speech of his Mexican-American subjects age 2-5, and Cohen (1976) finds frequent deviation in the formation of the past participle; some deviation he finds developmental in origin and other he attributes to English influence (<u>está sentado</u> > <u>está sentando</u> from <u>he is sitting</u> [down]). Difficulty with the preterite per se has not been substantiated by other studies, but the regulariza-

tion of irregular verb forms in child-language is well documented.
As to gender, Brisk (1976) found that at Grade One both monolingual Spanish-speaking children in Argentina and bilingual children in Boston were still in the process of acquiring article-
noun gender.   Similarly, Padilla and Lindholm (1976) noted that
gender in the interrogative word ¿Cuánto? did not appear in the
speech of their bilingual subjects prior to the age of 5.8.   Cohen
also found numerous instances of wrong gender in articles and demonstratives.   Brisk also reported greater difficulties with feminine nouns than with masculine nouns, which would seem to be related to Rodríguez-Bou's (1966) findings that the vocabulary of
preschool children contained a greater number of masculine nouns
than feminine.   Brisk's study also reveals greater gender problems
with nouns of neutral gender marking.   To our knowledge, the only
study which indicates any problems with the postposed adjective is
Elías's (1976) which finds this feature especially among children
(e.g., una español maestra).   Some instances of error in grammatical number were found by Cohen in article-noun agreement (un
papeles, el manos, etc.) and possessive and descriptive noun-modifiers (este casitas, mal cosas).   In adult speech, Elías reported
a single form of the question-word ¿Quién?, used with either the
singular or plural form of the verb (¿Quién van...?).

Influence from a Second Language (English)

     In 1973 we suggested that much of the influence generally as-
cribed to English was actually either syntactic or lexico-syntactic
in nature and that the latter should really be classified as syntactic, and we maintained then, supported in part only by Hernández
et al. ("Introduction," 1975), González (1968), and Cornejo (1969),
that the influence from English on the syntax of Mexican-American
spoken Spanish was indeed considerable.   So much supporting evidence has been added in recent years that we believe the validity
of our thesis is hardly questionable today.
     In the area of phonology, where English influence is less and
some of which is indeed questionable, recent evidence again sup-
ports and reaffirms the validity of the four areas of possible
phonological influence from English which we pointed out previously
(Matluck and Mace, 1973):   1) the weakening of intervocalic /y/
(e.g.:   eos, sía, cabeo, tortías < ella, ellos, silla, cabello, tor-
tillas); 2) the use of the English retroflex r as an alternate
syllable-final variant of /r/ (carne); 3) the sporadic occurrence
of the labiodental [v] allophone of the /b/ phoneme; and 4) the
high occurrence of the glottal stop [ʔ] across word boundaries
before a word beginning with a vowel ([el ʔ abrigo], etc.).   Sánchez (1972) adds a fifth area, that of intonation patterns, which
is greatly in need of additional investigation.   Sánchez (1972),
Elías (1976), and Phillips (1976) list the weakening of intervocalic /y/ as characteristic of two different Mexican-American dialects; Phillips attributes it to English influence; Elías and
Sánchez do not.   As definite English influence González (1974) and
Phillips cite labiodental [v] in free variation with bilabial [b]
in Texas and California respectively; Elías and Lastra (1969) agree

as to its occurrence, but deny the influence of English. Sánchez
and Phillips attribute to English the sporadic use of a retroflex
r in the Spanish of those areas, especially in the final cluster
/-rC/. Phillips reports a fairly high incidence of the separation
into separate syllables of vowels in contact across word boundaries. As to intonational influence from English, Sánchez notes
the frequent use in Mexican-American Spanish of the English /231↓/
pattern instead of the /1211↓/ pattern characteristic of declarative statements in Spanish. In addition, she also cites the following segments as influenced by English: 1) /u/ < /yu/ (comyuni-
car); 2) intervocalic /d/ crossing phonemic lines to appear as an
alveolar tap (puedo, medio, etc. > puero, merio), also noted by
González; 3) alternation of [č] and [š], also cited by Elías and
Phillips. The latter reports incidence of [θ] (theorías), of
voiced [z] in intervocalic of initial position ([zíper] < zipper);
and /-si/ > [š] (nashionalidad, etc.). The latter structure was
also found by Foster (1976) in El Paso.
     A final note on a phonological structure of great interest
and importance, in which English most certainly plays no part,
but which has now been reported at least three times to our knowledge for Texas and California Spanish, and which needs a sober
appraisal, we believe, in order that our data on Mexican-American
Spanish be scrupulously scientific and accurate. Sánchez,
Phillips, and Elías all report finding aspiration or deletion of
final /s/ in California and Texas. Elías says quite categorically that /s/ is either aspirated or deleted in syllable-final
position and indeed is "often" aspirated even in intervocalic
position, giving a wealth of examples throughout her study
(ehperate, ondehtá, ehcuela, [·leihémoseinglé] le dicemos en
ingles, etc.) that would lead one to believe that the Spanish of
the barrio in East Austin, Texas is, in this respect, a Caribbean
dialect, just like Puerto Rican, Cuban, and others. However,
that this is a regular, systematic feature of any Mexican-American
dialect is very seriously questioned by most investigators who
have spent long years working in the field of Mexican-American
dialectology. Sánchez states that it "aspirates in any position,"
and cites nojotros, dijir, puertah, ehte, but makes no further
reference to it, thereby giving much the same impression as
Elías. (The first two examples, of course, have historical and
morphological implications.) Of the three investigators, only
Phillips takes frequency of occurrence into consideration and demonstrates carefully (and correctly, we believe) that 1) the
phonetic realization is regularly a sibilant [s] before a pause;
2) that the tendency in Los Angeles is definitely not to "drop"
or aspirate final /s/; 3) that before a voiced consonant some
cases were found with [ʰ]; and 4) that before a juncture, a vowel
or a voiceless consonant it is almost always [s]. The key, as
always, to fully trustworthy dialect investigation is frequency of
occurrence. Before designating a phenomenon as characteristic of
a dialect, the linguist has the responsibility of determining how
often it does not occur as well as simply asserting that it does
occur or that it can occur.

Characteristics of English Spoken

In our 1973 study we demonstrated the magnitude of what we
considered the most critical of the problems facing (some or many)
Mexican-American children in the English-speaking school setting,
namely the loss of lexical and grammatical signals through under-
developed perception of English phonology. We demonstrated how
this faulty perception vitally affects not only his lexical and
grammatical failings but also his ability to learn as fast or as
efficiently in English as his monolingual English-speaking peers
in every area of learning. He has learned his English in a dual-
language setting in which Spanish is usually spoken in the home
but may not be the primary language of communication, and in
which English is the language he must use when he steps outside
the barrio or inside the school--an English judged by monolingual
standards alone. But the English he commands was learned in an
environment where the adult patterns which served as his model
were already infused with roughly two or three generations of
linguistic and cultural interaction in a lower socioeconomic-
level community.
    We also suggested that, apart from his adult models, some of
the additional factors which influence the English he speaks were:
1) second-language acquisitional factors, 2) native-language
(Spanish) influence, 3) the language of his peers, and 4) trends
in linguistic change.

Acquisitional

    We would like to focus our attention on acquisitional fac-
tors, reporting the findings of our own firsthand research and
citing evidence from other recent studies. Again we have analyzed
the pattern of errors found in the spoken English of the 119 K-1
bilingual children in our study 1) by semantic category, and 2)
within each of these semantic categories.

A. Errors by semantic category

    1. In kindergarten all semantic categories were proportion-
ally full at the middle proficiency level. At the higher proficiency levels, Number and Temporality produced the greatest frequency of grammatical errors. Case Relationship and Identification were only minimally represented and the categories of Classification, Negation, Interrogation, and Spatial Relationship
seemed to present very little difficulty.
    2. At Grade One, Number and Temporality errors were still
the most frequent, while those of Interrogation, Identification,
Case Relationship, Negation, Spatial Relationship, and Classification were still somewhat troublesome at the middle proficiency
levels, but were fast disappearing as problem areas at the higher
levels.
    Our research is still in progress, and unfortunately, we have
not yet been able to analyze the Grade Two data in this manner.

B. Errors within semantic categories

1. Number. The incidence of difficulty in this category remains among the highest throughout, even at the higher proficiency
levels. Most persistent at all grades and proficiency levels are
noun plurals and subject-verb number agreement of the /-z/ and
/ɨz/ types (balloons, brushes, plays) and irregular nouns and
verbs (children, has). Noun plurals with /-z/ decrease in difficulty after kindergarten, but errors in subject-verb agreement persist throughout the highest proficiency levels of first grade, as
is also the case for the irregular noun children and the pronoun
singular/plural contrasts (she/they; her/them). Gone as a serious
problem after the middle proficiency level of kindergarten was the
demonstrative pronoun number contrast of this/these.
2. Temporality. On the heels of Number as a source of difficulty throughout K-1 is the category of Temporality. Still-
lingering trouble spots even at the upper proficiency levels of
both grades are the following structures: 1) all past tense allo-
morphs (jumped, picked, played, painted), with /-t/ and /ɨd/ causing more difficulty to the upper levels than /-d/; 2) the periphrastic future (is going to eat, is going to put--difficulties
with this structure persist longer in production than in listening
comprehension); 3) the past progressive (was watching, was selling);
4) the present perfect (he's been), with the participle less persistent than the contracted he's. Still a source of difficulty
at the middle levels of proficiency of both grades but less so at
the upper levels are the past irregulars (went, saw) and the contracted form of the future (she'll).
3. Interrogation. This category was most troublesome at the
middle proficiency levels in such structures as 1) negative tags,
with three different items persisting at Grade One (...isn't he?,
...can't he?, ...won't she?); 2) word order of yes-no questions
(Is...tall man...?); and 3) the who/what question-word contrast
(Who's that?).
4. Identification. The highest frequency of errors in this
category, even at the upper proficiency levels of Grade One, was
the pronoun sex indicator (he/she, it/he, she, him, her). Mass
nouns vs. count nouns were also a source of great difficulty (a
desk, a clothesline, an ice cream cone, some milk, some meat), but
only some meat still remains a problem at the upper proficiency
levels of Grade One. Troublesome at kindergarten but not at Grade
One were lexical action verbs such as buy and play and the inclusion vs. omission of the copula (I am big, they are little).
5. Case Relationship. The most persistently troublesome
areas in this category were the /-s/ allomorph of the noun possessive and the noun-possessive word order in the cat's ear, but
children in the upper proficiency levels of both grades fared much
better with these structures.
A source of continuing difficulty, except at the upper proficiency levels of Grade One, were the following: 1) pronoun sub-
ject/object in two structures (he[is giving] him and the she, they/
her, them contrast); 2) pronoun subject/possessive (he [rode] his
bike]). A difficult structure only at the middle levels of kinder-

garten was the word order of the direct-object-plus-complement in the verb phrase ([He got a bike] for his birthday).

6. Negation. None of the structures in this category persisted at the upper proficiency levels of either grade, but two patterns provided a continuing source of difficulty at the middle levels: 1) the double negative (I don't [see] any...) gave much more trouble to kindergarten children than to first graders, but even in the latter group this pattern had a fairly high frequency of error; 2) the syntactic pattern of negative particle followed by a verb-negating particle (No, [he] didn't) continued being just as troublesome for first graders as for kindergarten children.

7. Spatial Relationship. Again, the upper proficiency levels in both grades had relatively few problems with this category, but at the middle levels several structures were a source of great difficulty: 1) the demonstrative pronouns this/that (This [is her dog and] that's [hers too]) had a very high incidence of error at both kindergarten and Grade One; 2) prepositional phrases such as on top of also persisted at both grade levels but with a lower incidence than the this/that contrast; and finally, 3) the directional preposition to (vs. from) was troublesome at kindergarten but not at Grade One.

8. Classification. As was the case with the two previous categories, none of the Classification structures exhibited a high frequency of error at the upper proficiency levels, but certain structures persisted with very high frequency across both grades. The possessive adjective/pronoun contrast her/hers ([This is] her [dog and that's] hers [too]) remains at the top of the frequency list at the middle proficiency levels of both grades. Structures which remained as trouble spots across both grades but dropped in frequency at Grade One were the following: 1) the word order of adjective plus adverb noun-modifiers (very easy job); and 2) the word order of possessive adjective plus descriptive adjective noun-modifiers (her little dogs). The inclusion/omission of definite and indefinite articles (the cat [played with] the ball; the [tall] man [is] a doctor), of moderately high difficulty at kindergarten, did not appear to be a serious problem in first grade.

C. Summary. Difficulties for Mexican-American children with number marking in English appear to be related to the acquisition of the unique features of the English number system, since the concept of grammatical number seems, for the most part, to be fully acquired by these same children in Spanish. The difficulty centers around the marking for number of English nouns, pronouns, and verbs. The only feature of the English number system that is not fully acquired in the early primary grades by monolingual English-speaking children either is the syllabic form /-ɨz/ of the noun-plural marker. Thus the acquisition of this allomorph may be related to developmental factors (Mace, 1972; Natalicio and Natalicio, 1971). Several second-language acquisition studies have shown that the third-person verb morpheme ranks relatively low in the acquisition order of English morphemes (Dulay and Burt, 1974; Fathman, 1975; Mace-Matluck, 1977). Cohen's study (1976) lends support to our findings in the category of Number. González (1977)

found that subject-verb agreement in English was the most common
deviation among the first-grade migrant children in his study.
     All of the Temporality structures which were a source of con-
tinuing difficulty for the children in our study throughout both
grade levels seem to be related to second-language acquisition,
with the exception of the present perfect and the /-ɨd/ allomorph
of the past tense. The perfect tenses appear to be acquired relatively late in both English and Spanish (Berko, 1958; Mace, 1972;
Mace-Matluck, 1977; Cohen, 1976; González, 1970). Both Cohen and
González report considerable difficulty with tense formation by
their subjects in Grades K-2 of Cohen's Redwood City project and
in Grade One of González' migrant study.

Influence from Spanish

     We have insisted previously that a very clear separation must
be made, in our analysis of his spoken English, between the child's
perception problems and his production problems, that in the area
of his production of spoken English the grammatical influence of
Spanish is very strong, but that a great many of his phonological
errors of production, although apparently influenced by Spanish,
are vastly reduced in significance (i.e., they do not result in
gross misunderstanding in the communication process). At the perception level, on the other hand, his phonological problems, both
phonetic and phonemic, combine in such an awesome way that they
are often the direct cause of the grammatical and lexical problems
which beset him in no small number indeed.
     We pointed out that in order to understand spoken English, the
Spanish-speaking child must learn a whole series of phonemic contrasts, both consonantal and vocalic, which he does not have in
Spanish (Saville and Troike, 1971), and that in order to understand,
he must learn them perfectly, not by intellectualization but by internalization. He must learn some 11 consonant contrasts that
do not exist in Spanish, that involve 14 phonemes, seven of
which do not exist in Spanish, all of which appear in word final
position in English, but only three of which appear in this position in Spanish. In addition, English has 178 consonant clusters
of two, three, and even four consonants, 160 of which can appear
in word-final position, and do so in thousands of words, while in
Spanish not one single Spanish word ends in more than one consonant
sound.
     As to vowels, English has one of the most complex vowel sys-
tems of any of the languages spoken today. The Spanish speaker,
whose five-vowel system is an extremely simple and stable one, must
learn an 11-vowel system, more than twice the number in his
own, not one of which is exactly identical to a vocalic segment in
Spanish, and which form seven acoustically similar English contrasts, so that again, and quite understandably, he has great difficulty in making--and hearing--the necessary contrasts. This
means that each pair of words in the thousands of possible contrasts
in which they appear will be heard as identical words until the
native-Spanish-speaking child has practiced and practiced and prac-

ticed, to the point where he can tell them apart every time he
hears them. Ninety-nine percent is not enough. In addition, in
the very important area of suprasegmentals (intonation, rhythm,
etc.) the English rhythmic system, with its very long syllables and
its very short ones in which the vowel is a short, indeterminable
schwa, also nonexistent in his own system, causes the child to
lose syllable after syllable, precisely in the area of perception.

Code Switching

     This phenomenon, one of the outstanding characteristics of
the language of Mexican-Americans and reflected in the speech of
virtually every Mexican-American adult, cannot, of course, be
mutually excluded from the headings of either the Spanish or the
English which the child speaks, since it is patently an important
characteristic of the models of both his languages.
     In 1973 we discussed some of the early investigations in the
area of code switching, citing works from Weinreich (1953), through
Gumperz and Hernández (1970). We also cited some examples, encountered in the speech of young children, of lexical switching
(Cornejo, 1969) and the syntactic switching (Cornejo, 1969; Lance,
1969b; Hernández, Cohen and Beltramo, 1973; Phillips, 1967).
     These early works' suspicions (pointing to the increasing
predictability of both lexical and syntactic switching) have been
confirmed again and again in more recent studies of adult bilinguals by Gingràs (1974), Reyes (1976), and Valdés-Fallis (1976),
Sánchez (1974), Elías (1976), and McMenamin (1973), and in the
even less-explored area of code switching by young children, in
studies by Cohen (1976), Genishi (1976), and García and Aguilera
(1978), indicating that children code switch much less frequently
than adults and even less so in the syntactic area. However, other
recent works suggest that perhaps this is not the case (Huerta,
1977; Valdés-Fallis, 1978; Elías, 1976; Zentella, 1978; and most
recently, Mace-Matluck, 1979, from data collected for the Southwest Educational Development Laboratory's Reading Research Project
in Rio Grande City, Texas).

The School Experience

     In summary, current research indicates that, upon his entry
into school at age 5-6, the bilingual Mexican-American child, like
monolingual children of the same age, has usually not fully acquired the structure of his home language, even though he may be
dominant in that language. At the same time many of these children do not have as much control of English as do their monolingual
English-speaking peers, since the former are often in the process
of acquiring certain language features unique to English which they
may have already acquired in their Spanish and which thus may influence how well and how rapidly the acquisition process proceeds.
Certainly, as Taylor (1975) points out, the influence of Spanish
is usually more marked at that time than it will be at a later age
when the child's proficiency in English increases. That he falls
behind his English monolingual peers in traditional school programs

is well documented, as is the fact that the gap tends to become cumulatively larger. It is our firm belief that this is due, in large part, to the limited control which the Mexican-American child has of the phonological system of English, and that this is manifested most severely and most damagingly in the area of perception (aural comprehension). Almost all studies dealing with the language difficulties of the Mexican-American child mention his problems with English pronunciation on the one hand, and with English grammatical patterns on the other, but few investigators link them together as related, nor do they see a cause-and-effect relationship between them; and with respect to the child's phonological problems, most of these studies persevere--as do most teachers--in their concentration on his <u>production</u> difficulties (oral performance, speaking). We have attempted to point out the nature and severity of his <u>perception</u> problems and to show how vitally they affect not only his morphological, syntactical, and lexical development, but also his ability to learn as fast or as efficiently in English as the monolingual English-speaking child.

Reading ability is, of course, one of the vital areas that affect overall school achievement. And it is certainly not uncommon to find a disproportionately large number of bilingual children in the overall school population reading well below their grade level. Our research in Seattle (Matluck and Mace-Matluck, 1977) showed a very strong and positive relationship between oral proficiency and reading achievement. Recent research by Fiege-Kollman (1977) and Barrera (1978) showed that oral language problems of Mexican-American bilingual children linger on in later years in their school experience with oral reading.

Finally, from the review we have presented on code-switching research, it is apparent that at the present time the results of that research have not yet clarified the enigma of just exactly how the child's acquisition of Spanish and English is affected by his contact with adult code-switching models, especially since findings seem to leave unresolved the question of the prevalence of code switching among bilingual children.

Appendix

Semantic Categories (Communication Concepts)

- I.   NUMBER: grammatical quantification, however achieved; specific to the items in each language selected for these tests.

- II.   TEMPORALITY: time relationships and the interrelated elements of tense, mood and aspect, primarily expressed (in English and Spanish) through the verb structure.

- III.   SPATIAL RELATIONSHIP: the concept of space and the relationship of objects in space.

- IV.   IDENTIFICATION: naming and/or labeling.

- V.   CLASSIFICATION: categorizing and/or assigning attributes.

- VI.   CASE RELATIONSHIP: the relationship of one sentence element (nominals, pronominals, noun-modifiers) to other sentence elements, designated generally through its form or its position in the sentence.

- VII.   INTERROGATION: seeking information or corroboration through the selection and/or arrangement of sentence elements, including the suprasegmental (i.e., intonation).

- VIII.   NEGATION: denying the existence or truth of what is expressed by a verb phrase.

REFERENCES

Barrera, Rosalinda B. 1978. The first-language and second-language oral reading behavior of native Spanish-speaking Mexican-American children. PhD Diss., Univ. of Texas, Austin.

Berko, Jean. 1958. The child's learning of English morphology. Word 14.150-77.

Bowen, J. Donald. 1974. New Mexican Spanish verb forms. Southwest areal linguistics, ed. by Garland D. Bills. San Diego CA: Institute for Cultural Pluralism/San Diego State Univ., pp. 157-66.

Brisk, M.E. 1976. The acquisition of Spanish gender by first grade Spanish-speaking children. Bilingualism in the bicentennial and beyond, ed. by Gary D. Keller et al. New York: Bilingual Press/Editorial Bilingüe, pp. 143-60.

Cárdenas, D.N. 1970. Dominant Spanish dialects spoken in the United States. Washington DC: Center for Applied Linguistics. iii, 46 pp. (Available through ERIC: ED 042 137.)

Clegg, J.H. 1969. Fonética y fonología del español de Texas. PhD Diss., Univ. of Texas, Austin.

Cohen, A.D. 1976. The English and Spanish grammar of Chicano primary school students. Studies in Southwest Spanish, ed. by J.D. Bowen and J. Ornstein. Rowley MA: Newbury House, pp. 125-64.

Cornejo, R.J. 1969. Bilingualism: Study of the lexicon of the five-year-old Spanish-speaking children of Texas. PhD Diss., Univ. of Texas, Austin.

Doyle, Vincent. 1976a. An empirical investigation of the reliability and validity of an oral proficiency test. PhD Diss., Univ. of Idaho.

_____. 1976b. A model for the development of language assessment instruments which insures psychometric quality. Unpublished paper presented at the Annual Conference of the Pacific Northwest Council on Foreign Languages.

_____. 1976c. An interim report on the progress of the joint C.A.L./U. of I. MAT-SEA-CAL project. Unpublished report submitted to the Center for Applied Linguistics, Arlington VA.

Elías-Olivares, L.E. 1976. Ways of speaking in a Chicano community: a sociolinguistic approach. PhD Diss., Univ. of Texas, Austin.

Ervin, S.M. and C.E. Osgood. 1954. Second language learning and bilingualism. (Supplement to) The Journal of Abnormal and Social Psychology 49:4(2).139-46.

Espinosa Sr., A.M. 1917a. The Spanish language in New Mexico and southern Colorado. Albuquerque: Historical Society of New Mexico, No. 14.

_____. 1917b. Speech mixture in New Mexico: the influence of the English language on New Mexican Spanish. The Pacific Ocean in history, ed. by H.M. Stephens and H.E. Bolton. New York: Macmillan, pp. 408-29.

Fathman, A.K. 1975. Language background, age and the order of acquisition of English structures. New directions in second

language learning, teaching and bilingual education, ed. by
M.K. Burt and H.C. Dulay, Washington DC: Teachers of English
to Speakers of Other Languages, pp. 33-43.
Fiege-Kollman, L. 1977. Reading in a second language. Occasional
papers on linguistics 1.40-52, ed. by J.E. Redden.
Foster, David W. 1976. The phonology of Southwest Spanish. Stud-
ies in Southwest Spanish, ed. by J.D. Bowen and J. Ornstein.
Rowley MA: Newbury House, pp. 17-28.
Genishi, Celia S. 1976. Rules for code-switching in young Spanish-
English speakers: an exploratory study of language socializa-
tion. PhD Diss., Univ. of California, Berkeley.
Gingras, Rosario C. 1974. Problems in the description of Spanish-
English intrasentential code-switching. Southwest areal linguistics, ed. by G.D. Bills. San Diego CA: Institute for Cultural Pluralism/San Diego State Univ., pp. 167-74.
González, G.A. 1968. A linguistic profile of the Spanish-speaking
first-graders in Corpus Christi. MA Thesis, Univ. of Texas,
Austin.
_____. 1970. The acquisition of Spanish grammar by native
Spanish speakers. PhD Diss., Univ. of Texas, Austin.
_____. 1973. The analysis of Chicano Spanish and the
'problem' of usage: a critique of 'Chicano Spanish dialects
and education.' Aztlán 3.223-31.
_____. 1974a. The acquisition of questions in Texas
Spanish. Southwest areal linguistics, ed. by G.D. Bills.
San Diego CA: Institute for Cultural Pluralism/San Diego
State Univ., pp. 251-66.
_____. 1974b. Potential negative interference from a
first language. A sociolinguistic analysis of the armed services vocational aptitude battery. Arlington VA: Center for
Applied Linguistics, pp. 60-71, 189-93.
Gumperz, J. and E. Hernández-Chávez. 1970. Cognitive aspects of
bilingual communication. Language use and social change, ed.
by H.H. Whitely. Oxford: Oxford University Press, pp. 111-25.
Hernández-Chávez, E., A.D. Cohen and A.F. Beltramo, eds. 1975.
El lenguaje de los chicanos: regional and social characteristics of language used by Mexican-Americans. Arlington VA:
Center for Applied Linguistics.
Huerta, Ana. 1977. The acquisition of bilingualism: a code switch-
ing approach. Working papers in sociolinguistics 39. Austin
TX: Southwest Educational Development Laboratory.
Keller, Gary D. 1976. Constructing valid goals for bilingual and
bidialectical [sic] education: the role of the applied linguist
and the bilingual educator. Bilingualism in the bicentennial
and beyond, ed. by G.D. Keller et al. New York: Bilingual
Press/Editorial Bilingüe, pp. 17-37.
Lance, D.M. 1969a. Dialectal and non-standard forms in Texas
Spanish. A brief study of Spanish-English bilingualism: final
report (research project Orr-Liberal Arts-15504). College
Station: Texas A & M Univ., pp. 45-68.
_____. 1969b. The mixing of Spanish and English. A brief
study of Spanish-English bilingualism: final report (research
project Orr-Liberal Arts-15504). College Station: Texas A & M

Univ., pp. 69-89.

Lastra, Y. 1969. El habla y la educación de los niños de origen mexicano en Los Angeles. Unpublished paper presented at the 1969 meeting of the Programa Interamericano de Lingüística y Enseñanza de Idiomas, São Paulo.

Lozano, A.G. 1974. Grammatical notes on Chicano Spanish. The Bilingual Review 1.147-51.

Mace, B.J. 1972. A linguistic profile of children entering Seattle public schools kindergarten in September, 1971, and implications for instruction. MA Thesis, Univ. of Texas, Austin.

_____ (-Matluck). 1979. Personal communication (Austin TX).

Matluck, Joseph H. 1976. Communicating in a foreign language: some sociolinguistic considerations. Proceedings, Pacific Northwest Council on Foreign Languages, 27th annual conference. Corvallis OR: Oregon State Univ., pp. 66-69.

_____. 1978. A conceptual model for the development of oral language assessment instruments. Unpublished paper presented at the Southwest Educational Research Association, 1st Annual Conference, Austin TX.

Matluck, Joseph H. and Betty J. Mace. 1973. Language characteristics of Mexican-American children: implications for assessment. Journal of School Psychology 11:4.265-86.

Matluck, Joseph H. and Betty J. Mace-Matluck. 1974. MAT-SEA-CAL oral proficiency tests: English, Spanish, Cantonese, Mandarin, Tagalog, Ilokano: field test edition in 6 volumes. Seattle: Seattle Public Schools/Arlington VA: Center for Applied Linguistics.

_____. 1975. Language and culture in the multi-ethnic community: spoken language assessment. Modern Language Journal 59.250-55.

_____. 1976. The multilingual test development project: oral language assessment in a multi-cultural community. ERIC: ED 119 489.

_____. 1977. The MAT-SEA-CAL instruments for assessing language proficiency. ERIC: ED 129 877.

McMenamin, J. 1973. Rapid code switching among Chicano bilinguals. Orbis 22.474-487.

Natalicio, D.S. and L.F.S. Natalicio. 1971. A comparative study of English pluralization by native and non-native English speakers. Child Development 11.1302-6.

Ornstein, Jacob. 1972. Toward a classification of Southwest Spanish nonstandard variants. Linguistics 93.70-87.

Padilla, A.M. and K. Lindholm. 1976. Acquisition of bilingualism: a descriptive analysis of the linguistic structures of Spanish/English speaking children. Bilingualism in the bicentennial and beyond, ed. by G. Keller et al. New York: Bilingual Press/Editorial Bilingüe, pp. 97-142.

Phillips, R.N. 1967. Los Angeles Spanish: a descriptive analysis. PhD Diss., Univ. of Wisconsin, Madison.

_____. 1976. The segmental phonology of Los Angeles Spanish. Studies in Southwest Spanish, ed. by J.D. Bowen and J. Ornstein. Rowley MA: Newbury House, pp. 74-92.

Rayfield, J.R. 1970. The languages of a bilingual community. The

Hague: Mouton.
Reyes, Rogelio. 1976. Language mixing in Chicano bilingual speech.
    Studies in Southwest Spanish, ed. by J.D. Bowen and J. Ornstein.
    Rowley MA: Newbury House, pp. 183-8.
Rodríguez-Bou, I. 1966. Recuento del vocabulario de prescolares.
    Río Piedras PR: Univ. de Puerto Rico.
Sánchez, Rosaura. 1972. Nuestra circunstancia lingüística. El
    Grito 6.45-74.
_____. 1974. A generative study of two Spanish dialects.
    PhD Diss., Univ. of Texas, Austin.
Saville, M. and R. Troike. 1971. A handbook of bilingual education.
    Washington DC: TESOL.
Talbott, B.L. 1976. The relationship between oral proficiency and
    achievement in a bilingual-bicultural elementary school. PhD
    Diss., Univ. of Idaho.
Taylor, Barry P. 1975. The use of overgeneralization and transfer
    learning strategies by elementary and intermediate students of
    ESL. TESOL Quarterly 25.73-107.
Troike, Rudolph C. 1968. Social dialects and language learning:
    implications for TESOL. TESOL Quarterly 2.176-80.
Valdés-Fallis, Guadalupe. 1976. Social interaction and code-
    switching patterns: a case study of Spanish/English alterna-
    tion. Bilingualism in the bicentennial and beyond, ed. by
    G. Keller et al. New York: Bilingual Press/Editorial Bilingüe,
    pp. 53-85.
_____. 1978. Code switching and the classroom teacher.
    Language and education: theory and practice, no. 4. Arlington
    VA: Center for Applied Linguistics.
Weinreich, U. 1953. Languages in contact. New York: Linguistic
    Circle of New York.
Zentella, Ana C. 1978. Code switching and interaction among Puerto
    Rican children. Working Papers in Sociolinguistics, No. 50.
    Austin TX: Southwest Educational Development Laboratory.

CONTRASTIVE LINGUISTICS AND THE PREPARATION OF BILINGUAL EDUCATION TEACHERS

DIANA S. NATALICIO

University of Texas at El Paso

Contrastive vs. Error Analysis: Background

There has been considerable discussion in recent years concerning the adequacy and appropriateness of contrastive analysis as a working hypothesis applicable to the second language learning context. This issue is not really new, although recent research in the area of error analysis has established· a new basis for criticism of the predictive model with which contrastive analysis has traditionally been associated. From the perspective of the teacher-educator, this debate is at once salutary and troublesome: salutary because fresh light is cast on accepted assumptions and practices, and troublesome because debates of this kind tend to emphasize extreme positions that are difficult to reconcile in applied settings. Still, the practitioner cannot simply ignore the issues involved. This paper attempts to describe briefly some of the issues that have arisen and to relate them to the teacher education context.

It is probably wise to define at the outset the principal terms that will be used here. Contrastive analysis has tradidditionally referred to the comparison of two theoretically com-

229

patible linguistic descriptions to determine similarities and differences which presumably facilitate or hinder second language learning. The emergence of error analysis, on the other hand, shifted the focus from linguistic models to learners' linguistic behaviors and specifically to their errors and the transitional linguistic competence they reveal. To explain learner errors, such analyses draw upon information from both native language acquisition research and contrastive analysis. Errors are defined as systematic target language deviations that reveal the status of a learner's transitional competence. They may be contrasted with mistakes, occasional, unsystematic aspects of performance such as slips of the tongue, that are of little interest to the linguistic researcher or the language teacher (Corder, 1976).

On the theoretical level, predictive contrastive analysis has typically been associated with a view of language learning as a process of habit formation. Thus, for example, both volumes on Spanish-English contrastive linguistics (Stockwell & Bowen, 1965; and Stockwell, Bowen & Martin, 1965) are based upon the notion of transfer.

A student may have some habitual responses which are contrary to the responses required for a new skill which he is trying to master (negative), or which are similar to the new responses (positive), or which have no relation to them (zero). This notion of transfer is applicable throughout the structure of the language: the sound system, the grammar, the vocabulary. (Stockwell & Bowen 1965: 9)

One of the results of the work of cognitive psychologists and of Chomsky and his followers in linguistics has been a growing acceptance of language learning as rule-governed and, as a result, an increased dissatisfaction with contrastive linguistic predictions that are based exclusively on notions of transfer and interference of language habits. This fundamental criticism of contrastive analysis is dealt with in great detail elsewhere (see Corder, 1967; Duskova, 1969; Wardhaugh, 1970; George, 1972; Diller, 1975).

Even if habit formation were acknowledged as a significant aspect of language learning, however, predictive contrastive analysis has tended to rely too heavily and often inappropriately on psychological research findings derived from transfer theory. As Carroll (1968) clearly pointed out, most psychological experiments upon which notions of transfer are based involve learning tasks that differ substantially from the usual language learning context (i.e., the difference between proactive and retroactive inhibition). The psychological data used to support contrastive linguistic predictions are simply not as relevant as has sometimes been claimed.

In addition to the overextention of psychological research data, contrastive analysis may also suffer from the intrinsic limitations of the linguistic descriptions that serve as a basis for its predictions. First, descriptions (of any language) are far from complete. Secondly, they may be seen as ignoring linguistic variation within both native and target languages. Most contrastive linguistic descriptions are based upon the language of idealized adult "standard-language" speakers; the appropriateness of applying such models to individual real-life speakers may be questioned. Extending the application of these idealized adult models to children is particularly vulnerable to criticism, and it is here that error analysis researchers (e.g., Dulay & Burt, 1972) have demonstrated most convincingly the limitations of contrastive analysis.

In addition to the theoretical weaknesses of contrastive analysis, there are also problems in applying the model to actual language learning contexts. The two most frequent criticisms of the predictive use of the contrastive model are: (1) it makes some predictions not borne out in language learner performances, and (2) it fails to predict some phenomena commonly observed in such performances. These are of course fundamental problems since one of the important applications of a contrastive model is as a basis for designing language teaching materials. Accurate predictions are essential if the model is to be useful; it is likely that materials based upon defective models will be pedagogically unsatisfactory.

The most extreme position taken by critics of the application of contrastive analysis to language teaching (e.g., Ritchie, 1967; Wolfe, 1967) argues that it has only a very minor--even a negative--role to play in second language teaching. In direct opposition, other researchers (e.g., Schachter, 1974; Schachter and Celce-Murcia, 1977) believe that in spite of some clear limitations, contrastive analysis offers certain advantages. They argue that an exclusive reliance on error analysis may result in conclusions as invalid as those generated by the predictive model, e.g., error analysis of unstructured spoken or written language may fail to take into account the learner's conscious or unconscious efforts at avoiding specific target-language grammatical constructions. Thus, the low incidence of a given error may lead through error analysis to the false conclusion that no learning problem exists, when in fact the learner's avoidance strategies have obscured significant problem areas.

The Teacher Education Context

As contrastive analysis underwent theoretical reevaluation by researchers, the significant development in U.S. educational policy marked by implementations of bilingual education began to have its own effects on the application of contrastive linguistics to teacher training programs. The growth of bilingual programs and the decline in foreign language enrollments created a need for adjustments in traditional teacher preparation. Most obvious were those changes involving the development of new courses and programs specifically designed to prepare teachers for bilingual classrooms. Less obvious, but of considerable importance, are the many adaptations that have been made in traditional university courses that were incorporated into bilingual certification

curricula. For example, courses in language teaching methodology, testing, or contrastive linguistics that had traditionally
been taught within foreign language education or ESL programs
were increasingly populated by a new and sizeable group of pre-
service bilingual education teachers whose needs and interests
differed considerably from those of the students who had regularly enrolled in them in the past.

In the specific case of contrastive linguistics courses, the
enrollment of large numbers of pre-service bilingual education
teachers appears to have brought about significant changes, not
only in suggesting modifications in course materials to adjust to
the interests and needs of this new student group, but also, and
perhaps more importantly, in highlighting the general problems
associated with teaching contrastive analysis to prospective
teachers. Although there was undoubtedly an awareness of at
least some of these problems in more traditional contexts, the
demands of preparing bilingual teachers seem to have exacerbated
them.

First, student teachers with little or no classroom experience tend to believe in the absolute veracity of predictions
generated by contrastive analysis. They become convinced that it
is their obligation to locate in learner performances the errors
predicted by the contrastive model; and in the search for errors,
the performance data themselves are often ignored--the more errors
they "find," the more successful they believe their search to be.
Such predetermined perception is particularly prevalent in the
analysis of oral language performances; that is to say, student
teachers hear exactly what the predictive model leads them to expect to hear, regardless of what actually occurs in a given performance. For example, a student-teacher who has recently been
exposed to the notion that initial voiceless stops are aspitated
in English and unaspirated in Spanish may hear aspiration errors
where none actually occur. Discrepancies between actual learner
behavior and perception of that behavior by student teachers are
likely to be smallest where constrastive analysis is most applicable, and here bilingual education becomes a factor. Because of
the nature of the model, contrastive predictions are more likely
to be accurate when applied to the performance of, say, a
secondary-level native-English-speaking student who is attempting
to learn Spanish for the first time; when the learner is a bilingual six-year-old, however, the model is less appropriate, and
perceptions colored by the model's predictions are often grossly
inaccurate.

A second and closely related problem with using contrastive
linguistic models in teacher preparation is that they tend to
lead to a conclusion that all native speakers of L_1 will experience the same problems when learning a given L_2. The predictive
approach's emphasis on linguistic descriptions rather than on individual speaker behavior may lead to the false conclusion that
anyone who is a native speaker of one of the languages described
will have internalized the grammar in question, and his/her behavior will therefore necessarily conform to the predictions.

Here again, an application to bilingual education teacher training tends to emphasize difficulties with the model. The lack of
recognition of individual learner differences that may result
from too faithful an adherence to the contrastive model's predictions is less obvious when the learners are mature, monolingual speakers learning a second language for the first time; they
are, relatively speaking, a homogeneous group. It becomes quite
salient, however, when the learners are bilingual first-graders
with widely heterogeneous linguistic histories. For example,
most monolingual English-speaking high school students experience
initial difficulty with article-noun agreement in Spanish, and a
prediction of this tendency would likely be accurate. A similar
prediction for bilingual first graders, on the other hand, will
probably miss the mark for most individuals in the group.

Underlying the aforementioned problems is a simple question
of focus. The predictive model tends to focus student-teachers'
attention on linguistic descriptions rather than on learners'
behaviors. They may preoccupy themselves with details of the
linguistic model (e.g., learning phonetic symbols), and fail to
see that these details are merely a means of achieving quite
another objective. The significant differences in maturational
levels and linguistic histories among bilingual elementary-level
pupil populations makes a focus on actual learner behavior absolutely critical.

This brief review of some of the problems connected with
using contrastive analysis to prepare prospective teachers clearly suggests that although there have probably always been problems in applying the model to teacher education, the preparation
of teachers for bilingual education settings has resulted in increasing the salience of these problems. One might easily conclude from the above that contrastive linguistics simply has no
place in the training of bilingual education teachers, but this
conclusion is probably incorrect.

The predictive contrastive linguistic model offers one significant advantage in preparing bilingual education teachers,
i.e., a framework within which to organize linguistic data. Inexperienced student-teachers usually do not know how to go about
deriving significant general patterns from a series of individual
errors that occur in learners' performances; that is, they cannot
do error analyses. They cannot distinguish errors from mistakes,
and they find it difficult to draw meaningful generalizations.
This tendency is particularly obvious when the prospective
teachers have linguistic histories that did not require them to
bring specific target language features to conscious attention.
Surveys of prospective ESL, Spanish and especially bilingual education teachers at the University of Texas at El Paso, for example, reveal two basic categories of students: (1) native
Spanish-speaking bilinguals, usually Mexican or Mexican-American
and (2) a small number of native English speakers whose foreign
language aptitude and Spanish language achievements are both considerably above average. Student-teachers whose personal language learning experiences have been relatively "trouble-free"

often have difficulty understanding the nature and magnitude of
the learning problems their future students will encounter. Thus,
although the contrastive approach may well result in some over-
generalized predictions on the part of the inexperienced student-
teacher, it does have the clear advantage of suggesting the sort
of analyses that may be conducted when attempting to understand
and evaluate the behavior of language learners.

We have attempted to argue here that a combination of the
theoretical reassessment of contrastive analysis over the past 10
years and the simultaneous application of this approach to more
heterogeneous learner groups as a result of the emergence of bilingual education have led to the development of more negative
attitudes toward contrastive linguistics than are probably justi-
fied. Although all of the criticisms of contrastive analysis
mentioned here have merit, they should lead us to consider more
realistic applications of this approach rather than to reject it
outright. Experience suggests that a less dogmatic, more re-
strained version of contrastive analysis, i.e., one that emphasizes analysis and deemphasizes predictions, is an important aspect of the preparation of bilingual education teachers.

REFERENCES

Carroll, John B. 1968. Contrastive linguistics and interference
     theory. 19th Annual Round Table: Contrastive Linguistics
     and its Pedagogical Implications, ed. by J. Alatis. Washing-
     ton, D.C.: Georgetown Univ. Press, pp. 113-122.
Corder, S. P. 1967. The significance of learner's errors. In-
     ternational Review of Applied Linguistics 4.161-170.
Diller, K. C. 1975. Some new trends for applied linguistics and
     foreign language teaching in the United States. TESOL
     Quarterly 9.65-73.
Dulay, H. J. and M. K. Burt. 1972. Goofing: an indicator of
     children's second language learning strategies. Language
     Learning 22.235-252.
Duskova, L. 1969. On sources of errors in foreign language
     learning. International Review of Applied Linguistics 7.11-36.
George, N. V. 1972. Common errors in language learning. Rowley,
     Mass.: Newbury House.
Ritchie, W. C. 1967. Some implications of generative grammar for
     the construction of courses in English as a foreign language
     17.45-69.
Schachter, J. 1974. An error in error analysis. Language Learn-
     ing 24.205-214.
Schacter, J. and M. Celce-Murcia. 1977. Some reservations con-
     cerning error analysis. TESOL Quarterly 11.441-451.
Stockwell, R. P. and J. D. Bowen. 1965. The Sounds of English
     and Spanish. Chicago: Univ. of Chicago Press.

Stockwell, R. P., J. D. Bowen and J. W. Martin. 1965. The Gram-
    matical Structures of English and Spanish. Chicago: Univ.
    of Chicago Press.
Wardhaugh, R. 1970. The contrastive analysis hypothesis. TESOL
    Quarterly 4.123-130.
Wolfe, D. L. 1967. Some theoretical aspects of language learn-
    ing and language teaching. Language Learning 17.173-188.

STUDENT REACTIONS AS INDICATORS OF TEACHING EFFICIENCY

ROBERT L. POLITZER

Stanford University

Overall Orientation, Source of Data

Sociolinguistic analysis of classroom language and teacher/ pupil classroom interactions is a rapidly growing field. On the other side of the Atlantic, scholars such as Barnes, Britten, and Rosen (1969) and Stubbs (1976) have called for sociolinguistically-based analysis of classroom language and the development of a comprehensive language policy. In an influential book, Sinclair and Coulthard (1975) developed a methodology for the analysis of discourse structures in the classroom. In the USA, a conference dedicated to the study of teaching dealt with "Teaching as a Linguistic Process in a Cultural Setting" and asserted that "the study of linguistic phenomena in school settings should seek to answer educational questions" (Gage 1974:1).

This article is an example of an investigation relating a linguistic phenomenon to an important educational variable, namely, teaching efficiency. The data and texts on which this article is based were gathered for purposes not directly related to those of the article. In an experiment recently conducted in the Center for Educational Research at Stanford (Politzer & Lewis, 1979), 19 teachers of third grade pupils (most of the latter speakers of Black English vernacular) were asked to teach a lesson

on the use of negation in English. Before and after the lesson,
pupils were given tests dealing with the use of negations (recognition of standard vs. non-standard forms, completion of
sentences, turning positive statements into negatives). The pupil post-tests were adjusted on the basis of regressions of post-
over pre-tests. Then the adjusted post-test scores in teachers'
classes were computed as measures of teaching efficiency displayed
during the lesson.

The lessons taught by the 19 teachers were videotaped,
and the videotapes were observed primarily for the purpose of determining whether teacher behaviors related to teachers' acceptance of Black English and any relation to teaching behaviors. In
general, the data relating teaching efficiency to accepting Black
English were inconclusive. It was decided, therefore, to take a
closer look at the lessons taught by the most and least efficient
teachers in order to generate new hypotheses concerning behaviors
related to teaching efficiency. The videotaped lessons of the
teachers who had the five highest and the five lowest ranks in
terms of teaching efficiency measures were transcribed in order
to facilitate analysis of classroom behaviors. The data on which
the teachers were assigned to the high (A) and the low (B) teaching efficiency groups are summarized in Table 1.

Table 1. Criterion Measures of Teaching Efficiency

A. Pretest and Post Test Data

	Pretest	Post Test
Teach N	19	19
Pupil N	228	228
Item N	22	31
Mean	15.70	16.83
S.D.	4.05	6.07
Reliability (Cronback's α)	.79	.84

B. Post Test Over Pretest Regression

Constant	B	Beta	Error	F. Ratio
9.52	.49	.65	.06	59.59

Table 1.   (Continued)

C. Adjusted Post Test Mean Scores of Classes A and B Group Teachers

| | Group A | | | Group B | |
Teacher	Mean	S.D.	Teacher	Mean	S.D.
I	19.61	2.81	VI	13.87	5.33
II	19.52	1.88	VII	14.88	2.60
III	18.60	3.55	VIII	12.07	4.03
IV	19.03	3.86	IX	12.09	4.17
V	19.01	2.58	X	15.16	5.65

One hypothesis, suggested by a cursory examination of the transcriptions, was that the pupils' discourse not teachers' discourse may be a sensitive indicator of teaching efficiency. Teaching involves communication. Pupils, especially third graders who are continuously responding to teachers' requests, may give us valuable clues as to whether teachers succeeded in communicating the intended content of the lesson. Therefore, an analysis focusing on the evidence of communication breakdowns furnished by pupil behavior was undertaken.

The choice of indicators as opposed to systematic observations of total classroom discourse can be criticized as being "capricious and arbitrary." Stubbs (1976:107) observed: "Different studies pick out a very mixed collection of linguistic items as 'indicators.' ... The linguistic items are selected, apparently according to the whim of the researcher, from different levels of language, including lexis (i.e., individual words), syntax (i.e., grammatical structure), semantics (i.e., meaning), and discourse (i.e., overall conversational structure)." The indicators selected in this article came from the latter category; while agreeing in principle with Stubbs' point of view, we nonetheless maintain that the particular indicator proposed for this study appeared to have a great deal of common-sense validity.

Classification of Student Reactions Interpreted as Indicators of Communication Breakdown

Much of the teaching performed in a third grade classroom takes the form of teacher requests followed by compliances by the pupils. Most of the requests are demands to supply information or to indicate that the information conveyed by the teacher has been understood. In order to document communication breakdown, it was decided to take a look at student reactions to requests related to instruction, especially those reactions that indicated that the intended communication had not been received or understood. Of course, the decision as to whether a reaction is indicative of a breakdown in communication is to some extent subjective. The decisions must ultimately be based on assumptions about motives--a shortcoming of perhaps all types of motivational (as opposed to purely structural) analysis of discourse phenomena (Humphrey, 1978); i.e., a student may give no reply or reply with I don't know to a teacher's question even though he knows the answer. Or an I don't know response may be expected by the teacher and be used for the purpose of demonstrating the need for an explanation.

After examination of three complete lesson transcripts, a categorization of student responses indicative of lack of student understanding and/or communication breakdown was established. The most obvious expressions of such student reactions were either "no response," don't know responses, or wrong responses to teachers' requests for information. In addition, two other categories of reactions indicative of misunderstandings were found: responses which did not seem to fit the request made by the teacher, and student reactions (some of them interpretable as student-initiated discourse rather than responses) which were indicative of students' surprise and puzzlement at the progress of the lesson.

The categorization system and specific example illustrating the categories are described below:

Category A: Student gives no answer or "I don't know" response.

   Example 1.

      T(VI): I am going to put up two sentences. Now I want you to tell me which one has a negative in it. (Writes: "Tricia should go to sleep. Tricia shouldn't go to sleep.") OK. Lucy.

      S(Lucy): (Silence)

   Example 2.

      T(VII): OK. Bobby Joe. What about you? Can you think of a sentence that you could use "not" in?

      S: Yeah.

      T: What?

      S: I don't know.

   Example 3.

      T(II): Who can raise their hand and tell me a correct way of saying it? Roscoe?

      S: Hm?

T: The correct way.

S: I don't know.

Category B: <u>Student makes a wrong response (usually in speech</u>, <u>sometimes in writing</u>).

   <u>Example 1</u>.

      T(V): Could you underline the negative for me? (The sentence, "Tricia never eats peanuts," is written on the board.)

      S: (Goes to the board, underlines <u>eats</u>.)

   <u>Example 2</u>.

      T(VIII): (In an exercise in which pupils are supposed to give examples of negative sentences:) Who wants to take <u>aren't</u>? <u>Aren't</u>. In the green group. Wanna take a chance at it, Jack?

         S: I can't read it. (An example of Category C.2, be-
             low.)

         T: OK. Well, would you take a chance at it for me,
             anyway?

         S: (Silence, an example of Category A, above.)

         T: Can ya think of something? Tracy, wanna help him?

         S: I aren't going to the park. (Category B)

   <u>Example 3</u>.

      T(IX): Think of a word that sometimes has a <u>no</u> connota-
              tion.

         S: Note.

         T: Not <u>note</u>.

Category C: <u>Student makes a response which, though not necessarily</u> <u>wrong</u>, is obviously unexpected (not the response expected by the preceding request on the part of the teacher).

Example 1.

     T(IX):   The words I want to talk about today are called...
There's, there is several ways of putting it. Several categories.
The one we're gonna [inaudible]...is called negation. OK?

Example 2.

     T(IX):   I don't have any brothers or sisters. Does that
have a negative in it?

     S: Yeah.

     T: What's the negative?

     S: You don't have no brothers or sisters. (Classified
as C, rather than B, because teacher expected identification of
the negatives, rather than a complete sentence.)

Example 3.

     T(VI):   (In an exercise in which class is supposed to turn
positive sentences into negatives, teacher writes on board: Stacy
jumps high.) Who can make this sentence into a negative? David?

     S: Stacy couldn't.

     T: Can you read the whole sentence....?

Category D: The student makes a remark or inquiry which indicates
lack of understanding of the teacher's intentions. (Since some of
the student initiations can be interpreted as unexpected responses
to teacher requests, the demarcation between Categories C and D is
not always clear. Cases in which it was difficult to decide between categorizations A and C were counted only once--either in
the C or the D category.)

Example 1.

     T(IX):   You better keep it to yourself till we get to you.

So that you can just hope that the person next to you doesn't say it.

        S: What did you say, Miss....?

Example 2.

        T(VI): Frank would like a new bicycle. Can somebody change that so that it has a negative in it? Tricia?

        S_1: (Silence--Category A, above)

        T : Which word are you going to change?

        S_2: Would.

        T : Would, and what am I going to change would to?

        S_3: (Totally perplexed) They wouldn't like a new bike?

(Student is evidently reacting to meaning of the sentence and not to the grammatical structure the class is supposed to practice.)

Example 3.

        T(VII): I'm going to ask you to do somethin' and don't get skiddish.

        Several students: Skiddish?

        T: Sorry, skiddish. You never heard of that? OK...,

Teaching Efficiency and Communication Breakdowns (Table 2)

    Table 2 shows the number of student reactions indicative of communication breakdowns recorded in individual teachers' classes. For four teachers (II, III, VII, VIII), the numbers arrived at by the author of this article were checked by another investigator, familiar with the category system but ignorant of the teachers' positions in either the high (A) or low (B) group. The data obtained in this reliability check are given in parentheses in Table 2. They show generally rather high interrater agreement (within the 100% to 80% range and no more than a difference of 1) at least as far as the figures for total N or indicators per teacher are concerned. Except for some possible mixups between Categories C and D, the observations are relatively reliable. (Categories A and B: no responses, don't know type responses, wrong responses also seem to be of a relatively low inference.)

Table 2. Numbers of Reactions Indicative of Communication Breakdowns by Classes and Groups

	Teachers	A	B	C	D	Total	Adj. Total	Rank (Adj. Total)
			Communication Breakdowns Category					
Group A	I	-	-	-	-	2	9.44	2
	II[1]*	(2)	2(1)	1(1)	0	5(4)	5.00	3
	III[1]*	(3)	3(3)	1(1)	-	7(7)	7.00	4
	IV	1	4	1	-	6	10.92	7
	V	-	-	-	-	0	0.00	1
Group Mean		-	-	-	-		5.47	(3.4)
Group B	VI	1	1	3	1	6	10.02	6
	VII[1]	2(2)	-	3(3)	1(1)	6(6)	17.16	8
	VIII[1]	3(3)	5(4)	3(2)	-(1)	11(10)	7.37	5
	IX	5	6	6	7	24	29.75	10
	X	3	7	1	-	11	15.73	9
Group Mean		-	-	-	-		16.01	(7.6)

*Significance of difference in ranks between A and B according to
the Kruskal-Wallis test of x^2 approximation of differences in rank
orders:

$$x^2 = \frac{12}{10(11)} \left\{ \frac{17^2}{5} + \frac{38^2}{5} \right\} - 3(11) = 5.06 \qquad p < 0.05$$

[1]Figures in parentheses indicate data obtained by second investigator for purpose of reliability check.

Comparison between teachers and teacher groups must take into
account the fact that the time segment observed was not the same
for all teachers' classes. While videotaping was supposed to take
place for a 20-minute period in all teachers' classes, actually
only Teachers X and III are represented by 20-minute periods.
For others, the observed time varied from nine to 30 minutes.
The actual number of observed communication breakdown indicators
were, therefore, adjusted to a 20-minute frequency (by multi-
plying the actual number as a factor of $\frac{20}{\text{minutes observed}}$).

The adjusted frequencies of indicators of communication break-down differentiate quite clearly between the A and B groups of teachers. The mean for the A group is 5.47; for the B group, it is 16.01. Four of the five teachers with the least number of such indicators are in Group A. The worst rank in communication break-downs for any A group teacher is No. 7. A non-parametric test of significance in rank orders between Groups A and B, the Kruskal-Wallis rank order test (Roscoe, 1969:300-05)--used here because of the small sample for which the usual parametric t-test may be too much affected by single scores--indicates that the rank order difference between A and B groups is well within the $p < 0.05$ level of significance.

Communication Breakdowns and Teaching Styles

The conclusions concerning the difference between A and B groups of teachers presented above must be qualified by two important observations: (1) The analysis was carried out on data originally gathered for purposes other than proving an hypothesis related to that conclusion. The results can, therefore, not be interpreted as proving an hypothesis but rather as suggesting one. (2) The hypothesis suggested by the data is, in a sense, not very satisfactory. One would expect the quality of teaching to be inversely related to the frequency of communication breakdowns. The hypothesis--even when proven--does not tell us anything about the teaching behaviors responsible for the quality of teacher/pupil communication.

Many of the indicators of communication breakdowns are unsatisfactory responses to teacher requests for information. This suggests the hypothesis that the relative frequency of these indicators may be influenced in turn by the frequency of teacher requests to provide information; thus the opportunity of not responding or responding with a wrong answer is a function of the number of information questions addressed to the pupil.

In order to investigate the hypothesis that the underlying teaching behavior distinguishing the A and B groups of teachers was the frequency of information requests addressed to pupils, all the requests made by teachers were analyzed. The requests concerned only with classroom procedures or discipline ("Be quiet," "Let's not talk at the same time," etc.) were not included in the analysis. The category of requests was defined according to the broad principles laid down by Labov (1970) (Labov and Fanshel, 1977): (1) there must be a need for an action which would not occur in the absense of the request. (2) The person to whom the request is addressed must have the ability to perform the action, and (3) must have the obligation to perform it. (4) The person making the request has a right to tell the addressee to perform the requested action. (It is difficult to imagine any social situation in which the rules of requesting are more clearly defined than in the teacher/pupil relationship.)

As will be shown in more detail in a study published elsewhere (Politzer, 1980), requests by teachers addressed to pupils fall almost without exception in the following linguistic categories:

(A) <u>Imperative</u>. Read it with your eyes. (T.III)

(B) <u>Direct questions asking for subject matter information</u>.
What's another way of saying <u>cannot</u>? (T.VI)

(C) <u>Questions soliciting actions like 'telling', 'saying',
'writing'</u>. Who can tell me what a verb is? (T.IV) Who wants to
read this sentence out loud? (T.II)

(D) <u>Overt expressions of the performative, i.e., spelling
out the making of the request or the obligation of performing the
action</u>. I want you to tell me which one has a negative in it.
(T.VI) You hafta read all the answer. (T.I)

(E) <u>Statement--"existential assertions" (see Labov and Fanshel, 1977) implying the request for an action to be performed</u>.
I can't hear you. (T.VII) (Meaning: Speak louder.)

(F) <u>Incomplete statements for which completion is expected</u>.
Instead of saying <u>should</u>, we say ... (Rising intonation) (T.III)

(G) <u>"Hortatory" request of the type, "Let's ...."</u> Let's
fix that right now! (T.IV)

Forms like "Your turn" or simply calling the student's name
are not included in the analysis because they are not really requests but simply "nominations," ways of channeling the request
already made towards a specific individual.
Of the categories mentioned above only Type B is by definition reserved for the information rather than the action-type requests. All others can be used for either purpose. Thus "Will
you read it?" (T.VI) (Type C) is a request for action. So is
"Can you underline the negative?" (T.VI) (Type C). "Don't you
know what <u>don't</u> means?" (T.VII) (Type C) is a request for some
kind of information. A direct imperative (Type A request) can refer to an action to be performed: "Fill in the blanks using
these words" (T.VIII). Or it can request information: "Tell me
where the <u>no</u> words are in that sentence" (T.V). The distinction
between "information" and "action" requests can thus not be made
on the basis of linguistic categorization alone and is at times
somewhat difficult to draw. In general, requests calling explicitly or implicitly for such performances as "telling" and "saying"
were interpreted as information requests. Action requests usually
call for such activities as "repeating," "underlining," "filling
in blanks," "saying out loud," "writing," etc.
In order to check on the reliability of the distinctions between information and action requests, the author asked another
researcher not familiar with the group affiliation of the teachers
to count the instructional-related action and information requests
of five teachers (III, II, IV, VIII, IX). The counts arrived at
in this reliability check are shown in parentheses in Table 3.
They show that in all cases, the interrater agreement is quite
high (above the 80% agreement level; e.g., 43 vs. 48 amounts to

43/0.48 or 89% agreement).

Table 3 also indicates that the ratio of action requests as opposed to information requests is clearly a factor distinguishing the A group from the B group teachers. The A group ratios of action to information requests range from 45 to 2.03. The B group ratios are 1 to 0.29. All of the A group teachers occupy the five highest ranks in the Action/Information request ratios, a fact that according to a test of significance of difference in rank order (Roscoe, 169:303-10) is significant at the p < 0.01 level.

Table 3. Action (A) and Information (I) Requests Made by Teachers

	Teacher	A Request	I Request	A/I	Teacher Ranks* A/I
Group A	I	45	1	45.00	1
	II	48(43)	23(26)	2.09	3
	III	77	38	2.03	5
	IV	43(40)	21(24)	2.05	4
	V	29	9	3.22	2
Group B	VI	13	13	1.00	6
	VII	5	17	0.29	10
	VIII	16(19)	39(40)	0.41	8
	IX	16(14)	50(47)	0.32	9
	X	15	16	0.94	7

*Significance of difference in ranks between Groups A and B according to Krustal-Wallis test of X-square approximation of differences in rank orders:

$$x^2 = \frac{12}{10(11)} \left\{ \frac{15^2}{5} + \frac{40^2}{5} \right\} - 3(11) = 7.15 \quad p < 0.01$$

What started as an inquiry into an indication of communicative breakdowns as shown by student reactions thus led to an hypothesis concerning teaching behavior. The more successful teachers were those who spent less time soliciting information from students and more time directing students to perform activities (writing, underlining, saying out loud) immediately related to the lesson and the test by which teaching efficiency was measured.

Conclusions

The pedagogical conclusions arrived at appear to confirm

others that stress the importance of a more directive and direct kind of teaching in the instruction of language arts and reading-- especially to children from minority groups (see also Becker, 1977). We want to emphasize, however, that the data examined were not gathered to prove an hypothesis concerning the effectiveness of directive teaching. Furthermore, the success of any teaching behavior is necessarily influenced by the criterion used for measuring that success. Requesting "actions," rather than information, may not prove a superior strategy if the criterion test consists in supplying information.

Nevertheless, the analysis of pupil indicators of communication breakdowns and the resulting study of action vs. information requests suggests that a motivational type of discourse analysis can be an extremely useful, sensitive tool for the identification of effective teaching strategies.

NOTES

[1]The data presented in this article were gathered in a research study conducted in the Center for Educational Research at Stanford, supported in part by funds from the National Institute of Education, U.S. Department of Health, Education and Welfare. The opinions expressed in this article do not necessarily reflect the position, policy, or endorsement of the National Institute of Education (Grant No. OB-NIE-G-0112).

REFERENCES

Barnes, D., J. Britton and H. Rosen. 1974 (=rev. ed.). Language, the learner and the school. Middlesex, England: Penguin Education Series.

Becker, W.C. 1977. Teaching reading and language to the disadvantaged--what we have learned from field research. Harvard Educational Review 47.518-543.

Gage, N.L., ed. 1974. NIE conference in studies in teaching. Panel 5: Teaching as a linguistic process in a cultural setting. Washington DC: National Institute of Education.

Humphrey. F. 1978. Structural versus motivational analyses of discourse. ERIC/CLL News Bulletin (September).

Labov, W. 1970. The study of language in a social context. Studium Generale 23.30-87.

Labov, W. and D. Fanshel. 1977. Therapeutic discourse: psychotherapy as conversation. New York: Academic Press.

Politzer, R.L. and S. Lewis. 1979. Teacher workshops, Black English test for teachers, selected teaching behaviors and their relation to pupil achievement. Stanford: Stanford University/Center for Educational Research at Stanford.

Roscoe, J.T. 1969. Fundamental research statistics for the behavioral sciences. New York: Holt, Rinehart and Winston.

Sinclair, J. McH. and R.M. Coulthard. 1975. Towards an analysis of discourse: The English used by teachers and pupils. London: Oxford University Press.

Stubbs, M. 1976. Language, schools and classrooms. London: Methuen.

EL LENGUAJE DE LA PUBLICIDAD EN PUERTO RICO—USOS Y EFECTOS DEL INGLÉS

MELVYN C. RESNICK

Florida Atlantic University

El abundante uso del inglés en el lenguaje de la publicidad es uno de los aspectos de la situación lingüística de Puerto Rico que más llama la atención.

No sólo en las áreas turísticas, donde cabe esperarlos, sino en toda la isla, saltan a la vista letreros de tiendas tanto en inglés como en español. Entre los ejemplos observados en Río Piedras, zona no turística del área metropolitana de San Juan, figura el UNIVERSAL TOW SERVICE. No hay que entender inglés para saber a qué se dedica la empresa, pues su letrero incluye la ilustración de un carro en remolque. Casi siempre se explica el nombre inglés de una forma u otra; en el caso de la ISLAND FINANCE CORPORATION la explicación PRESTAMOS PERSONALES aparece en letras rojas mucho más grandes que las del nombre de la compañía. El LIBERTY CARD AND PARTY SHOP vende TARJETAS HALLMARK (cards) y RECORDATORIOS PARA BODAS, BAUTIZOS Y FIESTAS (parties). El LU-AN WIG CENTER se dedica según su anuncio a la VENTA DE PELUCAS AL POR MAYOR Y AL DETAL.

En el caso de MARY'S GIFT SHOP, las explicaciones en la lengua vernácula son, que digamos, superfluas, en vista de que hay una exhibición diaria de regalos (gifts) y flores artificiales que llegan hasta la mitad de la calle.

Tales anuncios no se dirigen al visitante norteamericano, pues todos estos negocios quedan lejos de las zonas y rutas turísticas. HILDA'S DRIVING SCHOOL es una escuela de choferes en una urbanización residencial de clase media en Río Piedras.

Es común el uso del posesivo inglés en los nombres, como en HILDA'S DRIVING SCHOOL, MARY'S GIFT SHOP, BEBO'S BAR B Q, CHICO'S PLACE y ARI'S LIQUOR STORE. A veces resulta un híbrido léxico-morfosintáctico, como en el GARAGE JOHNNY'S, con palabras y morfología inglesas en una estructura sintáctica española.

El inglés publicitario, casi siempre en forma escrita, es común en toda la isla, como evidencia el PROFESSIONAL ELECTRONIC CENTER de la ciudad de Manatí. La "tienda por departamentos" B & B, también en Manatí, utiliza de provecho sus siglas para declararse en dos lenguas como BUENO Y BARATO y de BEAUTIFUL BARGAINS 'gangas bonitas'.

No insensible al valor comercial de la hibridación lingüística, una tienda ofrece cintas magnetofónicas español-inglesas: SPANGLISH TAPES.

El uso del inglés no se limita a negocios de una u otra categoría o tamaño. Desde las empresas más grandes como SEARS y J.C. PENNY hasta las más humildes, como el PEPIN BATTERY SERVICE, comparten las dos lenguas la tarea de llevar al público el mensaje publicitario.

El propósito del presente estudio es hacer un análisis sociolingüístico de los usos y efectos del inglés en el lenguaje de la publicidad de Puerto Rico.

Puerto Rico es un país bilingüe principalmente en el sentido de que en él se emplean dos lenguas oficiales. La mayoría de los puertorriqueños de la isla son, sin embargo, hablantes monolingües del español. Según los datos del Censo de Población de 1970, el 55.8% de los residentes mayores de 10 años de edad (330,429 de 591,699 personas) del área metropolitana de San Juan (municipios de San Juan, Carolina, Bayamón y Cataño) declararon que sabían hablar inglés.[1] El porcentaje para Manatí, ciudad distante de la capital que suplió varios de los anuncios incluidos en el estudio, es del 33.3% (8,028 de 23,877 personas).

Me parece que estos porcentajes son inflados, pues como el estudio del inglés es obligatorio en Puerto Rico desde el primer grado en adelante, aunque con resultados muy variados, cabe esperar que pocas personas admitieran que no saben hablar inglés, o que no saben hablar más que unas palabras sueltas en esa lengua. Sin embargo, el vocabulario pasivo inglés del puertorriqueño es considerable, aunque su competencia sintáctica es, en la mayoría de los casos, mínima o inexistente.

Dada esta circunstancia, la omnipresencia en el lenguaje de la publicidad de un idioma familiar pero fuera de la competencia lingüística de la mayor parte de la población, cabe investigar las siguientes cuestiones:

1. ¿Hasta qué punto entiende el pueblo puertorriqueño el lenguaje de los anuncios publicitarios escritos parcial o completa-

mente en inglés?
  2. ¿Por qué aparecen en inglés estos anucios? ¿Cuál es su
atractivo? Si no se entienden bien, ¿cómo operan para vender con
tanto éxito los productos y servicios que anuncian?
  Con el propósito de tratar de determinar hasta qué punto se
entienden los anuncios publicitarios en inglés, seleccioné varios
cientos de anuncios escritos parcial o completamente en esa lengua
y visibles en los negocios y los periódicos del área metropolitana
de San Juan y de la pequeña ciudad de Manatí. En ningún caso se
tomó un anuncio destinado para turistas ni visto en zonas o negocios frecuentados por ellos.
  Se reprodujeron de esta muestra unos 125 nombres ingleses de
empresas, productos y servicios, y otros nombres, frases y lemas
comerciales misceláneos, en fichas individuales. Éstas fueron pre-
sentadas una por una a 21 informantes en entrevistas individuales
en cinta magnetofónica. Cada entrevista duró aproximadamente 45
minutos.
  Los informantes eran de la clase media o media alta. Vivían
todos en el área metropolitana de San Juan, principalmente en Río
Piedras (17 personas), de donde provenía también la mayoría de los
anuncios encontrados en tiendas, y en Carolina (2 personas), Puerto
Nuevo (1) y Santurce (1).
  Los informantes se distribuyeron, en cuanto a sus edades y
educación, en los siguientes tres grupos generacionales:

GRUPO GENERACIONAL	HOMBRES	MUJERES	TOTAL
I. 14 - 18 años	3	4	7
II. 22 - 47 años	1	8	9
III. 53 - 77 años	3	2	5
TOTAL:	7	14	21

La falta de hombres en el grupo generacional II se debe a que la
mayoría de las entrevistas se llevaron a cabo durante el día, cuando éstos estaban trabajando. Esta situación se repite en las tiendas, pues no abren regularmente de noche ni los domingos.
  Todos los informantes sabían escribir y leer con facilidad, y
ninguno tuvo dificultad con las palabras españolas incluidas en las
fichas. Los informantes del grupo I eran todos estudiantes de escuela superior cuando se llevaron a cabo las entrevistas. Los del
grupo II habían terminado el cuarto año de escuela superior. Del
grupo III, todos habían alcanzado el octavo año escolar, exceptuán-
dose un señor de 77 años, autodidacto, que sólo llegó al cuarto año
pero obviamente lee mucho.
  Ninguno de los informantes habla con fluidez el inglés, y nin-

guno es de familia norteamericana. Tres habían vivido en Nueva
York entre dos y tres años; los demás no habían ido nunca a los
Estados Unidos o sólo habían ido de paseo. Como mencioné antes,
no es posible determinar el nivel de bilingüismo del puertorriqueño preguntándole si habla inglés, pues todos saben por lo menos
"un poco". Y, a pesar de que el puertorriqueño monolingüe no
habla inglés, no le es una lengua totalmente extranjera. Con todas
estas consideraciones, creo que se puede decir con seguridad que
once de los informantes no saben hablar inglés; siete saben expre-
sarse un poco; y con tal vez tres mujeres se podría conversar sobre
temas generales, aunque dos de ellas, estudiantes en una escuela
superior bilingüe, nunca han vivido en los Estados Unidos.
    Se le pidió a cada informante que leyera en voz alta el anun-
cio o parte de anuncio reproducido en la ficha y que luego tratara
de explicarlo en español. En los casos dudosos, se le hacía al
informante preguntas como ¿Para qué irías a esta tienda?, ¿Qué
venden aquí?, ¿Qué son bargains?, ¿De qué color es el strawberry?,
¿Cómo viene?, etc. Es decir, no se le exigía al informante una
definición o explicación precisa para catalogar su respuesta como
correcta: el strawberry (fresa) es una fruta colorada; el box
spring (colchón de muelles) es lo que va debajo del mattress (colchón); el mattress es lo que va encima del box spring; el American
cheese (queso americano) viene en /esláis/ (slices 'rebanadas').
etc. Éstas se consideraron como explicaciones adecuadas.
    Puesto que el estudio trata de la lengua escrita exclusiva-
mente, se eliminaron de la muestra después de hechas las entrevistas aquellas voces inglesas que resultaron ser de uso corriente en
el lenguaje hablado de Puerto Rico y que son por lo tanto casi
universalmente conocidas. Algunas de estas palabras aparecen a
continuación. Se dividen en dos grupos. En Grupo A incluye los
anglicismos corrientes pero con equivalente en el español de la
isla, como Beauty Salon y truck. El Grupo B contiene palabras sin
equivalente normal en el español puertorriqueño. Es decir, las
glosas españolas suplidas son desconocidas o desusadas en Puerto
Rico en la acepción indicada.

VOCES PUBLICITARIAS QUE FORMAN TAMBIÉN PARTE DE LA
LENGUA HABLADA

A. Voces con equivalente normal en el español hablado de
    Puerto Rico:

    beauty salon 'salón de belleza'
    truck 'camión'. Pronunciado /tro(k)/, /tro(s)/, esta
        última pronunciación debida tal vez a la confusión
        de /k/ > /Ø/ con /s/ > /Ø/. En plural, /tro(k)/,
        /tróse(s)/.

B. Voces sin equivalente normal en el español de Puerto Rico.
    Las glosas españolas son desconocidas o desusadas en la
    acepción indicada.

   hamburger 'hamburguesa'. Pronunciado /hambérger/.
   hot dog '(especie de) salchicha, perro caliente'
   tuna fish 'atún'. Tuna en este sentido es aceptado uni-
        versalmente como palabra española.
   box spring 'colchón de muelles'
   mattress 'colchón'. Colchón se refiere exclusivamente
        al colchón de muelles antiguo.
   closet 'armario para guardar ropa'. Armario se refiere
        únicamente al muebla antiguo.
   laundry 'lavandería comercial o la parte de la casa reser-
        vada para lavar y planchar ropa'
   dry cleaning 'establecimiento que se dedica a la limpieza
        en seco'
   dealer 'vendedor o agente autorizado, especialmente de
        automóviles'

    Se eliminaron asimismo varias voces cuya semejanza ortográfica
a palabras españolas facilitaba su inmediata comprensión, como mar-
garine, Pepín Battery Service y Professional Electronic Center.
    Finalmente, se excluyeron del análisis muchos anuncios que
contenían voces especializadas o técnicas, algunas de uso corriente
por segmentos de la población. Éstas se refieren a productos auto-
movilísticos, herramientas de carpintería, ropa destinada para cierto grupo generacional, etc., como en los siguientes ejemplos:

    VOCES PUBLICITARIAS ESPECIALIZADAS O TÉCNICAS, ALGUNAS
    DE USO CORRIENTE

A. Automovilismo:

   tires 'gomas, llantas'
   brakes 'frenos'
   power brakes 'servofrenos'. Sin equivalente español.
   power steering 'servodirección, dirección hidráulica'.
        Sin equivalente español.
   muffler 'silenciador'. También la adaptación ortográ-
        fica mofle, tomada universalmente como palabra
        española.
   tune-up 'afinamiento de motor'. Sin equivalente español.

B. Herramientas:

   jig saw Black and Decker 'caladora, sierra de vaivén, de
        marca Black and Decker'

254 FESTSCHRIFT FOR JACOB ORNSTEIN

C. Modas:

> camisas <u>en</u> <u>un</u> <u>surtido</u> <u>de</u> <u>colores</u> "groovy" 'chévere,
>   de moda'. Esta voz es corriente entre la juventud.

Llegamos, pues, a una lista de 51 ejemplos de voces y frases
no usadas corrientemente en la lengua hablada pero que se destacan
por su presencia en el lenguaje publicitario escrito, en anuncios
destinados a un segmento amplio de la población hispanohablante
de Puerto Rico. Con estos antecedentes podemos dirigirnos ahora
al primer problema planteado en este trabajo: ¿Hasta qué punto
entiende el pueblo puertorriqueño el lenguaje de los anuncios publicitarios escritos parcial o completamente en inglés?
    Se presenta en el Apéndice el análisis de las explicaciones
provistas por los informantes. Los anuncios aparecen en el mismo
orden que en las entrevistas, pero se dividen aquí en cinco tablas,
según el aspecto de la vida que tratan.
    Aunque hay pocos informantes para permitir que se haga un aná-
lisis estadístico detallado, ciertas tendencias son evidentes. En
el resumen presentado en la Tabla F, vemos que el promedio global
de contestaciones correctas en todas las cinco tablas anteriores es
del 53.8%. No hay diferencia entre hombres y mujeres: los hombres
explicaron correctamente el 53.0% de los anuncios y las mujeres el
54.2%.
    De los tres grupos generacionales, las ocho mujeres y uno de
los hombres del grupo II (quien regularmente se encarga de las com-
pras de la familia) tuvieron los mejores resultados, con un promedio global del 59.3%. En la Tabla A, NOMBRES DE NEGOCIOS, el grupo
II explicó correctamente el 65.3% de los anuncios; en la Tabla B,
ANUNCIOS Y LEMAS COMERCIALES MISCELÁNEOS, el grupo II explicó correctamente el 53.7%; en la Tabla D, el 56.8%; y en la Tabla E tuvo este
grupo el 66.7% de las respuestas correctas, resultados superiores
en todos los casos a los de los demás grupos generacionales.
    La inexperiencia del grupo I en el mercado se divulga en la
Tabla A, 46.4%; Tabla B, 42.9%; y en la Tabla D, 25.7%, o sea,
menos de la mitad del tanto de los otros dos grupos. Demuestra
el grupo I su interés en las modas saliendo en primer lugar en la
Tabla C (ROPA) con el 55.6%. Y, según la Tabla E, parece que el
grupo I sabe bastante de comida, bebida, y tabaco en inglés, con
el 58.1% de las respuestas correctas, pero no tanto como sus padres
del grupo II, con el 66.7%
    La protección del consumidor no parece ser el motivo de incluir
las palabras RAIN CHECK (Tabla B) en la propaganda semanal de Bar-
kers', cadena de "tiendas por departamento", pues sólo el 14.3% de
los informantes, o sea, tres mujeres, entendieron que al no encon-
trar la mercancía anunciada en el periódico, tenían derecho a pedir
un <u>rain</u> <u>check</u>, o comprobante, para poder comprarla en el precio
anunciado en una futura ocasión.
    Por otra parte, ¿por qué decirle a sólo el 33.3% de los clientes

potenciales que "traiga sus recetas a Walgreens y economice" (BRING
YOUR PRESCRIPTIONS TO WALGREENS AND SAVE)? La contestación, si uno
pregunta al gerente de la farmacia, es sencilla si no satisfactoria:
el anuncio viene en inglés, pues hay que ponerlo en inglés.

Sólo el 33.3% de los informantes sabían que GRAPEFRUIT JUICE
(Tabla E) es jugo de toronja. Casi todos los demás creían que era
jugo de uva, grape juice.

Había mucha variación individual entre los informantes de cada
grupo. A pesar de que ningún informante habla bien el inglés, varios
explicaron correctamente casi todos los anuncios. Otros ignoraban
casi todos. El grado de comprensión pasiva de cada individuo y su
nivel de bilingüismo activo en general parecen correlacionar posi-
tivamente con factores que incluyen el tiempo que él ha vivido en
los Estados Unidos, su sentido de solidaridad con los Estados Unidos y, muy importantemente, su nivel cultural-educacional.

Pasemos ahora al segundo problema planteado: ¿Por qué aparecen
en inglés estos anuncios? ¿Cuál es su atractivo? ¿Cómo operan para
vender con tanto éxito los productos y servicios que anuncian?

En algunos casos, el anuncio escrito totalmente en inglés desem-
peña un papel pequeño pero importante, el de apelar directamente al
nivel socio-económico más alto de la sociedad puertorriqueña. Así
es que un publicista explicó por qué sus anuncios para cierto res-
taurante eran siempre en inglés: el dueño quería atraer al ejecu-
tivo puertorriqueño, que siempre es bilingüe. El periódico El Mundo
publica en su edición dominical varias páginas de OPORTUNIDADES PRO-
FESIONALES y de EMPLEOS ESPECIALIZADOS. La mayor parte de los anuncios son escritos en inglés, aparentemente con el mismo motivo. Los
trabajos más humildes en la sección clasificada se publican generalmente en español.

Por otra parte, el uso del inglés coincide en gran medida con
el origen estadounidense del producto o de su concepto cultural.
Este parece ser el caso del ONE HOUR MARTINIZING, compañía norteamericana de lavado en seco que promete ONE HOUR SERVICE 'servicio
en una hora' (Tabla B), sin cobro adicional, NO EXTRA CHARGE. El
influjo norteamericana puede explicar también el letrero híbrido
CHICKEN A LA BAR B Q, o sea, 'pollo a la barbacoa' (Tabla E). Cla-
ro que el pollo es comida típica puertorriqueña, y el método de
asar a la parrilla antedata el descubrimiento de América. El voca-
blo inglés barbecue (Bar B Q), universalmente conocido, fue tomado
del español barbacoa, originalmente voz antillana que designaba la
plataforma para cocinar al aire libre. Sin embargo, el barbecued
chicken es un plato típico norteamericano cuya presencia en el
arte culinario de Puerto Rico es evidenciada por el uso del nombre
en inglés. Considere en cambio lo ridículo que sería anunciar
rice with chicken 'arroz con pollo'.

De igual modo, todos los bebés necesitan sus alimentos, pero
el concepto de BABY FOOD en potes (Tabla E) viene de los Estados
Unidos. El tuna fish (común en el lenguaje hablado) viene en lata;
no se le llama nunca atún, aunque la palabra española no es descono-
cida. Pero a nadie se le ocurriría vender codfish en vez del tradi-
cional bacalao.

Conceptos norteamericanos se ven también en LAY AWAY (Tabla B), nombre universalmente conocido del plan de separar la mercancía y sacarla después de pagada, y en SELF SERVICE 'autoservicio' y CASH AND CARRY 'pague y lléveselo'.

En algunos casos de coexistencia de nombres en las dos lenguas, los términos se distinguen semánticamente. La palabra strawberry (no incluida en el análisis por ser corriente en el lenguaje hablado) se refiere principalmente al sirop hecho de fresas, mientras que el equivalente español fresa designa generalmente la fruta fresca.

El término MATTRESS 'colchón' es de uso universal en Puerto Rico; no tiene equivalente en el español de la isla. Se coloca el mattress encima del box spring 'colchón de muelles', que tampoco tiene equivalente español. Éstos son, desde luego, los productos norteamericanos modernos. Antiguamente, uno dormía en una colchoneta rellena de guata que iba encima del colchón, que era un marco de madera con alambres entrelazados.

Pero los orígenes norteamericanos del producto o de su concepto no explican el tremendo atractivo que tiene el inglés para los publicistas y sus clientes. Tenemos que recurrir a otros medios para explicar el éxito del lema comercial WINSTON TASTES GOOD LIKE A CIGARETTE SHOULD 'Winston sabe bien como un cigarrillo debe saber' y para explicar la razón social Church and Tower, empresa (ya inexistente) que se dedicaba a instalaciones de comunicación. El nombre es traducción de los apellidos de sus dos dueños, Iglesias (Church) y Torres (Tower).

En vista de que el consumidor puertorriqueño de la clase media no parece entender el inglés de los anuncios publicitarios en la mitad de los casos, cabe preguntar cómo funciona un sistema de publicidad comercial en que el cero por ciento de los entrevistados' pudo explicar BUDGET BALANCING VALUES (Tabla B), letrero que gozó varios meses de prominencia en Pueblo, la cadena de supermercados más grande de Puerto Rico. La dificultad con este anuncio radica parcialmente en su vocabulario: poca gente sabe que budget significa 'presupuesto', pero se debe principalmente a la sintaxis inglesa en que la frase adjetival budget balancing va antepuesta al sustantivo values. Para traducir estas tres palabras al español hay que empezar por la última y leer para atrás, convirtiendo la frase nominal en una oración completa con cláusula dependiente: 'Valores que balancean el presupuesto'. Ninguno de los informantes pudo hacer esto, pero más significativo es el hecho de que ninguno pudo decirme de qué trataba el anuncio.

Dice Lisa Block de Behar en su valioso libro El lenguaje de la publicidad que no siempre es necesaria la comprensión del lenguaje del mensaje comercial: "Las referencias extranjeras estimulan una comprensión que excede la información denotativa en general o puramente designativa del nombre propio" (Block 1973:27).

La comprensión aludida, por falsa que sea, conduce al consumidor a creer que el producto anunciado es nuevo, diferente o mejor que sus competidores porque lleva la estampa de la lengua inglesa. Mediante los estereotipos y mitos, dice Block, "la propaganda difunde la ideología de la alta burguesía . . . Crea un consumidor fiel y entusiasta que comprueba en forma de experiencias vicarias

las satisfacciones que desde siempre sintió el consumidor de mitos"
(Block 1973:13).

Y "frente al español", opina Germán de Grande, "el inglés es
. . . no sólo un símbolo de superior status social, sino también el
pasaporte que da acceso al mundo mágico de la metrópoli" (Granda
1972:142).

La marca o el lema comercial en inglés engatusa: "Puertorriqueño, conmigo entras en la tierra de las maravillas del materialismo
americano. Cómprame."

No es lo mismo, pues, un Centro de Pelucas que un WIG CENTER;
los regalos se aprecian más si se compraron en un GIFT SHOP; y ¿quién
no quiere lucir la ropa puesta FRESH AS A FLOWER ... IN JUST ONE HOUR
por el proceso exclusivo de MARTINIZING, sobre todo si los pantalones
son de "KNIT" DOBLE, hechos de POLYESTER y comprados en BARGAIN TOWN
donde los baratillos son mejores?

Pero aunque se deje tentar por lo ajeno norteamericano, el puertorriqueño no es el tipo que deja que se le denigre lo propio. Un
colchón de cuna trae la siguiente etiqueta; se ve que no se da la
misma información en las dos lenguas:

THE ALL FOAM CRIB MATTRESS

SOLID FOAM 4" THICK	ANTI ALERGICO
EXTRA FIRM FOR RESTFUL SLEEP	LIMPIO Y SIN OLOR
FOAM NEVER NEEDS TO BE AIRED	RESISTENTE AL MOHO
EASY TO HANDLE	MANTIENE SU FORMA

REGULAR
27" X 52" X 4" THICK

OTRO
PRODUCTO DE CALIDAD POR

_____ DE PUERTO RICO
INC.

HECHO EN PUERTO RICO
POR
PUERTORRIQUEÑOS

NOTES

[1]U.S. Bureau of the Census, Census of the Population: 1970. Los
datos sobre habilidad para hablar inglés fueron derivados de las respuestas a la pregunta 16... [¿Sabe esta persona hablar inglés? Sí
__ No ___]. Estos datos fueron tabulados para la población de 10

años y más. Se catalogaron las personas como que sabían hablar
inglés si podían hacerse entender en inglés. Sin embargo, las personas que sólo sabían hablar pocas palabras en inglés, como 'Hello'
y 'Good-bye', se clasificaron en el grupo de los que no saben hablar
inglés.

REFERENCES

Blanco, Tomás. 1955. Anglocomodismos en el vernáculo puertorri-
    queño. Miscelánea de estudios dedicados a Fernando Ortiz.
    Vol. I. La Habana.
Block de Behar, Lisa. 1973. El lenguaje de la publicidad. Buenos
    Aires: Siglo Veintiuno Editores.
Cajigas, Teresa M. de. 1960. Phonemic modifications of anglicisms
    in Puerto Rican Spanish. Atenea [Mayagüez: Univ. de Puerto
    Rico] 1.51-8.
García Martínez, Alfonso L. 1960. Idioma y derecho en Puerto
    Rico. Revista del Colegio de Abogados en Puerto Rico 20.183-
    211.
Granda, Germán de. 1972. Transculturación e interferencia lingüís-
    tica en el Puerto Rico contemporáneo (1898-1968). 2ª ed.
    Río Piedras: Editorial Edil. (1ª ed. Bogotá: Instituto
    Caro y Cuervo, 1968).
Pérez Sala, Paulino. 1973. Interferencia lingüística del inglés
    en el español hablado en Puerto Rico. Hato Rey: Inter-American
    University Press.
Rosario, Rubén del. 1944. La influencia del inglés. El Mundo
    [San Juan], 13 de agosto, p. 6.
_____. 1955. Anglicismos generales. El Imparcial [San
    Juan], 26 de junio, pp. 6, 41.
_____. 1955. Anglicismos fantasmas. El Imparcial, 24
    de julio, pp. 36, 44.
_____. 1958. Consideraciones sobre la lengua en Puerto
    Rico. Sección III, "Elemento angloamericano". San Juan:
    Instituto de Cultura Puertorriqueña, pp. 9-10.
Tío, Salvador. 1954. Teoría del espanglish. [En su] A fuego lento:
    cien columnas de humor y una cornisa. Río Piedras: Univ. de
    Puerto Rico, pp. 60-245.
U.S. Bureau of the Census. 1972. Census of the Population: 1970.
    General Social and Economic Characteristics. Final Report
    PC(1)-C53 Puerto Rico. Washington DC: United States Govern-
    ment Printing Office.

TABLA A - NOMBRES DE NEGOCIOS

NOMBRES DE NEGOCIOS	HOMBRES #	% #7	MUJERES #	% #14	GG I #	% #9	GG II #	% #9	GG III #	% #5	TOTAL #	% #/21
Island Finance Corporation	5	71.4	10	71.4	4	57.1	8	88.9	3	60	15	71.4
Lu-An Wig Center	1	14.3	4	28.6	2	28.6	2	22.2	1	20	5	23.8
New York Fashions	4	57.1	14	100	4	57.1	9	100	5	100	18	85.7
Mary's Gift Shop	5	71.4	8	57.1	4	57.1	6	66.7	3	60	13	61.9
Universal Tow Center	2	28.6	3	21.4	0	0	3	33.3	2	40	5	23.8
Hilda's Driving School	7	100	14	100	7	100	9	100	5	100	21	100
Liberty Card and Party Shop	3	52.9	10	71.4	3	43.9	7	77.8	3	60	13	61.9
Bargain Town	4	57.1	3	21.4	2	28.6	3	33.3	2	40	7	33.3
% total		55.4		58.9		46.4		65.3		60		57.7

\# = Número de respuestas correctas.
% = #/n: Porcentaje de respuestas correctas = número de respuestas correctas/número de informantes.

TABLA B - ANUNCIOS Y LEMAS COMERCIALES MISCELANEOS

ANUNCIOS Y LEMAS COMERCIALES	HOMBRES #	%/7	MUJERES #	%/14	GG I #	%/7	GG II #	%/9	GG III #	%/5	TOTAL #	%/21
Lay Away	7	100	14	100	7	100	9	100	5	100	21	100
Self service	3	42.9	10	71.4	2	28.6	8	88.9	3	60	13	61.9
Open	7	100	13	92.9	7	100	9	100	4	80	20	95.2
Cash and Carry	3	42.9	5	37.5	2	28.6	4	44.4	2	40	8	38.1
Budget balancing	0	0	0	0	0	0	0	0	0	0	0	0
VALUES												
Beautiful bargains	3	42.9	3	21.4	2	28.6	3	33.3	1	20	6	28.6
Grand Opening	4	57.1	7	50	5	71.4	4	44.4	2	40	11	52.4
Estaremos complacidos de darle un "rain check" por cualquier artículo que no haya llegado a tiempo.			3	21.4	0	0	3	33.3	0	0	3	14.3
Stop paying high prices for your prescriptions	2	28.6	4	28.6	1	14.3	3	33.3	2	40	6	28.6
Bring your prescriptions to Walgreens and save	2	28.6	5	35.7	2	28.6	3	33.3	2	40	7	33.3
1 hour service	6	85.7	9	64.3	4	57.1	7	77.8	4	80	15	71.4
No extra charge	5	71.4	7	50	4	57.1	5	55.6	3	60	12	57.1
% total		50.0		47.6		42.9		53.7		46.7		48.4

\# = Número de respuestas correctas.
% = #/n: Porcentaje de respuestas correctas = número de respuestas correctas/número de informantes.

TABLA C - ROPA

ROPA	HOMBRES		MUJERES		GG I		GG II		GG III		TOTAL	
	#	% #/7	#	% #/14	#	% #/7	#	% #/9	#	% #/5	#	% #/21
"Shoes of the hour"	5	71.4	4	28.6	3	42.9	3	33.3	3	60	9	42.9
Shoes	7	100	13	92.9	6	85.7	9	100	5	100	20	95.2
Fabrics	4	57.1	9	64.3	6	85.7	4	44.4	3	60	13	61.9
Permanent Press	4	57.1	8	57.1	5	71.4	5	55.6	2	40	12	57.1
Walking shorts	2	28.6	6	42.9	2	28.6	6	66.7	0	0	8	38.1
Pantalones de pierna "flare"	4	57.1	8	57.1	4	57.1	5	55.6	3	60	12	57.1
Pantalones de "knit" doble	1	14.3	4	28.6	3	42.9	2	22.2	0	0	5	23.8
T-shirt	5	71.4	9	64.3	6	85.7	7	77.8	1	20	14	66.7
Briefs	0	0	1	7.1	0	0	1	11.1	0	0	1	4.7
% total		50.8		49.2		55.6		51.9		37.8		49.7

\# = Número de respuestas correctas.
% = \#/n: Porcentaje de respuestas correctas = número de respuestas correctas/número de informantes.

TABLA D - MUEBLES Y EFECTOS ELECTRICOS

MUEBLES Y EFECTOS ELECTRICOS	HOMBRES		MUJERES		GG I		GG II		GG III		TOTAL	
	#	%/7	#	%/14	#	%/7	#	%/9	#	%/5	#	%/21
Distinguir entre: Mattress tamaño Queen/Mattress tamaño King	5	71.4	7	50	3	42.9	6	66.7	3	70	12	57.1
Distinguir entre: Mattress twin set/ Mattress full set	2	28.6	11	78.6	2	28.6	7	77.8	4	80	13	61.9
Authorized Dealer Magic Chef Ranges	1	14.3	1	71.	0	0	1	11.1	1	20	2	9.5
Appliances	2	28.6	3	21.4	0	0	4	44.4	1	20	5	23.8
Westinghouse Appliances	5	71.4	$\frac{10*}{13}$	76.9	4	57.1	$\frac{7*}{8}$	87.5	4	80	$\frac{15*}{20}$	75.0
% total		42.9		46.4		25.7		56.8		52		45.2

* = Falta una respuesta.
# = Número de respuestas correctas.
% = #/n: Porcentaje de respuestas correctas = número de respuestas correctas/número de informantes.

TABLA E - COMIDAS, BEBIDAS Y PRODUCTOS DE TABACO

COMIDAS, BEBIDAS Y PRODUCTOS DE TABACO	HOMBRES #	% #/7	MUJERES #	% #/14	GG I #	% #/7	GG II #	% #/9	GG III #	% #/5	TOTAL #	% #/21
Delicatessen	3	42.9	6	42.9	2	28.6	5	55.6	2	40	9	42.9
Chicken	7	100	13	92.9	7	100	8	88.9	5	100	20	95.2
Chicken a la Bar B-Q	7	100	14	100	7	100	9	100	5	100	21	100
Baby foods	7	100	14	100	7	100	9	100	5	100	21	100
[Baby foods] strained	0	0	5	35.7	1	14.3	4	44.4	0	0	5	23.8
[Baby foods] Hi meat [strained]	1	14.3	10	71.4	4	57.1	6	66.7	1	20	11	52.4
Grapefruit juice	1	14.3	6	42.9	1	14.3	5	55.6	1	20	7	33.3
Cup cake	2	28.6	5	35.7	3	42.9	2	22.2	2	40	7	33.3
Black Out†	5	71.4	11	78.6	7	100	7	77.8	2	40	16	76.2
Boiled Ham	3	42.9	6	42.9	2	28.6	4	44.4	3	60	9	42.9
Roast beef	5	71.4	7	50	3	42.9	6	66.7	3	60	12	57.1
Beer	4	57.1	10	71.4	5	71.4	7	77.8	2	40	14	66.6
The beer that made Milwaukee famous	5	71.4	5	37.5	3	42.9	4	44.4	3	60	10	47.6
American cheese [Winston-20 Filter Cigarettes-]	5	71.4	13	92.9	5	71.4	9	100	4	80	18	85.7
Crush Proof Box	2	28.6	4	28.6	2	28.6	3	33.3	1	20	6	28.6
Winston tastes good like a cigarette should	5*/5	100	6*/10	60	4*/6	66.7	5*/6	83.3	2*/3	66.7	11*/15	73.3
Warning: The Surgeon General has determined that cigarette smoking is dangerous to your health.	5*/5	100	7*/10	70	5*/6	83.3	5*/6	83.3	2*/3	66.7	12*/15	80
% total		58.3		61.7		58.1		66.7		53.1		60.6

† = Coca Cola con helado (mantecado). Representación ortográfica errónea del inglés Black Cow
* = Faltan respuestas debido a la inclusión tardía de la ficha.
# = Número de respuestas correctas.
% = Porcentaje de respuestas correctas.
#/n: #/n = número de respuestas correctas/número de informantes.

TABLA F - RESUMEN DE TABLAS A - E

	HOMBRES	MUJERES	GG I	GG II	GG III	TOTAL
Respuestas correctas / Total de respuestas	187/353	382/705	174/355	270/452	125/251	569/1058
Porcentaje de respuestas correctas	53.0%	54.2%	49.0%	59.7%	49.8%	53.8%

ON TRANSFERENCE AND INVERSION

NICHOLAS SOBIN

Pan American University

0. <u>Introduction</u>. The questions of how and whether the syntax of one language can interfere with or ultimately influence
the syntax of another are of considerable interest to students of
bilingualism and of language change.[1] In discussing grammatical
interference, Weinriech (1967:29) quotes the extreme position
taken by Meillet that "'The grammatical systems of two languages
....are impenetrable to each other.'" Though some recent work
points in this general direction,[2] the amount of data on the subject is still scant and the issues far from settled.

This brief paper will study data from Spanish-English bilingual college freshmen in the area of questions and negative sentences, with particular emphasis on the main verb <u>have</u> (as in
'Max has a nickel.') The purpose of the study is to see what
these students produce in the way of transference-like data and
to see if we find grounds for rejecting the strongest position on
the transference of transformational rules, a variation of
Meillet's theme, that transformational rules do not transfer from
one language to another.

The data show some well-documented non-standard forms but
little evidence of transference of the relevant syntactic rules.
They also reveal an interesting and complex variance in the categorization of main verb <u>have</u> ($have_m$) as an auxiliary for forming

different syntactic types, a variance which is not limited to ESL
learners and which is not accurately described by the optional
status assigned to this phenomenon in other descriptions of $\underline{have}_m$.

1.1   Informants and materials. In the pilot portion of an
ongoing project studying the nature of bilingualism among students
at Pan American University,[3] students in a Fundamentals of Written
Composition class were given a questionnaire which was intended to
elicit a variety of basic phrase and sentence types. The fundamentals class is offered for freshmen who, on the basis of a writing sample, are judged by English instructors to have problems
producing standard English which would be a serious obstacle to
adequate performance in the regular first-semester composition
course. All but one of the 19 students in this particular class
were native speakers of Spanish from the Rio Grande Valley.

The questionnaire was administered informally. The basic instructions stated that this was not a test with right or wrong
answers, and that the student should give the responses which
seemed most natural. The instructions appeared on the questionnaire
and were also given orally to the class. Four students who could
not finish the questionnaire during the class period and who asked
if they could complete their questionnaires out of class were
allowed to do so.

The questionnaire consisted of a number of subparts, each of
which asked the student to produce or judge some phrase or sentence type. Among the tasks were the production of passives from
actives, actives from passives, questions and negatives from statements, the selection of prepositions and particles, and reflexivi-
zation. Here I would like to focus on the questions and negatives
which were produced.

1.2   YNQ's, WHO's, and Neg's. For brevity's sake, I will
assume some familiarity with the transformational rules thought to
be central to the formation of English questions and negatives.
Yes/no questions (YNQ's) utilize Subject-Auxiliary Inversion (SAI)
which places the first auxiliary verb (possibly $\underline{do}$) in pre-subject
position as in (1):

(1)   (a)   Is Max leaving?

(b)   Did Max leave?

Wh-questions (WHQ's) as in (2) involve Wh-Movement (WHM), which
moves a non-subject Wh-word to sentence initial position, and SAI.

(2)   (a)   Who is Max kissing?

(b)   Who did Max kiss?[4]

As to the formation of negative sentences, we will only be
concerned here with the fact that the negative element is placed
to the right of the first auxiliary verb (possibly $\underline{do}$), ostensibly
the same unit which is moved by SAI in questions, as in (3):

(3)   (a)   Max is not leaving.

(b)   Max did not leave.[5]

The rules mentioned above have Spanish counterparts. In YNQ's, Spanish has an optional rule of verb inversion (SVI) which places the main verb and any auxiliary verbs in pre-subject position as in (4):

(4)   (a)   ¿Está corriendo Max?

(b)   ¿Corre Max?

(c)   ¿Cuándo corre Max?

Cuando in (4c) has been placed sentence-initially by a rule essentially identical to WHM in English. Finally, the negative element no commonly appears in second position following the subject and does not intrude into the verb complex, as in (5):

(5)   Max no está comiendo la calabaza.

2.1   YNQ and WHQ responses. As mentioned above, students were given sentences with a variety of verb and auxiliary structures and asked to change them. In the section on YNQ's, they were asked to convert statements to YNQ's. In the section on WHQ's, they were given statements each containing a proform (e.g., 'Cesario went somewhere this morning.') and were asked to create WHQ's. In the section on negatives (see below), the students were asked to create a negative for each of various affirmative statements. In each section, along with brief written instructions, they were given one or more examples of the desired change.

The responses given on the questionnaire were either standard responses or commonly attested non-standard and learners' forms. In the case of YNQ's, one informant did not respond (though he responded to other preceding and following sections). There were a few non-standard auxiliary forms produced (e.g., "might been," "has earn"), a few responses where SAI was not applied resulting in some echo questions (e.g., "Yesterday Jack planted a tree?") and a couple of non-standard topicalizations (e.g., "A problem María has?"). A greater source of non-standard YNQ forms was what Dulay and Burt (1974:116) have labelled as 'two verbal words tensed' (e.g., "Did Jack planted a tree yesterday?"), and which they categorize as a developmental type of error for Spanish speakers learning English since this is a form produced by children learning English as a first language and bears no similarity to Spanish verb constructions. There were only 15 such YNQ responses. More interesting is the fact that eight (42%) of the 19 informants produced at least one such form on the questionnaire.

Another source of either non-standard or, in some cases, less common structures was what appeared to be a transference-like application of SVI. There were nine cases of main verb inversion among four different informants (21%) in the following sentences:

(6)   Has María a problem? (instead of 'Does María have

a problem?'; 4 instances; item VA 3.)

(7) Have you to go now? (instead of 'Do you have to go now?'; 2 instances; item VA 5.)

(8) Did they a lot of digging? (instead of 'Did they do a lot of digging?'; 2 instances; item VA 9.)

(9) Do you that first? (instead of 'Do you do that first?'; 1 instance; item VA 10.)

In most varieties of American English, have and do in the above sentences are treated as main verbs rather than as auxiliaries in forming YNQ's, as in the parenthetical sentences to the right of each example. However, for many speakers, (6) is acceptable; (7-9) by contrast seem completely unacceptable.

As to whether or not these examples indicate transference of SVI into English, certain facts suggest that they do not. For one thing each of the inverted main verbs is phonetically identical to an auxiliary verb which always appears in the inverted position in YNQ's. For (6) and (7) we have have as in 'Has Max left?' and for (8) and (9) we have supportive do as in 'Did Max leave?' Rather than transference of SVI, we might claim that have and do were categorized in these cases as auxiliaries by analogy to their phonetically identical auxiliary counterparts and subsequently inverted by English SAI. A simple theory of transference doesn't allow us to account for why inversion applied as it did and only in these cases. The English-internal analogy account, on the other hand, allows us to account for why this particular set of main verbs underwent inversion (as opposed to planted (VA 2)) and why more complex verbal structures included a main verb (e.g., should finish, has earned) were not inverted.

The range of WHQ responses was very similar to that of the YNQ responses just discussed. There were a few no responses, but every informant showed the ability to produce WHQ's. Occasionally, an incorrect Wh-word was used, a non-standard auxiliary-verb complex was produced, a preposition was omitted, and some echo questions were produced (e.g. "Cesario went where this morning?"). There were a total of 17 two-tensed-verb responses produced by eight different informants (again 42%, but not the identical eight who produced such YNQ's) such as: "Where did Cesario went this morning?" There were also some cases where WHM was applied, but not SAI, resulting in sentences like: "Where Cesario went this morning?"[6]

Of particular interest is the fact that in WHQ's there was only one clear instance of Spanish-like verb inversion. This occurred in response to questionnaire item VB 3: Max hit something in the dark. The response was: "What hit Max in the dark"?[7] As to this indicating transference of SVI, such a claim seems unlikely. First, transference-like verb inversion appeared nowhere else among the WHQ data. Second, a verb hit as it is used in VB 3

means something like 'involuntarily collide with.' In such cases,
'x hit y,' 'y hit x' and 'x and y hit each other' have very similar meanings. On purely semantic grounds, such a reversal of subject and object is completely conceivable. What this leaves us
with is the observation that any transference-like or analogical
application of SAI was almost entirely to YNQ's. This suggests
that the analogy theory proposed above for the transference-like
YNQ responses may not be sufficient to describe the cases where
ASI does and does not apply. If analogy alone was at work, then
we would expect the main verbs <u>have</u> to have been inverted in at
least some of the responses to questionnaire items VB 9 (Max had
to do <u>something</u> yesterday) and VB 10 (Maria had <u>something</u> yesterday) as in YNQ's. There were no such responses, however. The
four major categories of response were standard questions, two-
tensed-verb questions (e.g., "What did Maria had yesterday?"), non-
SAI question (e.g., "What Maria had yesterday?"), and echo questions. The main verbs <u>have</u> showed no susceptibility in WHQ's to
inversion as they had in YNQ's. Here, other nonstandard forms
seemed universally preferred to transference-like inversions.

   2.2 Neg and <u>have</u>$_m$ responses. The finding in the preceding
section that <u>have</u>$_m$ apparently inverts more readily in YNQ's than
in WHQ's naturally leads us to wonder about its treatment in negative sentences since there is variance in some dialects as to
whether <u>have</u>$_m$ is treated as an auxiliary or a main verb. In this
subsection, I will first briefly discuss the negative responses
generally and then the findings on <u>have</u>$_m$. The data to follow show
these informants to possess the apparatus within English grammar
to produce Spanish-like responses. The minimal production of such
forms seems to indicate a lack of pressure from L1. Comparison of
level of production of inverted <u>have</u>$_m$ constructions in negatives
and questions parallels native speakers' acceptability judgments
of such constructions which seems to indicate that the learners
are sensitive to an English-internal constraint on the use of
<u>have</u>$_m$ as an auxiliary in different construction types rather than
to pressures from Spanish.

   2.2.1 <u>Neg responses</u>. The responses to the portion of the
questionnaire asking for negative constructions were also either
standard or of non-standard types comparable to those in WHQ's
and YNQ's. Among them were two-tensed-verb negatives (e.g.,
"Max doesn't wants some cookies."), non-standard verb or auxiliary forms, and in a few cases, failure to produce a negative
sentence.[8]

   2.2.2 <u>Have</u>$_m$ responses. In standard English negative constructions, <u>have</u>$_m$ is sometimes treated as an auxiliary verb ([+Aux])
and sometimes as a main verb ([-Aux]), as illustrated in sentences
(10) and (11) respectively:

   (10) Max hasn't any money.

   (11) Max doesn't have any money.

In response to questionnaire item VC 4 ('Max has a little money.'),

Eight of the 19 informants gave a [+Aux] response like (10), seven gave a [-Aux] response like (11), three gave a response in which the distinction is not crucial, and one did not respond to this item. That is, 42% of all of the informants and 53% of the informants giving a commital response categorized $have_m$ as [+Aux] for forming the negative sentence.

Recall at this point that in YNQ's with $have_m$, the transference-like form is the one in which $have_m$ is treated as [+Aux] as in (6):

(6) Has María a problem?

Given the high proportion of informants treating $have_m$ as [+Aux] in negatives, and given the option of an acceptable transferencelike YNQ form whose production requires nothing more than this same categorization of $have_m$ (and SAI), one might expect a high proportion of YNQ's like (6). As already noted, this did not happen. There were only four [+Aux] responses to $have_m$ like (6). Also, there were no such transference-like WHQ responses. Of further interest is the fact that six of the eight informants who gave the [+Aux] response for the negative $have_m$ sentence also gave a non-standard response to the $have_m$ WHQ; three produced a twotensed-verb form ('What did María had yesterday?') and three produced an uninverted WHQ ('What María had yesterday?'). Thus, it is not the case that these informants had already learned the standard forms in deference to others.   Rather, six of these eight produced forms which were non-standard, like those produced by learners of English as a first language, and which were non-transference-like. In this case, the first language seems to have exerted little or no influence on which forms were produced, even where their production was possible completely within L2 by mechanisms the informants had shown familiarity with.

2.2.3 Native judgments on $have_m$. The informants' use or nonuse of $have_m$ as [+Aux] in negatives, YNQ's and WHQ's seems to parallel adult native English speakers' intutions on the use of $have_m$ as an auxiliary in these constructions. In an informal survey, ten Pan American University faculty and staff members from various geographic locales who were native speakers of English (one spoke British acrolectal Received Pronunciation [RP]) were asked to judge the acceptability of the three following sentences:

(12) Mary hasn't any money.

(13) Has Mary a problem?

(14) What had Mary yesterday?

For (12), 7 judged it acceptable,[9] 2 questionable, and 1 unacceptable; for (13), 5 said acceptable, 4 questionable, and 1 unacceptable; for (14), 6 said questionable, and 4 unacceptable.[10] Thus, (12) and (13) were partially acceptable, (most acceptable: (12)), and (14) was rejected. When asked to rank (12) - (14) as to relative acceptability, all ranked (14) as least acceptable, 7 ranked

(12) as more acceptable than (13), 2 ranked (13) above (12), and 1 could not decide between (12) and (13). The relative levels of production of these forms by the freshmen students follows these acceptability judgments, despite less than complete command of standard English and the potential pressure from Spanish towards forms like (13) and (14).

The fact that both native speakers and learners of English show this pattern suggests that it is not just a learned pattern in one of some dialects of English, but that it is due to some more fundamental characteristic of English structure or of the structure of languages like English affecting the language of both learners and adult speakers. Others have noted the apparent optionality of treating $have_m$ as an auxiliary in constructions like (12) and (13).[11] They characterize HAVE-Shift as being, "limited to certain dialects, in which it is optional." (1975:230). But the problem is more complicated. It is not at all clear why HAVE-Shift should be easier in negative derivations than YNQ derivations, and why it should be more highly restricted or impossible in WHQ derivations, even though the $have_m$ is still directly effected in WHQ's by just the same two rules as in YNQ's, namely, HAVE-Shift and SAI. Greater understanding of both learners' and other speakers' data awaits the further exploration of general syntax.

3. <u>Concluding remarks</u>. On the whole, bilingual speakers' treatment of questions and negatives gives us little reason to reject a hypothesis of non-transference of transformational rules.[12] Though the use of $have_m$ and a few other auxiliary-like items is occasionally transference-like, such uses seem to have reasons which are English-internal or acquisition-related. Obviously, this paper has presented only a small amount of data on limited phenomena. Further testing of the non-transference hypothesis will require much more research into a wide variety of syntactic phemonema and a deepened understanding of syntax generally.

NOTES

[1]Special thanks to Jon Amastae for reading and commenting on this paper. Any errors are my own. The activity which is the subject of this report was supported in whole or in part by the U.S. Office of Education, Department of Health, Education and Welfare. However, the opinions expressed herein do not necessarily reflect the position or policy of the U.S. Office of Education, and no official endorsement by the U.S. Office of Education should be inferred. The research reported here has been supported by an Advanced Institutional Development Grant (OEG-0-74-2511) to Pan American University, which support is gratefully acknowledged.

[2]See, for example, Ravem (1974), Schumann (1978:22ff.), and Cancino, et. al. (1978:218).

[3]For further demographic description of the Pan American student body, see Amastae (1978). Also see Willcott (1977).

[4]See Langacker (1974).

[5]Questions of the existence of a negative placement rule for either English or Spanish (see below) are not of immediate concern here, but do have an impact on the question of transference of transformational rules. See Culicover (1976:120ff.).

[6]In an independent discussion of such sentences, one informant told me that this and the preceding form were both acceptable and to an equal degree.

[7]A second possible instance involved the same sentence, but with who substituted for what.

[8]There was only one instance of a somewhat Spanish-like negative, produced by careting in a not to give, "Cesario not made the honor roll."

[9]'Acceptable' here includes the case where the informant would not use the sentence, but would not think it odd for someone else to use it.

[10]The RP speaker accepted (12) and (13) but rejected (14) as ungrammatical and knew of no varieties in which it was used.

[11]Interestingly enough, WHQ's are usually missing from such discussions. There are a few more acceptable inverted $have_m$ WHQ's such as 'What have you there?' but they seem idiomatic or frozen as indicated by the lesser acceptability incurred by minor changes, e.g., '*What had you then?' (c.f., 'What did you have then?').

[12]Schumann (1978:22ff.) claims positive transference of SVI for inverting the copula be. But there is the methodological consideration of how we are to mark those instances in which use of SVI is permissible. In the end, we seem to have little choice but to posit in the learner's grammar of English some sort of Subject-BE inversion rule. Early acquisition of BE-inversion may be related to the fact that BE-shift is generally much less subject to variance across English dialects than HAVE-shift (Akmajian and Wasow 1975:232).

Cancino, et. al. (1978:218) claim negative transference into English of not placement by Spanish speakers. However, the same pattern emerges in learners of English as a first language (Dulay and Burt 1974:117) and in ESL learners whose L1 does not follow this pattern (Ravem 1974:128). Also, there is doubt as to the existence of a transformational rule of negative placement in either Spanish or English (see Culicover 1976:120ff.).

REFERENCES

Akmajian, A. and T. Wasow. 1975. The constituent structure of VP and AUX and the position of the verb BE. Linguistic Analysis 1.205-45.

Amastae, J. 1978. Sociolinguistic background of PAU students. SWALLOW VII: Bilingual and biliterate perspectives, ed. by A. Lozano, Boulder: Univ. of Colorado, pp. 132-41.

Cancino, H., E. Rosansky and J. Schumann. 1978. The acquisition of English negatives and interrogatives by native Spanish speakers. Second language acquisition, ed. by E. Hatch. Rowley MA: Newbury House, pp. 207-30.

Culicover, P. 1976. Syntax. New York: Academic Press.

Dulay, H. and M. Burt. 1974. You can't learn without goofing. Error analysis, ed. by J. Richards. London: Longman Group Ltd., pp. 95-123.

Langacker, R. 1974. The question of Q. Foundations of Language 11.1-37.

Meillet, A. 1921, 1938. Linguistique historique et linguistique générale. Paris: Société de Linguistique de Paris.

Ravem, R. 1974. Language acquisition in a second language environment. Error analysis, ed. by J. Richards. London: Longman Group Ltd., pp. 125-33.

Richards, J., ed. 1974. Error analysis. London: Longman Group Ltd.

Schumann, J. 1978. The pidginization process. Rowley MA: Newbury House.

Weinreich, U. 1953, 1967. Languages in contact. The Hague: Mouton.

Willcott, P. 1977. A report on work in progress. Southwest areal linguistics then and now, ed. by B. Hoffer and B. Dubois. San Antonio: Trinity University Press, pp. 211-16.

LANGUAGE USAGE PATTERNS AMONG A YOUNG GENERATION OF CUBAN-AMERICANS

CARLOS A. SOLÉ

University of Texas at Austin

Recent sociolinguistic research on non-English mother-tongue maintenance in the United States seems to point to a correlation between upward social mobility and language shift (see for example Fishman and Casiano, 1971).[1] The question that remains today is whether favorable socio-economic conditions could not also work toward the establishment and maintenance of a coordinated and stable bilingualism rather than toward language shift as has been the case in the past.

The purpose of this study is to discuss the results of a survey concerning language usage patterns among adolescent Cuban-Americans--the third and most affluent sub-group of Spanish language claimants in the U.S. and the sub-group whose socio-economic profile contrasts sharply with that of Mexican-Americans and Puerto Ricans (see Arboleya, 1975).

This study is based on a survey conducted in Miami, Florida, during the fall of 1975. The participants chosen were high school students between the ages of 15 to 18 years of age, the first generation of Cubans raised and educated in the U.S. from elementary school on. To insure a heterogeneous sample, students from both public and private schools located in different sections of the city were selected. From a total distribution of 350 questionnaires, 268 usable responses were collected; these constitute the basis for this study.

The questionnaire had three main sections. In the first section, demographic data were elicited: age, sex, place of birth, years of residence in the United States, professional goals of the participants, educational and occupational status of the parents. Section two of the questionnaire dealt with language proficiency and language choice (Spanish or English) within a wide range of different contexts of social interaction and in relation to different age groups. Information was elicited concerning the participant's language proficiency and language dominance in all four skills (understanding, speaking, reading, writing), both developmentally and currently. The last section of the questionnaire was intended to elicit the respondent's attitudinal posture through a series of open-ended questions. Questions covered a wide range of topics such as: the importance of knowing Spanish, opinions concerning the on-going language shift perceived among the younger generation; the expressiveness of Spanish compared to English in relation to different topics or domains; the rationales of encouraging or discouraging Spanish maintenance; the disadvantages of using Spanish and the disadvantages of not knowing English; the measures necessary to insure Spanish maintenance; and attitudes towards bilingualism and on bilingual education. The following statistical analyses were performed on the data: frequency distributions, a varimax orthogonal factor analysis and an analysis of the effects of linguistic and socio-demographic variables upon differential language usage patterns.

It should be pointed out that the socio-demographic profile of the sample population proves that we are dealing here with an urbanized, socially and economically well-established ethnic group. The vast majority of the respondents were born in Cuba, 62% in Havana and 15% in other Cuban cities, while 12% were U.S. born. Of those born in Cuba, 48% arrived in the United States between the ages of 1 and 3 years, 27% between the ages of 5 and 8, and 22% between 10 and 12 years of age. Sex distribution was roughly the same: 49% were males and 51% females. This sample population is characterized by a high level of personal and professional ambition: 37% hope to obtain an M.A. degree, and 44% hope to achieve a doctorate degree either in medicine, law or the humanities. This is not surprising if one examines the high educational and occupational level of the respondents' parents: 85% of the fathers were educated in Cuba and today 20% of them are professionals, 5% are business owners or managers, 37% are white collar workers and 22% are skilled laborers. In 61% of the cases, the father's occupation in the United States coincides with the one held in Cuba.

The educational and occupational level of the respondents' mothers is also rather high: 24% of them finished high-school, 16% had some college education and 11% earned some kind of university degree. In 92% of the cases, the mothers were educated in Cuba. Nevertheless, only 51% of the mothers are holding a job today: 2% are professionals, 30% are white collar workers and the rest are skilled laborers.

Although the conclusions derived from the survey should not be generalized in an absolute manner to the entire Cuban-American population in the U.S., these results do have bearing on language usage patterns among members of this ethnic group. Apart from the fact that the sample may seem small in number--268 responses-- it closely reflects the socio-economic profile of the total Cuban-American population in Dade County as indicated by recent demographic surveys (see The Latin Community of Dade County..., 1975). On the other hand, because of the age bracket of the respondents, the sample population represents the demographic strata which ultimately will decide Spanish language maintenance among this group.

The results of the survey show that Spanish is the mother tongue of the respondents; 25% of them also learned English simultaneously with their Spanish during early childhood. This is not surprising if one keeps in mind that only 12% of the respondents were U.S. born, while 88% were born in Cuba. One should also remember that among this last group, 48% left Cuba at the age of 1 to 3 years, a very critical period in language acquisition. In spite of the fact that for 75% of the respondents, Spanish was the first language spoken during pre-school years, today only 26% claim higher Spanish than English proficiency, 39% claim to know English better, while 35% claim to be equally proficient in both languages. The different levels of current linguistic proficiency become clearer when percentages are examined according to different language skills. About 90% of the respondents claim to understand Spanish fully (only 10% claim partial understanding); about 68% claim to speak it fluently and 30% rather fluently; about 65% claim to have full reading ability and 38% partial command; 56% claim to have full command of writing skills while for 32% writing in Spanish is problematic. One may conclude, then, that proficiency in Spanish varies according to the linguistic skill considered, when it is a passive-receptive or an active-productive skill. Although the percentage claiming a high level or proficiency in understanding/speaking is very high, these percentages diminish considerably when one examines writing skills and even then, there are important differences between reading and writing ability ratings.

In spite of these differences in language skills ratings, the large majority of the respondents--78%--claim to understand and speak Spanish with equal proficiency, while 17% claim greater proficiency in the passive skills, (i.e., understanding as opposed to speaking, reading as opposed to writing).

The above percentages would seem to indicate a high level of oral language retention. Undoubtedly there is a high degree of linguistic continuity between childhood and adolescence. This may respond to several factors: 1) the home influence, since Spanish is the dominant language among the older generations; 2) the high demographic concentration of the group: 60% live in sections mostly populated by Cubans while another 21% live in sections where at least a third of the residents are Cubans or Spanish-speaking; 3) the influence exercised by social, cultural and religious Cuban organizations and institutions in that area; 4) the scope and success of bilingual programs in Dade County

(see Mackey and Von Nieda, 1977); and 5) the continuous flow of
Hispanophones through Miami, from South America and elsewhere.
    Although the respondents' oral command of Spanish is high,
their writing skills are limited in this language. On the other
hand, the respondents have also acquired an advanced level of proficiency in English, which was learned during the critical ages of
their social development. Once an individual acquires a second
language and this one happens to be the dominant language of his
geographic habitat, he is then faced with the problem of choosing
or alternating between the two.
    When one examines the question of linguistic choice among the
sample population, it becomes evident that alternating between
Spanish and English corresponds essentially to generational differences. It does not respond to differential code allocations
determined by socio-cultural contexts nor is it determined by
ideological considerations.
    The three generations of Cuban-Americans studied--grandparents,
parents and children--represent three functional linguistic groups
separated by age differences. The lack of reciprocity in language
usage between the groups corresponds to differences in language
proficiency in Spanish and English. Almost two-thirds of the members of the first or "grandparent" generation have little or no
proficiency in any of the skills in English; only 27% of the second
generation does not know English, while among the third generation
(our sample), English proficiency is universal.
    These proficiency differentials are clearly reflected in lan-
guage choice within the home. Spanish dominates in the communication between respondents and members of the oldest generation:
92% of them use only Spanish when addressing their grandparents
and older relatives while 90% of the first generation males and 98%
of the female members reciprocate it. It should be pointed out
that in one-third of the Cuban families within the sample, grandparents and/or older relatives live within the same household. An
extended family structure undoubtedly contributes to language retention.
    In the communication between respondents and members of the
second generation (parents, uncles, older relatives) the use of
Spanish diminishes. Almost two-thirds of the respondents--62%--
use Spanish exclusively when addressing members of the second generation; 21% use it most of the time, while 12% use English. Re-
ciprocal language use shows that 73% of the respondents' fathers--
74% in the case of mothers--use Spanish only and another 21% use
it most of the time (21% also in the case of mothers). In other
words, the second generation uses less Spanish and more English
than the third generation but there are no differences in language
choice according to sex among parents as occurs among grandparents.
Fathers and mothers of the respondents coincide in their language-
usage patterns.
    Spanish usage diminished considerably in interactions involv-
ing the respondents and their younger relatives. Instead, shifting
between the two languages and exclusive use of English prevails.
Among brothers and sisters only 25% use Spanish exclusively, while
41% use both languages and 38% prefer English almost always or

always. The same situation occurs in interactions with younger
relatives of pre-school age or who have just entered school: 43%
shift between the two languages when talking to these younger relatives, while 30% use mostly English. However, a considerable
percentage of these younger relatives use mostly Spanish when
addressing the respondents. From the above, it can only be inferred that although these younger children understand English
without any problem, they have not quite yet reached the same
level of oral proficiency as the respondents.

If one observes intra- and intra-generational social interaction beyond the home context, one can further corroborate that
there exists a correlation between age, linguistic proficiency
and language choice. In interactions with older second generation
neighbors, about 21% of the respondents shift between the two languages, 14% prefer mostly English and 8% use it exclusively. This
is indeed a rather high proportion if one keeps in mind the rather
recent Cuban arrival. On the other hand, if language usage within
the neighborhood is compared with that within the home where 12%
of the respondents shift between the two languages when addressing
second generation relatives, 3% preferring mostly English and only
2% using it exclusively, then there is no doubt that home language
usage patterns play a definite role in mother-tongue retentiveness.

Shifting between the two languages and preference for English
increases considerably among members of the third generation.
Among friends and neighbors of the same age group as the respondents, shifting between Spanish and English occurs in 50% of the
cases, while 33% use English exclusively. Social interaction between school-mates and close friends show similar ratings. This
trend towards English would seem to go against any possible influence that the barrio may have exercised in the linguistic continuity of Spanish.

The progressive displacement of Spanish among the young generation of Cuban-Americans seems more evident when one examines
the respondents' language usage patterns in contexts under personal control such as inner speech, prayer and the projected language choice with families of their own as well as mass media
contacts.

One-third of the respondents claim to use mostly English,
while another third shift between the two languages in inner
speech situations. Although two-thirds of the respondents attend
religious services conducted in Spanish, when it comes to actual
active participation in confession and praying, more than one-
third of them (44%) claim to use mostly English and 15% shift between Spanish and English. This apparent discrepancy could be
attributed to the fact that a full 40% of all religious services
held in Miami are actually conducted in Spanish.

English usage prevails even more significantly in mass media
contact. Miami has three Spanish television channels, one with
full programing and two with half-time programing in Spanish.
There are five radio stations with full-time Spanish language
broadcasting. Yet, only 20% of the respondents take advantage of
this important source of linguistic contact and even then, not as
their only source of information but in addition to the English

mass media.   Contact with the Spanish press on an exclusive basis
is claimed only by 8% of the respondents.
     Although at present there are about 20 Spanish publications
available in Miami (both magazines and newspapers--one of them, El
Diario de las Américas, with a daily distribution of 65,000 copies)
the Spanish press is an additional source of information for only
31% of our respondents.   The great majority of them--61%--claim to
prefer reading the English press exclusively.
     Shifting between Spanish and English or dominance of one or
the other does not assume the same proportions among all respondents.   Spanish language retention or its gradual displacement by
English is influenced by the following socio-demographic and linguistic variables: date of arrival in the U.S., educational and
occupational status of the father, occupational status of the
mother, and the respondents' linguistic proficiency level.
     Those respondents who are U.S. born or those who arrived in
very early childhood, whose linguistic proficiency is greater in
English than in Spanish, whose fathers possess a high level of
educational and occupational achievement, and whose mothers have
become part of the labor force use English far more often than
those respondents who arrived in later years, whose language proficiency is higher in Spanish than in English, and whose parents
possess a lower educational and professional attainment.
     It should be pointed out, however, that the correlation be-
tween educational/occupational level of the respondent's father
and the displacement of Spanish is not a linear phenomenon.   In
other words, it does not increase progressively from lowest to
highest.   The groups retaining Spanish most seem to be those respondents whose parents occupy either the lowest or the highest
point in the educational and/or occupational scales.   Professionals
and businessmen are less prone to retain Spanish.   The least retentive group are white collar workers (i.e., office clerks,
salesmen, public and private services employees.)
     Mother-tongue retentiveness among members of the lower occu-
pational level--blue collar and skilled workers--is easily understood as this labor force requires relatively little linguistic
competence in English.   On the other hand, at the highest occupational level we find that professionals are also highly retentive
as they primarily serve members of their own ethnic community.
The white collar worker, however, has closer contact with the dominant society due to the very nature of the services he offers.
     Therefore, we find in this middle bracket a labor force in
which knowledge of English becomes almost imperative.   This same
correlation has been noted with other immigrant groups of Hispanic
and non-Hispanic origin (see Fishman, 1966).
     In projected language usage with their future family, only a
small percentage of the respondents--10%--intend to use English
as the sole means of communication; half of the respondents in-
tend to use both languages while the rest--40%--intend to use
Spanish exclusively.   This is a highly idealized projection since
it does not reflect current language usage patterns among the respondents and their age peers.   As such, it is unlikely to materialize.

In spite of the fact that there are important external factors favoring Spanish language retention in Miami, the findings
of this study show that among the vast majority of the respondents, a coordinated and stable bilingual situation does not obtain.
    Language choice among this young generation of Cuban-Americans
does not respond to a diglossic system in which each language has
different code allocations according to different contexts of social interaction. Language choice seems to be determined essentially by the linguistic competence of the speakers, which in turn
is governed by generational differences, years of residence in the
U.S., and age at arrival. Language shift seems to have already
begun among young Cuban-Americans in spite of the recency of the
Cuban arrival and settlement. There is no doubt that this early
development has been largely motivated by their high educational
achievement and their rapid socio-economic establishment within
mainstream society, which has not been the case with other less
privileged ethnic communities, Hispanic or otherwise.
    Miami was officially declared a Bilingual City on April 6,
1973 (see Cruz, 1975). Whether or not this symbolic gesture will
in fact become a practical reality will depend largely on the role
of Spanish among the young and future generations. But we must
point out that if our research shows a trend towards linguistic
assimilation, the results of other studies on social adaptation
and acculturation among this population in Miami also indicate
greater facility for acculturation among the young (see Finemann,
1966).

NOTES

[1]The data gathering for the present study was made possible
thanks to a summer grant awarded by the Institute of Latin American Studies in 1975; the statistical analyses were funded by the
University Research Institute, both of the University of Texas at
Austin. I am most indebted to Dr. Herminia Cantero, Coordinator
of Bilingual Education, Dade County Public School System, for her
invaluable assistance in distributing the questionnaire. I am
also grateful to the schools' principals, teachers and staff for
their cooperation; but above all, my thanks to all those students
who by answering the questionnaire made this study possible. For
a move exhaustive and complete study, see my "Selección idiomática
entre la nueva generación de cubano-americanos," The Bilingual
Review 6:1, 1979.

REFERENCES

Arboleya, Carlos J. La colonia cubana, pasado, presente y futuro. Diario de Las Américas (Miami FL) 3 de septiembre, 1975.

Cruz, Amaury. 1975. Guide for Spanish translations of official Dade County documents. Dade County FL: County Manager's Office, Division of Latin American Affairs. (The resolution declaring Dade County a bilingual and bicultural administrative unit was unanimously approved by the County Commisioners of the county. An Office for Bilingual/Bicultural Affairs was then created.)

Finemann, Carol. 1966. Attitude toward assimilation: Its relationship to dogmatism and frigidity in the Cuban refugee. M.S. thesis, Univ. of Miami.

Fishman, J.A. et al. 1966. Language loyalty in the United States. The Hague: Mouton.

_____ et al. 1971. Bilingualism in the barrio. The Hague: Mouton. (Indiana University Publications, Language Science Monographs No. 7.)

Grebler, L. et al. 1970. The Mexican-American people: The nation's second largest minority. New York: The Free Press.

The Latin community of Dade County: A socio-economic and demographic study. 1975. Miami FL: Human Communications.

Mackey, W.F. and B. Von Nieda. 1977. Bilingual schools for a bicultural community: Miami's adaptation to the Cuban refugees. Rowley MA: Newbury House.

Meyer Rogg, Eleanor. 1974. The assimilation of Cuban exiles: The role of community and class. New York: Aberdeen Press.

Padilla, Elena. 1958. Up from Puerto Rico. New York: Columbia University Press.

Skrabanek, R.L. 1970. Language maintenance among Mexican-Americans. International Journal of Comparative Sociology 11.272-82.

Solé, Carlos A. 1976. El español en los Estados Unidos: Perspectiva socio-lingüística. Thesaurus 30.318-37.

Solé, Yolanda R. 1975. Language maintenance and language shift among Mexican-American college students. Journal of the Linguistic Association of the Southwest (LASSO) 1.22-46.

_____. 1977. Language attitudes towards Spanish among Mexican-American college students. Journal of the Linguistic Association of the Southwest (LASSO) 2.37-46.

Szapocznik, J., M.A. Scopetta, W. Kurtines and M. Aranalde. 1976. Acculturation: Theory, measurement and clinical implications. Unpublished report on a study conducted under NIDA Grant No. SH 81 DA (1699-02, Department of Psychiatry, University of Miami.

THE SPANISH/ENGLISH
CONTACT SITUATION
IN THE SOUTHWEST

YOLANDA RUSSINOVICH SOLÉ

University of Texas at Austin

In attempting to delimit what is to be understood by the Spanish/English contact situation in the Southwest one must begin by defining what is meant by language and what language means. Language may be defined in a narrow or a broad sense. In a narrow sense language is understood to mean the phonological, morphosyntactic and lexical subsystems that typify it. In a broad sense language is conceptualized as a behavioral manifestation inextricably bound to the sociocultural sphere in which it takes place, and the psychological matrix from which it emanates. In its broadest sense, language intersects with all aspects of psychosocial behavior, and as such is a means of interpersonal communication and influence whereby reality is mediated to the individual. But language besides mediating social reality is a symbol of social reality itself. As a symbol of social reality, language is a referent for loyalties and animosities, an index of social statuses and personal relationships, and a marker of situations and topics as well as a symbol of the societal goals and value systems that characterize every speech community (Fishman, 1972).

For certain objectives, the study of language may be legitimately approached from a strictly linguistic viewpoint. From such a viewpoint language is studied as a system, as a code detached from the speech community in which it is given. A strictly linguistic viewpoint may be a viable one when the purpose at hand is the study of phonological, syntactic or lexical features within homogeneous groups or across different subgroups who share a common tongue but do not differ significantly on more than one dimension. Broader objectives concomitantly call for less limiting approaches, in which in addition to linguistic features, sociolinguistic and psycholinguistic sources of variance are considered as well. Thus the study of language from the viewpoint of its social embeddedness implies going beyond the study of a code. It implies exploring linguistic behavior, the social organization of linguistic behavior, and the interdependence of both, as well as the study of behavior towards languages and their speakers. In taking the social matrix of language as a point of departure, there may emerge within a given language group different speech varieties associated with different statutes, topics, role-allegations, regional origins, ethnic membership, etc., which may or may not be acted and reacted upon differentially.

The study of the Spanish/English contact situation in the Southwest (or elsewhere in the United States) calls for such a multivaried approach in which the social realities, settings and psychological forces that have acted differentially upon the Spanish/English language are taken into account. When considering the variants commonly referred to as "Southwestern Spanish" or "Mexican-American English," one finds that both have been thought of as relatively stable and cohesive systems, in spite of existent group and regional differences. However, these assumptions of a uniform linguistic behavior or behavior towards either language are unlikely to be upheld if the social reality of its speakers is considered. Mexican-Americans are not a homogeneous group living in a homogeneous setting. They differ by immigrational distance, preimmigrational origins, educational level, regional distribution, and cultural orientation (Grebler et al., 1970). The linguistic variants known as Southwestern Spanish and Mexican-American English are, therefore, much more likely to be concealing than revealing of existing generational, regional, and social Spanish/English variants, of the continuities and discontinuities present in relation to other Spanish dialects, and of the resultant feasibility or futility of legitimatizing and institutionalizing supraregional norms for certain purposes within certain contexts.

It has been claimed that Southwestern Spanish is the most thoroughly researched and best described of any of the U.S. varieties of Spanish (Floyd, 1978). While the claim may be true quantitatively speaking, the focus of these studies has largely been lexical and phonological, only occasionally morphological and incidently syntactic. Sampling procedures used in collecting data have not followed strict criteria and samples obtained have by and large not been representative of any particular subgroup because location, group and context variables have not been adequately controlled. In view of the inherent limitations of the linguistic data and the sampling methods used to gather them, the existence or absence of what may or may not be an established internal standard for Spanish in the Southwest remains hypothetical and has yet to be described. Empirically, the needs for such a study are self-evident. Language factors are crucial to bilingual education pro-

grams, teacher training programs in bilingual education, the teaching of Spanish to native speakers, and the numerous federal and regional publications issued in Spanish.

Theoretically, the study of language variables in the Southwest offers a readily accessible testing ground for the many hypotheses related to linguistic change. Social change and dislocation,
upward/downward mobility, generational membership, and educational
levels are known to trigger and expedite linguistic change, bring-
ing about the loss or addition of rules and the restructuring or
reordering of some linguistic elements. Little is known about how
these changes occur, how and by whom they are initiated, and the
pace at which they spread or fail to spread from one subgroup to
another. It has been shown that speech variation among U.S. monolinguals is conditioned by age, education, occupation, and sex;
that language change may be triggered by different socioeconomic
groups and affiliative needs; that in first language acquisition
the speech of peers is more influential than the language of adults
(Kiparski, 1970; Labov, 1965, 1966). We do not know, however,
whether these forces are also operant among bilingual speakers in
the Southwest, whether speech variation, language change and language acquisition--whether in Spanish or English--respond to any
of the aforementioned or different factors. Among Mexican-Americans language change may or may not respond to different socioeconomic status. Social class differentials could be overridden by
ethnic membership. In first or second language acquisition, adult
speech could be more important than peer models due to possible
different reference norms. Insofar as language change is concerned,
ethnic distinctiveness could prove more crucial--at least among
some subpopulations--than changes introduced by generational factors and/or class distinctions.

From presently available data it is apparent that Southwestern
Spanish partly shares variable features with other Hispanic dialects and partly does not. Many of the linguistic variables found
in all Hispanic dialects respond to analogical leveling, similar to
that operant in child language (Solé, 1977). Analogical leveling
is, however, a descriptive rather than an explanatory term. We
have little understanding of how it does operate and what it responds to, whether singly or interactionally to simplicity factors,
frequency of items, the internal structure of the language and/or
other hitherto unexplored forces within the language or language-
learning setting itself. An intensive and extensive study of linguistic variability, both at the adult and child level, could answer some of these questions, and throw some light on the linguistic, psychological and social factors that influence these
processes.

If one goes beyond the Spanish language situation, and considers the differential interactions and involvement of Mexican-
Americans with the dominant society, the ramifications of language behavior and behavior towards language extend to other concerns such as bilingualism, language maintenance vs. language shift
(to English), attitudes towards usage of Spanish and English, towards language policies, and towards Spanish/English variants.

Of all the possible topics pertinent to the Spanish/English

contact situation, the one that has received the most attention
is Spanish language maintenance. Language maintenance among
Mexican-Americans in the Southwest has consistently been described
as exceptionally high. With some important qualifications, the
claim is true. The external strength of Spanish, that is, the
number of Spanish mother-tongue claimants as defined by the U.S.
Census--language spoken in the respondent's home during his childhood in addition to or to the exclusion of English--could hardly
be higher. Virtually all foreign-stock Mexican-Americans reported
Spanish mother-tongue in 1970 (Solé, 1975). The Census data are,
however, subject to many limitations and distortions as they do
not refer to the language actually learned or used by the respondent himself; do not contain any reference to the respondent's developmental or current linguistic proficiency; and do give preference to English when both English and another language are reported. The Census data, on the other hand, enable us to judge
the absolute or relative strength of non-English mother-tongues
within different subpopulations.

As a rule, all the large immigrant groups in the U.S. have
been characterized by a high degree of language maintenance.
Italian, Polish, Spanish, French and German, while changing their
ranking and numerical importance over the decades, still comprise
the largest numbers of non-English claimants (Fishman, 1966).
While these five groups, headed today by the Spanish-language sub-
group, could be said to be the most retentive ones, not all of
them have been equally retentive of their respective mother-tongues
within the same generation or across different generations. If
one examines Spanish language maintenance among Mexican-Americans
in terms of generational distance, it would seem that this factor
is irrelevant. Nearly all respondents of Spanish heritage in the
Southwest are of Spanish language as well. The Census data could
be interpreted to mean that a stable bilingual situation has existed across the decades, whether this in fact is true or not.

The existence of a stable bilingualism, however, has been
shown to be far from a reality among Mexican-Americans. More
Mexican-Americans in Los Angeles and San Antonio are comfortable
in Spanish than in English when bilingualism is measured by conversational fluency (Grebler et al., 1970). Neighborhood composition and social-class factors further affect an individual's
fluency in either language. Higher-income individuals in L.A.,
who live in neighborhoods containing few, if any, fellow ethnics,
are more likely to have greater competence in English than in
Spanish. Conversely, almost half of the low-income Mexican-
Americans in Los Angeles and San Antonio who live in ethnic
neighborhoods are not only more proficient in Spanish but have
very limited English ability. From these findings, it is clear
that the Census data is open to gross misrepresentations, as it
does not so much reflect upon Spanish language maintenance among
a bilingual population, as it reflects (in many instances) upon
Spanish-language usage due to lack of English proficiency. The
Census data further obliterate the fact that social class differentials, which have militated against language maintenance among

other immigrant groups, are presently also operant among subgroups
of Mexican-Americans as well.

Differential language maintenance and language shift in the
U.S. has primarily responded to demographic factors rather than
to the internal dynamics of a given subgroup. Language shift
traditionally has been dependent upon the socioeconomic and educational status of a given group, its demographic concentration,
the percentage of foreign-versus native-stock populations, and the
sustained or interrupted flow of new immigrants. Viewed from a
sociodemographic perspective, Spanish language-usage among Mexican-
Americans has more likely been perpetuated by their limited internal differential, the compactness of their settlements, their
low educational and occupational levels, and their segregations
from the mainstream society, than by ideological conviction or elaboration on behalf of Spanish.

To the extent that language maintenance depends upon sociodemographic factors, Spanish language retentiveness in the Southwest
can be expected to remain high for decades to come. Social mobility
within the minority group is slow. Up to the present, Mexican-
Americans have needed as many as three generations to approximate
the income status of the general Southwestern population. Mexican-
Americans remain now more so than ever one of the most conspicuous
examples of geographic concentration among national minorities in
the United States. The flow of new immigrants--one of the most
important sources of language maintenance--is higher now than in
the past. One third of all Mexican-Americans live at or below the
poverty level, and are for all practical purposes functional illi-
terates. Vast majorities of them are concentrated in low-skill
occupations and low-opportunity settings. Neither the present
economy nor ecology of the Southwest can absorb such vast numbers
of unskilled workers in the immediate future. Yet in comparison
with the past there is social change and progress. Today's generations have a greater educational attainment and occupational
status than their parents, who by comparison with other foreign-
stock populations have had the lowest educational and occupational
levels irrespective of decade of immigration. Mexican-Americans
today are linked to the city, whereas their ancestors were largely
rural dwellers. Spatial segregation from the mainstream society,
whether at work, home or school, while nearly absolute in the past,
is decreasing today in many settings. If integration is increasing, one may expect linguistic assimilation to occur as well. Today, the younger and better educated Mexican-American generations,
while still proficient in Spanish, are nonetheless more likely to
be English- than Spanish-dominant, more likely to use English or
both languages than solely Spanish in interactions with age peers
and younger interlocutors. Thus there is evidence of language
shift.

Evidence of language shift among Mexican-Americans would not
be of major interest in itself were it not for two factors. Only
a generation ago, they were thought of as unassimilable and alien
to the American way of life. Today, it is apparent that language
shift among them proceeds primarily in proportion to upward mobility within the larger sphere of American society as has been

the case with most other non-English-speaking groups. This finding,
of major social consequences, is of theoretical interest as well.
It allows us to explore a totally unexamined area: the actual contribution of sociodemographic factors in relation to language maintenance and language shift within a given setting, as opposed to
other factors, such as psychological and attitudinal forces, which
may enhance or inhibit the acquisition of second-language skills,
expedite language accomodation through a diglossic bilingual situation or precipitate language shift.

Very little is known about second-language acquisition among
immigrants, children or adults. Nor is bilingualism as a whole
much better understood, perhaps because it has generally been ap-
proached·from mechanistic and atomistic viewpoints. Psychologists
have most commonly studied bilingualism in terms of relative proficiency and effects upon performance as measured by fluency, speed,
flexibility, and translational facility. Linguists have most often·
studied the dependence/interdependency of the linguistic systems
among bilinguals. Sociologists have concerned themselves mainly
with exploring differential, non-differential code-allocations as
determined by domains of interaction, topic, repertoire, and
speaker (Fishman, Cooper and Ma, 1971).

While among monolinguals or incipient bilinguals the question
of language choice may readily be answered by considering language-
proficiency differentials, among relatively coordinate bilinguals
language choice cannot be expected to rest upon the purely mechanical aspects of language. The psychodynamics of language choice
among bilinguals living in an essentially monolingual host setting
would seem to be far more complex and conflict-ridden. Language
choice would seem to entail a resolution of various competing
forces: the personal need of the individual versus group demand;
the needs to preserve intra-group identification versus the desire
to identify with the outgroup; and the congruence/incongruence between the demands made by the ingroup versus the outgroup. Con-
flicting needs and demands could trigger feelings of ambivalence,
insecurity, and tension, which in turn could lead to vacillations,
retreat, and withdrawal from these demands. Overly aggressive demands to conform to the ingroup or the outgroup or public deroga-
tion of a given language or pattern of language distribution could
inhibit rather than facilitate second-language acquisition, could
retard language accommodation, and by prolonging the conflict
could trigger attitudinal aggression against the second language
itself. Language-usage patterns and ultimate language accomodation in conformity with ingroup and outgroup expectations, while
undoubtedly influenced by sociodemographic factors, are unlikely,
however, to be all-or-none processes. How conflictive linguistic
values and allegiances are resolved, how accommodation is best
achieved, and how these processes affect both language maintenance
and language shift in the American Southwest on an individual and
a societal basis, is a purely speculative matter, in need of docu-
mentation and analysis. Whether there is linguistic conflict or
not may partially be answered by the study of language attitudes.

The scope of language attitudes is far-reaching and its relevance obvious to the Spanish/English contact situation. Language

attitudes underlie language choice and differential code-allocations, language maintenance and language-shift processes, language
policies and planning endeavors, evaluations and devaluations of
speech varieties, and their reinforcement or displacement. The number of studies pertinent to language attitudes among Mexican-
Americans is, however, rather limited, and their origins recent.
The first studies appeared in the mid-sixties. From these studies
we have learned that language maintenance did not represent a consciously avowed goal among respondents in San Antonio in the sixties;
that the usage of Spanish was associated with considerable social
stress in domains other than those under private control, and that
mother-tongue continuity, when considered desirable, was not justi-
fied upon ethnic grounds such as the preservation of the group as
a distinct entity (which was perceived mainly in terms of its sub-
ordinate socio-economic status) but rather upon humanistic and
cultural values. If language maintenance succeeded, which it did,
it was due to habitual usage and other factors, rather than to
ideological elaboration or conviction. A large-scale more recent
study reinforces these findings. The Mexican-American population
of San Antonio, when asked what they would like to see their children retain of Mexican ways, gave priority to manners and customs
(38%) rather than to language (31%). Respondents from Los Angeles,
on the other hand, where Mexicanness is less of a liability because
of the greater permissiveness of the environment, the greater opportunity of upward mobility, and the greater English proficiency of
the Mexican-American population, gave preference to Spanish maintenance by a far greater margin (51%). In both San Antonio and Los
Angeles, the desire for language retentiveness seemed to be positively correlated with social status. It was mentioned far more
often among the well-to-do than the poor (Grebler et al., 1970).
    Ongoing changes within the ethnic community, progressive ur-
banization, greater educational attainment, and occupational diver-
sification--and within mainstream society, the civil rights movements and the bilingual education act--have lately facilitated the
rise of what is commonly referred to as the Chicano movement. The
Chicano movement brought along with it a profusion of political
and literary writings in which a reevaluation and ideologization
of Spanish is for the first time fully articulated. The goals of
the movement aim not only at improving the socioeconomic and educational status of the minority group, but its ethnic self-image
and status honor as well. Its adherents, responsive to the
heightened need for attaining group cohesiveness which might facilitate further socioeconomic gains, make frequent reference to
the Hispanic heritage--cultural and linguistic--as contrastive
components of self-identity, authenticity, and pride. While class
conflicts and discrimination might be the stronger driving force
behind the rise and growth of Chicano assertiveness than is the
will to ethnic distinctiveness itself, the effectiveness of the
movement is undoubtedly reinforced by its dual appeal to self-
interest and affective ties. Chicano nationalism (in the sense of
ethno-cultural identity, rather than political ideology linked to
the establishment of a separate territorial entity) has thus far
been primarily an urban and intellectual phenomenon. It has stirred

only the Chicano elites, its writers, leaders, and students, and among these just the younger generations. Whether it can or will mobilize the middle classes and the proletariat is far from certain. While ethnic unity itself is favored by vast majorities in such different settings as Los Angeles (81%) and San Antonio (90%), there is far less agreement on the reasons underlying this goal, and least of all when it comes to endorsing cultural unity. The attainment of political influence and social gains are far more commonly claimed than the notion of cultural unity, to which only a few subscribe, 11% and 17% in San Antonio and Los Angeles respectively (Grebler et al., 1970).

From these remarks it is evident that attitudes towards Spanish and language consciousness among Mexican-Americans are highly diversified. We know that Spanish language usage is associated with stress by some and with ethnic authenticity by others. However, we have very few indications of the individual characteristics that are correlated with differential orientations towards Spanish and the justifications that might be advanced in favor of its maintenance. While we have some knowledge about how some Mexican-Americans feel towards Spanish usage and Spanish maintenance, we have only scant data about the reactions certain Spanish/English variants elicit within the minority group of the mainstream society itself, and about attitudes towards language policies such as bilingual education programs. We know, for example, that Mexican-Americans are highly conscious of the potential or actual difficulties that ensue not only from limited English proficiency but from accented English as well. We know from recent research that these beliefs are introjections from outer realities rather than projections of inner fears.

English speech samples of Mexican-American children have been judged by Anglo teachers as considerably more ethnic and substandard as compared with speech samples of Anglo and Black children of equivalent socioeconomic background. Hesitancy, passivity, and low self-confidence have also been associated more often with Mexican-American children's speech than with those of other subgroups. In all instances, low class children have consistently been judged least favorable. We do not know, however, what levels of accentedness elicit these unfavorable evaluations, and which features are tolerated rather than stigmatized by the mainstream society.

There is general agreement that the language, languages or variety of languages a person speaks is often coupled, with or without justification, with a stereotypic level of education, social status, and personality traits. The study of speech or speech variants would be inconsequential were it not for the fact that attitudes are linked to behavior. Speech variants elicit stereotypes held by ourselves and others. Since we tend to behave in accordance with our stereotypes and our social reality, our expectations are shaped and molded by our motivations and attitudes. How a student, employee, patient, and defendant present themselves through speech has important consequences. Regional, ethnic or foreign accents may or may not erect a social barrier between the speaker and the member of the native speech community. On the other hand, a standardized language may or may not overcome racial, ethnic or social class barriers. Language extension or standardization programs in the educational sphere may or may not bring the desired results. Whether language extension programs are sufficient in themselves to bring about the desired results, or whether overt attempts at changing the attitudes and expectations of educators and the public at large are necessary, remains both unexplored and unknown.

We are equally ignorant about the attitudes held toward bilingual education programs, the rationales sustaining these programs, and the speech varieties implemented in classrooms. We do not know how parental, teacher, and administrator attitudes in this area may contribute singly or interactionally, negatively or positively, towards differential academic attainment among students and the smooth or disruptive functioning of the programs themselves. Ignorance in this particular sphere is difficult to comprehend, and impossible to justify, considering the human and economic costs involved.

Non-academics may wonder why the Spanish/English contact situation in the Southwest or in the United States at large deserves to be studied. Doubts are easily put to rest by invoking theoretical arguments or empirical consequences. Theoretically, the Spanish/English contact situation offers a readily accessible testing ground for the many existing hypotheses about dialects, language change, language acquisition, language maintenance, language shift, language attitudes, and language policies--in short, all the sociolinguistic and psycholinguistic topics that have received so much attention during the last decades in other settings with other populations.

Empirically, studies focusing on any or all of the above topics are more likely to rise rather than diminish in their importance and relevance. Today there are officially 7,200,000 people of Mexican origin in the U.S., concentrated largely in the Southwest. Because of the rate of natural increase among Hispanics at large, and because Hispanic immigration is running at the staggering rate of an estimated 1 million people per year, Hispanics may easily become the largest minority group in the U.S. within the next decade or two. While the Hispanic presence has been a palpable one in the U.S. for centuries, awareness of its scope and potential did not dawn until the 1960's. In the future, the Hispanics' very numbers guarantee they will play an increasingly important role, and that increasing attention will be paid to them, their language, language variants, language attitudes, and language needs.

REFERENCES

Fishman, J. A. 1966. Language loyalty in the United States. The
    Hague: Mouton.
_____. 1972. The sociology of language. Rowley, Mass.:
    Newbury House.
Fishman, J. A., R. Cooper and R. Ma. 1971. Bilingualism in the
    Barrio. The Hague: Mouton.
Floyd, M. B. 1978. Verb Usage in Southwest Spanish: A Review.
    The Bilingual Review/La Revista Bilingüe 5.76-90.
Grebler, L., J. Moore and R. C. Guzmán. 1970. The Mexican-American
    people. New York: The Free Press.
Kiparski, Paul. 1970. Historical linguistics. New horizons in
    linguistics, ed. by J. Lyons. Baltimore: Penguin Books.
Labov, William. 1965. On the mechanism of linguistic change.
    GURT [=Georgetown Univ. Round Table] 18.91-114, ed. by
    Charles W. Kreidler.
_____. 1966. The social stratification of English in
    New York City. Washington, D.C.: Center for Applied Lin-
    guistics.
Solé, Yolanda. 1975. Language maintenance and language shift
    among Mexican-American college students. Journal of the Lin-
    guistic Association of the Southwest 1.22-49.
_____. 1977a. Language attitudes among Mexican-American
    college students. Journal of the Linguistic Association of
    the Southwest 3.37-46.
_____. 1977b. Continuidad/discontinuidad idiomática en
    el español tejano. The Bilingual Review/La Revista Bilingüe
    4.189-199.
Williams, R., J. L. Whitehead and L. M. Miller. 1972. Attitudinal
    correlates of children's speech characteristics. USOE Research
    Report Project, No. 0-0336.
Williams, R., J. L. Whitehead and J. Traupman. 1971. Teacher's
    Evaluations of Children's Speech. Speech Teacher 20.247-254.

LANGUAGE AND DIVERSITY:
A SOCIOLINGUISTIC PERSPECTIVE

ROBERT N. ST. CLAIR

University of Louisville

Linguistic variations continue to create a nemesis for the theorist. Under the tradition of American structuralism, this problem was labelled as one of free variation and conveniently dismissed as irrelevant data. Those attempts to seriously deal with "free variation," on the other hand, explained how such patterns of fluctuation were related to the history of different settlement and migration movements common to the history of dialect geography. When dialectology expanded its focus to include the study of social dialects, it provided a new focus for the study of language differences. Dell Hymes (1962), for example, addressed the concept of the "ethnography of speaking" in which the various factors affecting social dialects were outlined: the setting (locale, situation), participants (sex, age, status), topic (religion, politics, etc.), and function (request, command, rituals). The trend since then has been one of quantifying those parameters of linguistic variation.

The incorporation of these social variables into transformational grammar has been the concern of a number of scholars who have sought to objectively measure these various parameters of the ethnography of speaking. These include the works of William Labov (1969), Charles-James Bailey (1972), Henrietta Cedergren and David Sankoff (1972), David DeCamp (1971), and Derek Bickerton (1971). Several of these scholars have employed the Guttman

Scale for the analysis of qualitative data; and some have sought
other forms of quantification in their quest for a more definitive
statement on language variation.

What is missing in this research on variation is a coherent
theory which adequately incorporates the findings of both sociology and linguistics. In particular, the interface between these
two disciplines requires a larger focus from which new questions
can be raised. Because each academic discipline brings with it a
different set of theoretical assumptions and methodological practices about language and society, these perspectives cannot be
readily integrated into a larger framework until the conflicts
which result from the disparities in their fundamental concepts
are resolved. In essence, the linguist has been oblivious to the
theoretical models and the methodological practices which form
the mainstream of sociological research.

The Sociological View of Diversity

Ferdinand Tönnies (1957) made a basic distinction prior to
the turn of the century between two kinds of group behavior:
Gemeinschaft and Gesellshaft. Emile Durkheim (1933) expanded
this dichotomy and embellished it with a new theoretical framework. His concern was with the social division of labor and how
individuals participate as members of a group. Although this concern may not appear to be overtly paradoxical, it should be. As
Durkheim noted, when the individual associates with a group and
identifies with it, he or she no longer exists as an individual,
but as a depersonalized member of the group. Even more perplexing
to Durkheim was the fact that a mulitiplicity of individuals can
function in the creation of an ordered society. The resolution of
these problems for Durkheim was to be found in the concept of
solidarity. He postulated two different kids of societies and
characterized them in terms of their sense of group allegiance.

In the Gemeinschaft group, the individual has a sense of belonging which is shared with the community. They basically share
the same range of emotions, cherish the same social values, and
hold the same things to be sacred. An informative explication of
this concept can be found in The Sacred Canopy by Peter Berger
(1969). It deals with the sociology of religion and provides an
illuminating discussion of how a sense of community is socially
constructed and organized throughout the sociopolitical processes
of reality confirmation and maintenance.

The Gesellschaft model of society is based on a sense of
organic solidarity in which people experience a fragmented social
world. They sense a greater degree of differentiation in dealing
with one another; they vary substantially in their panorama of
emotions; the values which they cherish find no common bond; and
the things which they consider sacred are no longer strengthened
by a communal spirit of devotion and participation. Peter Berger,
Brigette Berger and Hans Kellner (1973) have characterized this
state of affairs in their research on the role of consciousness
in modern society.

These forms of social solidarity lend themselves to further comparison. Consider, for example, the analogy of the shoe-maker in a tribal community where the individual is in total charge of the productive process. Since the individual artisans within this Gemeinschaft model share the same sense of awareness of creativity, they experience a common bond of collective consciousness. By way of contrast, the productive process of shoe-making in the Gesellschaft model is fragmented and alienating. The factory worker participates in only a small part of the total product and has a separate and distinct function in the total process. The bond of solidarity which unites him with his fellow workers is a fragile one. When pressures occur which add to the strain of social interaction, it may lead to the eventual fragmentation of group solidarity or anomie. This state of affairs is also known as alienation and is a favorite theme of existentialism (Barrett, 1962). It should be noted that Durkheim not only developed these complementary models of group cohesion, but also envisioned them in evolutionary terms. They represent a natural transition from the strong Gemeinschaft bonds of the tribal community to the fragile and alienating co-existence of the Gesellschaft networks which characterize the modern industrial society.

Another concept of immediate interest and importance to the sociologist is Durkheim's concern for social facts. It should be noted that Durkheim was raised within the tradition of positivism which dominated the intellectual climate of 19th century Europe. According to this tradition, science was defined in terms of the natural sciences with its methodological concerns for quantification and formal laws of operation. In particular, Durkheim wanted to emulate the outstanding success of the science of physics with its commitment to objectivity. As a consequence, he developed the concept of a social fact and argued that it bears a necessary relationship to physical facts in that they can both be discerned by observation, reside outside of the subjectivity of the individual, and provide constraining forces of human behavior.

Saussure and the Sociology of Language

When the work of Ferdinand de Saussure is investigated, several structural parallels with the work of Durkheim begin to emerge (Doroszewski, 1933). This link with the positivistic tradition is evident in the dichotomy which he created in his lectures in general linguistics (Saussure, 1966) between the concepts of langue and parole. The former was seen as a social phenomenon whereas the latter only pertained to the individual. But langue is more than a social phenomenon. It represents a linguistic fact which exists outside of the speaker. It is a fact which can be discerned by other observers. And it is a fact which has a constraining effect upon its human environment. This common social bond, according to Saussure, was shared by all members of the speech community. Langue, therefore, is an expression of collective conscience and belongs to linguistic community which is bound by the Gemeinschaft bonds of solidarity. When Noam Chomsky (1965) developed his argument for a distinction between competence and performance, he drew upon this Saussurean dichotomy. What is important about this history of ideas from a sociological point of view is that Chomsky's search for an "ideal speaker-hearer in a homogeneous speech community" is comparable to Durkheim's concept of a collective consciousness. Hence, upon closer investigation several theoretical inconsistencies among linguists in their assessments of language in a social context begin to emerge. Emile Durkheim viewed society as organized diversity and accepted a Gesellschaft model of language. Ferdinand de Saussure, on the other hand, limited the study of language to speech communities in which the objective consistency of linguistic facts was of paramount importance. His model of language is based on the Gemeinschaft model. Noam Chomsky has also followed this restricted view of language and has defined his concept of linguistic competence within the framework of the Gemeinschaft model. Within this framework, diversity cannot exist. It is not a part of the parameters recognized by this framework. It assumes linguistic homogeneity. Hence, such models cannot begin to explicate the concept of linguistic diversity and are doomed to theoretical dissonance and experimental failure.

Phenomenological Sociology

    Although some sociologists concur with the Gemeinschaft model of language in which speech communities are united by a common code, this view is not shared by those who operate within the phenomenological tradition. They would argue, by way of contrast, that language exists in the form of a plurality of codes which are socially distributed. Those who take this position base their assertions on the tradition of Wissenssoziologie (Schultz, 1967). More recent explications of this framework are referred to in the field as the sociology of knowledge (Berger and Luckmann, 1967; Holzner, 1966), cognitive sociology (Cicourel, 1974), existential sociology (Lyman and Scott, 1970), and phenomenological sociology (Psathas, 1973). These scholars all agree that the organization of reality is socially constructed. What this means, in effect, is that not everyone has the same way of defining the sociolinguistic context nor do they bring the same kinds of knowledge and experience to bear in the symbolic interaction with others. People experience multiple realities and diverse interpretations of social behavior and these also vary from one context to the other. But they even differ on how language is used in the same social context because of how people define the context of the situation. Their selectivity of perception is guided by different experiences within their own bibliographical histories and from the different social expectations which they have come to experience within their own repertoire of symbolic interaction. This model of linguistic diversity contrasts substantially with the positivistic tradition of sociology where language is viewed as a constant and is the shared experience of all the members of the community.

    What is significant about this phenomenological approach is

not only that it incorporates language into its framework but that
it also considers it to be of paramount importance in the organization of social knowledge. As Peter Berger and Thomas Luckmann
(1967) have argued, language performs several major sociolinguistic
functions. It objectifies the construction of social reality into
discernible units of human interaction. These emerge in the form
of episodes and social situations. It also signifies the meaning
behind human behavior through the expression of verbal signs. In
addition, it typifies experience by labeling it and channeling it
into verbal categories which provide a focus for social expecta-
tion. Finally, language does not only mediate the various parameters of social perception, but also transcends the social construction of reality by providing discernible instruments by which
such experiences can be probed and evaluated. According to this
view of sociology, the processes of role modelling are not only
socially distributed, they are also incomplete. What this means
for the study of language, then, is that if linguistic communities
exist in the form of regional and social dialects, they exist in
various stages of development and evolution. What is commonly referred to as the language of a nation, for example, is no more
than an official dialect and represents the common medium for the
political communities of government with their power over the mass
media, public schooling, and the legitimation of literature. Obviously, there are many who do not share this standard form of language. However, even those who profess to know the standard dialect of the nation in which they reside, differ radically in their
linguistic competence, patterns of expression, and intuitions about
its use in different social contexts. Hence, variation is a
natural part of language and is characteristic of the high level ·
of diversity associated with complex modern society.

Conflict Models of Language

As noted previously, the standard theory of language is based
on the Gemeinschaft model. This is evidenced in the traditions of
structuralism espoused by Ferdinand de Saussure and Noam Chomsky.
Hence, it is not surprising that this model is also associated
with the dependency principle in dialectology. This is because
it assumes that all variations in the dialects of a language depend on the same underlying forms at the systematic phonemic level. By contrast, the independency principle holds that different
clusters of linguistically related systems can co-exist indepen-
dently on one another (St. Clair, 1973; 1974). These systems are
related through a diversity of socio-historical and political factors and they range over a wide spectum of differences which contrast from the homogeneity of mutual comprehension at one end to
the heterogeneity of non-intelligibility at the other. Whereas
the dependency principle can only account for mutual intelligibility, the Gesellschaft model with its independency principle can
also account for other forms of communicative interaction, i.e.,
non-reciprocal communication, latent communication, and non-
intelligibility (St. Clair, 1973; 1974).

	Dependency Principle	Independency Principle
Social Model	Gemeinschaft	Gesellschaft
Modes of Communication		
a) Mutual	X	X
b) Non-Reciprocal		X
c) Latent		X
d) Non-Intelligible		X
Theoretical Base	Positivistic	Phenomenological
Linguistic Model	Structuralist	Neo-structuralist

     The phenomenon of non-reciprocal communication forms one of
the modes of interaction between linguistically related systems.
It occurs whenever the speaker of one system understands the dialect or language of the other, but not vice-versa. An example of
this phenomenon can be found among speakers of Black English and
those of standard English. The former can understand the latter,
but not vice versa. This phenomenon can also be documented
among generically related languages not both spoken in a single
polity. Speakers of Spanish and Portuguese are familiar with
this problem and have noted that the latter can usually understand
the former, but not vice versa. Latent communication is another
mode of linguistic interaction and results when both speakers in
a non-reciprocal situation can eventually speak to each other in
their own languages or dialects without substantive loss of comprehension. Anyone who has been caught off guard by the sounds
and the syntax of a new dialect can attest to this form of communication. But the experience need not be limited to dialects,
as speakers of historically related languages soon come to more
fully understand each other with the passage to time. Non-
intelligible genetic systems represent one of the extreme forms
of interaction. These systems are the result of an eventual lack
of comprehension between historically distant languages or dialects which have undergone substantial modification with the
passage of time and have been restructured to the point of linguistic anomie. What is significant about the independency principle is that it can not only account for the different modes of communication among dialects, but also among genetically related
languages.

If there are so many difficulties with the dependency principle, why does it continue to remain as the dominant model within linguistics? Part of the answer to this question is best explained in terms of how sociolinguists view diversity. Most have failed to recognize the anomalies which exist within their own theoretical frameworks. They have also remained oblivious to the concept of diversity in the sociological literature and the implications that this has for their own models. But there is still another reason why the dependency principle remains as an incorrigible postulate. It rests on the Aristotelian tradition of classification. According to this framework, the members of a class are either characterized by means of a common element or they are designated by merely enumerating the elements in an ad hoc fashion. Obviously, the first form of classification has been used exclusively in dialectology. It underlies the assumptions upon which Bloomfield (1933) and Hockett (1958) have drawn their dialectal atlases, and it underlies the quest for unique abstract forms on the systematic phonemic level within generative dialectology (Halle, 1962). Given the choice between a definitive classification of dialects and a mere amassing of apparently ad hoc forms into a class, it is understandable why linguists have consistently found refuge in the former.

The question of how to classify things became one of the major concerns of Ludwig Wittenstein. In one of his later works, Philosophische Untersuchungen, Wittgenstein (1963) found himself addressing this issue. He was attempting to classify language games and was perplexed by the fact that these games all differed from one another. They shared some features in common, but there was no unique defining feature by which Wittgenstein could successfully classify all of these events under the rubric of language games. It was during this moment of dissonance that Wittgenstein argued effectively against the Aristotelian system of defining class membership. He resolved this problem in a metaphorical sense. He initiated his concept of the family resemblance model. The members of a class need not be united by a common defining element, Wittgenstein noted. They may share a family resemblance. Just as in the picture of a family gathering in which there is no one feature defining the group, so it is in language games. In each case, there is an overlap of features behind a network of relationships. This digression about Wittgenstein and his attempt to resolve the dichotomy of Aristotelian logic is informative because it provides some insight into the linguistic classification of languages and dialects.

Given the Gemeinschaft model of language, one could argue that there are many linguistic communities in which a homogeneity of form and structure exists. This highly restricted view of language underlies the rationale behind the dependency principle. The problem begins to emerge when one attempts to relate these isolated coherent systems within a larger framework. What unites regional and social dialects? Can the dependency principle acount for highly disparate reconstructions of language in which the various modes of communication exist? Obviously, there are limitations to the dependency principle. What this means, in

essence, is that linguists must begin to look elsewhere for solutions to problems of linguistic diversity. It is in this context that the family resemblance model of Ludwig Wittgenstein
begins to form a plausible hypothesis. It states that linguistic
communities can be related to others through an overlapping network of common features. Some dialects may have a rule in common,
others may have a form or two which they share. These various relationships can range from a high degree of overlapping to almost
none. The former is characteristic of mutually intelligible dialects and languages and the latter can be found among non-intel-
ligible disparate systems. It should be noted that this model of
family resemblance is not new to dialectology. It can be found
in the study of dialectal speech chains such as the one which runs
from Paris, France, to Rome, Italy (Bloomfield, 1933). Hence, the
independency principle is not inconsistent with linguistic tradition.

     Another aspect of the mutual comprehension model or Gemein-
schaft model of dialectology which needs some elaboration involves
the problem of human information processing (Hart, 1977; Lindsay
and Norman, 1977). The dependency principle is attractive to
psycholinguists because it allows them to handle linguistic diversity according to their template model (Neisser, 1967). Perhaps a more insightful model of human interaction can be found
within the tradition of symbolic interactionism (Hewitt, 1976;
Faules and Alexander, 1978; Manis and Meltzer, 1972; Simmons and
McCall, 1966). What makes this approach interesting is its attempt
to operate outside of the Aristotelian laws of the excluded middle
and the law of identity. According to the former, the first operation involves the logical division of objects into disparate classes. Once this has been accomplished, the law of identity holds
that identical things all share the same properties. If this model of classification seems familiar, it is. This is the same
framework upon which the dependency principle operates. It is
also the basis for experimental psychology with its emphasis on
absolutes and constants. In their co-authored work, Hugh Mehan
and Houston Wood (1975) have openly addressed these issues. They
aruge that social events are not networks of caused events, nor
are they amenable to literal description. When people speak to
one another, they do not adhere to the law of the excluded middle
or the law of identity. These are not normal uses of language.
It can be occasionally found in a law brief or in a natural
science position paper, but it remains outside of the normal use
of symbolic interaction. Not only are the objects of one's conversation not readily separated into logical divisions, they are
not even constant or stable properties. The meanings of the social world shift over the course of an interview or a conversation.
They display little or no constancy. But the law of identity
holds that every word must mean the same thing to every person and
that constancy is the basis for mutual comprehension. Obviously,
the positivistic quest for consistency must be forsaken. The resolution of this problem can be readily found within symbolic interactionism. It allows diversity to thrive within a family re-

semblance model and assumes that people have different repertoires of cognitive strategies which they employ in defining the context of a situation. It allows for continual evaluation and reinterpretation of events; and it is not hampered by variations in linguistic judgments, the instability of dialects, and the wealth of linguistic diversity.

In a recent monograph, William Labov (1977) voiced some concern about his inability to consistently define linguistic data. He notes how unreliable linguistic judgments are. He questions the stability of idiosyncratic dialects; and he mentions several contradictions which he has noted between actual linguistic behavior and the introspective judgments of speakers. It should be noted that Labov is working within the Gemeinschaft model of linguistics; and as a consequence, it is not surprising that he has encountered some difficulty in coping with the problems of diversity. His model was not meant to resolve such problems. It will always lead to theoretical anomalies and experimental inconsistencies.

Concluding Remarks

If sociolinguistics is to become a viable model of language and society, it must incorporate many of the insights which have evolved over the last two centuries in sociological theory. Although linguists have operated on the principle that language coheres as a system of collective competence, this Gemeinschaft model of language has led to a host of anomalies. When these anomalies are viewed from an interdisciplinary perspective, they clearly divulge the nature of the problem. Linguists have been using the wrong tools. They have attempted to cope with problems of diversity when their own models, by definition, do not even consider such problems to legitimately exist within their domain of investigation. What is needed, of course, is a further clarification of just what these models entail. If the linguist is to continue to work with the dependency principle, he or she must severely restrict research to highly homogeneous linguistic communities. If, however, the linguist wishes to account for a wider range of linguistic phenomena, then he or she should recognize the fact that diversity is a normal aspect of everyday language. Hence the relevance of the independency principle and the conflict model of language which is based on phenomenological sociology.

Some linguists may feel that this shift toward existential sociolinguistics is unscientific. Such is not the case. By giving up the Aristotelian laws of the excluded middle and identity, one does not give up science. This is tantamount to the reduction of the postulates in mathematics and its resulting creation of new systems such as Abelian rings or quarternions (Kramer, 1970). Another form of misunderstanding may come from the experimental psychologist or the linguistic methodologist who feels that the abandonment of these Aristotelian laws of logic leads to incoherency. This is not so. Anyone who is familiar with the research traditions of cognitive sociology or symbolic interactionism knows that the question is not one of methodology. The problem involves the proper combination of research tools with theoretical models. Some forms of methodology need to be complemented by other forms of investigation as they do not provide an adequate examination of the phenomenon under study.

The approach advocated in this essay is not new. It is consistent with the research models employed by ethnomethodologists. This fact is important because this field of study represents a synthesis of the methodology of positivism in all of its richness and the phenomenological sociology of the humanists with their concerns for such important phenomena as consciousness, intent, value, and interpretation. If linguists are to be able to cope with problems of linguistic diversity, they can find comfort in this new theoretical framework of existential sociolinguistics.

REFERENCES

Bailey, Charles-James. 1972. Variation and linguistic theory. Arlington VA: Center for Applied Linguistics.

Barrett, William. 1962. Irrational man: A study in existential philosophy. New York: Doubleday Anchor.

Berger, Peter. 1969. The sacred canopy: Elements for a sociological theory of religion. New York: Doubleday Anchor.

_____, B. Berger and H. Kellner. 1973. The homeless mind: Modernization and consciousness. New York: Vintage.

_____ and T. Luckmann. 1967. The social construction of reality. New York: Doubleday Anchor.

Bickerton, Derek. 1971. Inherent variability and variable rules. Foundations of Language 7.457-492.

Bloomfield, Leonard. 1933. Language. New York: Harper and Row.

Cedergren, Henrietta and David Sankoff. 1972. Variable rules. (Unpublished ms.)

Chomsky, Noam. 1965. Aspects of the theory of syntax. Cambridge MA: M.I.T. Press.

Cicourel, Aaron. 1974. Cognitive psychology: Language and meaning in social interaction. New York: Free Press.

DeCamp, David. 1971. Toward a generative analysis of post-creolization of language. Pidginization and creolization of language, ed. by Dell Hymes. Cambridge, England: Cambridge University Press.

Doroszewski, W. 1933. Quelques remarques sur les rapports de la sociologie et la linguistique. Journal of Psychology 30.82-91.

Durkheim, Emile. 1933. The division of labor in society. New York: Free Press.

Faules, Don and Dennis Alexander. Communication and social behavior: A symbolic interactionist perspective. Reading MA: Addison-Wesley.

Halle, Morris. 1962. Phonology in a generative grammar. Word 18.54-72.

Hart, David. 1977. Introduction to human information processing. New York: Wiley and Sons.

Hewitt, John. 1976. Self and society: A symbolic interactionist social psychology. Boston MA: Allyn and Bacon.

Hockett, Charles. 1958. A course in modern linguistics. New York: Macmillan.

Holzner, Burkart. 1966. The construction of social reality. New York: Schocken.

Kramer, Edna. 1970. The nature and growth of modern mathematics. Vol. 1. Greenwich CN: Fawcett Premier Books.

Labov, William. 1977. What is a linguistic fact? Lisse, The Netherlands: Peter de Ridder.

Lindsay, Peter and Norman Davis. 1977. Human information processing. New York: Academic Press.

Lyman, Stanford and Marvin Scott. 1970. A sociology of the absurd. Pacific Palisades CA: Goodyear Publishing.

Manis, Jerome and Bernard Meltzer, eds. 1972. Symbolic interactionism: A reader in social psychology. Boston MA: Allyn and Bacon.

Mehand, Hugh and Houston Wood. 1975. The reality of ethnomethodology. New York: Wiley and Sons.

Neisser, Ulric. Cognitive psychology. New York: Appleton-Century-Croft.

Psathas, George, ed. 1973. Phenomenological sociology. New York: Wiley and Sons.

St. Clair, Robert N. 1973. The independence principle in dialectology. Language Sciences 27.23-27.

_____. 1974. Communication across linguistically related systems. Linguistics 126.83-95.

Saussure, Ferdinand de. 1966. Course in general linguistics. New York: McGraw-Hill.

Schutz, Alfred. The phonomenology of the social world. De Kalb IL: Northern Illinois University Press.

Simmons, J.L. and George McCall. 1966. Identities and interactions: An examination of human association in everyday life. New York: Free Press.

Tönnies, Ferdinand. 1963. Community and society. New York: Harper Torchback.

Wittgenstein, Ludwig. 1963. Philosophical investigations. New York: Macmillan.

THE PROBLEM OF COMPARING
VARIABLE RULES ACROSS DIALECTS:
SOME EXAMPLES FROM SPANISH

TRACY D. TERRELL

University of California—Irvine

The purpose of this paper is to demonstrate that in order to characterize the phonology of dialects it is necessary to determine the complex systems of constraints which may operate on a single variable phonological rule. I will attempt to show this by examining the operation of two related phonological processes of Spanish which are used in many dialects: the aspiration and deletion of word final /s/.

The importance of dialect comparison for linguistic theory has been accepted for many years and was emphasized within the school of generative phonology by Robert King in 1969:

> The topic of central interest in historical linguistics
> is linguistic change... whatever else we may do in the
> name of historical linguistics at bottom we are dealing
> in matters at first or second remove from change in a
> language or a language family. But before saying what
> we can about linguistic change we shall make what at
> first glance seems a detour to concern ourselves with
> the question of dialects and their differences. This
> is really not a digression because any change--our para-
> mount concern--is ultimately rooted in the process of
> two dialects having become different. Dialects in
> other words provide the most direct evidence regarding

change at our disposal. Our immediate job is to
clarify the notion of difference between related
dialects of the same language for without understanding dialect differences we cannot hope to
determine with any precision how those differences
have arisen; that is to say we cannot determine
what has changed or indeed for that matter what
change really is.

According to the structuralist theory, phonological dialect
differences were characterizable in terms of phonemes, allophones,
and their distributions. Within the generative model emphasis in
analysis changed from the allophonic level, which is the source
for most phonological dialect variation, to morphophonemic variation, which for many languages does not change greatly from one
dialect to another.[1] In articles which were influential in the
formative years of generative phonological theory, it was suggested
(Halle, 1962) that a certain class of dialect differences might
result from different extrinsic ordering of phonological rules in
various dialect areas. King (1969) in his elaboration of these
ideas proposed that the differences between dialects might be for-
mulated in five ways: (1) restructuring of underlying forms (in
structuralist terms, this would usually imply a change in the phonemic system); (2) the addition of a phonological rule to the
phonological component (in dialect terms, a rule might be adopted
in one dialect but not in another); (3) the loss of a phonological
rule (which when applied to dialects, results in the same situation
as the preceeding point); (4) a different order for phonological
rules, the original proposal of Halle which has proved to be of
little or no validity; and (5) the simplification of a phonological
rule, by which was meant changes in the specification of a rule in
terms of distinctive and redundant phonological features.
      The generative model in addition proposes a distinction be-
tween rules of obligatory application and those of optional application. However, studies of Labov (1963, 1965, 1966, 1971, 1972a,
1972b) and others (Labov, Yeager, Steiner 1972) of English and
American dialects have demonstrated that this division is not adequate for the explanation and characterization of the phonological
variation which one finds when examining normal speech. Labov's
proposal for a new model which can account for variable application of phonological rules has created new possibilities for the
description and explanation of dialect differences and finally for
phonological change itself. Labov's model is essentially a quantitative model based on the assumption that variability is inherent
in the phonological system used in natural speech. Those of us
who have worked directly with the speech of a large number of informants know that there are very few cases in which one can make
completely categorical statements and for this reason alone an
accurate description of dialect comparison must be more complex
than was suggested by either structuralists or generativists.
      Let us first review what we know about dialect comparison.
We know that dialects may differ because of different phonemic
systems.[2] For example, the variety of Spanish spoken in northern

Spain (as compared with the Spanish of the Caribbean) normally has two phonemes in its inventory which Caribbean Spanish lacks; the zeta /θ/ of zapato ('shoe'), cine ('movies'), and the palatal lateral /λ/ of llamar ('to call'), and llorar ('to cry'). Even in the case in which two dialects make use of the same phoneme, it is still possible that they differ in terms of the phonetic character of the principal allophone of that phoneme. For example, the voiceless anterior fricative, orthographically j or g (before e, i,), may be uvular, velar or pharyngeal with varying degrees of friction according to the dialect area. This sort of difference may be represented formally in terms of redundant phonological features.

We also know that two dialects may differ in terms of phonological rules. The famous distinction between the Highlands and Lowlands dialects of Spanish (Canfield, 1962) is based mostly on the presence and absence of certain phonological rules. For example, aspiration and deletion of syllable and word final /s/ is not normally used in most of the Highlands dialects while they form a part of the normal speech patterns in the Caribbean, the River Plate region, and other areas of the Spanish-speaking world. A rule of lateralization of syllable- and word-final /r/ found in various areas is another example of dialect differentiation in terms of the presence or absence of a phonological rule.

There are also different dialects which share essentially the same phonemic system, the same rules for redundant features (i.e., the same allophones) and the same principal phonological rules, but are still different. I will try to show that at least some of these differences may result from a different system of constraints of a single phonological rule.[3]

The phonological process which has been studied most, and for this reason lends itself better to a comparative study, is the process of aspiration and deletion of word final /s/. We will define the subset of the ocurrences of the phoneme /s/ to which the rules of aspiration and deletion apply as the variable (s). Variable (s) is syllable-final esto 'this' or word-final años 'years.' In speech these rules are variably applied and constrained by both extralinguistic and linguistic factors. In the areas in which these rules are used, virtually all speakers of Spanish use them in their speech; there is yet no conclusive evidence that there are speakers who delete (s) and do not aspirate nor are there speakers who aspirate without deletion.[4] We know that the specific use of these processes varies according to area, social class, and speech style. These are sociolinguistic constraints and an account of this variation will be the basis for a sociolinguistic study of Spanish phonology. In this report I wish to concentrate on linguistic and geographical variables and have chosen data from a single socioeconomic class--middle--within a single speech style-- free conversation (semiformal). The interviews from which the data are taken were recorded in the various capital cities, for the most part by natives from those cities.[5]

The rules of aspiration and deletion have been the focus of considerable theoretical discussion of their formulization in terms

of generative rules.[6] For the purpose of this report I will simply say that the speaker may eliminate completely the variable
(s) under conditions which I will discuss in some detail. If he
does not eliminate (s), he selects between sibilant allophones
which I will represent with the symbol s̲ and aspirated allophones
which I will represent with h.[7]

   In the studies done so far, the rule of deletion has shown
the most complex conditioning. This is logical if we consider the
practical effects of the two rules. With the deletion of (s) all
phonetic representation of the phoneme disappears. This has the
potential of disturbing the morphological system since (s) represents the plural morpheme for various grammatical classes:[8]
nouns, pronouns, and adjectives. In addition, the final /s/
functions as a part of the verbal morphological system: hablamos̲,
tienes̲, antes̲, entonces̲. Aspiration, on the other hand, cannot
affect the grammatical system at all since it consists merely in
the change of one phonetic representation for another; the phoneme
continues to be present.

   In view of these observations it is not surprising that the
process of elision is affected by grammatical-functional constraints
while the choice between sibilant phones or aspirated phones is constrained almost entirely by phonological factors. This observation
is valid for all of the informants I have studied to date and it is
probable that it stems from universal linguistic tendencies. However, within this general picture in the specific detail of the
function of aspiration and deletion there are interesting differences, differences which will help us in the formulation of a model
of dialect comparison. The model I propose will be a descriptive
model only which will serve as a first approximation to a basis
which we need in order to arrive at our true goal, which is the explanation, both synchronic and diachronic, of these differences.

   Let us look first at the constraints on deletion. In all the
studies of application of final /s/ deletion by middle class
speakers, there exists a strong constraint to preserve some phonological indication of plurality in the noun phrase. This retention
of /s/ may be in form of a sibilant or aspiration, and normally
appears on the first element in the noun phrase: los̲ americanos̲
avaros̲, dos̲ chicas̲ lindas̲, mis̲ padres̲. The other /s/'s of the noun
phrase, syntactically redundant, are deleted frequently by all
speakers I have studied; however, it operates with variable strength.

   One of the differences between Spanish dialects with regard to
the operation of deletion stems from the possibility of the influence of phonological factors in its operation. In the following
Table (I), I have represented the effect of the three most important
phonological contexts: preconsonantal (los̲ niños), prevocalic
(los̲ amigos) and prepausal (ya se lo dijimos).
   The Caribbean differs from Argentina in that in the former the
phonological context does not seem to condition deletion. It is
probable that this difference is representative of two different
diachronic stages of development. An examination of the index
of deletion shows that deletion is far more advanced in the
Caribbean: 26% Cuba, 29% Puerto Rico, 22% Panama (Cedergren
1973 for middle and upper groups), Caracas 35% versus 15% for Buenos

I

Deletion constrained by phonological context

(a) /s/ is deleted more before a consonant, less before a vowel, and even less before a pause:

_____C > _____V > _____P

Buenos Aires

(b) /s/ is deleted more before a consonant, less before a pause, and even less before a vowel (see Longmire, 1976):

_____C > _____P > _____V

Mérida, Venezuela

(c) Phonological context is not a constraint on deletion:

_____C ≅ _____V ≅ _____P

Havana, San Juan, Panama (Cedergren, 1973), Caracas.

Aires. I hypothesize that when deletion began to spread the phonological conditioning operated the same as for aspiration. However, as the rule was used more and more frequently the chances for disturbing the morphological system became greater and grammatical conditioning became part of the rule's operation. The Spanish of Buenos Aires is in a stage in which grammatical conditioning interacts with phonological constraints. I predict that with an increase in the rate of the application of deletion, the phonological constraints will become less and less important.

If the speaker does not delete /s/ he must choose between aspirated or sibilant phones to represent the phoneme. There are three constraints on this selection, all phonological, which function differently according to geographic area. The norm for all speakers is to use aspirated allophones in word-internal position; however, in certain areas it appears that speakers react to a following voiceless dental stop /t/ by retention of a sibilant in a higher number of cases. In these informants it becomes very difficult to classify the phone in this position because of the mixture of sibilance and aspiration. This effect was noted in San Juan and Havana but it was minimal and the overall sibilant retention rate was only 6% (San Juan) and 3% (Havana). Cedergren does not mention such a constraint for her informants and an index of only 2% sibilant retention (Panama) would support her omission of any discussion. On the other hand, Longmire found in the Spanish of Mérida, Venezuela, that the use of sibilant in this position reaches a mean of 15% (Longmire 1976:100) and Terrell found a mean of 12% for Porteños (Terrell 1977). Longmire suggested that the

retention of a sibilant was related to the particular character
of the sibilant in Mérida which according to her is more dental.
This may be the case; however, it is also possible that the retention of sibilance before /t/ is simply a case of the remains
of an earlier stage before aspiration had reached category status.
The effect of a following /t/ has also been noted for some informants from Cartagena, Colombia, and Guayaquil, Ecuador, although
I do not know if this feature can be attributed to all speakers
of those areas. It is possible that this constraint on sibilant
retention divides the area of aspiration into two zones: the
Antilles and South America.

The constraint which most affects the choice between sibilant
and aspiration is the general phonological context. In all dialects aspiration is favored in preconsonantal position. On the
other hand, in the case of a following vowel or pause, there
appear to be differences according to the area of origin of the
speaker.

Contexts which favor sibilance

Pause favors s̲ more than a following vowel favors s̲

_____ P > _____ V

in Havana, San Juan, Panamá, Mérida, Caracas.

Vowel favors s̲ more than a following pause favors s̲

_____ V > _____ P

in Buenos Aires.

I suspect that the explanation for this division is purely
diachronic. The adoption of aspiration and deletion is much more
advanced in the northern areas than in the River Plate region.
This may be shown by comparing the indices of sibilant retention
in prevocalic position:

Buenos Aires:	88%	Caracas	16%
		Havana	18%
		San Juan	22%
		Panamá	20%

The final feature which I will discuss is more complicated

II

Dialect Comparison of the Variable Constraints on Aspiration and Deletion of /s/ in Spanish.

	Phonological context conditions deletion.	/t/ favors retention of sibilance.	Sibilant retention favored by pause more than vowel.	Stressed Vowel differs from unstressed vowel for sibilant retention.
1. Panama - 22167 cases 79 informants	no	no	yes	yes
2. Cuba - 8077 cases 22 informants	no	no	yes	yes
3. Puerto Rico - 20344 cases 18 informants	no	no	yes	yes
4. Venezuela, Caracas - 18608 cases 24 informants	no	yes	yes	yes
5. Venezuela, Mérida - 8147 cases 49 informants	yes	yes	yes	?
6. Argentina - 14674 cases 24 informants	yes	yes	no	no

than the others since it involves an interaction of two constraints: the phonological context, in this case /s/ before a stressed vowel, and a functional constraint, the class of modifiers which appears in the first position of a noun phrase. In the case of this combination, that is, first position noun modifier followed by a stressed vowel (dos años, mis hijos, los otros), the retention of a sibilant is almost categorical in the speech of the informants studied. This phenomenon was first noticed by Ma and Herosimchuk (1971) in their study of mainland Puerto Rican speech and later examined in more detail by Cedergen (1973) for the speech of Panama. It surfaced again in the studies by Terrell (1975a, 1975b) for both Cuban and Puerto Rican speech. On the other hand, this constraint does not operate as such in Porteño speech since the presence of any following vowel, stressed or unstressed, in any grammatical class whatsoever, causes almost categorical retention of a sibilant. The following table presents a summary of the constraints discussed in this paper.

We have seen that a single phonological process can produce different surface phonetic configurations as a result of a different system of constraints on the application of the rule. We have discovered at least two sorts of differences:

(1) The presence or absence of a specific constraint; examples: the phonological conditioning of deletion, the effect of /t/ on sibilant retention, the effect of a following stressed vowel on sibilant retention of determiners.

(2) A different ordering of constraints; example: the relative strength of a following vowel or pause on the application of aspiration and sibilant retention.

With these examples I have tried to show that the determination of the system of constraints which operate on the application of a variable rule of phonology is necessary for a complete description and explanation of dialect comparison. It should also be evident that studies of the dialects of Spanish and especially those of the Caribbean offer an opportunity for the construction of theoretical models which will enrich our understanding of not only phonology, but of linguistic change in general.

NOTES

[1]See Harris, 1972, for an example of generative dialect study in Spanish.

[2]I use the term phoneme in its normal sense, not in the sense of morphophoneme.

[3]Also inherent in the problem of dialect comparison is the problem of the relationship between the individual speaker and the

speech community of which he is a part. See Terrell 1977b for
further discussion.

[4]Although some observers have tried to separate these two processes by means of sociocultural differentiation (Becerra, 1976) or
geographical differentiation (Canfield, 1962), I personally have
seen no proof of a speaker who aspirates and never deletes on any
occasion. Fontanella de Weinberg (1973:54) reports that 10 of
her 60 informants did not delete /s/ even in the most informal
of speech situations. However, from her article it is impossible
to determine the total number of cases of /s/ examined and it is
probable that with a greater N, cases of deletion would appear. In
my own study of deletion in the speech of Porteños, all informants
deleted final /s/ (see Terrell 1977), although some exhibited rather
low rates of deletion. The other possibility is more interesting.
There may indeed be speakers for whom deletion has become categorical. In this case restructuring of words without underlying /s/
must occur, eliminating the possibility of aspiration. Although I
believe such speakers exist, there are none reported to date in the
literature.

[5]Almost all of the tapes which I have used are taken from the
collection of the Latin American Urban Areas Dialect Project. (See
Lope-Blanch 1969.)

[6]I myself have vacillated considerably and, in spite of the
amount of attention given to the problem, am not really happy with
any of the results. For discussion see Longmire, 1976, ch. 2.

[7]There are those who argue that another important step in the
weakening process is the complete assimilation of the /s/ when in
preconsonantal position resulting in a sort of geminate consonant.
This is the analysis used by Longmire in 1976. Becerra in his
study of the Spanish of Cartagena (Colombia) says that complete
assimilation (gemination) is the most common variant in informal
speech (Becerra, 1976:9). I am more in agreement with the traditional analysis in which the geminate is analyzed as a natural
variant of aspiration in preconsonantal position. Malmberg (1950:
158-9) discussed this problem in some detail and concluded that /h/
better represented the infinite number of phonetic variations which
aspiration undergoes according to context. (See also Terrell 1977.)

[8]The supposed system of seven vowels which reportedly functions
to signal plural when deletion has applied does not exist for Cuban
speakers and I doubt that it exists for other speakers of the
Spanish Caribbean. (See Hammond 1973 and Resnick and Hammond
1975.)

REFERENCES

Becerra, Servio. 1976. Consonantes implosivas en el español de
Cartagena de Indias (Colombia): Implicaciones sociolingüísti-
cas. Paper read at the Modern Language Association's annual
meeting.

Canfield, D.L. 1962. La pronunciación del español en América.
Bogotá: Instituto Caro y Cuervo.

Cedergren, Henrietta. 1973. The interplay of social and linguistic factors in Panamá. PhD Diss., Cornell Univ.

Fontanella de Weinberg, M.B. Comportamiento ante -s de hablantes
femininos y masculinos del español bonaerense. Romance Philology 27.50-8.

Halle, Morris. 1962. Phonology in generative grammar. Word 18.54-
72.

Hammond, Robert M. 1973. An experimental verification of the phonemic status of open and closed vowels in Spanish. M.A. Thesis,
Florida Atlantic Univ.

Harris, James. 1973. Morphologization of phonological rules.
Paper read at the Third Linguistics Symposium on Romance
Linguistics, Indiana Univ.

King, Robert. 1969. Historical linguistics and generative grammar.
Englewood Cliffs NJ: Prentice-Hall.

Labov, William. 1963. The social motivation of a sound change.
Word 19.273-309.

_____. 1965. On the mechanism of linguistic change.
GURT (Georgetown Univ. Round Table) 18.91-114.

_____. 1966. The social stratification of English in
New York City. Washington D.C.: Center for Applied Linguistics.

_____. 1971. Methodology. A survey of linguistic sci-
ence, ed. by W.O. Dingwall. College Park MD: Univ. of Maryland
Linguistics Program.

_____. 1972. Sociolinguistic patterns. Philadelphia
PA: Univ. of Pennsylvania Press.

_____. 1972. The internal evolution of linguistic rules.
Historical linguistics and generative theory, ed. by R. Stockwell and R. Maconley. Bloomington IN: Indiana Univ. Press.

_____, M. Yaeger and R. Steiner. 1972. A quantitative
study of sound change in progress. Philadelphia PA: U.S.
Regional Survey.

Longmire, Beverly J. 1976. The relationship of variables in
Venezuelan Spanish to historical sound changes in Latin and
the Romance languages. PhD Diss., Georgetown Univ.

Lope Blanch, J.M. 1969. El Proyecto de estudio coordinado de la
norma lingüística culta de las principales ciudades de Ibero-
américa y de la península ibérica. El Simposio de México, ed.
by J.M. Lope Blanch and others. Mexico DF: Univ. Nacional
Autónoma de México.

Ma, R. and E. Herasimchuk. 1971. The linguistic dimensions of
a bilingual neighborhood. Bilingualism in the barrio, ed. by
J.A. Fishman, R.L. Cooper, and R. Ma. Bloomington IN: Indiana

Univ. Press.
Malmberg, Bertil. 1950. Etudes sur la phonétique de l'espagnol parlé en Argentine. Lund, Sweden: C.W.K. Gleerup.
Resnick, Melvyn C. and Robert H. Hammond. 1975. The status of quality and length in Spanish vowels. Linguistics 156.79-89.
Terrell, Tracy D. 1975a. Aspiration and deletion of final /s/ in Cuban Spanish. Manuscript (to appear in Hispania, 1979).
_____. 1975b. Sobre la aspiración y elisión de la /s/ implosiva y final en el español de Puerto Rico. Manuscript (to appear in Nueva Revista de Filología Hispánica.)
_____. 1977. La aspiración y elisión de /s/ en el español porteño. (Manuscript.)
_____. 1978. Aportación de los estudios dialectales antillanos a la teoría fonológica. Corrientes actuales en la dialectología del Caribe hispánico (Actas de un Simposio), ed. by Humberto López Morales. Río Piedras PR: Editorial Universitaria/Univ. de Puerto Rico, pp. 217-238.

IS CODE-SWITCHING INTERFERENCE, INTEGRATION, OR NEITHER?

GUADALUPE VALDÉS

New Mexico State University

In the last several years, renewed interest in the study of bilingualism has led to the investigation of a very common language-contact phenomenon known as code-switching. At the same time, this same interest has once again led to the examination of the exact classification of code-switching within the definitions of the two processes known as interference and integration. The purpose of this paper is to recall previous discussions relating to this same problem, to review some recent attempts at establishing definitions of types of code-switching, and finally, to emphasize the difficulties surrounding the strict classification of code-switching given the varying interpretations of both interference and integration as well as new evidence concerning the very nature of language alternation.

Definitions of Interference and Integration

Interference is defined by Weinreich (1953) as "those instances of deviation from the norms of either language which occurs in the speech of bilinguals as a result of their familiarity with more than one language." Integration, on the other hand, is defined as being interference at the level of language as opposed to speech. "In language," Weinreich states, "we find interference phenomena which, having frequently occurred in the speech of bilinguals, have become habitualized and established." Haugen (1956), presenting a slightly different viewpoint, defines interference as the overlapping of two languages and integration as the regular use of elements of one language in the other--a use which is characterized by morphological and phonological adaptation. Mackey, however, defines interference (1970) as "the use of elements from one language while speaking or writing another." He adds that interference is characteristic of the message and not of the code. By this definition, the insertion of an element of one language (language A) into the context of the other (language B), whether adapted or unadapted, will be judged interference if such an element is not considered a part of language B by its community of speakers. Clearly the problem here, as Mackey himself pointed out, is determining the exact classification of a given item. Not only must the researcher be aware of levels of both morphological and phonological adaptation, but he must also be conscious of the fact that "... the question of whether or not a given element belongs to both codes or only to one does not take a yes/no answer. It is also a matter of degree." (Mackey 1970). Thus in spite of an item's continued use in language A, it can best be considered a part of language B if members of a community use that one form, and only that one form for a concept when speaking in language B.

More recently, researchers have tended to dismiss both the concepts of interference and integration as misleading and as part of a trend in the study of bilingualism which Fishman (1968) has categorized as a preoccupation with finding "smears of wet paint." He and others have suggested that languages in bilingual communities can in most cases not be looked upon as two pure and distinct languages, which influence one another because they are in contact. Instead they have argued persuasively that norms found in such bilingual communities will not be identical to those monolingual societies. For that reason, they have insisted, it is important that researchers describe not how existing bilingual speech is different from the monolingual norm but how norms and varieties actually in use in such communities are used by bilinguals in everyday interaction.

Currently, then, it is far more stylish to speak of a bilingual repertoire and to examine how a bilingual uses such a repertoire for various needs and purposes than to make long "laundry lists" of integrated items. The concept of interference has fared no better, and at the moment even the second-language teaching field has abandoned its belief that all errors are the product of a learner's first language.

Definitions of Code-switching vis à vis Interference and Integration

Given the above and the fact that the study of code-switching has stemmed from the work of the very researchers who have argued against the constructs of interference and integration, it is ironic that so much time and attention has been devoted to the problem of the classification of code-switching vis à vis these

two concepts.   Initially, code-switching was defined by Haugen
(1956) by comparing it with the other two processes. He defined
code-switching as the alternating use of two languages which permits a bilingual to avoid interference in the strict sense.   He
added that if a bilingual masters both phonetic systems there is
no real interference, but merely successive stretches belonging
to different languages. Since that time, code-switching has been
given a slightly different definition by each researcher who has
studied it. The majority of these researchers have attempted
(though their individual concerns may be informed by various
schools of thought or various disciplines) to include or exclude
certain types of switches by claiming they are more accurately
described as either interference or integration. In this section,
the positions of four different researchers will be discussed.

A.   Hasselmo

Hasselmo, a follower of Haugen, defines code-switching (1970)
as the introduction, into the context of the discourse of one language, of stretches of speech which exhibit the phonological and
morphological features of the other language. He prefaces this
definition, however, with a discussion of the difficulties to be
faced in determining the differences between code-switching, interference, and integration. He says (Hasselmo, 1970:180):

> The occurrence of an item that shows a high degree
> of social integration would then be interpreted an
> instance of integration, the occurrence of an item
> that shows a low degree of social integration as an
> instance of code-switching. However, items that show
> overlapping of two phonologies and or morphologies can
> also be referred to a third category, that of inter-
> ference in the strict sense, which thus serves as a
> classificatory slot for both imperfect integration as
> well as imperfect code-switching.

Following this line of reasoning, it is soon obvious that in
utterances such as:

(1)   Me dijo mi mamá que I have to study.   (My mother told me
      that I have to study.)

and

(2)   Tengo la waist twenty-nine. Tengo que reduce.   (I have
      a twenty-nine inch waist. I have to reduce.)

the real question is whether English elements are being used in a
Spanish context (involving Mackey's definition of interference)
or whether there are alternating stretches of English and Spanish
which do not betray either phonological or morphological overlap
from the other language. If the latter interpretation is true,

then such switching is not a deviation from the norms of a given language, but rather a change in norms. From this perspective the interpretation of a given segment of speech by the researcher becomes central to the classification process. He may, like Hasselmo (1970), be forced to establish what the phonology and morphology of each language is for each informant studied.

   B. Gumperz

   Seemingly at a very different end of the spectrum in the study of bilingualism, Gumperz also defines code-switching by rejecting certain instances of language mixing. In his study of code-switching among Mexican-Americans (1969), he excludes the types of switches known as "identity markers." He argues (Gumperz 1969:5):

> Not all instances of Spanish words in the text are necessarily instances of code-switching. Expressions like ándale pues, dice [he says] are normally part of the bilingual's style of English. Speakers use such expressions when speaking to others of the same ethnic background in somewhat the same way the Yiddish expressions like nebbish, oi gewalt, or interjections like du hoerst characterize the ingroup English style of American jews. They serve as stylistic ethnic identity markers and are frequently used by speakers who no longer have effective control of both languages.

   While not specifically mentioning integration, Gumperz is arguing that words or phrases in one language which are part of code A in a particular community cannot be considered true switches in spite of the fact that they were originally a part of code B. One can interpret this to mean that the use of such identity markers results, not in a change in language but rather in a case of integrated elements belonging to the informal register used by bilinguals when speaking to persons of the same ethnic background. For Gumperz, there are apparently two categories: code-switching and integration (identity markers and loanword nouns). Since he does not seem to be concerned with phonological adaptation, one assumes that he is not concerned with interference, that is (in Hasselmo's terms), imperfect code-switching or imperfect integration.
   Interestingly enough, the problem of classification is no less severe for the researcher following Gumperz than it is for the researcher following Haugen and Hasselmo. The decision of whether or not a specific identity marker is or is not code-switching must be based on an awareness by the researcher of the fluency in each language of each informant and of the presence or absence of the identity marker in question in the codes of the bilingual speakers of the area. There is considerable similarity between this problem and the much-discussed question raised by Mackey (1970) concerning the difficulties of differentiating between interference and integration, a process which must involve

establishing the vocabulary availability of each speech community.

C.   Gingràs

Much related to Gumperz's position is Gingràs' (1974) concern with whether one is dealing with an instance of code-switching in certain types of intrasentential alteration or with some sort of lexicalization. He argues that in the sentence

(3)   Mi grandfather vive en Albuquerque.   (My grandfather lives in Albuquerque.)

grandfather may be an English term used for abuelo or a case of lexicalization in which it has replaced the native word in that specific Spanish dialect. He comments (1974:169):

If the speaker knows the word abuelo, we may have an instance of lexical substitution. If not, we might have a case of lexicalization. I reserve the term "substitution" for what an individual does and the term "lexicalization" for what speakers of a dialect may have done. Where it becomes particularly difficult to distinguish between code-switching and either substitution or lexicalization is in sentences of the following types:

(6)   Dijo que iba downtown.
      'He said he was going downtown.'

(7)   Me dijo que se fue yesterday morning.
      'He told me he went away yesterday morning.'

In (6) the adverb downtown might be an instance of substitution, that is, the speaker may have decided to substitute al centro with the equivalent English word downtown or it might be an instance of code-switching in that the code has switched from Spanish to English at the point where the adverb is introduced; in (7) the temporal adverb presents a similar problem of interpretation. Of course, in either case, it might be an instance of lexicalization. It should also be pointed out that in dealing with observational data, it's difficult to sort out problems of various kinds due to interference between the two codes. Since interference appears to be a result of performance factors (assuming we have the case of a coordinate bilingual who can keep his two codes fairly separate), I will also try to ignore cases of bilingual interference, since I have no interest in performance factors at this time.

Gingràs himself stresses the difficulties of trying to include or exclude specific instances of language alternation as code-

switching. He points out how the question is further complicated
by the presence of interference which may occur between two codes.
He is careful, however, to emphasize the fact that when dealing
with interference, one has now moved into the area of performance.
   Clearly, and regardless of their position with regard to interference, both Gumperz and Gingràs are concerned with differentiating between code-switching and integration (identity markers
which are part of a code, and lexicalizations which are part of
dialect). Both researchers suggest that regardless of morphological or phonological assimilation, an element from language A,
used in the context of language B, may still be seen as an integrated form. Gingràs further refines the previously discussed
classification by differentiating between "substitution" (what a
speaker does) and interference (a result of performance factors).

   D.   Reyes

   More recently, Rogelio Reyes has argued that while most sentences which contain elements from two languages qualify as interference under Weinreich's broad definition, such a classification glosses over a number of important linguistic processes.
Moreover, he maintains (Reyes, 1976:184)

      ... the term interference seems to imply an invol-
      untary process whereby the speakers fail to communi-
      cate according to the model that he attempts to use.

He identifies, instead, three different types of language mixing
as they are found in Chicano communities:

   (4)   Yo sé porque ('I know, because') I went to the
         hospital to find out where he was at.

   (5)   Hizo improve mucho.   ('She improved a lot.')

   (6)   Taipeo las cartas.   ('I type the letters.')

Type A, as in (4), for which Reyes uses the term code-switching,
consists of changes which occur at discernible syntactic junctures.
Type B, as in (5), consists of single lexical items--most specifically English items which depend on a Spanish frame for their interpretation. Type C, as in (6), consists of single lexical items
which are adapted both morphologically and phonologically. Reyes
offers the term spontaneous borrowing for Type B changes and incorporated borrowing for Type C changes.
   In many respects there are parallels between Gingràs' category of substitution and Reyes's category of spontaneous borrowing.
In both cases these investigators are responding to a need to
differentiate between interference (caused by performance factors,
implying a failure to use a given model) and a process which,
while spontaneous, is predictable and regularly used.
   Summarizing the four approaches discussed above, it will be
seen that in each case each investigator has attempted to come to

terms with what Haugen (1956) claimed to be the most significant
question in dealing with bilingual speech: how to decide whether
a given stretch of speech is to be assigned to one language or to
another. For Hasselmo, the degree of social integration of an
item as well as morphological and phonological characteristics
are basic to such a decision. He emphasizes, however, that using
such a definition, the researcher must establish what the phonology and morphology are for each language for each informant studied. Gumperz, on the other hand, is concerned with differentiating between code-switching which is really a change in languages,
and instances of integrated items (identity markers) used habit-
ually in a given code. He does not, however allude to the difficulties, for the researcher, of determining at what point the use
of given items can be considered a part of a community's bilingual
style. Gingràs excludes interference from his consideration and
yet establishes a classification which includes three processes:
code-switching, substitution, and lexicalization. He rejects the
inclusion of a single lexical item in one language, used in the
context of another, as an instance of code-switching. However,
his categorization of processes stresses his conviction that, regardless of morphological or phonological lack of adaptation,
there is a difference between the process of substitution and that
of interference. The former three-part classification (interference, integration, code-switching) is now refined to interference, substitution, lexicalization, and code-switching. Reyes,
though offering a similar four-part refinement, describes slightly
different categories of language mixing. Interference is defined
as involuntary. Spontaneous borrowing is defined as the use of
lexical items in one language which depend upon the other for in-
flectional interpretation. Incorporated borrowing is defined as
the use of single lexical items which have been assimilated morphologically, and code-switching as a term is restricted to those
instances of language change which take place at syntactic junctures and which have their own internal syntactic structure.
Table 1 presents the four positions summarized above.

Other Current Approaches to Definitions and Classifications

While not all researchers currently working in the area of
code-switching have devoted time and effort to the definition of
the phenomenon vis à vis interference and integration, all investigators have found themselves (given the various definitions
in use at present) forced to define, before beginning a discussion
on the subject, exactly how they are using each term. This section will briefly review a number of current approaches.
Pfaff (1975), while reviewing the disagreement among researchers as found in the work of Gumperz and Hernández, Gingràs,
etc., elects to establish her own classification of code-switching
(consisting of four different types) which, in fact, disregard
the questions studied above. She defines Type 1 as typical of
casual interaction between peers and close friends on everyday
topics, and characterized syntactically by a high frequency of

Table 1

DEFINITIONS OF CODE-SWITCHING VIS A VIS INTERFERENCE AND INTEGRATION

Hasselmo	Gumperz	Gingràs	Reyes
Interference: items overlapping of two phonologies or morphologies		Interference: a characteristic of performance	Interference: an involuntary process, failure by the speaker to use a model he attempts to use
Integration: items which show a high degree of social integration	Code-changing which involve the use of identity markers, loan word nouns (integrated as part of the code.)	Lexicalization: items which are a part of a dialect	Incorporated borrowing: single lexical items incorporated morphologically
Code-switching: item which shows a low degree of social integration	Code-switching: code-changes at the word, phrase, clause, and sentence levels, not including items described above.	Code-switching: language changes which do not involve either interference, lexicalization or substitution	Code-switching: language changes which take place at syntactic junctures and which have their own internal syntactic structure
		Substitution: lexical items in individual uses which are not incorporated into the opposite language	Spontaneous borrowing: lexical items in one language which depend upon the other for inflectional interpretation

switches which occur either at surface sentence breaks or at independent or dependent clause breaks. She adds that conjunctions,
in this type of switching, may occur in either language, as may
adverbial and prepositional phrases. One or two word switches
may also occur. Type II is defined as typical of casual or more
formal interactions which are mainly in Spanish. Syntactically
this type of switching is characterized by the use of loan words.
"Deep S" switching was infrequent in this type of switching, although sentence introducers and tags occurred relatively frequently. Type III is defined as the jargon of the bato loco.
This type of switching is characterized by exhibiting, in a primarily Spanish context, frequent switches into English of single
nouns, verbs, adjectives and set phrases.
     Closely following Pfaff's (1976) approach to the question of
definition, McClure (1977) believes it is advantageous to study
the interplay of the various language contact phenomena rather
than segregating them. She thus proposes, for her own work, two
broad classifications: code changing, which is the complete
shift to another language system at the level of the major constitute (e.g., NP, VP, S); and code-mixing, the individual's use
of opposite language elements which cannot be considered community
borrowings. Again, like all four investigators studied above,
McClure excludes integration, the process of incorporated borrowing, from her very broad classifications. She argues further that
"phonology is only one clue in disambiguating the status of opposite language elements, because they often contain a mixture of
English and Spanish sounds." In this instance, McClure shares
Hasselmo's concern.
     Quite different in orientation is the position taken by Di
Pietro (1976) who defines code-switching as "the use of more than
one language by communicants in the execution of a speech act."
Stressing the complexity of the phenomenon and the various theoretical viewpoints from which it has been approached, he suggests
that in studying language alternation as part of a set of verbal
strategies which bilinguals use in order to influence the out-
comes of their conversations with one another, it is perhaps not
crucial to provide clear definitions of when an item is a code-
switch and when it has been integrated into the grammatical system.
     Generalizing, it can be said that the concern with defini-
tions, exclusions and inclusions by present researchers is closely
related to the focus of their study. Of the researchers concerned
with syntactic constraints on code-switching, Pfaff finds it
necessary to propose her own classification, Poplack (1977) explains both her inclusions and exclusions, while Timm (1975) adopts
a very broad and traditional definition. Researchers like McClure,
who are concerned with child language and the use of code-switching
by children, will find that they must adopt a system for talking
about development levels with regard to language alternation; while
researchers interested in bilingual speech who are concerned with
quantifying frequencies will find that they must develop a definition which facilitates counting different types of phenomena.
Examples of such latter tendencies can be found in the work of

Valdés-Fallis (1978) and Dearholt and Valdés-Fallis (1978).

The interest in constructing models whether of bilingual competence (Bautista, 1973) or performance (The Second Foundation, 1978) will inevitably lead to the formulation of definitions either as a starting point or as a body against which the appropriateness of a model is tested. At the same time, ethnographic approaches to the study of language in bilingual communities will result in descriptions which are more concerned with the function and use of either pure or different "mixed" varieties in the community than with establishing frequencies. Definitions in this case will be related, as in Elías-Olivares (1976), to the overall differences between "mixed" varieties. On the other hand, work which relates to speech-act theory (Di Pietro, 1976 and Valdés-Fallis, 1979) will be more concerned with how bilinguals use language to carry out actions than with classifying the different varieties of language alternation.

It does not seem, in the light of the above considerations, that the identification of code-switching as interference, integration, or neither will be established in the near future. Indeed it is evident that continued research in the area brings forth additional complications in the classification of this phenomenon. For example, current work on the relationship of language alternation at the word level to short term memory and to accomodation between speakers, as well as a closer view of the mechanism known as triggering (described by Clyne, 1967), suggests that previous perspectives which moved toward a rigid labeling of all types of code-switching were, to a degree, simplistic. It seems likely that the issue may be further confused by the finding of additional evidence for the fact that code-switching can resemble interference in certain factors and integration in certain others. At the same time, it may be possible to argue that a number of other types of switches can only be seen as the avoidance of both processes in the strict sense (as Haugen suggested) by switching languages. Some will continue to insist that code-switching should be defined as the introduction, in the context of one language, of stretches of speech which exhibit primarily the other language's phonological and morphological features. These researchers will continue to insist also that code-switching is a separate process from interference and integration. Similarly, others will eliminate from their definition of switching all types of language alternation which seem to be closely related to either interference or integration. This concern with classifications, inclusions, and exclusions, however, rather than a trivial exercise, is an important on-going contribution to the study of bilingualism. In each instance, researchers are re-examining established definitions and in doing so they are discovering both the limitations of these definitions in general and the necessity for renewed attention to the labeling mechanism, a process which can all too often restrict the complete understanding of complex problems.

REFERENCES

Bautista, María Lourdes S. 1973. A model of bilingual competence
    based on an analysis of Tagalog-English code switching. Philip-
    pine Journal of Linguistics 6.51-89.
Clyne, Michael G. 1967. Transference and triggering. The Hague:
    Martinus Nijhoff.
Dearholt, D.W. and G. Valdés-Fallis. 1978. Toward a probabilistic
    automata model of some aspects of code-switching. Language
    and Society 7.411-419.
Di Pietro, Robert. 1975. Code-switching as a verbal strategy
    among bilinguals. Paper read at the Linguistic Symposium,
    University of Wisconsin-Milwaukee.
Elías-Olivares, Lucía. 1976. Ways of speaking in a Chicano speech
    community: A sociolinguistic approach. PhD Diss., Univ. of
    Texas-Austin.
Fishman, Joshua. 1968. Sociolinguistic perspective on the study of
    bilingualism. Linguistics 39.21-49.
Gingràs, Rosario. 1974. Problems in the description of Spanish-
    English intrasentential code-switching. Southwest Areal Ling-
    uistics, ed. by G.D. Bills. San Diego CA: Institute for Cultur-
    al Pluralism/San Diego State University, pp. 167-74.
Gumperz, John and Eduardo Hernández-Chávez. 1969. Cognitive as-
    pects of bilingual communication. Language Behavior Research
    Laboratory Paper #28. Berkeley CA: University of California.
Hasselmo, Nils. 1969. How can we measure the effects which one
    language may have on the other in the speech of bilinguals?
    Description and measurement of bilingualism, ed. by L.G. Kelly.
    Toronto: University of Toronto Press, pp. 122-41.
_____. 1970. Code-switching and modes of speaking.
    Texas studies in bilingualism, ed. by Glenn Gilbert. Berlin:
    Walter de Gruyter, pp. 180-210.
Haugen, Einar. 1956. Bilingualism in the Americas: A bibliography
    and research guide. Tuscaloosa AL: University of Alabama
    Press.
Mackey, William F. 1970. Interference, integration and the syn-
    chronic fallacy. GURT (=Georgetown University Round Table)
    #23, ed. by James E. Alatis. Washington DC: Georgetown Univer-
    sity Press, pp. 195-223.
McClure, Erica. 1977. Aspects of code-switching in the discourse
    of bilingual Mexican-American children. GURT 1977, ed. by
    Muriel Saville-Troike. Washington DC: Georgetown University
    Press, pp. 93-115.
Pfaff, Carol. 1975. Syntactic constraints on code switching.
    Paper read at the annual meeting of the Linguistic Society of
    America.
_____. 1976. Functional and structional constraints on
    syntactic variation in code-switching. Paper read at the
    Chicago Linguistic Society (Parasession on Diachronic Syntax).
Poplack, Shana. 1977. Quantitative analysis of constraints on
    code-switching. New York: Centro de Estudios Puertorriqueños.

Reyes, Rogelio. 1976. Language mixing in Chicano bilingual speech. Studies in Southwest Spanish, ed. by J. Donald Bowen and Jacob Ornstein. Rowley MA: Newbury House, pp. 183-88.

The Second Foundation. 1978. Relational network approaches to code-switching. The fourth LACUS forum, ed. by Michel Paradis. Columbia SC: The Hornbeam Press, pp. 250-62.

Timm, L.A. 1975. Spanish/English code-switching: el porqué y how-not-to. Romance Philology 28.473-82.

Valdés-Fallis, Guadalupe. 1978. Code-switching among bilingual Mexican-American women: Towards an understanding of sex-related language alternation. International Journal of the Sociology of Language 17.65-72.

_____. 1979. Code-switching as a deliberate verbal strategy: A microanalysis of direct and indirect requests among bilingual Chicano speakers. Discourse processes: Advances in research and theory (forthcoming).

Weinreich, Uriel. 1953. Languages in contact. New York: Linguistic Circle of New York.

PIDGINS (AND CREOLES?)
ON THE U.S.-MEXICAN BORDER

JOHN T. WEBB

University of Iowa

Jacob Ornstein was one of the first to point out the amazing diachronic and synchronic spread of language varieties on both sides of the border. Central to this vast spiderweb are continuums from the Spanish of Mexico to the English of the USA, and back again. In point of fact, however, the continuum includes a respectable number of special speech types, some of which have been indiscriminately labled "pidgin," "creole," and the like. In the case of each type, we might profit from an examination of possibility, neither rejecting nor accepting out of hand an "indiscriminate" or folk characterization.

Some investigators have seriously suggested longtime pidginization at the meeting point of Spanish and English, usually singling out the basilect, often called pachuco (more accurately, caló, which is not the same as pochismo; see Webb et al., 1978: 175-176). Such language is used most proficiently by monolingual Spanish-speakers, who rarely mix in any English at all. Lexical elements from English, already naturalized in similar speech of urban Mexico, and possible syntactic interference from Anglicized Spanish along the border, are the only effects I have been able to find in "deepest" caló. However, as low-life caló filters upward into popular, informal Spanish--along the border and in the interior of Mexico--much more English presence is felt.

It is this more popular "counter-prestige" language that has been most often studied and labeled, usually in the few impressionistic works that have subsequently come to the attention of competent scholars. Voegelin and Voegelin (1964) argue that, given sufficient context, a Spanish-English bilingual could interpret the calques and loanwords that make caló unintelligible to native speakers of ordinary Spanish. This is true to the extent that such authors are referring to poverty-level, ghetto-dwelling Mexican-heritage Spanish-speakers on the U.S. side, and of the lower classes just across the border in Mexico. This "language" is understood principally by males, but is also widely understood by more females than some Mexican and Chicano investigators would like to admit. Although at the popular level there are fleeting phenomena, deepest caló does not change steadily in order to preserve its role as a language of concealment; on the contrary, it is quite conservative in all areas of grammar, is often comparable to and occasionally identical with similar speech of Mexico and Madrid, and has great similarity to concealment codes in Chile, Peru, Brazil, France, Italy, and even beyond the Romance-speaking world. Such relexification as does take place, even from English, is often for purposes of con- rather than di-vergence. Its speakers often do not consider it a language of concealment, which further adds to the confusion on the part of native speakers of more socially acceptable registers, to say nothing of that of academic researchers, particularly those who have experienced little of street life.

Caló basilect is at best barely comprehensible to fluent speakers of what might be loosely called "Mexico City standard." Additionally, its most adept users rarely know much English, and little English is involved in its form or content. On the other hand, speakers approaching the acrolect of standard Spanish may consciously include random caló expressions in informal dialogue, much as American-English speakers may purposely use what they consider to be "slang." (Note that speakers of "model language" are not always available to caló-speakers, principally because of social distance.)

The acrolects of bilingual English-Spanish speakers often differ from standard Mexican Spanish or standard American English only in distinctive pronunciation, particularly in patterning. Alongside the continuums, there have been pidgin adjustments (as well as contributions to caló--see Webb, 1976), adjustments between groups of Native Americans (cf. Brandt and MacCrate, 1979), various Europeans, and others; persons such as those who might wish to identify themselves as Arabs, Jews, Chinese, Russians, etc., have often purposely acquired and developed varying degrees of fluency or not-quite-fluency (perhaps particularly true in the case of ethnic "Gypsies") in the languages with which they wished to have contact, hoping to survive, yet also hoping to preserve some degree of their own culture. To some extent, just as a "special" or typical English may be spoken by many Native Americans, so in Mexico many indigenous populations speak a special Spanish easily identifiable by other Spanish speakers. In addition, ad-

justment has been made to and by other groups, such as French- or
Japanese-speakers, though more rapid blending with the English or
Spanish of their neighbors is often involved. No major social institutions, such as schools or churches, have promoted significant
study of other than the dominant languages until quite recently
(despite the large-scale projects of the Mexican government in the
1930's, which in the long run did little to preserve Native American tongues).

    With increasing urbanization in both Mexico and the USA, and
with growing big-city problems along the border, one observes an
increase (particularly among young people) in both the rejection
of "rustic" speech and the acceptance of "counter-prestige" language (street talk, delinquents' speech, etc.). Caló has developed not from a pidgin but from a transfer of language features
from local groups to students enduring compulsory schooling or
vocational training; this transfer is reinforced by exposure to
informal situations on the street or at home, and by local teachers,
though these teachers may attempt to reproduce the acrolect, and
though they may "correct" their students. Very recently, street
speech has begun to spread into all public and private domains.
With the growth in numbers of speakers one finds reinforcement of
features of English-Spanish blending and of caló. While English
has greatly affected syntax and morphology in border-Spanish varieties, a great deal of "obvious" differences from standard Spanish
nevertheless stem from non-standard international Spanish expression, including borrowing from Romanés, the ethnic tongue of the
"Gypsies" (Hymes 1971, p. 86, note 4; Webb, 1976).

    With the advent of technology and the increase of mass commu-
nication, remnants of earlier contact vernaculars are now often
limited to older persons and to the countryside (as with cowboys,
for example). Big-city Spanglish (or ingléspañol), together with
caló, varies in importance for outsiders; it has survival value
for Latin Americans along the border waiting for an opportunity
to cross into the United States and afterwards living in Mexican-
American ghettos; it has utility for those attempting to exploit
extra-legal opportunity at the border, or for law-enforcement
personnel (including English speakers) attempting to control such
opportunity. For residents along the border, such language offers
an alternative code or style. Attempts of outsiders to reproduce
such speech may cause annoyance or ridicule. Short-term visitors
are often "dealt with" through purposely faulty reproduction of
the alien tongue. The acrolect is approached normally only after
and through formal schooling.

    On the border, and particularly in the city, each speaker has
available to him, differentially, a number of varieties or lects
of speech. During a conversation he is able to move from one to
another according to his sociolinguistic capabilities, which define
his position on a predominantly Spanish or English continuum (this
continuum normally reflecting the medium of education). Position
on the continuum is determined by individual range of language
ability coupled with socioeconomic and educational factors, in turn
leading back to the type and number of subvarieties at the indivi-

dual's disposal. In general, the higher on the scale of subvariety he is able to produce in "formal" speech, the greater will be the range of the continuum which is available to him. (Speakers may be equally proficient in Spanish and English, but tend to be pre-dominantly English- or Spanish-speaking when using a higher lect.)

Figure I

ACROLECT

"standard
Mexican
Spanish"

"standard
American
English"

"caló"

basilect

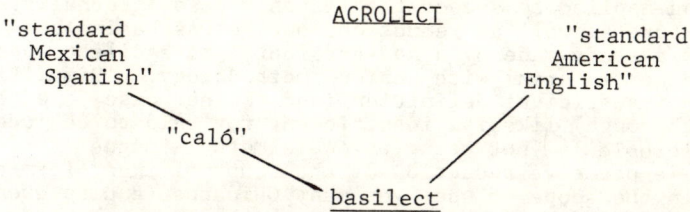

The mixture of English and Spanish, from acrolect to basilect (see Figure I), is unlike a pidgin in that it is not drastically re-duced in lexicon or syntax, and unlike a creole in that it may be used inter- and intra-ethnically, as first, second, or third in a repertoire, and does not always correspond to either dominant official language (given a particular political territory). It is like a creole in serving where a formerly rigid social stratifi-cation has partially broken down. (As the reader is aware, pidgins commonly lack standardization, autonomy, historicity, or vitality, whereas creoles should have vitality, should have native speakers, normally do not function as a lingua franca, and are not used as one of several native languages.)

Our basilect is similar in structure to a number of creoles in having more than one copula, occasionally having a variable lack of copula, having variable non-marking of number and person, and variable marking of past tense in the verb and in phonemic and phonic variation from the standard language (its superordinate being one of the official languages of the territory). It is also similar in having transference of features from several ethnic lan-guages into its own standard (if such a thing can be defined), and in not being used as a lingua franca in the wider community. And, further, it is not just a set of deviations from a standard, whether dimly perceived or otherwise.

Ingléspañol or Spanglish is the best major candidate on the border for major pidgin-creole status. Starting from English or Spanish acrolects, its continuums end at a basilect, a near-convergence, caló, proficiently used only by those fluent in in-formal Mexican Spanish, and itself of mixed international ancestry. Caló almost meets the criteria for a "creoloid" as defined by Platt (1975: 372): it has similar structural variables based on the same standard language; it did not develop from a pidgin but by another process; it developed from the transference of features into a type of "standard" of its own from the languages of un-

related ethnic groups; its primary superordinate language is one
of the official languages of its area; it is used as one of several native types of speech within the community. But contrary
to Platt's criteria, caló is not also usually used as lingua
franca in inter-ethnic group communications within the community
where it is one of the subvarieties. (Speakers of caló may avoid
its use even with English-dominant persons of Mexican ancestry,
to say nothing of situations involving still other languages.)

Hymes (1971: 70) understandably takes exception to the term
'pidgin' being applied to speech that is only used internally, despite its mixture as well as reduction, but he was basing his
evaluation on a study made by a non-acrolect, non-basilect speaker
who collected her material with dubious methodology. 'Simplification' is an insufficient definition (and, in our case, one that
is far from thorough); likewise insufficient for caló to be judged
'pidgin' or 'creole'is 'not being anyone's mother-tongue.'

In caló we perceive reduction of the scope of inner form and
restriction in the scope of use; yet many Chicanos, and an even
greater percentage of Mexicans, would see both narrowness and
breadth in the creativity of such as buti, a Romanés expression
glossed as 'very, much,' as in the following: un buti de 'a large
quantity of,' buti lágrimas 'many tears,' buti loco 'quite loco
(in whichever of many possible definitions),' de a buti volada 'in
a real hurry' (this last may occasionally have hypercharacteriza-
tion of gender as in de a buta volada), or in the gigantic family
centering on madre (many native speakers do not realize that desmadre is a standard term for 'overflow'). ATM /ateéme/, the
letters or their names standing for a toda madre 'at full speed';
de poca madre 'with little or no proper upbringing,' and its abstraction pocamadrismo; me importa madre 'it doesn't matter to me
at all' and the related social behavior meimportamadrismo; chinga-
madral 'enormous quantity'; and on and on and on, to the point
where one might comment ¡qué desmadre! Now it might be objected
that most of these expressions could only fully be understood by
a "real" insider, and that though casually understood by most
Spanish-speaking Chicanos and Mexicans (and a good number of
Anglos), the expressions are not accepted by most as used or
usable. In that case, I must suggest a thought from Weinreich,
Labov, and Herzog (1968): truly homogenous systems are not functional.

Much investigation needs to be carried out and must be based
on valid data. Brandt and MacCrate (1979) have shown that even in
non-standard language evidence can be ferreted out and interpreted with some assurance of accuracy. Webb (1976) is being expanded into a full dictionary of caló, to include exemplary
sentence-frames. In an area, however, where socioeconomic and
other prejudice still exists, researchers need to take more than
a quick plunge; the field needs to be carefully examined for re-
curring phenomena, for possible trends and trajectories. The
Southwest, as Ornstein has often pointed out, is a vast laboratory; when we learn to make the best use of it, it may lead to
discovery and implications for other areas. For instance, in-

sights gained along the border may help answer the major question posed by Ian Hancock (personal communication): Why, with an apparently almost ideal setting, has Mexico not produced an important creole language?

REFERENCES

Brandt, Elizabeth, and Christopher MacCrate. 1979. Multi-lingual variation or contact vernacular in the Southwest: 'Make like seem heap injin'." Presentation at 43rd International Congress of Americanists, Vancouver, Canada.

Dumas, Bethany K., and Jonathan Lighter. 1978. Is slang a word for linguistics? American Speech 53:1.5-17.

Hymes, Dell H. 1971. Pidginization and creolization of languages. Cambridge: Cambridge Univ. Press.

Labov, William. 1971. Notion of 'system' in Creole studies. Hymes 1971:447-472.

Mühlhäusler, Peter. 1974. Pidginization and simplification of language. Pacific Linguistics, Series B, No. 26. Canberra: Australian National University.

Ornstein, Jacob. 1970. Sociolinguistics and new perspectives in the study of Southwest Spanish. Studies in Language and Linguistics: 1969-70, ed. by R. Ewton and J. Ornstein. El Paso: Texas Western Press, pp. 127-184.

Platt, John T. 1975. Singapore English speech continuum and its basilect 'Singlish' as 'creoloid.' Anthropological Linguistics 17.363-374.

Taylor, Douglas. 1971. Grammatical and lexical affinities of Creoles. Hymes 1971:293-296.

Valdman, Albert, ed. 1977. Pidgin and Creole linguistics. Bloomington: Indiana Univ. Press.

Voegelin, Charles F., and Florence M. Voegelin. 1964. Pidgin-creoles. Anthropological Linguistics 6.39-71.

Webb, John T. 1976. Lexical study of Caló and non-standard Spanish in the Southwest. Ph.D. Diss., Univ. of California, Berkeley.

_____, Carol Longoria, and Moisés Andrade. 1978. Geological search of form and content in Mexican-Chicano caló. Bilingual and Biliterate Perspectives, ed. by A. G. Lozano. Boulder: Univ. of Colorado, pp. 174-186.

Weinreich, Uriel, William Labov, and Marvin Herzog. 1968. Empirical foundations for a theory of language change. Directions for historical linguistics, ed. by W. Lehmann and Y. Malkiel. Austin: Univ. of Texas Press, pp. 95-195.

OHIO UNIVERSITY LIBRARIES

1000621624

P 26 .07 F4

A Festschrift for Jacob
Ornstein :